HUMAN RIGHTS, GENDER AND THE ENVIRONMENT

HUMAN RIGHTS, GENDER AND THE ENVIRONMENT

Manisha Priyam
Krishna Menon
Madhulika Banerjee

Pearson

Original edition, entitled *Human Rights Gender and Environment*, 6 by Priyam/ Banerjee/ Menon, published by Pearson Education Ltd., Copyright © 2009.

ISBN 9788131713259

First Impression, *2009*
Twelfth Impression, 2023
Thirteenth Impression, 2024

Published by Pearson India Education Services Pvt. Ltd, CIN: U72200TN2005PTC057128.

Head Office: 1st Floor, Berger Tower, Plot No. C-001A/2, Sector 16B, Noida - 201 301, Uttar Pradesh, India.
Registered Office: Featherlite, 'The Address' 5th Floor, Survey No 203/10B, 200 Ft MMRD Road, Zamin Pallavaram, Chennai – 600 044.
Website: in.pearson.com; Email: companysecretary.india@pearson.com

Printed in India at Repro India Limited

Contents

SECTION II GENDER

SECTION III ENVIRONMENT

Preface and Acknowledgements

This book was attempted primarily to help students at the University of Delhi through the foundation course entitled 'Human Rights, Gender and the Environment' in the newly structured BA (Programme) syllabus introduced in 2004. This textbook attempts to introduce to the students *the basic arguments* in each dimension of these issues, as spelt out in the syllabus, and to provide further reading that they could easily find in most college libraries today. The important point is about the arguments. In social science, there are no correct answers or positions. For every issue, there are different points of view that are called *arguments*, arrived at after a great deal of research and analysis. The learning process in the social sciences is the process of understanding different kinds of arguments and also how to decide what is good analysis and what is poor. It is also about learning what is right and what is wrong, but that depends upon your own point of view about the world. For that, exposure to others' views is very useful. We hope that this book opens a window to a great world of ideas and encourages you to venture into other new ones.

It was the energy and enthusiasm of Kamini Mahadevan that initiated the process of writing, refereeing and reworking the manuscript, as also coordinating between the three authors who were writing for a textbook for the first time. All three authors would like to acknowledge and express their deep appreciation for her help and support. Later, the other editors at Pearson took over and provided support as well, which we would all like to acknowledge. We would also gratefully like to acknowledge the detailed reports of the referees that undoubtedly enriched the text in both form and content.

In addition, all three authors have specific acknowledgements to make. Manisha Priyam would like to thank John Harriss for being a constant source of encouragement and for helping her structure many parts of the section on human rights. She would also like to thank the support of the library of the London School of Economics, where she is a doctoral candidate, with procuring much of the material required for her section. She would like to gratefully acknowledge Radhika Kumar for her substantive research assistance and Babuji who would look at the manuscript with longing, hoping it would become a book, sooner rather than later.

Krishna Menon would like to thank Nivedita Menon for being her friend. She would also like to thank Kamini Mahadevan for offering this project. Krishna would like to thank all the wonderful, bright young women who opt for the course 'Women and the Political Process' as part of their BA Political Science (Honours) programme at the Lady Shri Ram College. From them she learns and because of them she is. Krishna Menon would like to thank her parents and sister and her partner, friend and husband, Suresh, and last but not the least her daughter—the young and enthusiastic Meenakshi, who also illuminates her life.

Madhulika would like to thank Mahesh Rangarajan for his great help and support with books and ideas and Chandni Khanduja's untiring research assistance over many months, without which the section on environment could not have been written. The National Centre for Biological Sciences, Bangalore, provided an office and computer at a very crucial phase of the writing, and Apurva's wonderful home and support at that time helped complete the section, finally. She would also like to thank her students in the 15 C optional class over the years in which it was written for bouncing off ideas, her husband Yogendra for happily taking over the family front in periods of intense writing despite his own commitments, her parents for just always being there and Minoti and Jamuna for their able support in the house.

All three authors of this book are teachers at heart, and their ultimate achievement will be that the students are able to relate to this book and make sense of the issues with its help. Comments and criticisms are most welcome, so it can be improved for the future, as required.

Manisha Priyam
Krishna Menon
Madhulika Banerjee

Introduction: Understanding Social Inequality

This book is about trying to understand three significant issues in contemporary societies around the world—human rights, gender and the environment. You must have noticed that if you look out from a building from different points, the same 'outside' looks different every time. So, the view 'outside' depends on the vantage point you adopt for it. What is more, you cannot have all the views at once—you have to choose what seems to give you the best view, or the biggest view, or whatever you really wish to be able to see. Likewise, we will discover that there are many ways of 'seeing', 'understanding' or 'explaining' any social issue, depending on which vantage point of explanation you choose. These are known as perspectives and are used to offer some common thread of explanation to any set of issues. For the purpose of analysing the three series in this textbook, the perspective is that of social inequality. The reason for this is that the issues embodied in each of the above three are, in a significant way, about one kind of inequality or another. Gender is an expression of the inequality between men and women, and the issue of human rights arise precisely because some human beings are not treated by others even with the basic respect due to a fellow human. We will also find that so many of the problems of environment are caused by the unequal relations human beings have with nature—that is, most human beings feel superior to nature and want to simply 'use' it, or some human beings believe they have greater rights over the resources available in nature than others.

Yet, these can at best be viewed as preliminary explanations from the choice of inequality as the common thread. In order to fully appreciate how this actually works, it is very important to understand what social inequalities are all about, the different forms they could possibly take and which of these would be pertinent to understand these apparently different and unrelated issues. This chapter aims to do precisely that, in the following manner. It will introduce the idea of inequality in the social sciences through a real-life example. This will point towards four main categories of social inequality: caste, class, gender and ethnicity. So, there will be four main sections discussing each of the four categories, which will contain:

- An overview of the debates on them.
- The relationship between them and each of the other categories, e.g., class–caste, class–gender, class–tribe and likewise in each of the rest.
- Their significance in understanding the issues of human rights, gender and the environment.

WHY INEQUALITY? WHY NOT SIMPLY DIFFERENCE?

In everyday life, we observe that there are many differences amongst people—they are of different ages, they speak different languages, they wear different kinds of clothes. Each of these could simply mark the fact that people have different tastes, or customs or culture, and that is why there are differences between them. Sometimes, however, these very differences can be such that they make one seem superior than the other, one more powerful than the other or enable some to take advantage of social opportunities, while others are unable to do so. Above all, it is the last characteristic that ensures that groups of people in this category remain in that position for generations, for a long period of time in histoy. These are instances when differences become inequalities. We will try to explain this with the help of a real-life example, discussed in Box 1.

Are These Differences Instances of Inequalities?

The account of Dharavi (Box 1) could read simply like a description of differences, which do not amount to inequality. One particularly poignant statement from one of the older inhabitants seems to indicate this. She says, 'See, Mumbai is not like our *desh*. Here people from 50 villages have come to live. It is *Allah ka gaon*.' But delving deeper in the stories that Kalpana Sharma tells in the book, *Rediscovering Dharavi,* shows other layers.

The first question that arises is what is the reason for these particular communities, and not others, to have come here? The history of each community gives us the answer to this. Beginning as a simple fishing village, this area of Mumbai slowly accommodated people from several places that could not sustain their livelihoods anymore and were in dire economic

BOX 1

Dharavi: A Case Study of Differences and Inequality in Real Life

Dharavi, a large sprawling area inhabited by thousands of people, has the distinction of being known as 'Asia's biggest slum'. In a fascinating book[1] about this place in Mumbai, Kalpana Sharma describes the lives and worlds of the people that live in it. Here, we will pick some parts of the description from the book for our purposes. The first thing that strikes about this place is the *different kinds of people* that live in Dharavi. A survey in 1986 found that more than one-third of the people living there were from Tamil Nadu. The rest of the population consists of people from Maharashtra, the *Kolis* from Gujarat, the *Kumbhars* from Andhra Pradesh, people from Karnataka and Kerala, and from Uttar Pradesh—especially Azamgarh and Jaunpur districts—and even from Haryana. There are a growing number of people from Bihar and Orissa (Sharma 2000: xxxi). Probing further shows even more details of social distinctions—the Tamils are from three different castes: the *Adi Dravidas*, the *Nadars* and the *Thevars*. The Kumbhars are a close-knit community without caste divisions amongst themselves in Dharavi, while those from Uttar Pradesh (UP) are Muslims, very conscious of the divisions between themselves, those of *Barelvis* and *Deobandis*. While for most of the century that these communities have come to settle close to and live with each other in Dharavi, there was no real tension between Hindus and Muslims. This was, however, broken in 1992, after the demolition of the Babri Masjid in Ayodhya, when there were in fact riots between Hindus and Muslims here, as in most parts of the country. But the majority of the communities that live in Dharavi, regardless of which part of the country they are from or what work they do, are Dalits. While most of the above divisions remain on the lines of community, which principally means a common area of origin and language, *Valmikis* (a section of the Dalit community) that have migrated from Haryana and other parts of the country, live together in one part. Of them, the ones from Haryana particularly remain aloof, to the extent that they might not pick up Marathi even after years of living in Mumbai.

Further, people here do *different kinds of work*. The original inhabitants of Dharavi were the Kolis, a traditional fishing community, with a claimed unique fishing technique. But now they have, by and large, switched to brewing country liquor, also a specialty of the community. A majority of the people work in the leather-goods business, both in tanneries and finished goods. These include people from Tamil Nadu and UP, some of whom knew this work before they arrived and others who were farmers earlier, but practically destroyed by drought conditions. When their kinfolk and caste members opened tanneries in Dharavi and needed workers, they went back to their native areas to recruit them. The Kumbhars from Saurashtra were traditional potters who continued their profession when they came to live in Dharavi, joining the potters already living there. There are some originally nomadic and performer groups like the *Konchikoris* and the *Gondhali Samaj*, which now have turned to other avenues of making income. At the same time, there are parts of Dharavi where people who work elsewhere (as blue-collar workers in multinational companies, the railways, the municipal corporation, and so on) live, because they were not provided housing. There is a general sense that in the last few years the number of migrants from Bihar and Orissa has gone up substantially, but there are no dependable figures that precisely establish this.

The layout of Dharavi gives an indication of *different living patterns of people*, despite 'slum' being the overall term for this area. While most of it comprises places where there is a mixture of Hindus, Muslims and other religious groups, and people from north and south, some parts can easily be identified with the communities that inhabit them. Kamaraj Nagar, the main area of the Tamil homes is spotlessly clean, with each house having a little sit-out decorated with rangoli. The areas dominated by the Muslims often have narrow winding lanes and two- or three-storey high structures, reminiscent of similar areas in north India. The Kumbhars have small homes dominated by the potter's wheel and a courtyard common to four or five homes in which there are shared kilns for firing. Yet, there are parts of Dharavi where one can see high-rise buildings, proper roads and pavements and swank, modern air-conditioned showrooms displaying beautifully finished leather products.

Given how they live and work, *one sharp difference* is that of *attitudes of men and women to life and the future*. For men, Dharavi is a place of opportunity, providing work and sustenance. For women, it means living in cramped surroundings, lack of privacy, difficulties of water and sanitation, and often carrying a triple burden of work—running the household, bearing and rearing children, and doing something to earn some income as well. They work in their homes and also have to take up not just one but often two jobs. These reasons often make them crave for their native villages which, despite the poverty and the lack of toilets, were at least open and clean, and could be easily accessed by them. In some communities, the practice of men marrying more than once continues.

need. For the original inhabitants of the village, the Kolis, life was transformed right where they lived because of two 'developments' way beyond their control. First, the factories upstream at Chembur started to discharge untreated effluents into the stream that came into the Mahim creek. As a result, the fish started to smell of kerosene and became impossible to sell. Also, the reclaiming and building up of land all around, especially along the Mahim–Bandra stretch meant that Mahim creek, the very place where they did their fishing, dried up. In order to continue making a living, they then started to use the other skill they had—brewing country liquor, the specialty of which was brewing with salt water, and thereby, have managed to retain some distinctiveness stemming from their identity.

The Kumbhars fled from prolonged drought in Saurashtra and the Tamil tanners from Tirunelveli (originally small and marginal farmers) were also wiped out after years of drought. This is also true of many of the newer migrants, except that they come from the recently impoverished areas of Bihar and Orissa. The tanners from UP simply could not sell their wares back at home and came away to Mumbai where the markets were better. Thus, the bottomline is that each of them came here to find employment which they could not find at home.

Many of the communities that arrived here to escape dire economic need had to, additionally, either lose out on the skills they had earlier, or practice them at a subsistence level, only slightly better than where they came from. In this are implicit two kinds of economic inequalities—first, of unequal development because their area lacked development and they could not continue to work there, which meant that they became economic and environmental refugees; the second is of work in relation to skill—while the work they got in Mumbai paid them better than what they received back home, the innate nature of the work did not use their skills and kept them at subsistence level, hence not effectively pulling them out of the cycle of poverty they were born into. This is true of a number of different communities, particularly of those nomadic and performing communities like the Konchikoris, whose tale is a sad one of combining the skills they had with acquiring new ones. At the same time, they were also dealing with living precariously, choosing sites simply because there was none other available, and constantly being evacuated from them by either government demolition drives or property dealers.

At the same time, there are different kinds of inequalities, some newly created and others a repetition of the old ones. For instance, Valmikis across communities came to live and work here for precisely the same reasons as the communities discussed above. Yet, the fact that they live separately in one area repeats the very old social practice that has served to reinforce their social position. And most of them continue to engage in the traditional occupations of cleaning in public or private buildings, and the women do domestic cleaning labour. On the other hand, other Dalits and OBCs, especially from Tamil Nadu have been able to send their children to school and, by the second or third generation, are on white-collar jobs in the railways and information technology industry. This implies that the caste differences between people that live here make for, and reinforce, inequalities between them.

One of the most significant stories of inequality is possible, perhaps, in terms of living space. While this place is a picture of enterprise and hard work, the forces that control it are way beyond it—a nexus of government officials, property dealers and Mumbai's underworld. And often, the differences visible in the layout of Dharavi is a result of the power games played by these sets of people and their differential relationships with people that live in it. The attitude of the government has vacillated between ignoring them, because they are 'illegal properties', to not being able to overlook, because such large numbers of people that obviously live and belong to the city have serious political and economic significance, if not simply as human beings. This, sometimes, means 'beautifying' the city by clearing the people out of these places and relocating them out of sight of the city's elite. Only sometimes have 'slum development' programmes provided some benefits like water and electricity. In other instances, it has involved the relocating of the tanneries and high-rise buildings being built in those areas. And from these, one can see how Dharavi has been redeveloped only around its periphery, while its heart remains untouched. This has been taken up by many citizens' groups and social movements in Mumbai, in an attempt to defend the rights to a livelihood and space of those that have made Dharavi their home. And this is the story of slums in all our big cities, whether Delhi or Mumbai or elsewhere.

Not only are the otherwise common inequalities of the division of work between men and women prevalent here but are heightened in this context with women having to carry the burden of extra income. Further, given that these areas are not provided with basic services like healthcare and sanitation, and lacking the help they would have had with bearing children back in their villages, the cases of infant and child mortality are fairly high. In the instances of men of some communities continuing the practice of more than one marriage, it has the worst consequences for the women involved. Given the constraints of space, it often means that a family of a man with three wives and their children might have to share a tiny living space and meagre resources of food and all else. This naturally puts enormous strain on already difficult relationships between men and women, and among women.

Sharma's book provides many more such examples, were we to continue this exploration. For our purpose of understanding social inequality, we can now attempt to cull out some *general characteristics* of 'real' society from the above description and *the lessons on inequality* we draw from them. Then we will be in a position to understand the definitions of such terms as caste, class, gender and ethnicity that we are required to apply in this course to understand larger issues of human rights, gender and the environment.

How Do We Define Inequality?

Simply put, inequality is the absence of equality. But then, what is equality and how is it to be achieved? These are some of the fundamental questions for the social sciences and even though they have been explored a great deal in the literature on politics and sociology, it is difficult to put an exact meaning to it. Here, we will quickly explore some aspects of this literature and try to make sense of this idea by relating to our earlier example, if necessary.

Equality for human beings is usually thought of in two ways: the first that all human beings *are* born equal, and therefore, should be treated as such; the second that all human beings *ought* to have an equal share in economic goods, social opportunities and/or political powers among people. If we truly believe in both of these, then each needs to find expression in the way in which society and polity are organised and conduct themselves, and vice versa. From our discussion of Dharavi, it is not very difficult to recognise that neither of these two principles of equality is being fulfilled—quite to the contrary. Hence, inequality is the hallmark of this site that we have chosen.

The next step we need to take is to understand *the nature of these inequalities*. For this, we need to understand the ways in which the differences between people are articulated. For example, one way is to divide people on the lines of languages they speak. This would demonstrate the differences between them in a simple manner. But when people are separated into castes, the differentiation is not along horizontal lines, but vertical; that is, in the caste 'system', some castes will always be superior to others. Thus, a caste society structurally and systematically reproduces these differences. In this instance, the differences are no longer simply differences between equal people, but ordered in a hierarchy and therefore unequal. Similarly, the difference between men and women, which is basically natural, acquires a hierarchical character in society because of the power relations between them. This is the sense in which class and ethnic differences are not so simple; they are also hierarchically ordered. Once we recognise the different kinds of differences and inequalities that exist, we need to understand the relationship between them because they do not exist as separate entities. Simply put, a person such as a very poor Brahmin is an example of intersecting differences, wherein one scale puts him at the top and the other at the bottom. So, there are different forms of inequality, which need to be understood.

Forms of Inequality

The differences and inequalities discussed above coexist and operate simultaneously. Sometimes they can reinforce, making a life situation very complex; they may not be equally salient at all times. What is important to remember when dealing with so many categories is that none is more real than the other. Gupta (1992) warns that asking questions like: 'Is caste more important than class?' or 'Does gender matter more than class?' are actually false questions because they do not help us understand the complex reality any better. Instead he argues that social inequalities are already existent in societies and the ways in which they individually manifest are complex and difficult. Further, they exist in connection with other inequalities and we need to look beyond the obvious and trace those interconnections.

Beginning to understand social inequality requires that we recognise that most societies are a complex web of different people. The basis of these differences are also varied; that is, it could be occupation, culture, region of habitation, customs, and so on. Over time and with different experiences, these differences acquire an order amongst themselves, when some become more important than others. This is known as hierarchy.

> Hierarchy implies the regular ordering of a phenomenon on a continuous scale ...Height, weight, income and even power (once it has been quantified) can be arranged in a hierarchy. Hierarchy is but one form of social stratification and it certainly does not constitute the essence of social stratification. But not all systems of stratification are hierarchical
>
> (Gupta 1992: 6).

And specially, a more general term, which is difference, often describes social stratification which in societies can be understood in terms of distinct categories like caste, class, gender, ethnicity, race and community. These categories are meant to explain the kinds of strata or levels prevalent in every society. Sociology shows how these categories have come about and interact with each other in ways that are unique to the history, culture, economy and politics of a particular society. This course focuses on the caste, gender, ethnicity and class, and their interconnections. While

BOX 2

A Note on 'Commonsense'

'Commonsense' is something that all of us possess, despite ourselves. In the course of our own socialisation (that is, the context of our education, growing up, and so on), we acquire knowledge and understanding about a large number of things about life around us. The work of social science, however, is to look beyond the obvious, and unravel multiple layers and intertwining of the operation of different aspects, which can have the effect of actually complicating, or worse, confusing you, because it might contradict what you already know to be the 'truth'. But that is actually the beginning of understanding society—when we force our commonsense back and see aspects that we did not know existed and which prove us wrong and make us want to deny them. In this book, we will try to follow this pattern as far as possible—begin with the commonsense on any issue and then slowly progress to a sophisticated understanding of the issue.

each of these brings a large number of people a common defining characteristic and an organising principle of society, it does not rule out differences on a large number of other counts.

Indian society represents a social system characterised by pervasive inequalities that have become a way of life. To understand the nature of this way of living, we need to consider the plural divisions and their related ideologies that characterise social life. These divisions both cut across and interconnect caste, class, ethnicity and gender to each other.

CASTE

We all know about caste, or so we think. Let us take surnames. In most cases of people we meet, or interact with, or people reported in the media, we can tell which caste they belong to, by looking at the name. At the same time, we also register *where* in the hierarchy of caste they are located.

Why don't you have a discussion in the class about the castes that people belong to and see if you can address the following questions in the following order:

- Does everyone know their caste?
- Who does? Where do they come from originally?
- Who do not? Do they have any particular reason for not knowing so?
- Ask how many people would face stiff opposition, if they wanted to marry outside their caste.

Do you discover a large number of the most amazing things, somewhat along the following lines?

- That while most surnames might indicate the caste directly, many may not; for example, Singh, Chaudhary, Rai/Roy, Rao, and such others may indicate *jati*/region, but may not because many of them originated as titles. Thus, we find that people of the same caste use different surnames and those of different castes use same surnames.
- There are so many social groups, but each contain so many different castes; for example, the Malyalis or Gujaratis, which are social groups, would have caste divisions amongst themselves.
- As regards social groups, if you were to compare the caste groupings on the basic four-fold classification of Brahman–Kshatriya–Vaishya–Shudra, it would not be possible to make a one-to-one correspondence each time.

- What is more, within each of these broad caste categories, there would be many differences, and often no agreement between who is hierarchically superior or inferior.
- It is almost always argued that castes are basically occupational groups and so the caste system is simply an indication of the division of labour in a society.

So if all of these are true in some sense or the other, then what is caste actually?

Defining Caste

Caste is a form of social stratification unique to the context of Hinduism in South Asia of which three dimensions are most well known:

- Caste divisions originated in traditional occupations.
- Caste is always inherited and perpetuated by complex rules of marriage within the larger boundaries of caste and the specific ones of *jati*. Each *jati* consists of lineages that dictate where each person may acceptably marry.
- Caste order carries hierarchy within it, that is, hierarchy is innate to it and is related to who may perform and participate in religious rituals and who are definitely outside of it.

All three aspects are equally significant in the working of caste as a social category. This is particularly important in order to recognise the manner in which caste works as a basis of social inequality rather than merely social difference. In this section, we will examine the literature in the discipline of sociology, which has studied caste most closely, and try to understand how they interpret it (see Box 3).

BOX 3
How Sociologists Study Caste?

Most of these studies are based on close observations of the way of functioning of caste hierarchy by the authors, through a method called 'fieldwork'. By this method, the researcher spends many months or sometimes more than a year, with the community or group they are studying, observing their rituals, customs, restrictions and rules, from which they derive an understanding of how caste functions. Naturally, they are actually based on small-level and micro-level reality, but can be generalised to the entire society. But this is different from the mass-scale studies of the society as a whole, by counting numbers of people in different caste groups and the relationship between them, and so on, the outcomes of which we will discuss in the next section called Caste in Contemporary India.

According to scholars such as M. N. Srinivas and G. S. Ghurye, the three pillars of the caste system are broadly as follows:

1. **Hierarchy** which is derived from birth and traditionally prescribed status, and ranks unequal groups and all that is associated with each into a hierarchy of high and low.
2. **Pollution** which is the central principle that enables this ranking and permeates all aspects of caste society, that is, people, groups, things, occupations and even the body are separated into the pure and the polluted, and thus clean or unclean, and therefore ranked high or low.
3. **Segmentation** or division which refers particularly to the fact that castes are subdivided or segmented into smaller subsections called subcastes, which are different yet not unequal and function as parts of the whole caste via the principles of fusion and fission. Each of these subcastes has its own subculture and way of life within the parameters of its larger caste identity.

The caste hierarchy and separation between castes is maintained with the help of certain restrictions:

1. There is restriction of **behaviour**, through who one marries. This is also called the rule of caste endogamy, as one only marries one's equals and so within the caste.
2. **Interaction** with people of other castes is regulated through acceptance or non-acceptance of food and water also called the 'rule of commensality' where one eats only with his equals and accepts only uncooked food from his non-equals or food cooked in ghee from his non-equals, as ghee is pure (therefore you find *prasad* is either made in ghee or is dry).
3. **Monopolisation of hereditary occupations** is again very central to the system because what you do is who you are and vice versa. Thus, an upper-caste person follows what are called clean occupations such as priesthood or land-based occupations that do not 'defile' or pollute, whereas a low-caste person does work that is unclean, polluting and defiling such as the work of a sweeper or a cobbler, which places him at the bottom of the hierarchy as 'untouchable'.
4. **Restrictions on dress, speech and custom** also prevail, and what an upper-caste person wears, speaks or does may not be done by others. The lower castes cannot even live in the same kind of houses as the upper castes, or for that matter, are also restricted from living in the same streets/village area as other castes or walking the same streets, sharing the same wells, temples or cremation grounds. In fact, there are regions in Maharashtra where the lower castes had to not only wear a broom around their waist to sweep the ground behind them as they walked, but also were not allowed to walk through

the streets of a village while the sun was high as their shadows would be long and may fall upon an upper caste.

5. Every caste group and village also has a caste or village panchayat which ensures through punishment that rules of the caste were strictly followed by its members.

If we look at the caste system, we find that it is a system that divides and, indeed, puts people in hierarchies in all areas of life. What makes it rigid and discriminating is that this ideology is also translated into visible markers of difference, that is, social stratification is translated into social segregation.

Central to understanding the caste system is the need to examine the ideology of pollution which is in fact the principle around which the system is built and kept alive in *ritual* terms (see Box 4). According to this principle, everything can be characterised as having certain degrees of pollution which make that person or thing or act defiling/polluting and give to it a rank which can be high or low. Thus, people are ranked by birth and occupation they follow which may be clean or unclean, and people, according to Srinivas, are polluted daily by acts such as eating, defecation or menstruating because all biophysical processes and emissions from the

BOX 4

Louis Dumont

A very significant contribution in the understanding of the caste system and the idea of pollution comes from the work of Louis Dumont. For Dumont, caste was a system grounded in religious ideology and hierarchy. At its core was a system of oppositions and inclusions, or complementary hierarchical relationships of purity and pollution between each caste. In other words, for Dumont, there was a fundamental opposition of the pure and the impure which formed the base of the system. It divided castes but also enabled interactions between them because, for Dumont, the caste system was a system of hierarchy where the parts of the whole were ranked in relation to the whole. Thus, the dominance of the Brahmin would be insignificant if there were no King to protect him and the King would not be king if the Brahmin were not there to do his coronation. Likewise, the dominance of the Brahmin would fail if there were no untouchables to take away his impurities.

Dumont's work is believed to epitomise what is regarded by critics as the Brahmainical view of caste. In other words, for Dumont, castes stood in a relationship of complementarities and encompassment to each other, that is, dependent yet separate, where the status of each was derived from the purity or pollution of the caste above or below. Dumont and the work of others who stressed the importance of hierarchy in caste has been questioned as ignoring the importance of difference and what significance the system has for the untouchables.

body, including hair and nails, are considered to be sources of pollution. Even the human body is separated into the left and right with the former side considered less pure than the latter. Because pollution is so important and essential to ranking, avoidance becomes the basis of interaction/non-interaction between castes and creates the hierarchy and degrees of un-touchability.

Thus, Dipankar Gupta (1992) writes of the importance of the former when he says that caste must be understood as based on the principle of natural superiority and bodily purity, and the externalisation of internal differences. When these differences become visible and demonstrable (through restrictions and behaviour patterns) we have social stratification. He argues for how there may be a single criterion of differentiation but the social display of these differences may be plural, and express the inequalities between groups through social segregation. For Gupta, the interaction between hierarchy and difference is seen most clearly in relations of caste and class.

Therefore to understand caste, it becomes important to also look at these inter-relations that caste has with other institutions. Thus, we find that caste and class are intertwined in various ways. In rural India, there is an extensive nexus between the relationships based on caste and land such that there arises an economic hierarchy of class that parallels the social hierarchy of caste. Marxist scholars who have studied agrarian relations in India speak of the cumulative nature of the inequalities that arise consequently. Simply put, we find that in relation to land ownership and working on land, the upper castes are the owning classes (*malik*), the middle castes are the tenant classes (*kisan*) and the lower castes are the landless labourers or the lower classes (*mazdoor*). In other words, the hierarchy of caste and status ranking is paralleled by an economic hierarchy and class divisions. Such an agrarian class structure based on unequal distribution of land, attached social privileges and disadvantages could be found in most regions.

Attempts to understand this nexus between class and caste have been the core of many studies on village-India over the decades. Andre Beteille's (1965) study of Sripuram in Tanjore examined the nature of the nexus, and how changes take place when politics and power enter into the equation and create a dispersed system of inequality where caste status no longer determines other identities. Beteille believes that the mutual relations between these categories constituted the heart of the agrarian hierarchy and that an understanding of caste would be incomplete unless these relations were understood.

The very same authors will be referred to again in the section on class and it will become clear how the point at which one is standing to see anything changes the nature of the view.

Caste in Contemporary India

What is especially important though, for the purposes of this book, is to understand the way in which caste operates in contemporary India, taking into cognizance the vast changes that have taken place in the social, and by implication, caste structures through processes of education, migration and new professional groups. These changes have created new elites that dominate economic, social and political life, and over the years, democratic politics has created movements and opposition to this domination by marginalised groups. This politics of marginalised groups has, in many instances, overlapped with those of many backward castes. Now, at the time of the adoption of the Constitution, there was a clear recognition of inequality fostered by caste and, together with a commitment to eradicate untouchability, it yielded the policy of reservation in educational opportunities and jobs in the public sector. This has been in place since then, but two distinctly opposite evaluations are available. One, that it has served the purpose of promoting the interests and enhancing the capabilities of the castes and groups that needed it, and the other that it has simply served to skew relations in society, jettisoned merit and ought to be discontinued if we are to develop in any substantial way. These positions were first openly and sharply brought into the public space during the controversy over the government's decision to implement the Mandal Commission Report, which recommended extending the umbrella of reservations to include another category of lower castes, the Other Backward Classes (OBCs). So, the 1990s saw a co-termination of increasingly voluble, assertive, even belligerent backward-caste politics on one hand and the Mandal controversy on the other. In this context, the understanding of caste provided by mainstream sociology proved inadequate. As Satish Deshpande (2003: 103) pointed out:

> much of anthropology has dealt with caste in terms of religious texts, ritual status linked to notions of purity and pollution, and rules and customs about marriage (endogamy) and food-sharing (commensality). This is, indeed, a far cry from the rough and tumble of competitive caste politics in independent India, especially in the Mandal era.

He argues that a certain commonsense on caste exists amongst the powerful new classes referred to above and this commonsense view 'shapes sociologists and is also shaped by them' (ibid.: 104–5). While this point may be debated on its own, for purposes of understanding caste in contemporary India, we will follow his carefully articulated 'commonsense' on caste and the arguments that a sociologist can offer to counter them, in the light of his better understanding of contemporary society.

Deshpande poses four points that he believes are what 'most urban, educated, middle-class (and therefore largely upper-caste) Indians would tend to think of caste inequality' (ibid.: 105). They are (ibid. 105–6):

1. Caste inequality is a social evil, ... after things have been changing rapidly, ... Reservation has provided very real benefits ... but this is being monopolised by a minority within the group ... now involved in the electoral arithmetic of vote banks ... not warranted.
2. Caste has been given a new lease of life by its encashability in politics. Since politics is dominated by the numerically stronger lower and middle classes, the upper castes are now facing a very real reverse discrimination.
3. More objective criteria sensitive to individual contexts are needed ... Particularly with respect to job reservations, the principle of compensatory preferences has been overextended, and this has resulted in the 'murder of merit'.
4. ... By and large, the upper castes have given up their prejudices and moved beyond/out of caste. Ironically, today it is the lower and middle castes who are the main props for the continuance of this pernicious system.

By way of response as a sociologist whose responsibility is to help people understand societies better, particularly their own, he poses counters to the commonsense 'as questions that remain unasked'. So,

1. ' ... the condition of all social groups, including the lowest castes and tribes, has improved today. But by how much has it improved? How have the lowest castes/tribes fared in comparison to the rest of the population?'
2. ' ... the massive social reality (is) that the overwhelming majority of those in the 'highest' or most preferred occupations are from the upper castes, while the vast majority of those in the menial and despised occupations belong to the lower castes.'
3. 'We must also ask if particular *occupations* continue to be dominated by particular caste-clusters and whether this makes for a recognisable pattern systematically linking privilege or disprivilege to caste' (ibid.: 107). That is, if an overwhelming majority of people in the media, especially in senior positions, continue to be from the upper castes, then the presence of one OBC or SC person anywhere cannot be taken to be an example of, or be successful in, delinking caste from occupation. There is something in the system that allows the domination to continue. Now, this is what needs to be understood, if the true character of inequality is to be understood, while recognising that, indeed, caste is a very significant aspect of it.

Deshpande's task is difficult because there have been no systematic attempts to collect information on caste.[2] So, he argues that on the basis of careful reading of data collected by the Government of India, namely the Census (that does not list all castes), the National Sample Survey Organisation (that lists the poor and some castes) through the massive monthly per capita income and expenditure, it could be clearly concluded that 'caste continues to be a major fault line of economic inequality in contemporary India' (ibid.: 109). And so, he (ibid.: 116) concludes by stating firmly:

> Despite the major phenomenon of the rural OBCs—itself a residual, unexamined category that deserves more careful attention—caste inequality has been flourishing in rural and especially in urban India. These data are from a very large, national survey; they report proportions averaged across thousands of cases—they cannot be dismissed as being due to inter-individual differences or statistical accidents. The differences between caste groups are too strong and too stable to be artifacts. We have to make the necessary effort to transcend the commonsense view and re-examine the question of caste inequality seriously.

CLASS

In everyday parlance, class is used a lot—to denote social and cultural differences in terms of education, upbringing or manner, or a level of poverty, or even to indicate those who rule as different and apart from those that are ruled. Thus, we use the word in different senses—in social terms, and to refer to economic power or political status. But these are not limited to a colloquial usage of the word *class*. Indeed, the sociological literature also explores these different dimensions of class to understand how it operates in society. The study of sociology separates each of these meanings in terms of hierarchy and difference (as discussed earlier), and helps us to recognise which of the meanings of class helps us best to understand inequality, which is, as we have repeated many times already, the focus of this book. Thus, explaining class in terms of economic characteristics locates it as a category of *social strata* (level), while the others, social and political, locate it as a category of *social structure*. The first locates class to help understand *social inequality*; the second, *social difference*.

DEFINING CLASS

The following three assumptions are common to all conceptions of 'class' (Ossowski 1963):

BOX 5

Cases of Caste Inequality

Here are brief accounts of two stories on caste, one by the veteran journalist, P. Sainath, on a village in UP, from 1987, and the other from Bombay in 2005. These stories cover the ground reality of India that the majority in the media never report:

Sherpur is a village in UP that fought the British for independence. In this struggle for independence, both upper-caste Bhumihars and the Dalits participated. But till today, all 3,500 Dalits here are landless and, in 1975, in a flare-up over wage-rates, the Dalit basti was burnt down. Whenever there are jail-bharo agitations and the jails are over-full, the police arrest six or seven Dalits on the pretext of 'conspiracy to stage a robbery', put them in jail, have them clean up 'all the excreta, vomit and the rubbish of jail bharo' and then release them. 'The Dalits here are not free', Shiv Jagan Ram, a Dalit leader says. 'No independence, no land, no learning, no assets, no jobs, no health, no hope. Our freedom is slavery.'

('Forgotten Freedoms: Sherpur: Big Sacrifice, Short Memory', *The Times of India* 1997)

Chandrakant Sasane is 31 and belongs to a scheduled caste. He holds an MA degree in social work. He said that though he was selected for the position of lecturer at Mumbai's N. G. Acharya and D. K. Marathe College of Arts and Science, the college did not appoint him to the post ... Still, using the Right to Information law, he asked for documentary evidence from the college as well as from Bombay University. On 14 September 2004, a Bombay University selection committee—with seven of its eight members present—unanimously selected Chandrakant Sasane for appointment as lecturer to teach the Foundation Course in Philosophy at the college. The post was reserved for SC/ST and six candidates had been interviewed. The selection committee also included the Principal Dr D. M. Muley and the Head of Department, Professor A. V. Desai, of the same college. On 16 September 2005, the university followed up and sent a recommendation to the college to appoint him.

(Shailesh Gandhi, www.indiatogether.com, 22 Feb 2006)

1. It constitutes a system of the most comprehensive group in the social structure.
2. It has a relatively permanent membership.
3. It concerns a system of privileges and discriminations not determined by biology.

Other characteristics normally associated with class are:

- A vertical order: superior /inferior status.
- Permanent class interests and conflict.
- Class consciousness and action.
- Relative isolation.

What follows is a brief discussion on each of these characteristics and their theoretical basis. Thereafter, we will move to understanding those aspects that help us better understand social inequality and the issues to be covered in the later sections of this book. To understand class as a social group, we go back to the definition we began with—one that is predominantly defined by economic interests, or the economic base. Each class has access to some part of the 'material base' of society, that is, any resources, natural or human-made that can be used to live on or provide income, such as land, forests, or anything. Given that all production takes place in society by using any or all of these resources, the power of each class depends on its control over these resources. It also follows that this power will bring them into conflict with others in society and the resolution of conflicts may result in some classes gaining greater control and, hence, greater power than before.

Karl Marx is most often associated with his perspective on class. It is very important to clarify at the very outset that the 'commonsense' on Marx, whereby people believe that he stood for two classes—the bourgeoisie and the proletariat—is a gross mistake. Therefore, criticism about Marx's position on class on these grounds is completely misplaced. Then what is it that we need to know of Marx? First, we will clarify what he understands by the concept of class itself. Second, we refer to his understanding of the relationship between different social classes and social change.

Marx's concept of class does not separate the economic, the social and the political. In fact, he argues that class can be understood as a social category that is *located at the confluence of* economy, society and polity. Thus, he identifies each of them by their economic role or position, which then shapes the social world they inhabit and the culture they fashion. Consequently, the combination of the economic role or position, and their social world shapes, also, their political consciousness. This is how he demonstrates the confluence of the three in the concept of class. But what is more, the significance of each of these is not equal—causal priority is accorded to the economy, which is privileged over, or is more important than, the other two levels of society and politics. In short, the concept of class is the centrepiece of the core causal sequence proposed by Marxist theory wherein what you *are* (at the economic level) shapes what you *experience* (at the social level) which ultimately determines what you *do* (at the political level) (Deshpande 2003: 126). Marx's truly distinctive contribution to class is his identification of specific combinations of economic, social and political conditions, in different historical epochs called 'modes of production'. For each, depending upon its character he identifies social classes. Thereby, the merchant class in feudalism would be very different from that under capitalism and also play a different social and political role.

Marx believed that the great achievements of capitalism were not available to the majority of the people, who actually did the hard labour that made it possible. Thus, capitalism needed to be overthrown, and a more just and equitable society be brought in its place. In analysing how it could be done and by whom, Marx offered, amongst other things, the analysis of social classes under capitalism, especially the industrial working class. This class had been created by the movement of people away from the countryside, thereby breaking out of the deep inequalities perpetrated by the shackles of feudalism and opting for the relative freedom of wage-labour. That is, under industrial capitalism, they became free to go to the employer that paid them more, rather than have to stick to the one they were born to serve, as under feudalism. However, Marx demonstrated by careful analysis (called the use-value–exchange-value analysis) that this system was based on a deep economic inequality, i.e., of the capitalist keeping the lion's share of the profit and thereby creating and perpetrating a new form of inequality, *which has the pretence of equality*.[3] Thus, this pretence is a *contradiction* within capitalism, which claims to help establish democracy as the organising principle of politics by breaking up the old feudal order. Thus, it will need to be overthrown, to be replaced by one that is truly democratic. In Marx's understanding, a truly democratic state is one in which those that live by the hard labour of their hands must have equal position in social and political terms as those that live by the labour of their minds (intellectuals and professionals) or the use of their capital (capitalists). And this would be possible, if the main source of inequality, that is, the ownership of capital, were to be completely changed, and instead of it being in the hands of the few, it becomes commonly owned by *society*. Thus, when capital moves away from the capitalist to the society, it can become the basis for *socialism*.

At the heart of this transformation is the requirement for the industrial working class to become conscious of this contradiction they are in. Then, they need to find ways and means of translating this new consciousness into political action. Marx argues that this is possible when they themselves become critical of the system, and if other social classes, such as intellectuals and professionals (that also developed under capitalism) would take this up as a political cause. They would do this not out of philanthropic intent, but because they believe in its liberating potential. Thus, when they are able to consolidate this consciousness, they would be able to challenge the system by a revolution.

It is in this context that we can understand two aspects of his thought, the focus on the two classes of capitalism, and his contempt for the peasantry. He recognised a number of other classes in several of his works like *Class Struggles in France*, *The Eighteenth Brumaire of Louis Bonaparte*, and in his analysis of the historical background of capitalism in the other modes of production like feudalism, slavery and primitive communism. But he *concentrated* his analysis on the bourgeoisie and the working class of industrial capitalism for two reasons: (1) that the antagonism between them represented the *principal contradiction* of capitalism, and (2) the potential for revolutionary change lay in this contradiction being overcome. As he famously observed (in the *Theses on Feuerbach*), the role of the philosopher was not merely to interpret or analyse the world, but also suggest a way to change it, make it better. Further, he saw the peasantry as but a part of the old, oppressive feudal system, representing its lack of dynamism and accepting the exploitative social relations and political power it lived in. According to Marx's analysis of history, all modes of production break up when significant economic changes take place, thus pushing changes in social and also political structure, and consequently giving way to the new. That is exactly how the feudal mode of production became capitalist in most parts of Europe and it would be a matter of time before the rest would follow. The peasantry would be significant in terms of being able to follow the lead of the new industrial working class, not having a historical role to play by itself. This is why Marx did not accord the peasantry any role in modern historical changes and famously called them 'a sack of potatoes', in direct contrast to the industrial working class. This part of Marxian analysis has important implications for understanding social inequality with the help of the criterion of class in developing countries. At a very broad general level, it means that unless they arrive at a certain level of industrialisation, they cannot expect to have a dramatic social/political change.[4] It may also mean excluding the majority of the population from analysis and a potential for change. This could not possibly be a serious option for sociologists and anthropologists working in India and other developing countries. So, we find that a fair amount of scholarship, not as 'conceptually rich or plentiful as material on the caste system' (Gupta 1992: 230) but significant enough for our purposes, is available on class in contemporary India. This is what we examine next.

Class in Contemporary India

In order to understand classes in contemporary (postcolonial) India, we need to look at the broad economic structure comprising the industrial, agrarian and tertiary sectors. Each of these is not homogenous or uniform by any chance. In all three, the amount of capital invested indicates the different kinds of labour used and the power relation between the capitalists (owners) and labour. In industry, this would include the range from big steel and heavy manufacturing companies to small-parts manufacturing companies or power loom textile making industry; in agriculture from capital-intensive farming to traditional low-intensive farming, as in large farms using heavy machinery, chemical fertilizers and pesticides to small farms completely run by family labour and organic inputs; and in the tertiary sector, from highly skill-based institutions like management companies to low-skill or lowly paid skill-based occupations like those of barbers or cobblers. It is in accordance with the proportion of capital that both the volume of labour and the power relations between the owners and labour would be understood.

Additionally, in both the industrial and the tertiary sectors, the 'organised' and 'unorganised' sectors need to be differentiated. Definitions are difficult, but, by and large, organised sectors are those in which laws about the hiring and firing of workers passed by the government are applicable, because the units of manufacture would be properly registered and would be paying taxes. Unorganised sectors are those in which neither is the case. So, in the latter, the power relations between owners and workers are even more strongly in favour of the owners, because in case of any crisis, typically, the worker has hardly any right to justice. In the agricultural sector, the landholding pattern is a very important factor for understanding agrarian social classes and inequality in that context. In most areas, the landholding pattern dates back to the colonial period and in others, to the precolonial. In only some was it changed or influenced in the postcolonial period following a number of state and other political interventions like the Zamindari Abolition Acts, the Bhoodan movement, the Naxalite movement and the initiatives of the Communist governments specifically in Kerala, West Bengal and Tripura.

Following Marx, all of these together would then demonstrate the inequality between the different social classes. But it is important to remember that this category intersects with the other categories being discussed, as do the inequalities resulting from it. Naturally, the inequalities resulting from class can never be studied in isolation from those resulting from the others. We will broadly focus on the industrial labour force, the agrarian classes and the 'middle class'.

The Working Classes

The labour market, as Holmstrom (in Gupta 1992: 257) describes it,

> appears to separate people into at least three groups, ... These three kinds of people have different chances in the job market, different earnings and working conditions, often live in different places and have different friends; though kinship and friendship can cut across these boundaries. First, there are the permanent organised-sector workers, including factory workers as

> well as government and office employees ... This group shades into workers with fairly regular employment unprotected by law, including all the workers in small firms and 'temporaries' etc. in large ones.

He further identifies 'a fourth group: the self-employed, ranging from those depending on one or a few customers who can dictate terms, to independent craftsmen like carpenters who have a real market for their work ...' (in ibid.). What is important to ask, he suggests, are really three sorts of questions: about real differences in economic conditions and life-chances ... about social maps—the differences and alignments that people think are important; and about the social worlds they live in.

The Agrarian Classes

Thorner describes the agrarian social classes in his classic work, *The Agrarian Prospect in India* (1976). Researching the country's changing agrarian structure he (in Gupta 1992: 262) found that it

> is, after all, not an external framework within which various classes function, but rather it is the sum total of the ways in which each group operates in relation to other groups. We will find that some of these relations are defined and enforced by law. Others are customary. Still others are of a flexible or fluctuating character.

As an illustration, we may cite that while it is known that the basic agrarian classes are landlords, tenants and labourers, it is not a given that each of them are constituted by separate individuals. In fact, any individual may inhabit one or more of the classes. On the other hand, as indicated earlier, different parts of the country have class categories remnant from the colonial or earlier times, while others may be more recent. What Thorner (in ibid.: 263) tries to do is to

> set up criteria which will help us marshal these divergent systems of tenure and cultivation into usable categories, ... by asking the form in which the income is obtained from the soil, ... what type of rights are enjoyed and ... how much land is held under these rights.

Collecting and anlysing data based on these questions, Thorner (in ibid.: 265) formulated his three-fold classification of the agrarian classes, 'the *maliks* or proprietors, the *kisan* or working peasants and the *mazdur* or agricultural labourers.[5] The key to the division is the total amount of actual labour contributed to the production process and share in the product.' This key, he (in ibid.: 265) combined with the Permanent Settlement landholding pattern introduced by the British, in which he recognised two dimensions:

> One, the British insistence upon the State's prerogative as ultimate owner and below it, elaborate sets of inferior claims were defined and put into writing. This resulted in a development that was common to the country, that is, 'Whatever the particular form of land system that was followed, it served to confirm the right of one group of holders to a share in the produce of the land, whether or not they participated personally in the productive process.'

Unfortunately, the legislation enacted in the postcolonial period to restore the traditional rights of actual cultivators served only to consequently entrench them as rentier peasants. Hence, the structures of inequality were deeply entrenched by this system.

Dhanagare (1992), the other well-known analyst of agrarian classes in India, sought to apply the Marxist model of categorising classes in peasant societies in a more obvious manner. While he agreed with the basics of Thorner's scheme, he felt it needed to be taken forward by redefining the specific sub-categories within the classes (which have not been discussed earlier in this book) and also relating them to 'broader and more widely used conceptual models in contemporary sociology, ... in the study of peasant societies' (in ibid.: 273), like rich, middle and poor peasants. However, he was careful to state, by regrouping Thorner's classification, that each category that developed was regionally specific and that more often than not the terms rich, middle and poor peasants were better understood in qualitative terms, rather than quantitative. Most importantly, however, Dhanagare (in ibid.: 274) is conscious that

> obviously there is some risk in using a 'class' model in analysis of an agrarian social structure in a traditional society such as India. But the risk must be attempted if any meaningful historical and comparative sociology of peasant movements in India is to be attempted.

In further descriptions of the agrarian classes, however, both Thorner and Dhanagare were careful to identify them on the basis of castes or caste groups, which we will take up for discussion when we talk of the interconnections between caste and class.

The Middle Class

Let us begin with a set of questions: Who is the 'middle class' in India? What are the two ends of which it is in the middle? Why is it important to study the middle class when we are trying to understand social inequality? These questions, or the opinions we have on them, are part of everyday discussion amongst most of us that study in universities in India. And so, there is a 'commonsense' about them, which is normally absent from discussions about the other two classes we have discussed before. This 'commonsense' can become a better and more nuanced understanding, if complemented with rigorous analysis. That is precisely what we hope to be able to do in this section. Unlike on the other two classes, there is very little up-to-date material that addresses these questions, but one study by Deshpande (2004) is available and we will turn to it for the very interesting set of insights it offers.

Going by the conceptual basis of analysing classes, we need to identify the three components—economic, social and political. In economic terms, the middle class has been conceived of as a purely economic segment of consumers, particularly since the 1990s, a potential market for the international corporations that were keen to enter the Indian market. Deshpande (2004: 134) says that we 'have to determine where to draw the lines that distinguish the middle class form the other classes. ' At the same time, his worry is, 'Is the middle class a purely negative and residual category, or should it also involve some positive characteristics?' (ibid.). At the end of a discussion that involves a critical examination of data, he gives us significant ideas:

> that when it is defined as a class of consumers, its size may be very large by world standards, but it is a very small proportion of the Indian population;
>
> that this proportion is the top 10 or 15 per cent of the income distribution of the population—so it is not really in the 'middle' of the population at all!
>
> that there are two parts of the middle class—the elite fraction (the intelligentsia) and the mass fraction (the middle middle and the lower middle)—difficult to measure, but can be differentiated for purposes of understanding their role, particularly in matters political, as examined later.[6]

Next, we try to understand its social significance. Deshpande (ibid.: 129) points out that

> the 'common man'... manages to convey a powerful sense of middle-class identity that claims to be 'common' both in the sense of something that is *shared* as well as *widespread*. Further along, ... is inflated into a larger sense of legitimate representativeness—the 'middle class' is projected as the social group that is best qualified to represent the whole of society.

But the really important question is: How can a class that is at the top 10 per cent of the population be a good representative of the rest? This term is actually derived from the experience of the Western industrialised nations where, Deshpande (ibid.: 131) points out, 'There is some justification—at least in purely numerical terms—for the representative claims of the Western middle classes, if identified broadly as "middle income" groups. Matters are starkly different in poor countries like India.'

Then what is the political significance of this class? And to go back to our question: Is it pertinent to the study of inequality? Satish Deshpande again offers a powerful set of explanations, summarised here.

a. The middle class in post-independence India is entirely a product of the regime of Nehruvian 'development'. It was visualised mainly as a scientific–technical process which would be brought about by experts, on behalf of and for people who needed and wanted it. This automatically implied two things: that the middle class, which could afford and also acquired such technical and scientific education, were given pride of place, were the 'nation-builders' and so enjoyed moral legitimacy; and the other, that in this model, the illiterate and the dispossessed, who were naturally also the poor, remained outside the glory of this activity, just hungry mouths to feed, with no contribution to make. This implied that they did not know anything of value for modernisation and that they were a burden for the country, no glory. (This has very great significance for the debates on environment, which you will also find in the relevant section of this book.)
b. Because of its unique access to education, relationship of access to all the other classes and the ability to articulate, the middle class expresses the policies of the ruling bloc as those that are the most appropriate for the nation as a whole. Whenever there are doubts or active opposition to them, make sure that these are quelled or 'adjusted'. Thus, as Deshpande (ibid.: 139 emphasis original) puts it, 'it is the class that *articulates* the hegemony of the ruling bloc; it both (a) *expresses* the hegemony ...; and (b) *mediates* the relationship between classes within the ruling bloc, as well as between this bloc and other classes'.
c. The elite segment (referred to above) specialises in the production of ideologies; for example, in producing ideas on the 'appropriate Indian' identity, how important the corruption of politicians is, the meaning of secular versus the religious, what is the 'correct' form of dress, language, behaviour, mannerisms, and such that affect the everyday lives of people, consciously as well as unconsciously. The mass fraction would believe and follow these ideologies, thus giving them a solid base in society, which is necessary for any ideology to be of any lasting value. So, they would be responsible for the dissemination of these ideas.

All of these are *political* roles, inasmuch they have the *power* to continuously set the modes in which people think and act. This leads us to the final question: what does this have to do with the social inequality? By now, I am sure you know where to look for this answer. It is in the relationship that this class would possibly have with the other classes in society. For instance, if it sets the agenda for 'modern development', then what does it imply for 'the voice of the people' in setting development agendas? That it does not exist, or that the poor and illiterate are incapable of articulating it, or that they themselves are the voice of the people? Would any of them be actually true? Some of the debates on the first two questions are dealt with in the section on environment.

CLASS AND CASTE

Gupta (1992: 4) argues the basic theoretical position that

> it is not at all the case that a society should exhibit only one form of social stratification. ... the caste system ... coexists with occupational stratification, linguistic stratification, sexual stratification and religious stratification (to name a few). It is important ... to remember that each of these forms of stratification have their own axial principles. In fact, he argues that the question often asked whether caste is giving way to class is an outcome of conceptual fogginess. There is no reason to believe that if there is caste, there cannot be class, nor is it the case that as one grows the other must wane. We should not forsake an elementary methodological tenet, namely, that a concept should be independently defined ... Caste and class after all do not constitute a continuum. ... The covariation between one or more forms of stratification asks for a higher order of explanation, and not the abandonment of one for the other, e.g., caste for class or class for caste.

In this respect, the work of Beteille is significant in that it analyses the changing relationship between castes and the classes they belong to, especially as it is manifest in political power, in his study of Tanjore district in Tamil Nadu. He demonstrates how traditional dominant castes that lost their position of economic superiority as a result of a number of different factors from the early twentieth century onwards also had to give up their position of being the political elite. Yet, this has not always meant for them having to shift from being landowners to tenants and cultivators. Further, the history of the various anti-Brahmin movements like those of the Justice party and the Self-respect Movement, supported by education of the non-Brahmins, spreading their word through their own press and creating a space eventually in the most important vehicle of politics, the Indian National Congress, shows the growing political power of these castes, not fully linked to their economic power, at least not to the majority of them. Also, the focus of the movement, Beteille points out, 'is not in its practice an attack against a particular economic class, but against Brahmins in general, whether they are landowners, school-teachers, clerks or temple priests' (in ibid.: 347–48). Thus, he concludes that 'It is *the anti-Brahmin movement rather than class conflict* between the landowners and the landless that has dominated political life in this area over the last forty years. ' While he acknowledges that, 'No doubt, the anti-Brahmin movement has been viewed by many in the idiom of a class struggle', he is not convinced that it can be explained as *caste struggle translated to class struggle*. The point that is relevant for our basic level of understanding in this course, however, is that there are struggles against inequality, and these struggles are marked by the context in which they are carried out. In this context, there are overlaps of economic and social inequality, and exploitation, and people are able to creatively respond to these overlaps by innovative strategies.

Perhaps one of the best illustrations of the confusion that surrounds this issue between caste and class has been exemplified by the agitations on the Mandal Commission in 1991 and those protesting the government's move to extend reservations, in the summer of 2006. While those were clearly on the issue of caste, those protesting were from the self-declared 'middle class', which, Deshpande points out in the work cited before, is a code word for the 'upper caste'. This could be a point of discussion in a class, by looking closely at the arguments Deshpande makes in his book and the nature of the controversy in the two instances.

A NEW INSIGHT ON SOCIAL INEQUALITY

It is rare to find insights on fundamental categories of society. More often than not, analysts tinker at the edges of concepts, most often content to making adjustments in those that already exist. Initiatives that challenge received concepts and offer new ones, because they are not convinced of the explanatory value of what exists, are one-off developments. Gadgil and Guha's work *Ecology and Equity* (2000) dares precisely to do this. They address a fundamental discomfort that has been evident in the discipline of sociology for a long time (see Guha 1982), in which the study of society is limited to the study of just people amongst themselves, whereas a basic reality is that the relations between people are very significantly dependent on how they relate with nature. So, both people and nature need to be studied together, if we are to correctly characterise social structures, social categories and, hence, social inequality. Their studies of the impact of development policies on people and ecology pushed them to recognise that the frameworks of class or interest group or indeed caste were not adequate to exactly explain the myriad changes occurring in India. All social groups were in one way or another dependent on ecosystems, but their relationship would vary greatly. And so, when ecosystems changed, different social groups would clearly be asymmetrically or unequally affected, contributing to rising inequality. Yet, the traditional castes/classes/interest groups were not the same as these social groups—often they would cut across, though sometimes they did not. But these changes urgently needed to be explained, documented and resolved.

So from the points of focus as the social groups and the ecosystems, they developed three categories that best explained this relationship—ecosystem people, ecological refugees and omnivores.[7] Four-fifths of India's rural people, over half of the total population, depend on natural environments of their own locality to meet most of their material needs. They cite the reality that

> the bulk of the poor, or even the not-so-affluent, must scratch the earth and hope for rains to grow their own food, must gather wood or dung to cook it, must build their own huts with bamboo or sticks of sorghum dabbed with mud and must try to keep out mosquitoes by engulfing them with smoke from the cooking hearth.
>
> (Gadgil and Guha 2000: 3)

These are *the ecosystem people*. Further they (ibid: 4) state that

> as the natural world recedes, so shrink the capacities of local ecosystems to support these people. Dams and mines, for instance, have physically displaced millions of peasants and tribals in independent India. Others have fled as forests, and with them, springs have vanished. These people constitute the ecological refugees who live on the margins of islands of prosperity, as hawkers and domestic servants of Patna or Hyderabad.

And finally, the remaining one-sixth of India's population is the real beneficiaries of economic development—they enjoy the produce of all aspects of nature, while paying next to nothing for it. After Raymond Dasmann who calls them 'biosphere people', Guha and Gadgil (ibid.) feel 'they might equally be termed omnivores'. They do provide a lengthy explanation of this category and also the problem of reducing this huge population to these three, fully conscious of the overlapping criteria hard to fit in any one of these categories. But they (ibid.: 5) argue that 'we are nevertheless convinced that a majority of the Indian population is covered by them. More crucially, from a socio-ecological point of view, we believe our categories to be a great improvement on the more conventional ones

...' It would be interesting and important to incorporate these in future analysis of Indian politics, society and economy, some of which will be attempted in the section on environment.

GENDER

This is one of those terms that definitely needs to be understood in two ways: what *it is* and what *it is not*. Perhaps the reverse order would be better.

What Is Not Gender?

- It is not about studying women to the exclusion of men.
- It is not about pointing out that women are actually superior to men.
- It is not about stating that all women are always and only ever subjected to discrimination, abuse and exploitation and that all men are responsible for it.

What Is Gender?

- It *defines the relationship* between men and women.
- It denotes that this is unequal, with men having more power over women as a basic principle of society, on the basis of a larger social reality.
- It believes that it is *not possible* to locate the differences between men and women in nature; that is, it does not accept that this inequality can be attributed to the *fact* of their being biologically different.
- It *locates these differences in the social structure* that specifies roles, identities and positions of power for men and women.
- It does not deny that men are discriminated against or are exploited; rather it tries to focus on the inequalities women suffer, in the context of the larger inequalities in society.

Two ideas/concepts are very significant in the study of gender—patriarchy and feminism. Both of these are examined in great detail in the section devoted to gender in this book. So, here we need only to refer to some points of significance. First, relating to the 'commonsense' on these ideas. Of all the concepts discussed in this introduction, the maximum 'commonsense' exists on gender. Like with all else, all concepts have to be historically and contextually located. Unfamiliar information, unknown facets and unpalatable truths need to be equally welcomed, and this is probably most true of gender. And this is equally difficult and necessary to do, by both men and women. Second, and very importantly, *neither* of these terms—feminism, gender or patriarchy—*is only about women*. I reiterate, they are all about men *and* women. The layers in which these and others (which will be eventually introduced) operate will confuse, but will eventually reveal.

Gender in Contemporary India

What seems to be the 'commonsense'? That lots of women are educated, work outside the home, have the rights of all citizens, wear what they want, have property, break conventions and are important political leaders. So, is there a gender issue at all in contemporary India? The answer is, as always, we need to look at what exists beyond the obvious and see what we find.

The first issue is *of numbers*: How many women work outside the home? How many women actually get an education and to what level? What proportion own property and do they control it?

The second is of the *actual power/control* women have in situations in which they are definitely better off than before; for instance, women earn independent incomes, but how many of them are actually able to decide how it is to be used? Or, that they have equal rights as their brothers to inherit property from their parents—but how many of them actually get it? And how many of them are persuaded/pressurised by the parents or by social norms to concede this right? And why does that happen?

The third issue is of control in those respects that they ought to have, but do not. The arenas of fertility (the right to decide when and how many children to have, whether to abort female foetuses or not, when to stop having children), pursuing higher education in order to have a professional career (instead of accepting that education is good for bringing up children, or even just to have a job that supplements the family income), right to family property instead of a dowry or a big wedding, the right to political action, representation and organisation are just some of the many unresolved, indeed, very conflict-ridden ones in India today.

The fourth set of issues are those that are confronted by women that might actually give the impression of them being the most liberated and, therefore, without problems—gender-based discrimination against women scientists,[8] artists, sportswomen (a great example being the women's cricket team that actually has won more matches in international cricket than the men's team), media, and so on.

It is possible that other sets of issues can be identified, but we can begin with these. A great many developments have taken place in the issues of gender in India, and both mainstream social and political movements, as well as more clearly committed feminist movements have been responsible for these changes. Much of this will be discussed in the section on gender, so what we will concentrate on here are the interconnections of gender with other social categories and how these embody social inequality.

The recognition of the existence of inequality between men and women in contemporary India goes back to the colonial period, mainly in the social reform movements that worked towards women's education and the initiatives taken by the political movements to include women in their activities.

Relationship with Other Categories

The most obvious intersection of inequality is that of *gender* and *class*. The concept of patriarchy explains the division of labour within the household and how all women are discriminated against in that. But in society, the differences in class (which we have defined as the difference in access to natural/material resources of production) have meant that women have had to suffer doubly. This has been true of both modern as well as older systems of production.

Caste and *gender* are also closely related. Patriarchy and gender-based discrimination have found support in the caste system when the position of women is reduced to that of an untouchable in given contexts in relation to the ideology of ritual pollution. It is common knowledge that caste-based norms ensure that women do not participate in rituals when menstruating, in many instances debarred from cooking or entry to the kitchen. Additionally, when they are widowed, they are avoided and deprived of social visibility. Also, no woman has a permanent caste identity since it changes at marriage, but carries the burden of upholding family and caste honour. This is particularly significant in the expectations of behaviour when their caste is attempting mobility, as shown by Srinivas's work on 'Sanskritisation'. Srinivas uses this term to describe ways in which lower castes attempt to break out of the characteristics that signify their caste by emulating or imitating behaviour or practices of upper castes. While this idea and its veracity has been intensely debated amongst sociologists, what is very illuminating is how one of the clear indicators of this process is the changed behaviour of women. Lower-caste women have regularly worked in the fields, done hard labour and moved about freely, mostly because the gendered division of labour demanded it. But with any sign of upward mobility, they are confined to the household, expected to cover whatever body part is considered erogenous to that particular region/caste/ethnicity. Uma Chakravarti's body of work has illustrated another dimension of this relationship, historically. It is discussed in great detail in the later section and, hence, will not be taken up for discussion here.

Gender and *ethnicity* is perhaps one of the most difficult intersections to explain, not least because the term *ethnicity* itself is fraught with contradictory meanings. So, we will take this up after the basics on ethnicity have been discussed.

ETHNICITY

Ethnicity is the principle that denotes differences in culture between groups. These differences may be religious, linguistic or of a whole way of life. It is interesting to note that ethnicity is the most recent of the social scientific categories. In the last 100 years in India and elsewhere, modern nation-states have emphasised uniformity in order to foster unity amongst people, but often these national identities resulted in playing down special characteristics of communities that gave them a distinct character. This could mean loss of language in the public realm, loss of control over resources for local development, or, even more serious, systematic removal of people of specific origins from positions of power and authority. In extreme instances, these took the form of pogroms against whole communities as in the case of the Jews in the Holocaust, and derecognising language and ritual practice as in the case of the Basques in Spain. These communities then felt it necessary to assert their difference and fight for its recognition, often by violent means, and sometimes through methods of persuasion, rather than be subsumed by the dominant identity.

An example closer home is that of Bangladesh. When East Pakistan was created during the time of the partition of India, the logic was the dominance of Muslims living in that part. Hence, the religious identity was accorded higher significance. However, in the functioning of the Pakistani state, the people of East Pakistan felt that their identity as Bengalis was being completely subsumed, even denied because of the language policy of using Urdu. Hence, this gave rise to a militant movement which ultimately resulted in the creation of Bangladesh. The point, relevant for us here, is that the concept of ethnic identity usually crystallises or becomes significant when it is challenged. At the same time, it is important to remember a point that will be discussed in detail later. That is, that in no conflicts over ethnicity is the sole issue that of identity. Referring to the point about power made in the earlier paragraph, it is when loss of power over economic resources, or positions of authority, is seen to be systematically suffered by a certain group or community that the issue of identity becomes a rallying point. Thus, the larger political and economic context is very important to understand the issue of ethnicity.

There is a difference in the focus of much of the European/American literature and the Indian on ethnicity. While the former are significantly concerned with the relationship *between* ethnicity and race, the latter has been centred on the differences in culture *within* a broad racial group.[9] That is, within the broad Indo-Aryan racial group, the basic ethnic differences that can be identified would be on the basis of *language*. Within the issue of languages, too, there are differences. There are the inequalities between Hindi and the other 'dialects' spoken in the upper Gangetic plain, like Avadhi, Khadi, Bundelkhandi, and such other, and conflict and struggles between Hindi and other South Indian languages. Over time, the issue of ethnicities has been highlighted not simply when there have been conflicts between identity per se, but is cases of access to and distribution of natural or material resources. This is most evident in the conflicts between migrant labour and the original inhabitants of pockets of prosperity. By that definition, these are most often in urban areas.

Ethnicities in Urban India

To return to the example we began this chapter with, a great number of ethnic groups were visible and listed in a survey of Dharavi. They come from different parts of the country, speak their own languages, follow their customs and the like, known as 'markers'—those that mark them out to belong to a certain ethnic group or identity. What is more, they continue to use these markers for at least a generation or two, after which it sometimes gradually disappears as people may absorb other markers from the local community, or some which are adopted generally by everyone. Examples of the latter being the switch in women's dress from saris to 'salwar-kameez' or to trousers and shirts for men. 'Commonsense' indicates that these are done for simple considerations of utility and availability. Yet, it is not as simple or straightforward as it might appear. It often involves considerable debate, sharp differences between generations, between men and women, and very often the resolutions themselves continue to be contested socially even when they are accepted. The main reason for the debate and conflicts within the communities over the change in markers is the fear of what sociologists call 'assimilation', or a loss of distinctiveness of identity, which is the one part that remains accessible to communities that leave their place of origin to live elsewhere. Further, assimilation is also an indicator of loss of power or position to the greater power of the local culture or 'markers', and therefore, sensitive members would naturally want to counter it from the point of view of keeping control over their cultural identity. However, this sensitivity may often take the form of an exercise of power of one generation over another or more commonly of the patriarchal view over women. Often, it is women who are required to carry markers of distinction rather than men, though that may not always be the case.

India, by the admission of an anthropologist, is a tough case for the development of a general theory of ethnicity or nationalism. It is a country with deeply embedded hierarchies and considerable internal cultural variation (Eriksen 1993: 156). Ethnicity has been most strongly articulated around linguistic and tribal identities, and in this book, we will concentrate on tribes or adivasis as we call them.

Tribal India

The ethnicity discussion in India is dominated by that on 'tribes'. The official terminology adopted for them has been 'adivasis', which translates to 'original inhabitants of the land', in itself contentious and difficult. But the people it seeks to describe are to be found in all kinds of natural habitat in India—in forests, hills, deserts, plains—the commonality precisely in their habitat and culture being close to nature. A whole host of issues have developed around the adivasi since the colonial period and continues to this day, with the controversies over the Tribal Land Rights Bill raging all over the country. We take up each of these for discussion by turns.

What Is a Tribe?

Tribes in India can be understood basically from two broad sources—one, the Constitutional definition of a scheduled tribe. The other, from the studies conducted by sociologists (Beteille 1960, Bose 1971, Ghurye 1963, Roy-Burman 1994, Singh 1993, Vidyarthi and Rai 1977) on different tribes and the generalisations they have arrived at. In most 'tribes', according to this literature, there is an all-pervasiveness of religion—almost all members believe in animism, and observing the forms and practices are an important part of their life. This characteristic gives most tribes a kind of homogeneity—that is, everybody follows these, rather unlike in castes, where each caste has smaller groups of 'jatis' that have their own variants of rituals and practices. Also, there is no real hierarchy—there is a kind of equality among the members, which also makes for the absence of exploitation of some groups over others a part of the structure of the tribe itself. In fact, it has been observed that often the members of a tribe come together to fulfil common goals—build homes, harvest crops, hunt, and so on. Most tribes also have distinct taboos, customs and moral codes, usually very different from the Hindu caste society. But Xaxa (1995: 1520) argues that

> these sets of attributes ... are not possessed by a large number of groups identified as tribes in India. And even groups that do subscribe to these attributes have dissimilarities. At one end, there are groups that have all these features, and at the other are those that hardly show these attributes. The large majority of the groups, however, fall somewhere in between.

In fact, he believes that 'the only thing the tribes seem to have in common is, as Beteille puts it, that they all stand more or less outside Hindu civilisation' (ibid.).

Following from this is one of the most important issues for tribes in India—their relationship with the Hindu caste society. As tribal communities have lived separately from, but in close interdependence with, Hindu caste communities in different parts of the country, the most common interpretation of this relationship has been that of their assimilation or transformation into castes. Given that tribal communities also pursue certain occupations like agriculture or iron-mongering, they are often transformed into the corresponding castes prevalent in the closest Hindu society. N. K. Bose called this the Hindu method of tribal absorption, whereby they are absorbed into the caste hierarchy—but what is important to note is that this usually takes place at the bottom of the hierarchy. This process has been happening for a long time in some cases like those of Bhils, Bhumjis and Raj-Gonds, such that over time these castes even develop many sub-castes like Hindu castes. Various anthropologists, referred to above, have offered their classification of tribes on the very basis of the kinds of relationships they establish with the Hindu society. However, Xaxa believes most of these to be inaccurate and negates the whole idea of assimilation being so significant that tribes in India are being overwhelmingly transformed into castes.

Further, other studies also show that it is not necessary that assimilation is the only relationship between tribals and Hindu communities. For example, in the Nilgiri Hills, where the Todas and Kotas live side by side geographically, the Todas as a pastoralist group provide all the dairy needs of the Kotas, while receiving all other goods from the Kotas and other neighbouring castes. While these processes are essential to their ways of life, they do not impinge upon the identity of the two groups which have remained distinctive over a period of time. Thus, harmonious existence between tribal and non-tribal groups allows for a confident culture and helps maintain peace over a long period of time.

Following from the conceptualisation of tribes offered by anthropologists is, however, a far more fundamental issue that is pointed out by Xaxa in the conclusion of the article referred to above. He argues that tribes can be seen simply as a form of society, in which there are people of one kind, belonging there according to some common set of rules, as also other boundaries of language, culture and politics. Instead, two other perspectives, the first that of seeing a tribe as 'a distinct type of society, with positive and negative features (all in relation to 'modern society')' and the second of seeing them 'as representing a socio-political formation which, with the passage of time, will move on to a new stage such as nation, nationality or nationhood', have overshadowed the earlier argument. Thus, tribes are seen 'primarily as a stage and type of society … primitive, illiterate and backward societies. With the onset of changes in the features that constitute its specific features through education, specialisation, etc., … it is no longer considered tribal society, … but become caste society or peasant society' (ibid.: 1524). Thus, the idea that a 'tribe' is 'outside civilisation' is firmly entrenched in the minds of both social scientists and ordinary people.

Another significant interaction that tribal societies have had has been with the Indian state. The Constitution envisaged a special responsibility for the state in welfare programmes for the tribes, which has been translated into a number of programmes, ranging from specially focused development programmes to reservations in educational institutions and employment avenues. Yet, somewhere, something has gone wrong with both the conceptualisation and the implementation of these projects. The other dimension of the interaction has been certain assumptions guiding basic relations with the Indian Union in the first place, as in the case of the tribes of the Northeast India. The antagonistic relationship laid by both of these, together with the 'commonsense' about tribes (discussed just before), is the basis for people of the tribes in India to feel less than equal to others in India. Hence, we will briefly refer to these here.

Antagonism of the tribal people with the modern state began at the time of the British when economic dominance amounted to exploitation, and spilled over to social and cultural exploitation as well. History has powerful stories of rebellions by different tribal communities against these different kinds of exploitation. But what helped to make people see it for what it was and brought them together to oppose it was, first, to posit the exploiters as 'outsiders' and, then, try to assert their identity with respect to them. Thus, the solidarity of tribal identity helped mobilise them into powerful political forces.

What is important to understand is that in post-independence India, too, the state has been perceived as the 'outsider' by many tribal people—though for different sets of reasons. In much of the Northeast, for instance, the government of independent India simply substituted for the colonial British that had robbed them of their proud independence, particularly because it was assumed that they would want to join the Indian Union. Thereafter, things became worse because in the new political system, they had a miniscule presence because their numbers were unfavourable to the rest of the people in the country. In the new administrative framework, all kinds of unfamiliar people came to live and work in their regions and given that development planning was almost entirely carried out in New Delhi, it was deeply resented that their desires, opinions and methods found no place in government functioning. While this was a characteristic of planning and development practice for the whole country, reactions to which came from everywhere eventually, in the Northeast it seemed like an enhanced persecution and neglect. Again, the opposition to this, then, took the form of asserting tribal identities and seeking secession and independence from the Indian Union. In other areas where tribal lands and forests have been used for 'development' purposes, like in Jharkhand, Madhya Pradesh and Orissa, the projects have had the immediate effect of uprooting tribal people from their lands, livelihoods and, hence, their very basis of life and culture. The benefits of this development, which is the reason for undertaking this, are meant to be in the 'national interest'. What it means for those that lose in the first instance is that unless they can be shown how exactly they will benefit as and when the nation does from this very act of uprooting, it is hard for them to believe what the state says. While there is no doubt that there is some benefit from these development projects, no government has been able to actually make sure that it reaches those that gave up everything for it. In this context, it can only seem to the tribal people that the state is especially hostile to them. This, then, is what makes for the feeling of being treated unequally despite being equal and free citizens of India.

It is also very important to remember that the effectiveness of government welfare and other development policies might have been able to offset these sentiments. While this is not the place to discuss the policies in detail, one comment on the reservations policies could be made here. In the context of tribal populations particularly, the usefulness of reservations in higher education and jobs is largely dependent on the preliminary access to some level of infrastructure—primary education, health services, and income-generating activities—to be able to make use of them. In the absence of any of these, and the well-known inefficacy of government welfare projects, in most instances, they remain where they are. This is another reason that contributes to a feeling of inequality.

The third aspect of the relationship between tribals and others has been their conversion to other religions, predominantly Christianity. This has been extremely contentious and important in the context of Indian politics of the last two decades in particular. Yet, a detailed discussion of this would be outside the scope of this book.

INTERCONNECTIONS AS EVIDENT IN THE ISSUES OF HUMAN RIGHTS, GENDER AND THE ENVIRONMENT

Interconnections between class, caste, gender and ethnicity, the four social categories that are sought to be explained in order to explain inequality, actually explain many significant issues in contemporary politics, especially those of human rights, gender and environment. One of the most interesting studies that have established interconnections between these categories has been Gadgil and Guha's (2000) work referred to earlier in the section titled 'A New Perspective on Inequality'. The new classifications/categories of people offered in their analysis embody these interconnections as well as intersections from a specific ecosystem point of view. Novel in approach and rich in political economy bases and archival and oral content, they provide an insight into methods of analysing social reality, while also presenting a different picture of the reality itself. This is what we require, if we are to understand and apply what we learn from this course. This is a relatively new perspective, by which unequal structures in society are not viewed in terms of their parallel existence, but an effort is made to trace and develop the complex interactions between them. This helps to demonstrate why some situations are worse than they need be, because they might illustrate some aspect of social inequality that is not self-evident, sometimes even to those that are interested in it.

Some of the interconnections have already been explained above and some require detail. From here, we adopt a slightly different approach. A series of stories that demonstrate these interconnections have been collected and have been presented. Each story will be followed by a series of questions that can be points for discussion in a class, in a canteen, at home, in the neighbourhood, anywhere and an analysis of the problem.

Unemployment and Migration

Fifty-six Biharis were murdered in Assam in November 2003, over a week of sustained ethnic violence. In the face of intense competition for the semiskilled D category of jobs (requiring a minimum of eighth standard education) in the Indian Railways (the single largest employer in the world), targeted bloodshed was the answer. A mere 2,750 vacancies in Assam had attracted 20,000 prospective applicants from Bihar. This prompted the local ULFA (United Liberation Front of Assam) to call for protection of employment opportunities for the sons-of-the-soil. Eleven wage labourers were also brutally murdered because they hailed from Bihar. But what is the root of a force so vicious and desperate that it instigates mass murder on ethnic lines?

The root of the problem is 'jobless growth' in the Indian economy; that is, despite an acceleration in the growth rate in India, the pace of creation of work opportunities has not kept pace with the growing requirement. The reason for the phenomenon of jobless growth could be that growth in India has essentially been capital intensive. Further, the public sector is in the process of shedding excess labour in the name of downsizing for meeting the efficiency challenges of market competition.

This trend of rising unemployment is compounded by the existence of regional imbalances in development within the country, which have collectively accelerated the phenomenon of migration. This increase in migration is essentially due to regional differences in the population pressure on land, inequality of infrastructure, industrial development, and modernisation of agriculture. (Adapted from Narayan 2004, 'Unemployment and Migration'. www.indiatogether.com.)

Gender and Class

Years of hardship and back-breaking labour in the drought-stricken agricultural fields of Mhaswad village in west central India have worn 64-year-old Sumantai Limbrao Gaekwad to the bone. A single woman by choice, she walked out on her husband two decades ago and survived as a daily wage labourer earning a miserable Rs 2.10 per day. Yet, Sumantai's eyes sparkle today with a new zest for life. Perfectly turned out in a traditional silk sari, her jewellery-laden daughter in tow, the sexagenarian says: 'All that's in the past now. I have built my own house and have my own flowers and condiments shop in the temple complex.'

Sumantai's story captures in a nutshell how a group of assetless, rural women have created, and now operate, a bank for themselves. The Mann Deshi Mahila Sahakari Bank (Mann Land Women's Cooperative Bank) of Mhaswad village is unique in the fact that it is the country's first rural cooperative bank of its kind: *for* and *by* women. The absence of formal education has not deterred these women from managing a system of microcredit that is suited to their needs when the big nationalised banks have failed to see any value in serving them. In the process, they have changed the quality of life in their villages by empowering themselves economically, educationally and politically. Now, even the big nationalised banks want them as clients. (Sen, September 2002, 'You Can Bank on It'. www.indiatogether.com.)

Agrarian Classes and Migration

The poverty of agrarian India has the most astonishing fallouts of all, aggravating and creating overlaps in already deep structures of inequality. It is not possible to provide a countrywide picture, but a few instances will be cited here from news stories done by committed journalists in the non-mainstream media. The first is that of Katabanji, a small town in the Bolangir district of Orissa. This place has seen no industrialisation or development, but is by now known for its large-scale migration of poor labour to other industrial parts of the country every year. When the rural credit folded in early 1990s, Sardars, the middlemen or labour contractors, began to coax the poor people and farmers of these poorest areas of the country into migrating for work to other states where the rich industrialists, brick-kiln owners or road contractors savour the cheap but skilled labour. It's a mutual need. The industrialists in other states need cheap labourers, and the gullible farmers or the landless labourers here need work round the year. As a result of being fortunately located in the axis of this need, the contractors have become millionaires over the last few years and live in islands of prosperity in between the ever-increasing misery and deprivation of the poor. With a dropping rate of rural employment in this region, villagers who are reeling under abject poverty and drought of policies accept deals of loans against harvest-time financial needs unhesitatingly. They then pay back the loans with high interest rates from the earnings they make over the next six months, little knowing that those earnings, if they got to keep them, would definitely improve their status. So, it is in the interest of the contractors to not simply send them across, but to keep them in penury so they have a captive labour force.

While this has been happening for the past two decades, exploitation is taking an even uglier turn now. From women being forced into prostitution to migrants being served with highly adulterated food, it's all happening out there. Since the deals are struck in Orissa, but the labourers work in other states, the labour machinery of the host state can't act against the contractors. Yet, even in cases of exploitation of labourers where the state can act, it does not always do so, because the very officials, including the local police, the Railway Police Force, the office of the Labour Commissioner and many more high-profile officials, get their kickbacks from these Sardars. (Adapted from Hardikar 2004, 'Orissa's Labour Industry'. www.indiatogether.com.)

This concludes our overview of 'Understanding Social Inequality'. In the next section of the introduction, we will examine the impact of globalisation on specific categories of people—peasants, workers, adivasis, Dalits and women.

GLOBALISATION AND ITS IMPACT ON WORKERS, PEASANTS, ADIVASIS AND WOMEN

The first question to be addressed in this section is why we are expected to address the issue of globalisation as a part of this introduction. There are mainly two reasons for this. The first, this is the most significant phenomenon that has dominated world affairs in the last two decades and needs to be understood properly. The second, that globalisation has a special relationship to the problem of social inequality, which we have been discussing in the previous pages. Broadly, there is one school of thought that believes that the phenomenon of globalisation is what will eliminate social inequalities across the globe because it offers greater opportunities for economic participation to all. There is another school that believes that the processes of globalisation actually make inequalities worse than before. Once we know the arguments of both sides, it becomes easier for us to take our own stand on these issues. After all, that is the ultimate purpose of learning about ideas.

In this part, therefore, we will do the following:

1. Explain globalisation, its historical evolution and significance. For this, we also present insights into accounts offered by different authors, to show the diverse ways in which it is understood.
2. In separate sections, we will discuss the impact of globalisation on women and workers, and how the impact of globalisation on the environment affects peasants and adivasis. These will also provide links with the earlier section in which we have explained the concept of social inequality using these categories.
3. Finally, the layout of the chapters of the book will be explained, so that you can find your way around them.

What Is Meant by Globalisation?

Globalisation is widely believed to be a phenomenon of the late twentieth century, but, in fact, many of its features were evident long before then. Charles Oman in his essay titled 'Globalisation, Regionalisation and Inequality' has identified three distinct waves of globalisation. The fifty years leading to World War I witnessed a strong wave of globalisation characterised by rapid expansion of trade and international investments. The second wave of globalisation was in the 1950s and 1960s; this wave weakened by the 1970s. The creation of the international financial institutions, the World Bank, the International Monetary Fund and the signing of the General Agreement on Trade and Tariffs made possible two broad trends. The first was that the badly damaged post-War economies of Western Europe and Japan were given financial support by the United States. Also, this being the era of decolonisation followed by a surge towards *development* by the Third World countries, it meant that a lot more global financial flows in the form of aid began across the world. From the 1980s, Oman suggests that we are in a new phase of globalisation. The current wave of globalisation owes its origins to a number of developments. Deregulation of markets in advanced countries, the expansion of microelectronic-based information and communication technologies, and the globalisation of finance have contributed to the current phase of globalisation. These last three that Oman suggests are very distinct developments and let us take a minute to understand them.

Deregulation of markets in advanced countries means that the government's control over those doing business was reduced, in order that doing trade and commerce was made easier. This meant that those who were already producing in surplus and had restrictions on their ability to export were given more freedom, which certainly improved their economic condition. It was on the basis of this experience that it was argued that if the same were done for business and markets everywhere, the overall economic condition would improve. However, there are very important qualifiers here. First, as Steven Kent Vogel has shown in his work, *Freer Markets, More Rules: Regulatory Reform in Advanced Industrial Countries* that in the advanced industrialised countries, governments have reorganised their control over markets and businesses, while introducing more competition and reducing the number of rules governing it. Thus, they have introduced liberalisation along with reregulation. Further, each country does this in many different ways—so there is no formula for how liberalisation or de/regulation ought to be done. Third, it is the states themselves, rather than the private interest or pressure groups, that have driven this process. So, in fact, they have *not* become weaker and are not subject to greater international pressures.

The expansion of microelectronic-based information and communication technologies is more familiar to most students. We have all observed how information and communication have become more accessible to a larger number of people and at a much faster pace. This does help to bring people that live far away from each other not only in terms of distance, but also in terms of cultures, resources, languages and ideas closer to each other. This provides an opportunity for people to learn from each other, participate in an exchange of ideas and even debate with each other. This is perhaps the one most important development of recent times that has given rise to the idea of the *global village*. Yet, this is possible only when people have access to this technology which, in spite of it becoming so much cheaper than before, remains outside the reach of a majority of the planet. Also, many languages in which people speak, read and write are not yet used on the Internet, not to mention that basic literacy is not accessible to all that might otherwise be able to have opinions and ideas worthy of exchange. For businesses, the most important usefulness of these technologies has been their ability to use the cheap labour markets outside of the advanced industrial countries to carry out their jobs. This phenomenon is known as *outsourcing* and the organisations that conduct them are called Business Process Outsourcing Units or BPOs.

The globalisation of finance[10] is the third dimension that needs to be understood. Finance has been a very important part of the functioning of capital, since about the late nineteenth century. Its significance has increased, especially at the international level, during the twentieth century, such that investments are made across the world, and banks compete with each other in offering lower interest rates in order to attract more capital towards them. Transactions can be made very quickly across the world, that too with electronic support—remember there is no physical movement of goods here, it is just money that moves—and it needs to move in those places where investors think there is a real possibility of return. This also means that big investors decide what is profitable and what is not and so decide where money should go. But there are governments everywhere with rules of how money can or cannot be transferred, so this requires an international regulatory mechanism and one that is as supportive of this as possible. The globalisation of finance is about how banks and international investors negotiate with governments and international financial institutions like the International Monetary Fund and the World Bank and national governments to have their way in this movement of capital. So we can see that the second and third waves of globalisation are linked to each other particularly through the globalisation of finance capital.

Globalisation and Workers

Another very important aspect of globalisation is that of the creation of the global work/labour force. This is linked to both global finance and the new technologies of capital that we have just talked about. In the 1980s, it was recognised that the expensive and organised labour force of the advanced industrial countries would make it hard for capitalists to continue functioning there and earn very high profits. Their profits were sought to be shared by the workers and the latter also asked for large number of other benefits like health and safety. So investors decided to take their investments to those countries where cheap labour was available and could carry out instructions for making products that were designed in the country of origin of the capital. This generated a large number of industries in the Third World that generated employment opportunities, no doubt. There were important qualifiers though. In the early years, it meant the creation of workspaces that were not according to any norms of safety or health, hence the name *sweatshops* for them came to be widely used. Also, these workers were employed on contract basis which gave enormous power to the employers—for salaries, for the period of appointment, to ban any kind of unionisation—in short those very initiatives that gave the working class in the advanced industrial countries their fair share of the gains of industrialisation. Many kinds of critiques of these practices emerged internationally. One was *the feminisation of labour*, which we shall look at in the section on globalisation and gender. Another was from a lobby of consumers who believed that they would not like to buy cheap products from those countries where the people manufacturing them did not enjoy civil, political or even human rights. These issues are taken up in the section on globalisation and human rights.

In the 1990s, the focus of international investments shifted to the industries based on information technology, as discussed above. The creation of the BPOs has generated new kinds of debates, the most important of which is that the young people being employed are being used at a very basic level of computer literacy and the relatively higher salaries and perks available in this industry gives an illusion of early achievement. But the possibilities of growth in this sector are limited and that become evident to the work force possibly at a point in which personal growth and diversification in other industries is no longer possible. This is bound to create anger and resentment and the results of this cannot be envisaged just as yet.

Globalisation and Gender

Contemporary globalisation has resulted in increased access for women to wage labour through the existence of global markets. But the consequence of these expansions has not been an entirely happy one. Many of the new feminised workplaces offer miserable working conditions, poor salaries and are highly stressful. Most women have been pushed into the highly flexible labour market with no certainties. Remasculinisation is a trend witnessed since the 1990s in the *maquiladora* or manufacturing sectors because of increasing automation guided by the conventional idea that only men can handle heavy machinery.

A more alarming trend in female work participation triggered by globalisation is the increased levels of women's participation in the informal sectors of the global economy. A very disturbing trend is the expansion in the global market in domestic servants, mail-order brides and prostitutes. These can hardly be seen as positive developments in the context of female work participation triggered by contemporary globalisation. On issues other than employment—for instance, global finance—there has been very little effort to allow women an entry into the world of credit market that is largely controlled by men. Despite alternatives like small microcredit groups (one of which, the Grameen Bank, is discussed in the section on gender in this book), the mainstream of global finance remains male-dominated.

Once again, the limitation of state activities aimed at mitigating the impact of inequities has had a far worse impact on women than on men. Charged with the principal responsibility of being caregivers and nurturers, women have been adversely hit by the cutting of government programmes and funding for the care of children, senior citizens and the sick. Decreasing food subsidies has also had a negative impact on women. Women seem to have to bear the burden of neoliberal global economics far more than men. In this context, therefore, it is pertinent for us to take up the issue of gender and understand it.

Globalisation, the Environment and Impact on Peasants and Adivasis

Simon Retallack in his paper 'The Environmental Cost of Economic Globalisation' has argued forcefully that creating increasingly global and unfettered markets for trade and investment has undoubtedly increased destructive impact of economic activity upon the Earth. He identifies specific ecological problems that are a direct consequence of the boom in world trade and economic integration. The boom in world trade has meant greater transportation; this has meant a direct increase in air pollution with an adverse impact on the global climate. Another consequence has been bio invasion, the movement of organisms and other creatures in the ships, cargo and other modes of transport often leading to a complete extinction of the local species. The tearing down of trade barriers has meant the spread of lifestyles and products which when used are highly polluting, the spread of the motor car as the primary means of transport is a case in point resulting in increased air pollution and more greenhouse gas emission. The increasing flow of new products into the new markets in addition to the already existing markets has resulted in greater exploitation of the raw materials required to manufacture these products. Mining, felling of trees, fishing has all reached new heights of exploitation. Intensive mining or soil use, for instance, creates heightened levels of environmental damage.

Yet, there is no escape since globalisation is based on ever-increasing abilities to export. The logic of production under globalisation is governed by the logic of free trade based on the idea of economic specialisation (for example, in 1990 all the diamonds produced in Botswana were for export) and the need to pay off debts to Northern banks, hence the need to earn foreign exchange. The global expansion of computers, plastic, steel, cars, chemical and oil-refining industries have resulted in serious implications not only for biodiversity but also for public health.

Michael Redclift and Colin Sage in their essay titled 'Resources, Environmental Degradation and Inequality' identify four important parameters for this discussion.

1. The unequal distribution of historical responsibilities for global environmental changes, especially climate change.
2. Global changes have disparate impacts on different regions and peoples in the world, for instance, global climate change in all likelihood would be prejudicial to countries within the tropics and as a result they would be subject to more incidence of cyclones, increasing aridity of soil and resultant food insecurity.
3. The poorer countries are more concerned with questions of local-level 'livelihood' issues like safe drinking water and adequate diet. The richer countries show greater concern about issues like climate and population.
4. The failure to address the problem of distribution, which to a great extent could help, solves many global environmental problems.

From the perspective of the developing countries, distributive issues are most important and form their central concern in the new policy agenda labelled Global Environmental Change (GEC). Countries of the South are not as worried about the issues of climate change and biodiversity losses; thus, most of them see the GEC as being a Northern agenda. There are other more crucial consequences of globalisation that the countries of the South are more concerned with. The structural adjustment plans, the impact of liberalisation policies and the consequences of international debt repayments exert a far more severe and immediate impact on the lives and environment of the poorer nations than anticipated changes in the climate. Thus, the countries of the North and South are unable to share their concerns in the context of globalisation and its impact on the environment.

There is little doubt about the environmental vulnerability of the countries of the South. However, it also needs to be mentioned that the definition of an environmental problem is itself culturally specific, reflecting social and cultural assumptions. Daily life and its assumptions and practices constitute the 'filter' through which people make sense of the 'global' environmental problems. In the poorest countries, the environmental problems refer to issues of health, shelter, water and food. In newly industrialised countries with rapid growth rates, high levels of pollution become very often the most important environmental problem. In the advanced countries, unseen issues like climate change, exposure to various harmful radiations, etc. become the primary issues requiring people to fight for greater civil liberties and freedom, the right to information and other similar rights. Thus, the agenda is very different depending upon the location.

In this sense, the environmental impact in the south is most on two vulnerable sections of the population that are directly dependent on the natural resources, the environment. These are peasants and adivasis. As long as agriculture is driven by chemical fertilisers, pesticides and genetically modified seeds, all of which are part of the scientific and industrial agendas of the advanced industrial countries forcefully arguing their way into the development, scientific and industrial agendas of the developing world, these sections have little chance of independent survival. They lose many things—their knowledge of natural farming, their stock and diversity of seeds, methods of planting and harvesting, cultural practices of exchange and equally their economic independence in conducting their lives, whatever little they had of it in the first place.[11]

The Three Sections in This Book

You are now ready to go in the details of the three sections of this book: human rights, gender and the environment. You will see that each of these constitutes a separate section under which the different dimensions of that issue are explored. The first section, on human rights, begins by exploring its conceptual basis and then puts it in its international and national context. It proceeds to analyse the human rights of marginalised groups and the character and issues of the human rights movements in India. The second section, which is on gender, you will find, follows a similar pattern—beginning with the conceptual basis of patriarchy by which gender is best understood, then putting it in the relevant context of culture and history. The issues of women and development, the changes they have gone through and the debates they have generated are covered next. It also discusses the institutional and legal context of women's issues, the controversial issue of representation and reservation, while detailing finally the women's movement in India. The final section, which is on environment, too begins with the conceptual frame and goes on to discuss the institutional context of the United Nations Programme. Thereon, specific issues of the environment are taken up in an international context, followed by the environmental policy and movements in India.

We hope that you are able to follow and really utilise this book.

NOTES

1. The case study that is reported is entirely derived from Kalpana Sharma's book, *Rediscovering Dharavi: Stories from Asia's Largest Slum*, published by Penguin in 2000. Hence, phrases and sentences are not separated in quotation marks.
2. For those who are interested in how the calculations are done despite this and the issues on this aspect should read the detailed discussion by Deshpande in the book cited.
3. This has a reference to a big body of literature on the character of modern liberal democracy, which overlapped with the development of capitalism and both are seen as partners in 'modern development'. But that is a separate set of issues that we cannot go into here.
4. Again, on this issue reams of analysis are available, but this is not the place to refer, in any significant way, to it. Those interested will need to look at the literature on political economy of development.
5. How he calculates this and the debates that followed are fascinating, but could not possibly be summarized here. All college libraries stock Thorner's work and many of the debates are to be found in the *Economic and Political Weekly*, a journal published from Bombay and highly reputed and respected internationally.
6. Deshpande is very careful to reiterate that not all of this can be exactly measured by the available data; hence, it must be used very carefully at a tentative level for purposes of analytical understanding.
7. In fact, this formulation came partly as a response to the critique, and from their point of view, a misunderstanding of their analysis of the caste system and its significance for ecology, stated in their first book *This Fissured Land*. For a full discussion, see their 'Introduction to the Omnibus Edition' (2000: x-xi).
8. See Bal, V. 2004. 'Women Scientists in India: Nowhere near the Glass Ceiling'. *Economic & Political Weekly*, 39(32). 7 August.
9. It must be stated, however, that some differences of race are to be found in India too, as in the case of the North-East. These are inescapably connected with differences in ethnicity but much of the debate remains about whether culture or race should be highlighted, or indeed it can be at all understood outside the spectrum of political economy and state sovereignty concerns. So, it will not be discussed in the context of the category of ethnicity.
10. See two easily available, very good introductory books: Kavaljit Singh (2000). *Taming Global Financial Flows: Challenges and Alternatives in the Era of Financial Globalisation*. New Delhi: Madhyam Books; and Porter, Tony (2005). *Globalisation and Finance*. London: Polity Press.
11. There is considerable literature on this in India and internationally. For a start, the fortnightly magazine *Down to Earth*, published by the Centre for Science and Environment, New Delhi, and Vandana Shiva's writings are most helpful. Some of these are referred to later in this book in the section on the Environment.

SUGGESTED READINGS

Hurrell, Andrew and Ngaire Woods (eds) (1999). *Inequality, Globalisation and World Politics*. New York: Oxford University Press.

Scholte, Jan Aart (2000). *Globalisation–A Critical Introduction*. New York: Macmillan.

Shaw, Martin (ed.) (1999). *Politics and Globalisation*. London: Routledge.

Goldsmith, E. and Jerry Mander (eds) (2001). *The Case Against the Global Economy*. London: Earthscan.

Gills, Barry K. (ed.) (2000). *Globalisation and the Politics of Resistance*. Basingstoke and New York: Palgrave.

Deshpande, Satish (2003). *Contemporary India*. New Delhi: Viking Press.

Mohanty, Manoranjan (ed.) (2004). *Caste, Class and Gender*. New Delhi: Sage

Eriksen, T. H. (1993). *Ethnicity and Nationalism: Anthropological Perspectives*. London: Pluto Press.

REFERENCES

Bal, V. (2004). 'Women Scientists in India: Nowhere Near the Glass Ceiling'. *Economic and Political Weekly*. 7 August. pp. 3647–3652.

Beteille, A. (1960). 'The Definition of Tribe'. *Seminar*, No. 14.

Beteille, A. (1965). *Caste, Class and Power: Changing Social Stratification in a Tanjore Village*. Berkeley: University of California Press (also published by OUP, Delhi in 1966)

Bose, N. K. (1971). *Tribal Life in India*. Delhi: Government Publications.

Deshpande, S. (2004). *India: A Sociological View*. New Delhi: Penguin.

Dhanagre, D. N. (1992). 'The Model of Agrarian Classes in India'.

Dumont, L. (1972). *Homo Hierarchichus: The Caste System and Its Implications*. London: Paladin (also published by OUP, Delhi in 1988).

Gadgil, M. and R. Guha (2000). *Ecology and Equity*. New Delhi: Oxford University Press.

Ghurye, G. S. (1950). *Caste and Class in India*. Bombay: Popular Prakashan.

Ghurye, G. S. (1963). *The Scheduled Tribes*. Bombay: Popular Prakashan.

Gupta, D. (1991). (ed.) *Social Stratification in India: Readings in Sociology and Social Anthropology*, New Delhi: Oxford University Press.

Holmstrom, M. 'Who Are the Working Class?' in D. Gupta (ed.) *Social Stratification*. New Delhi: Oxford University Press.

Sharma, Kalpana (1991). *Rediscovering Dharavi: Stories from Asia's Largest Slum* Penguin (2000).

Marx, K. (1850). *The Class Struggles in France*: *The Eighteenth Brumaire of Louis Bonaparte, Theses on Feuerbach* (all available in Collected Works or individually published by the USSR Academy of Social Sciences).

Ossowski, S. (1963). *Class Structure in the Social Consciousness* (tr. Sheila Patterson). New York: Free Press of Glencoe.

Roy-Burman, B. K. (1994). *Tribes in Perspective*. Delhi: Mittal Publications.

Singh, K. S. (1993). 'Marginalised Tribals'. *Seminar* 412.

Srinivas, M. N. (1952). *Religion and Society Among the Coorgs in India*. Oxford: Clarendon Press.

Thorner, D. (1992). 'The Agrarian Prospect in India' in Gupta (ed.) *Social Stralification*. New Delhi: OUP.

Vidyarthi, L. P. and B. N. Rai (1977). *The Tribal Culture in India* Concept. Delhi: Publishing Company.

Xaxa, V. (1999). 'Transformation of Tribes in India: Terms of Discourse'. *Economic and Political Weekly*. June 12. 1519–24.

Section I Human Rights

1

Thinking About Human Rights

HUMAN RIGHTS: VARIOUS MEANINGS

At first sight, the opening remarks of this text may seem to embody a sense of ambiguity, a feeling that is deepened when combined with the relative ease with which we see and hear the term human rights being employed for different political purposes. It is also used to describe, at times even justify, contrasting political events. Waging of wars and pursuit of peace may both be justified on the grounds of human rights. The differences in *meaning* may reflect substantive arguments about the contents: which rights are *human*; are civil and political rights the core of human rights, or does the ambit include economic, social and cultural rights as well? Are individuals alone the bearers of rights, or can there be rights of collectives? Some collective rights even cross the path of individual rights—enforcing religious rituals on members of a group, expelling individuals for non-conformity with group directives. Honour killings, the practice of circumcision, expelling members from a caste by caste panchayats are some examples. There may be moral dilemmas about how to interpret a particular right, and whose rights to prioritise in case of a conflict. How does one prioritise the right to life of a foetus, when the mother might want to exercise her individual choice and opt for abortion? Arguments from different cultural viewpoints contest the universality of these rights, and may even insist on different perspectives of human rights.

Take, for example, the case of Turkey. In deciding on the case of Turkey's accession to the European Union (EU), the country was put on a human rights watch of sorts and asked to improve its human rights records as a pre-condition for its accession. While human rights was primarily about the guarantee of a secular set of rights to its citizens by the Turkish state, observers did point out that the debate was more than just about human rights. Turkey is a predominantly Muslim country, and the EU is considered essentially a Christian club (on the basis of the religious affiliation of the countries that currently constitute this group). Was the rights yardstick being strictly applied to Turkey on account of the differentness of the religious affiliation of its people? In other words, was the use of the human rights yardstick political in this case, specially as many countries of Eastern Europe had been admitted to the Europe Union without necessarily going through a similar process?

Another point of contention lies in the fact that external aggression may be justified by invading powers in the name of protection of human rights, as in the case of Iraq. Saddam Hussein's regime was said to violate human rights of its own citizens, especially of those with a Kurdish origin. Human rights groups, on the other hand, complain of rights' violations by the invading powers, as in the case of Iraqi prisoners or the prisoners held by the US at Abu Gharib. The prison of Abu Gharib was in news for the abuse of prisoners by the US soldiers.

Often, there may be conflicts on what a particular human right means and whose rights are to be prioritised in case of a conflict. These may be in the nature of moral dilemmas or even real conflicts amongst groups. The current debate on the right to abortion is a case in point. Feminists argue in favour of women's right to decide and reaffirm control over decisions relating to her body, whereas the church has often argued for the right to life of a foetus. Feminists further argue that the stand of the church in this case represents a religious conservatism in acknowledging women's rights. Another challenge to the common perceptions of human rights pertains to the right to end one's life. Euthanasia, or the right of a terminally ill or practically dead person to end his/her life, is an example. The moot question is whether the right to die in such cases violates the human right to live. Also, who exercises this right in case the patient is not in a condition to do so?

Substantive differences, thus, exist on which set of rights to prioritise, whose view to follow, and what the core meaning of a right is. These questions underlie the debate on the concept of human rights. Reflections on these questions and differences of opinion are inevitably the background of conceptualitising human rights.

In the political context of the Cold War, countries in the Western bloc emphasised upon civil and political rights, whereas those in the Eastern bloc stressed upon social and economic rights. Leaders such as Julius Nyerere in Tanzania, a poor developing country, also called for the eradication of poverty, and collective social and economic development, before people could have these rights.

A further set of arguments points towards the cultural embeddedness of the human rights debate in the West and calls it a Eurocentric concept with an excessive focus on individual rights. Arguments from an Africanist (pertaining to the African) position on these rights, due to the sociocultural and political preferences of Africans, emphasise the importance of the collective. It is, indeed, in contrast to the priority of the individual, as in the Western conception of rights. Struggles of individuals and collectives, the world over, on a variety of issues—ranging from environmental destruction and displacement, violation of citizens rights by their own states such as police or prison atrocities, Dalit struggles against the assault on their dignity and equality to struggles for rights for people such as the gay community—launched in the name of protecting human rights are examples cited by this perspective. Hence, it seems that the stance that accords priority to colletive is more valid than the Western stance of priority to the individual.

Such contrasting usage, stemming from the varied purposes and substantive disagreements about what human rights denote, are not just about meanings. They also convey to us the political nature of the concept. On one hand, while it seems to embody a 'universal' rhetoric implying an acceptance all over, on the other, it is a contested concept. As Steven Lukes notes, '... in some sense, it is accepted virtually everywhere. It is also violated virtually everywhere, though much more in some places than in others.' Further, he feels that '... its virtually universal acceptance, even when hypocritical, is very important', for this is what gives it a political leverage. As Lukes observes, despite the challenges from several quarters, 'virtually no one actually rejects the concept' (Lukes 1997: 233).

What is it, then, that gives human rights a unique standing amongst political values and such international official recognition? What is the basis for the consensus around human rights principles? Are these principles above statutes and states? If so, what is the appropriate relationship between democracy and human rights? Why have human rights become a symbol for expressing individual and collective aspirations? Why are human rights the principle for grant of legal entitlements by states?

In this chapter, we answer some of these questions; first, by analysing the concept, and second, by looking at the creation of the concept through a process of political engagements, and then examining some of the challenges to the concept from the standpoint of other cultural and religious doctrines. The concluding section outlines some of the current challenges to the concept.

The subsequent chapters of this section look at the universal declaration of human rights and its implementation through the UN mechanism, and finally, the struggles of various marginalised groups for human rights in India. As Francesca Klug notes, the concept is a creature of politics, not above politics. The process of understanding the concept must be situated in a political engagement, of people's struggles against abuses (Klug:

2004). Our deliberation, henceforth, on the concept of human rights, its emergence in international discourse, and its acceptance the world over would be premised upon such a politicohistorical context.

THE CONCEPT OF HUMAN RIGHTS

To understand the concept, it is useful to begin with locating it within a discussion of rights. What does it mean to have a right? In common usage, the word *right* refers to both *being* right and *having* a right, that is, *rectitude* and *entitlement*. The first refers to certain accepted standards of acting virtuously or righteously; statements of the kind 'what ought to be done', are examples of the this kind. In this sense, being right is opposed to being wrong. Donnelly (2003: 7-9) points out that such claims of righteousness draw attention to standards of moral conduct and, in terms of action, refer to the dutybearer's obligation for approximating such standards. In simpler terms, it is a duty to be right, that is, to maintain the standards of moral conduct. The second connotation of the word 'right', interrelated with the first one, refers to *entitlement*. In this latter sense, one may have a right to something, and its non-fulfilment allows him/her to claim that the particular duty be performed to fulfil his/her right. The right-holder has a special title to enjoy her right Non-fulfilment of a right does not mean that the right ceases to exist. This conceptualisation of right, in terms of rectitude and entitlement, is suggestive of an interactive relation between right and duty. To simplify it, right-holders and dutybearers are intertwined and no right is possible without duty and vice versa.

To explain the concept of rights, we have used the classic analysis of rights to be found in Wesley Hohfeld's *Fundamental Legal Conceptions* (1919), analysing types of legal rights. As is evident, having a right implies the existence of a relation between a right-holder and a dutybearer, and an object of that right, which the right seeks to achieve. Claim rights, which involve a specific duty, as also the right-holder's claim that his/her right be fulfilled, are considered to be rights in the strict sense by Hohfeld.[1] In actual practice, claim rights coexist with other forms of rights. Taken together, the four types of rights that Hohfeld distinguishes are liberties, claims, immunities and powers. A liberty right imposes no duties on anybody. Nobody is under any obiligation to perform necessarily so that this right may be realised. People in Hobbes's hypothetical state of nature have such rights. The liberty right of one man does not infringe upon the similar rights of another man. Claim rights impose performance of duty on another. Immunities are more like exemptions from law. An example is diplomatic immunity. Powers are rights that a sovereign may have to determine the rights of others. The power of the right-holder to press for the enjoyment of his/her right distinguishes rights from any other type of benefits. Human rights are rights of exceptional importance and belong to every individual by virtue of being a human. The specific characteristics of these rights are that they are *equal*, every human being is endowed equally with these rights, *inalienable*, in the sense that they cannot be taken away, and *universal* in that they are rights of all human beings.

HUMAN RIGHTS AND MORALITY

Human rights need to be distinguished from values that underlie other rights, such as equality, liberty or simply other important moral values such as love, care or respect. At the outset, it must be pointed out that while rights are important, they do not constitute the whole of morality. Not all aspects of morality or simply 'that which is right' are achievable through right claims. A child for example, requires love of his/her parents, but how do we translate it in the language of rights? Also, a conception of social good may precede, and even have priority over individual's claims. Furthermore, understanding and recognising diversity and difference, has led to a realisation that there may be individual, as also a collective basis for rights.

For many moral and political values worth realising, such as liberty or political participation, human rights provide a specific mechanism by which the values are achieved. Donnelly points out that not all good things are the object of human rights. The emphasis on human rights means the selection of some of these for advancement through a specific mechanism that of rights (Donnelly 2003: 10–11).

In case of human rights violation, whom does a claim lie with, or who has the obligation to perform a duty for the realisation of these rights? The strictly legal interpretation would place the responsibility on the state. In many instances, however, the violation of human rights may be done by non-state groups or individuals. In the infamous Bhopal Gas Leak Case, whereby many residents in the vicinity of the Union Carbide factory were adversely affected, by the leaking of the poisonous gas M.I.C. on 3 Dec 1984, the violator of human rights was a multinational or a conglomerate. Also, the feminist critique of human rights as being excessively preoccupied with the public sphere, points to the importance of looking at the private sphere where a regular gender based discrimination violates the human rights of women. The instance of domestic violence in the private sphere is a case in point. Similarly, the practice of caste-based discrimination in spheres of private life calls for the broadening of the ambit of human rights. In all these instances, however, it is still possible to place the onus on the state and point to its duty or obligation to make possible the realisation of human rights.

CRITIQUE OF THE CONCEPT OF HUMAN RIGHTS

While acceptance of the concept of human rights is commonplace, scepticism about the concept exists too. Alisdair McIntyre feels that the concept of human rights is as fictitious as that of 'Utility' advanced by Jeremy Bentham and other utilitarian philosophers. According to the utilitarian philosophy, the facts of 'pleasure' and 'pain' should be the governing principles, and not something vague or fictitious. The objective of politics and morality is to attain the greatest happiness of the greatest numbers, something that can be measured in a concrete way. The only type of right that utilitarians accept are legal rights. Belief in human rights is like belief in 'witches and unicorns'; it is an act of superstition. He feels that every attempt to find reasons to believe that such rights exist has failed (Lukes 1997: 238–9). Probably, some part of such reservation emanates from the manner in which the human rights discourse is embedded in the language of rights. The 'object' of such rights, probably, may not be something tangible that we can feel in a concrete way. But it is an entitlement to a 'moral' right. The problem is, also, one of specifying what in the ultimate analysis is the 'foundation' or even the ethical justification for such rights. We will address these two issues in the following section on human rights. But before we do that, it is appropriate to consider some of the other objections to the concept as well.

Richard Rorty considers human rights as a matter of 'sentimental imagination' rather than rational calculation. He seconds McIntyre and considers human rights to be a matter of belief, without theoretical foundations. He points out that slave drivers, rapists, ethnic cleansers, and such others can continue to perpetrate their violence without an iota of guilt, as they do not consider the objects of their violence to be humans. Even if one were able to prove the absolute existence of a human right, it would make no difference (Rorty 1993). Such critiques pave way for a discussion on the foundations of human rights. Only by implementing the sensibility stemming from the above stated critique would a better understanding of the concept of human rights arise.

LOOKING FOR FOUNDATIONS: HUMAN RIGHTS AND NATURAL RIGHTS

It is a commonly held view that the concept of human rights derives from 'natural rights'. This relationship can be analysed at two levels. First, tracing the history of the origin of the concept of human rights along with natural rights, in a sense of human rights chronologically evolving from natural rights; and second, analysing the manner in which the tradition of natural rights provides an ethical justification to the concept. The second way is a more analytical-conceptional way of looking at the relationship. Of course, these two are not watertight compartments; looking at the history helps understand elements of the concept. It also helps us in locating the concept within a political discourse, rather than leaving it outside the realm of political conflict and struggle.

The classic statement of natural rights theory is to be found in the works of John Locke, the seventeenth century English philosopher. According to Locke, every human being has certain rights derived from nature. So, the starting point of his theory is a fundamentally egalitarian belief about the right of every human being. The source of this right is not the government or its laws, rather it is a 'state of nature' characterised by an absence of government. Each individual has an obligation to God, who wills the preservation of humankind. This imposes an obligation on everyone not to harm the life, liberty and property of others. Since men are rational, they come to know the laws of nature. Why then do men leave the state of nature? When each man becomes his own judge, conflict arises. The 'social contract' amongst men sets up the civil society and government is set up as a 'fiduciary'[2] with the expressed purpose of protecting natural rights through a known/established law. If this trust is violated, people have a right to revolt. Thus, a condition of legitimacy of government is the protection of natural rights. Protests by people, for example the Narmada Bachao Andolan, against the state's failure in discharging its fiduciary duty are commonly found in a vibrant democracy.

Moving ahead, it is important to note the similarities in ideas between the modern concept of human rights and Locke's version of human rights.

- Both begin with a belief in equal rights of all human beings.
- Natural rights and human rights are endowed to human beings; it is the duty of government to protect these rights.
- Protection of rights is a yardstick of legitimacy of governments.

The crucial difference between the two is that human rights do not subscribe to the affinity of natural rights to religious origins. In an attempt to gain universal acceptance from societies and communities with different religious beliefs, it clearly steers away from religious foundations without necessarily replacing them with any other. Freeman (2002: 10) notes that 'human rights had to be *abstracted* from particular religious and ideological beliefs, but the character of that abstraction was not clear. The declaration says little about the source of these rights ...' Critics of human rights praxis, in the wake of the global war on terror, note that such secular foundations have been put to question by state action of some powerful states post 9/11; terms used to describe terrorism or Saddam's rule of Iraq such as 'evil regime' or 'collective sin' signify a fusion of religious and political ideologies in recent times.

Also, Locke's conception is a strictly individualistic conception of right, and his theory exhibits a tension between individualism and community. The premise that every human possesses natural rights justifies, consequentially, considerable inequality in making individual labour the basis of private property. Critics, such as C. B. McPherson (1962), dub Locke's theory as 'possessive individualism', despite certain moral limits on the right to property as conceived by Locke. For Locke, the right to private property was not that of unfettered greed. He also spoke about subsistence rights of the poor. But his thinking provided the justification for private property.

The modern human rights theory is said to be a restatement of Locke's theory, with a secular core. There were, however, discontinuities in Locke's statement of natural rights in the seventeenth century and its modern restatement as secular human rights. (It is wrong to see human rights as having sequentially evolved from Locke's statement of natural rights.) The theory declined in the eighteenth century. Its principles were incorporated in the working of Constitutional monarchy in Britain, after the Glorious Revolution of 1689, but were more clearly evident in eighteenth century America. The American Declaration of Independence (1776) affirmed as 'self-evident' that all men are created equal and are endowed by their creator with the inalienable rights to life, liberty and the pursuit of happiness. The declaration also stated that it was the duty of the government to protect these rights. A government could be legitimately overthrown if it failed to do so. A severe limitation of this statement of rights, as also the Bill of Rights included as an amendment to the American Constitution, was that it was tolerant of the institution of slavery.

The French Declaration of Rights of Man and Citizen (1789) included the right to liberty, property, security and resistance against oppression. This declaration also affirmed the preservation of these natural rights of man as the objective of every political association.

The main attacks on Locke's conception of natural rights came from Burke, Bentham and Marx. These are being briefly discussed here for two reasons. First, these attacks can, to a certain measure, be extended to apply to the concept of human rights as well; and second, for their impact on the modern concept of human rights. Edmund Burke considered natural rights to be a useless metaphysical abstraction. Although he never completely rejected the concept of natural rights, he felt that the real rights of men were social, not natural. He also criticised the universalism of natural rights theory for its failure to take account of national and cultural diversity (Freeman 2002: 27). A stronger criticism came from Bentham who held natural right to be a nonsense. He considered these to be vague and argued that disputes over rights were likely to be settled through violence. Therefore, rational laws were needed, which could calculate pleasure and pain to the individual. The principle of utility was suggested by him as an alternative and a concrete way of determining the good of society. The only rights recognized by him were legal rights.

Marx was critical of the individualistic premise which was the basis of the conception of natural rights. It looks at man as a *being* separate from community and also from nature with which man has an intrinsic relationship. This conception was neither natural nor universal. It was the *egoistic individual* created by bourgeois philosophy that was being projected as a 'universal' category. Powerful as Marx's critique was, Freeman notes its inadequacy in not being able to assess the need for protection in the form of rights, or in the face of abuse of state power (Freeman 2002: 29–30). What happens when the state violates the rights of individuals?

Today while human rights undoubtedly have a neo-Lockean ring, for a long time these rights (human rights) were interpreted strictly as legal rights, in the Benthamite tradition. The strictly individualist structure emphasized in the early days has largely been put aside in favour of a frame of reference that recognizes rights of groups as well. In addition, the advocates of cultural diversity have critiqued the claim to universalism of human rights.

The importance of natural rights of individuals in the social sciences declined in the wake of massive changes brought about by industrialization. In the new order of priorities, there was a desire to be scientific, systematic and empirical. This pre-occupation with evolving a science of society led to a neglect of the concept. It was the horrors of Nazism that led to a revival of the concept after the Second World War. The indulgence of Nazi Germany in persecution and genocide did not ascribe much relevance to a neutral term such as 'freedom'.

Klug (2004) calls it a *second wave* of rights. While the first wave was concerned with the rights and liberties of individual citizens within their nation-states, the second was concerned with creating a better world for everyone.

THE PHILOSOPHICAL MODEL OF THE UNIVERSAL DECLARATION OF HUMAN RIGHTS (UDHR)

The term 'human rights' was not a part of common usage until its incorporation in the UDHR. The drafters of UDHR drew upon ethical thinking from all major religions, as also from liberal, socialist and other secular thinking. Aware of the religious, political and ideological diversities of its members, the UN deliberately did not ground these rights in any particular philosophy. The only clear philosophical commitment made in UDHR was against the Nazi ideology. The substitution of the term 'natural rights' by 'human rights' was done to steer clear of the controversial religious implications of grounding rights in nature. Human rights, thus, were conceived to provide the *values for a godless age*.[3] Thus, the scheme of discussion on rights moved away from the framework of natural rights without necessarily subscribing to a new one. Though the new concept of human rights is a pragmatic, moral and politically useful concept, it is philosophically 'ungrounded', that is, it does not have any 'foundations' like the earlier one which was premised upon natural rights.

An important consequence of leaving the core hollow was that it made possible the acceptance of these rights across a wide spectrum of ideological and religious beliefs, thus, imparting a 'universal' appeal to it. It is not a comprehensive moral and/or political philosophy by itself; rather it is compatible with a range of positions/perspectives.

Claims of universalism notwithstanding, UDHR was open to criticisms of being rooted culturally in the West and of ignoring the diverse conceptions of rights around the world. This challenge to universal claims of human rights from particular cultures is discussed in the following section.

Universal Human Rights, Particular Cultures

The absence of 'philosophical foundations' of the concept, and the Universal Declaration's claim to universalism has been responsible for a prolific debate on the possibility of non-Western conceptions of human rights. These arguments often apply the concepts enumerated in UDHR and elaborate on how such concepts, as also the practice of human rights, can be found right across cultures. Adamantia Pollis and Peter Schwab argue that all societies, culturally and historically, manifest conceptions of human rights. Yogindra Khushalani takes the claim forward when he argues that the concept of human rights can be traced to the origin of human race itself (Pollis, Schwab and Khushalani, cited in Dannelly 2003: 71). These arguments are refuted by others, such as Donnelly (2003: 71), who hold that non-Western cultural and political traditions, like the pre-modern West, lacked the practice as well as the concept of human rights. According to this, human rights first emerged in the West in response to social changes produced by modern markets and states (ibid.). This argument confirms the 'cultural rootedness' of the concept in the modern West (a particular culture, rather than in all cultures, at all times). In other words, it highlights a particularism with which the concept of 'universal' human rights is endowed.

Let us now examine what the alternate conceptions of human rights, such as Islamic, Africanist and 'Asian values', have to state. When pushed to their extremes, the arguments about Asian, African, or Islamic values may call for an abrogation of the 'universal human rights regime'. In another sense, the arguments arising from different contexts (i) advance different standpoints, (ii) enable a healthy cross-cultural dialogue among ideas, and (iii) constitute such differences as a central feature of the contemporary discourse on human rights. The dialogue between these various conceptions, from different cultural viewpoints, also provides a method of interrogating one's own culture from the standpoint of others.

Islam and Human Rights

Contemporary literature attempts to elaborate human rights as listed in the declaration or other treaties and conventions, and finds the source of these rights in the *Quran*. Further, the attempts to ground human rights in the Quran and other holy texts of the Muslims take the conception of universal human nature and ethical universalism as emphasized in the Quran as their basis. Many authors such as Tabandeh hold that the contemporary human rights doctrine merely replicate what has already been stated in the 1,400-year old Islamic ideas. Scholars such as Khalid M. Ishaque (1974: 32–38) list out 14 specific human rights as recognised by Islam by virtue of their being granted by God. Donnelly, however, argues that these 'rights' are merely duties of rulers and individuals, and not equal and inalienable rights of all human beings. The lists of rights, tendered by the religious scriptures, involve either rights-less duties, or rights simply given the predominance of religious status in them. They are not rights of human beings in the legal and social sense because they do not take into account human fallibility. Nevertheless, it is not to be missed that Islamic scriptures and practice call upon Muslims to treat each other with respect and dignity, and to pursue personal well-being as well as social justice. These values remind of those outlined in the Universal Declaration. However, the difference between the claims of universal human rights and those of the Islamic origin is not denied.

Othman points out the difficulty of accepting the UN Convention for Elimination of Discrimination against Women in Islamic Societies. He feels that the method of reform should be through internal dialogue within the society or culture. On the other hand, Freeman critically notes that the problem with the above advocacy is about an alternate course of action in case the internal dialogue fails. To put it simply, what would be a way out of the crisis if the religious take on human rights result into violation of rights in other ways. Further, Othman points out that Islam has a conception of the individual as a right-bearer, as Muslims are obliged to resist oppression. Even in this argument, however, a gap between the obligation of a Muslim as against a non-Muslim is clearly discernible. The moral equality of all human beings, irrespective of religious differences, is basic to the human rights discourse. In many instances, the concrete directives of the Shari'a, such as stoning to death on charges of theft, are in conflict with the prescriptions of Article 5 of the UDHR which forbids cruel punishment (Freeman 2002: 112–113).

The fine points of this debate, however, do not deny the substantive similarities at the level of basic values between Islam and the UDHR model, and do not in any way suggest any fundamental incompatibility. Unless we appreciate these differences in social practice, we would, according to Donnelly (2003: 77), continue to delude ourselves about the past and obscure central elements of the meaning and importance of human rights today.

African Values and Human Rights

The 'Africanist' writings on human rights include a critique of the language of individual rights in Western conceptions. It emphasises on a collectivist notion of rights in the African tradition and advances evidence of certain social practices in many traditional African societies as akin to that of human rights.

The term 'Africanist' does not describe a synthetic argument on human rights from an 'African' viewpoint. On the contrary, it consists of a wide variety of positions. One of the early contributions is that of Issa Shivji and Josiah Cobbah who argue that there is very little written on the distinctive African conceptual and philosophical foundations of human rights. What exists may at best be simply an 'African ethno-philosophy' of human rights, or attempts to show the Western viewpoints and their Marxist critiques, or Western style condemnation of human rights in Africa (Ibhawoh 2001: 49–50).

Several African and Third World writers reject the view that the concept originated in the West and was subsequently transplanted to the rest of Africa. Mahmood Mamdani argues that wherever oppression occurs, there are rights, and no continent has monopoly over this phenomenon (Ibhawoh 2001: 52). Further, Ibhawoh cites Paulin Hountondji's views that challenge the Western origin of the concept. Arguably, what can rightly be attributed to the West and the Enlightenment tradition is locating the discussion within a formally articulated philosophical system. As Ibhawoh quotes,

> Western philosophers produced not the thing but the discourse about the thing, not the idea of natural law or human dignity, but the work of expression concerning the idea, the project of its formulation, explanation, and analysis ... in short, a draft of the philosophy of human rights.

Yogindra Kushalani, Okey Martin Ejidike and Makau Wa Mutua are amongst those who argue for a distinctively African conception of human rights. Ejidike points out that the traditional Igbo society recognised rights and accepted philosophical principles similar to, but necessarily different from, the present set of human rights. Mutua examines the legal, political and social norms governing pre-colonial Africa, and finds that the notion of rights informed the notion of justice. Although these were community-centric, they supported a measure of individualism. The notion of rights emphasised on community orientation, cooperation, commitment to family and deference to age. It was a 'matrix of entitlement and obligations which fostered communal solidarity and sustained the kinship system'. This was the basis of African conception of human rights (Ibhawoh 2001: 54).

Critics point out that such rights were typically assigned on the basis of social roles and status within the community. According to Donnelly, African society had concepts of human dignity that simply did not involve human rights. Further, the idyllic picture of a community was often painted by elites and rulers to hide human rights violations. Also, the main interests served by the appeal to the traditional African values, is predominantly for the male, and to that extent, it is a patriarchal construct.

An interesting set of arguments that is advanced, keeping the particular African situation in mind, relate not to the African worldview or the concept of human rights in traditional Africa. They rather relate to the need to prioritise social and economic rights over civil and political ones. This need arises from chronic poverty and underdevelopment that postcolonial African societies face. Julius Nyerere's arguments for collective social and economic development taking priority is a case in point. Often dubbed the 'full-belly hypothesis', meaning that civil and political rights can be enjoyed only after poverty is reduced, the clear merit of this argument is the introduction of postcolonial structural constraints in the debate on universal human rights. The other clear contribution of this debate is stressing upon the idea of groups, duties, social cohesion and communal solidarity as valid norms. Also, it associates the concept of human rights with a wider set of social struggles.

Asian Values and Human Rights

The Bangkok Declaration of Asian states (1993) issued at the end of a preparatory regional conference for the subsequent World Conference in Vienna in the same year, brought the issue of a 'distinctively Asian point of view on human rights' to the forefront. This was noted by Bilahari Kausikan (1993) in his widely noted article entitled 'Asia's Different

Standards'. Joseph Chan interpreted this as 'Asia's challenge to universal human rights'. In the debate that ensued, it seemed that even regional political leaders were beginning to ask for a redrafting of the declaration because it was viewed to be clearly incompatible with Asia's values and traditions. Freeman notes that while cultural relativism had a role to play, yet far more crucial to explaining this cultural assertion was the fact that these Asian countries were significant economic powers. They were being translated into soft 'ideological' power assertion. What were the core values, then, that were being put forward in this alternate conception?

Central to the alternate conception was the Confucian perspective on human rights. The idea of human rights was said to have developed very early in China; in fact, as early as 2000 years ago. The Confucian code talks of individual's right to personal dignity, but this right has to be acquired by living up to the code. Donnelly argues that this is not an inalienable human right as it has to be acquired, and therefore, runs the risk of being lost. Further, cultural differences between Asia and the West lead to an emphasis on a different set of rights; for example, Confucianism draws our attention to the respect of the elderly. Freeman notes that approaching human rights from such different perspectives enriches our understanding of human rights, and these principles become acceptable to people in diverse cultural settings.

The approach of the UN, as evident in the Vienna Declaration and Programme of Action, adopted by the World Conference on Human Rights (1993), has been to reaffirm the universality, not the significance of particularity of different cultures, regions and religions, without necessarily committing itself to any of these different principles. The debate is still an open one, and the claim of 'universality' is still being contested from many different quarters. Taking this debate to the context of India enriches our understanding a little more.

The Caste and Human Rights

The caste system in India denies the equal worth of all human beings, and clearly contradicts the basic human rights principle. In this system of ideological beliefs, an individual is assigned a place/status by birth, which translates into one's social class. Duties and obligations are assigned on the basis of one's position in this hierarchy. Extensive social practices of discrimination and rules of marriage help to maintain social distance.

Caste was also an economic system in that one's location in the hierarchy decided what profession one had to take. Economic and political power rested with those higher up the social ladder, and the ideological power of the *Brahmans* or the priestly caste helped to maintain belief in the legitimacy of the system. The theoretical model of caste was that of *varnas,* four levels of hierarchy with *Brahaman*, *Kshatriya*, *Vaisya* and *Sudra* classes with corresponding occupations of priesthood, warrior, mercantile and servile classes. In fact, caste existed as *jati*; that is, numerous local social groups arranged in hierarchy, wherein those at the bottom and those outside the purview of the caste system were systematically discriminated against, and denied even the status of a human being. Needless to say, Indian society vis-à-vis caste system is essentially discriminatory and, thus, promotes violation of human rights.

With a glimpse of the diverse positions on human rights, it is pertinent to note as to how UDHR puts the same.

THE CONTENT OF HUMAN RIGHTS

The Universal Declaration of Human Rights (UDHR), and other covenants draw up an elaborate list of rights as human rights. These are generally divided into

- civil and political rights, and
- economic and social rights.

The two sets of rights are incorporated in two different covenants, meaning thereby that they are accepted by those states that ratify these covenants. This option of incorporating the two sets of rights in two different covenants was a means to accommodate the 'Cold War' ideological divisions, wherein the two sides placed different emphasis on the two sets of rights.

The two sets of rights differed in the obligations they placed on the state in terms of their implementation. Many of the civil and political rights were immediate obligations on the states, and inalienable rights of the citizens/persons by virtue of their being humans. Whereas, on the other hand, the social and economic rights were made contingent to the capacity and resources available with the states for the realisation of these rights.

A further source of difference was supposed to be the justiciable character of civil and political rights, whereas for the realisation of social and economic rights one could move to the courts. In a large way, this distinction was the result of the strictly legal interpretation of rights—a narrow focus from which the discourse on human rights has moved away. Later, the critical developments in the stance on human rights lay bare the pitfalls of UDHR's conceptualisation.

It suggests that human rights are not made by some 'supernatural' source and placed for interpretation in the hands of judges and courts of law; they are not above the political struggles of people. They are a creation of politics and there is an important linkage between people's struggles, social movements and the contours of human rights. The increasing emphasis on the realisation of social and economic rights as well is evident in the approach that the judiciary is taking. These are discussed in detail in the Indian context in Chapter 3. In brief, this presents the latest development in the conceptualisation of human rights.

Now, there is a growing emphasis on a third generation of rights that focuses on the fulfilment of minimum needs. Right to development is an essential part of the so-called third generation rights. The votaries are participants in the people's struggles, NGOs and the international agencies. The idea of development as a right had received emphasis as early as the 1960s, when the newly independent states of Asia, Africa and Latin America realised that their formal equality with other nation-states made little sense, unless their right to development was established. While the earlier set of rights placed an obligation on the states for their realisation, the new emphasis on the rights to development implied an obligation of the 'rich' states of the North to help the poorer states mainly in the South. In 1988, the General Assembly adopted a declaration on the Right to Development.

HUMAN RIGHTS AND CITIZENSHIP RIGHTS

It is important to understand the relation between and distinction of human rights and citizenship rights. We learned in the previous section about the theory of natural rights suggesting that certain rights, belonging to human beings, are in fact natural rights. The theory also secularises the concept, that is, draws it out of the Christian natural law tradition and says that human rights belong to all human beings by virtue of being human. Hypothetically speaking, human rights belong to human beings even if they did not live in the framework of a state, or any other form of political society. On the other hand, citizenship rights refer to those rights that belong to those who are members of a particular state. They include many human rights listed in the declaration, or conceived in other charters and treaties, but many rights of the citizens may not be 'human rights'. The French Declaration of 1789 noted this distinction between the rights of citizens and the rights of man.

A number of rights of the citizen, as we see them today, parallel the charter of human rights promoted in the UN Declaration. In the case of India, we will see in Chapter 4 that the rights outlined in the Indian Constitution are similar in content to those in the two key covenants on civil and political rights, and social and economic rights. Human rights provide the moral horizons for the struggle for citizen's rights.

Historically, there have been conceptions of citizenship and citizen's rights, without having a notion of human rights. In Aristotle's theory, set in the Greek city-states, there were citizens with rights but not everybody was a citizen. Slaves, women and children did not have any rights. Women and slaves were meant only to assist the head of the household who was both a man and a citizen. Citizen's rights are fundamental which implies that they are above the tribulations of day-to-day politics.

CHALLENGES TO HUMAN RIGHTS

In a global scenario characterised by the end of the Cold War, the coexistence of human rights with global capitalism is a reality. Globalisation itself is a complex concept. Analysing its impact on human rights is, therefore, not a simple issue. There is a sense in which globalisation is a threat to human rights. The concept of sovereignty of the nation-state, which is fundamental to the international human rights regime, is being challenged by globalisation. There are many instances of human rights violation by powerful multinational conglomerates. Some of these MNCs have greater power than many small, poor states. Systematic evidence on violations by MNCs may be difficult to collate in many cases.

Another set of influences of globalisation on the human rights discourse is the emphasis on its universal character. In an era of globalisation, human rights is often associated with free trade, liberal democracy and the idea of international citizenship. Proponents of neo-liberalism even see free trade as the vanguard and disseminator of rights. The emphasis on 'minimum needs protection of the poor' is viewed as creating safety nets of minimum guarantees for them, while allowing the untrammelled expansion of global capitalism. There are, thus, critics who see a dangerous alliance between human rights discourse and global capitalism. On the other hand, numerous struggles against globalisation for survival, livelihood and the call for sustainable development find support in the human rights discourse.

An important set of challenges to the concept has emerged from the 'Global War on Terror', launched after 9/11. Klug notes that when these rights were becoming values for a godless age and belief in human rights substituting religious belief, the discourse received its greatest challenge from the actions of powerful states against terrorism. In this new context, many developments seem to be undermining the values that human rights stood for. There has been a fusion of religious and political ideologies, whereas the human rights discourse has moved away from affiliation with

'God' or religion. The rule of law has been suspended many times to fight the new enemy, and Western states routinely cite security threats as grounds for suspending rights that had been secured through struggles of people (Klug 2004: 570).

The key challenge is to see that the dynamism of these principles, in guiding the struggles of people and shaping state action contingent on the belief in the power of the people, is kept alive even in the face of such threats.

NOTES

1. In the Hohfeldian scheme, liberty rights exist in the absence of any rule or duty to the contrary. For example, violent acts may specifically be barred in law, but if one is attacked, one has a liberty right to act in self-defence and use reasonable force in doing so.
2. The dictionary meaning of the term *fiduciary* is a specialised job of looking after diverse interests. 'Government with fiduciary duty' means its responsibility to take care of rights of humans to which they are naturally entitled.
3. This term is borrowed from the title of a book by Francesca Klug, *Values for a Godless Age: The Story of the UK's First Bill of Rights,* Penguin, 2000.

BIBLIOGRAPHY

Beetham, D. (ed.) (1995). *Politics and Human Rights*. Oxford: Blackwell.

Donnelly, J. (2003). *Universal Human Rights: In Theory and Practice*. Ithaca and London: Cornell University Press.

Evans, T. (ed.) (1998). *Human Rights Fifty Years On: A Reappraisal.* Manchester: Manchester University Press.

Evans, T. (2000). *The Politics of Human Rights: A Global Perspective*. London: Pluto.

Freeman, M. (2001). 'Is a Political Science of Human Rights Possible?' *Netherlands Quarterly of Human Rights* 19(2): 123–139.

Freeman, M. (2002). *Human Rights: An Interdisciplinary Approach*. Oxford: Polity Press.

Ibhawoh, B. (2001). 'Cultural Relativism and Human Rights: Reconsidering the Africanist Discourse'. *Netherlands Quarterly of Human Rights* 19(1): 43–62.

Ignatieff, M. (2001). *Human Rights as Politics and Idolatry*. Princeton, NJ: Princeton University Press.

Ishay, M. (ed.) (1997). *The Human Rights Reader: Major Political Essays, Speeches and Documents From the Bible to the Present*. New York: Routledge.

Ishaque, Khalid M. (1974). 'Human Rights in Islamic Law'. *The Review of the International Commission of Jurists.* 12(June): 30–39.

Jones, P. (1994). *Rights*. Basingstoke: Macmillan.

Klug, F. (2004). 'Human Rights Above Politics or a Creature of Politics?' *Policy & Politics* 32(4): 563–572.

Lukes, Steven (1997). 'Five Fables about Human Rights' in M. Ishay (ed.) *The Human Rights Reader: Major Political Writings, Essays, Speeches, and Documents from the Bible to the Present.* London: Rontledge.

McPherson, C. B. (1962). *The Political Theory of Possessive Individualism.* Oxford: Clarendon Press.

Mutua, M. W. (2000). 'Politics and Human Rights: An Essential Symbiosis' in M. Byers (ed.) *The Role of Law in International Politics:Essays in International Relations and International Law.* Oxford: Oxford University Press.

Rorty, R. (1993). 'Human Rights, Rationality, and Sentimentality'. *On Human Rights: The Oxford Amnesty Lectures 1993.* S. S. A. S. Hurley. New York: Basic Books 111–134.

The Economist (2001). 19–21 August.

2

Human Rights, Laws and Institutions: The International Context

HUMAN RIGHTS AND THE UNITED NATIONS: THE UNIVERSAL DECLARATION OF HUMAN RIGHTS AND OTHER COVENANTS

The United Nations (UN) is the lynchpin of the international human rights regime. The norms, decision-making procedures and institutiontional initiatives of the UN are considered exemplary and accepted by states as binding in many human rights issues and areas. The Universal Declaration of Human Rights (UDHR), various covenants and the monitoring bodies set up by the UN are part of the global framework for thought and action on human rights. The UN charter makes it explicit that one of the principal aims of the organisation includes 'promoting and encouraging respect for human rights and . . . fundamental freedoms for all without distinction of race, sex, language or religion' [Article 1 (3)]. Further, the charter also envisages that its member states would take joint and separate action in achieving universal respect for and observance of human rights.

The incorporation of an explicit human rights agenda in the UN is significant not merely in terms of its place in the chronology of events, but also conceptually. It provides a new rationale for human rights as well as a concrete foundation for international action in this area. In stating that human rights derive from the inherent dignity of human beings, it sets aside the natural law framework and ensures an agreement on norms or principles of decision making and action, rather than on specific stated values, or comprehensive philosophical positions. Such a strategy has been successful in garnering support for the UN human rights agenda from different countries, irrespective of their regional and religious affiliation.

Concerted international action in support of human rights under the auspices of the UN is an advancement over the principles that existed prior to the World War. International law principles prior to the First World War were concerned with state actions in the international arena alone. In the domestic arena, the principle of state sovereignty was left untouched, even if the state concerned was engaged in violating human rights, as we understand them today. The sovereign was considered the sole source and arbiter of the rights of its subjects. Abuse of these rights, even in the form of torture, summary execution or arbitrary arrest and detention were taken up at the international level and became issues of interstate relationships, only when rights were violated of a person who happened to be a citizen of another state (Kingsbury 1994: 240). The claims of the individuals and groups against their own states were on a weak footing, as also the possibility of intervention in the affairs of another state, on the grounds of violation of universal and inalienable rights of its citizens.

The League of Nations, set up after the First World War, did not make a mention of human rights. Nor did any of the post-war treaties focus on a universal charter of rights with international guarantees. But underpinnings of a conceptual movement forward were evident, as nations did seem to be admitting the possibility of individual and group claims against their own states. The main focus in the League of Nations was on the guarantee of fair treatment to minorities, and clauses to that effect were included in the post-war settlements. These clauses were, however, not seen as breaking new grounds, but simply extending protection that powerful Western powers had already practised amongst each other, when their subjects travelled to other parts of the world (China, Ottoman Empire, and so on), mainly for trade. The weak powers of enforcement at the disposal of the League and its inability to mobilise any action to stem the horror of the Nazi atrocities were decisive events in mobilising international thought to agree upon a core set of obligations of states to all citizens.

Dealing with Nazi Germany after the war led to an agreement on an important principle of human rights. The argument that there were general principles of law that should form the standards of conduct for every civilised society, and that these were the core obligations applicable to all sovereigns, were upheld in the Nuremberg trials. Germany was penalised for war crimes and for 'crimes against humanity'.

Over the years, states have put on themselves necessary obligations of self-restraint, and are now trying to achieve the decent conditions of living for their citizens. Under these circumstances, it is hardly surprising that the UN incorporated an explicit reference to human rights in the charter. But it remained political, in that the 'collective will' that built the consensus around adopting human rights, was unable to overcome the hurdles of national sovereignty. The charter broadly prohibited, for instance, the use of force in case of violation of human rights; a prohibition that, in fact, would shelter the existence of human rights violating regimes in many countries.[1]

The context of the Cold War further conditioned the politics around the adoption of a human rights framework in the UN. The erstwhile USSR felt that the UN should mainly limit itself to the aspect of proclamation of human rights, its enforcement being essentially a matter of domestic action. The political nature of this consensus was evident in the process of adoption of the Universal Declaration. Further, the political and ideological mindset of the Cold War had an impact on the conceptualisation of human rights as well, the differing emphasis on the two sets of rights—civil and political, and social and economic rights. Coupled with a legal–positivist understanding of rights ('rights are what the law gives us as rights'), civil and political rights were considered hierarchically superior and justiceable in comparison to social and economic rights that were merely a guide to policymaking. The practical implication of this was the splitting up of the 'Bills of Rights' into two categories by the UN. International practice, however, for a long time would consider human rights as civil and political rights alone. The emergence of the Universal Declaration on Human Rights is against this backdrop.

THE UNIVERSAL DECLARATION OF HUMAN RIGHTS (UDHR)

The Context

The idea of drafting an International Bill of Rights (IBR) had been mooted since the early days of the UN. It moved a step forward when the Economic and Social Council (ECOSOC) set up the Commission on Human Rights, and entrusted this as one of its primary tasks. Faced with contentious ideological and political differences, as evident in the contrasting stands taken on national sovereignty and relative differences of emphasis on individual as opposed to common interests in the conception of rights, the commission decided to adopt an alternative mechanism. The draft bill was divided into three parts—first, a set of general principles that the General Assembly could ratify; second, a covenant applicable to the countries that signed them; and finally, the enforcement mechanisms. A committee of the General Assembly, the Third Committee on Social, Humanitarian and Cultural Affairs deliberated this draft in over a hundred meetings. The UDHR was finally adopted by the UN General Assembly on 10 December 1948 with 48 votes in favour and eight abstentions. [2] It is important to note that neither in the Third Committee nor in the General Assembly were any negative votes cast against the Declaration.

The questions that were raised in the first chapter underpin the philosophical model of the declaration. An understanding of the philosophical model of the declaration can also shed light on the relation between the international politics of that time and the thought process.

The Philosophical Model of the Universal Declaration: Beyond Natural Rights

Analysing the philosophical character of the declaration, Freeman (2002: 35) notes that the Human Rights Commission was aware of the religious, political and ideological diversity of the UN members, and it deliberately did not ground these rights in any particular philosophy. The only clear philosophical commitment made in the declaration was against the Nazi ideology. The substitution of *natural rights* by *human rights* was probably an attempt to move away from the controversial philosophical implications of grounding rights in nature.[3] In a similar vein, Donnelly (2003 :40-41) remarks that the nature of consensus underlying the declaration is an overlapping, political consensus, in contrast to a comprehensive moral or a religious doctrine. This means that the declaration is compatible with a range of comprehensive philosophical positions, with a fundamental belief in the moral equality of all human beings. Perhaps, a pragmatic approach makes it possible for a range of political and religious belief systems to subscribe to the UDHR.

However, this approach still leaves the declaration open to the charge of a Western liberal bias. In principle, the universality is called into question by two sets of arguments. First, there is the charge of an inherent Western liberal bias, evident in the emphasis on the individual rather than the collective, and on rights rather than duties. The second set of arguments, recently visible in the debate between Asian values and the 'universality' of human rights, questions whether there can be a universally valid definition of human rights in a culturally diverse world. Kausikan (1993) in an article titled *Asia's Different Standards* argues that the Bangkok Declaration of Asian States of 1993 (a preparatory regional conference for the upcoming World Conference in Vienna in the same year), charted out a distinctively Asian point of view on human rights. Dr Mahathir Mohammed, the then Prime Minister of Malaysia was reported to have asked for a redrafting of the Universal Declaration.[4] The approach of the UN, as evident in the Vienna Declaration and Programme of Action adopted by the World Conference on Human Rights 1993, has been to reaffirm the universality, not the significance of particularity of different cultures, regions and religions, without necessarily committing itself to any of these different principles. The debate is still an open one, and the claim of 'universality' contested from many different quarters.

This debate in no way, however, undermines the historical significance of the declaration as one of the most widely cited sources of authority on human rights in international law. Its echoes are to be found in regional declarations on human rights, and in national constitutions the world over. The declaration is also a source of inspiration and support to numerous human rights activists, struggling on various issues. Despite the dispute over the universality of the declaration, there is an agreement on the content of UDHR. It is important to note that the content of the declaration is suggestive of the philosophical tenets too.

The Content

Article 1 affirms the fundamental equality of human beings, that is, all are born free and equal, endowed with dignity and rights. Freeman (2002: 37) notes that while there is an echo of Locke and the French Revolution in this article, this is not 'unreconstructed natural rights theory' but a liberal response to Fascism. This is further evident in Article 2, which affirms the principle of non-discrimination. Everyone is entitled to all the freedoms set forth in the declaration regardless of race, colour, sex, language, religion, political opinion, birth, social status and property. Articles 3 to 5 confer on the individual what is referred to as the *personal integrity rights*. Article 3 affirms the right to life, liberty and security of person. Article 4 prohibits slavery and slave trade. Article 5 prohibits torture, and cruel and inhuman treatment. The intentions of this article are further addressed in a specific covenant to this effect adopted by the General Assembly in 1984.

The declaration includes both legal rights of the individual (Articles 6–12), and social and economic rights (Article 22–27). The relative emphasis between the two sets of rights has been a matter of extensive debates and ideological posturing within the UN. UDHR has been accused of being biased towards legal provisions of civil and political rights, rather than social and economic rights. This debate is discussed in the context of India, on the issue of the relative importance of the Fundamental Rights and Directive Principles in the following chapter.

The legal rights of the individual and individual freedoms (Articles 6–21) ensure:

(a) the right to recognition everywhere as a person before the law,
(b) the right to effective legal remedy,
(c) theright of protection from arbitrary arrest, detention and trial,
(d) everyone is equally entitled to a fair and public hearing by an impartial tribunal,
(e) the right to seek asylum away from persecution.

The freedom of an individual includes that of movement, opinion and expression, thought, conscience and belief, freedom of peaceful assembly and association. Further, the individual is also free to take part in the government of his country. The right to property as elaborated in Article 17 is considered a weak right, and is left out in both the later covenants. Its nature, that is, whether it should be regarded as a human right, is still a matter of debate.

Article 22 says that everyone has the right to economic, social and cultural well-being, indispensable for the dignity and progress of the individual. The realisation of these rights are made dependent on the resources of the state and are said to be 'weak rights'.

Article 25 states the right to an adequate standard of living for individual and his/her family. This includes food, clothing, health, and the cover of social security in case of loss of livelihood, disability or other circumstances beyond his/her control. Minority rights do not find a mention in the declaration, except as an indirect reference to everyone's right to participate in the cultural life of the community (Article 27) . It was only in 1992 that the UN declaration of support for this issue moved centrestage with the Minority Rights Declaration (MRD) .

The rights spelt out in UDHR are said to be indivisible and interdependent. Simply stated, this means that one set of rights cannot be violated in order to fulfil another. Also, many rights are interdependent—one sets out the preconditions for the operation of others. For instance, the guarantee of fundamental equality is basic to the legal rights conferred on the person. In practice, the issue of indivisibility cannot be interpreted very mechanically. States may prioritise some rights and sometimes exercising some rights may violate others. The basic issue once again appears to be the difference in emphasis between civil and political rights, and economic, social and cultural rights. The two separate covenants, discussed below, embody the approach of the UN and many non-state actors working in the field of human rights. Till recently, the approach was a legalistic approach that interpreted human rights as civil and political rights. As fundamental political divisions of the world such as the Cold War come to a close, the human rights agenda of the UN has expanded to focus on *third generation rights*. These include the right to development, and many collective and group rights, such as rights of indigenous people or minority rights. As the 'legal' approach of an earlier era is put aside in favour of a more inclusive definition of human rights that includes individual as well as group rights, the issue of relative importance of one or the other set of rights slowly seems to be getting marginalised.

Two Key Covenants

1. International Covenant on Civil and Political Rights (ICCPR) In 1966, two important international treaties, the International Covenant on Civil and Political Rights (ICCPR), and the International Covenant on Social and Economic Rights (ICSECR) were opened for signature. They came into force in 1976, when the necessary 35 signatures were received. Together, the Universal Declaration and these two covenants are known as the *International Bill of Rights*. The ICCPR contains civil and political rights of the individual. At the moment there are 154 state parties to the covenant.[5] It contains 53 articles, 27 of which are substantive. In addition, there are two optional protocols that the states are at liberty to sign.[6] The first optional protocol gives the Human Rights Committee the competence to examine individual complaints with respect to human rights violation only for states that are party to the protocol. It, also, has a second optional protocol related to the abolition of death penalty by states that sign it.

Article 1 deals with the right of self-determination. Article 2 places an obligation on the states to take all the necessary steps for the implementation of rights of the individual as recognised in the covenant. The covenant includes personal integrity rights, legal rights and individual freedoms, more or less as outlined in UDHR with the exception that ICCPR does not include a reference to right to property, and includes an additional right to self-determination. In the event of an emergency, certain rights are likely to be curtailed by states, but some rights are 'non-derogable' even in the event of an emergency. These include the right to life (Article 6), prohibition of slavery (Article 8), torture (Article 7), right to be recognised as a person before law (Article16), and the freedom of thought, conscience and religion (Article18) . The covenant also envisages the setting up of the Human Rights Committee, a body of independent experts meant to monitor the implementation of ICCPR. The role of this body will be dealt with in some detail in the following section on Implementation Mechanisms.

2. International Covenant on Social and Economic Rights (ICSECR) The International Covenant on Social and Economic Rights (ICSECR) includes the right to fair and equal wages, equal pay for equal work by men and women, right to form trade unions, right to strike, protection of children from social and economic exploitation, and compulsory primary education, right to health, adequate standard of living and the right to culture.

The obligation for implementation that is placed on the states appears to be the basic difference between the two sets of rights. While states are urged to take all the necessary steps to ensure the rights outlined in ICCPR, in case of ICSECR, the states are asked to progressively ensure their implementation. Availability of resources has been cited as a real constraint on the states in order to ensure these rights. As discussed earlier, an exclusive legal focus on the interpretation of rights meant that civil and political rights were considered to be a 'superior' set of rights than social and economic rights. In fact, a strictly legal interpretation saw human rights only as justiceable civil and political rights. With issues such as addressing poverty and development becoming a key focus of international human rights activism, this strict legalistic interpretation is no longer tenable.

Developments in international law have strengthened the obligations on states to achieve these rights. In 1986, a group of distinguished international law experts met at the University of Limburg, Maastricht, and developed what is known as the Limburg Principles, that is, guidelines on states' obligations to implement ICSECR. These were strengthened by a further meeting in 1997 in Maastricht. These developed the Maastricht Guidelines on violations of economic, social and cultural rights. The guidelines clearly reflect the consensus, even within the legal community, on the states' responsibility and accountability to ICSECR.

Other Covenants

The other important human rights covenants are as follows:

- Convention on the Elimination of all Forms of Discrimination Against Women (CEDAW)
- Convention on the Rights of the Child (CRC)
- Convention Against Torture and Other Cruel, Inhuman or Degrading Treatment or Punishment
- International Convention on the Elimination of All Forms of Racial Discrimination

These and other covenants provide the basis for single issue human rights regimes, such as women's, minority or children's rights, or issues like racial discrimination and torture.

The CEDAW was adopted by the General Assembly in 1979 and came into force in 1981. Theoretically, feminist thinking challenged the traditional conception of human rights as they focused exclusively on the public sphere and states' obligations, rather than on the issue of male domination in the public sphere. Efforts of feminists were responsible for the UN Charter making a reference to equal rights for men and women, UDHR prohibiting discrimination against women, and for the setting up of the Committee on the Status of Women. It was this committee that drafted CEDAW. Despite formidable challenges of resource constraint, and opposition from conservative states, CEDAW does provide a substantial charter of rights for women. The specific obligations on states include measures for

- eliminating prejudices and stereotyping of sex roles,
- suppression of all forms of trafficking and exploitation of women,
- elimination of discrimination in political and public life,
- equal participation of women at the international level,
- absence of discrimination in education and employment, and other social and economic rights.

Subsequent efforts made in the 'Decade for Women', 1975–85, led to the recognition by the General Assembly of specific women's rights in various fields such as political participation, health, nutrition, employment, agricultural production and marketing, access to credit and many other rights. There was an important shift of focus from specific issues to 'mainstreaming' gender in all aspects of UN planning.

The Convention on the Rights of the Child was adopted in 1989 and came into force within a year with the necessary signatures obtained. The corresponding monitoring body is the Committee on Child Rights.

IMPLEMENTATION MECHANISMS: CHARTER AND TREATY BODIES

The Universal Declaration and other covenants are not merely statements of intent, they are meant to be a guide to action as well. Together, they provide the basis for a system of rules and implementation procedures centred on the UN, and build what is 'termed as the norms for a global human rights regime'. This elaborate system consists of a variety of institutions ranging from multimember, intergovernmental bodies to those made of independent experts or even the single member office of the High Commissioner for human rights. A large array of UN bodies are engaged in the process of implementation. Depending upon whether their source of origin is the UN Charter or various treaties, these are subsequently classified as charter or treaty bodies. Apart from the charter/treaty bodies, the UN commission is an all-encompassing body for the debates over issues, formulation of obligations and implementation of the enshrined norms. The variety of activities that the various UN bodies engage in includes (i) standard setting and clarifying what individual rights should be (ii) recommending measures to realize these rights, and (iii) humanitarian assistance.

Before we look at the UN bodies, working specifically on the human rights alone, it may be useful to look at the role of the policymaking bodies, the General Assembly and the Security Council. Standing at the apex of the UN institutional pyramid, the General Assembly has had an instrumental role in setting standards, and in protection and promotional activities. Its role in overall policy supervision, provision of resoures—human and financial—sets out the broad parameters of the pursuit of the human right agenda. Further, the UN Commission on human rights works under the direct supervision and control of the Economic and Social Council (ECOSOC); the ECOSOC falls under the monitoring purview of the General Assembly. The third committee of the GA is known as the Social, Humanitarian and Cultural Committee. Many of its other committies and auxilliary bodies assist with the upholding and implementation of human rights framework. The International Law Commission participates in standard setting; special committees of the GA have taken up issues such as decolonization, apartheid, and difficult international situations such as the Palestine issue. Since the 1990s, it has steered international action in focussed areas of activity, necessary for the realisation of human rights such as the decade for Right of Indigenous People (1994–2004).

The Security Council, which has primarily been charged with the maintenance of international peace and security, did not, for many years, consider human rights as a cornerstone of its activities. The stituation had, however, changed by the 1990s. The entire perspective to human rights changed. These were issues that merited humanitarian assistance. The denial of the human rights were considered the key reason for armed conflicts in many parts of the world. Thus human rights was taken as integreal to implementation of 'peace and security', the key activity of the Security council. Specially, the office of the High Commisioner has played an important role in integrating the human rights agenda to all aspects of the working of the UN.

UN Commission on Human Rights

Since 1946, it is the principal forum for negotiating international human rights norms, including the Universal Declaration and the covenants. It is now involved in standard setting in a number of important areas. It is an intergovernmental body and its members are nominees of the states/ national governments. In the past years, it has also acquired some monitoring powers, especially those devolved upon it by resolution 1503 of

ECOSOC. It authorises the commission to investigate cases of gross human rights violation. The criteria of admissibility is stringent, so not all reports qualify for its investigation. Only cases of gross and systematic violence are covered; individual cases or particular abuses are not covered. The powers of enforcement are weak—only a handful of cases ever reach this stage. 'Enforcement' means making the publicly available evidence at hand to the commission. The autonomy of the commission is also questioned as it consists mainly of state representatives. As a result, this also largely remains a promotional mechanism, weak on enforcement. Its practical value is the pressure that it can exert on states in the international community.

The Human Rights Committee

One of the major treaty bodies is the Human Rights Committee. It is a treaty body, set up in 1976, to monitor the implementation of the covenant on civil and political rights. It consists of 18 independent experts elected for a four-year term by state parties. The task of the committee includes a review of periodic reports of compliance submitted by the states. The reports so submitted are of varying quality—while some are detailed, others are a farce. Also, only parties to the covenant report to this body. However, with a majority of the countries of the world being members of the committee, this is not a limitation on the working of the committee. Information exchange does happen, though powers of monitoring are weak.

High Commissioner for Human Rights

The High Commissioner for Human Rights also looks into the cases of violation. The Vienna Conference of 1993 emphasised the special vulnerability of certain groups such as women, children, minorities, migrant workers and refugees. It opened the way for the appointment of a high commissioner for human rights. The approach of the working of this office combines investigation and advocacy. The high commissioner travels widely, makes public statements, and frequently engages in dialogue with governments to strengthen national human rights protection. Mary Robinson's tenure (1997–2002) as High Commissioner has gone a long way in establishing the public face of this office. She assumed office at a time of great change and geared up the office to face the challenges to human rights, associate new actors, and persuade a respect for fundamental rights and freedoms in the global arena. She also carried forward Secretary General Kofi Annan's agenda of intergrating human rights concerns in all aspects of the working of the UN. Navanethem Pillay, a South African Tamil, is the current high commissioner.

Assessing the role of the UN in promoting and protecting human rights is a difficult task. Simply classifying the experience is difficult, partly because of almost 60 years of experience, the number of nation-states involved, and the number of cases of human rights violation brought before it. The political character of the consensus underlying the concept and the UN mandate for action means that the efforts of the UN have been dependent on the initiatives of the nation-states. So, while the focus has been on the UN, the scenes of action lay elsewhere. Some of the conceptual challenges to the concept (as exemplified in the Universal Declaration), especially those coming from the debate about Asian values have been dealt with earlier. This section, therefore, limits its attempts to highlighting some of the challenges and limitations faced by the implementation mechanisms, and the significance of the UN-led global human rights regime.

Challenges to the UN-led Human Rights Global Regime

In an earlier era, the main challenges to the UN-led human rights regime came in mainly from Cold War. Both parties to the conflict the Eastern and the Western bloc, used the human rights argument to critique the opponents' economic and political systems, and eventually the ideologies on which they were based. The erstwhile USSR and the Eastern bloc countries were criticised for the absence of political rights, democracy and freedom of expression of its citizens, while the Capitalist Block was criticised for its inadequate attention to economic and social rights. The collapse of the USSR and the end of Cold War meant an extension of civil and political rights to countries of Eastern Europe, though the challenges are still many. Today, the key human rights challenges come from new political institutions and challenges to minority rights.

In the former Yugoslavia, for instance, there was a Serb minority in Croatia, three minority populations in Bosnia–Herzegovina, and an Albanian minority in Kosovo. The wars and oppression of minority populations in these countries involved gross human rights violations, such as mass murders, rapes and ethnic cleansing. Yet, the UN was unable to intervene militarily. Finally, in 1999, NATO intervened militarily, and there were still charges of gross human rights violations of Albanians, as also war casualties among civilians.

Gross violations of human rights still continue. In the case of Rwanda, the UN was unable to prevent the genocide, despite early warnings. However, what the UN was successful in doing both in the case of Rwanda and earlier in Yugoslavia, was the setting up of international criminal tribunals. Human rights of undertrials from the Iraq war, held by the USA at the

Guantanamo Bay continue to be the focus of international attention. It needs to be seen what role has the UN envisaged for itself in negotiating rights with a superpower.

Limitations of Implementation Mechanisms

The treaty- and charter-based working of the monitoring bodies has led to the emergence of widely accepted norms in various fields of operation, and considerable promotional activity, but very little international implementation. The nature of this regime is such that authoritative action is the result of conscious political decisions to be made by the state actors alone. Donnelly dubs the UN-led regime a 'declaratory' regime, moving beyond which has proved difficult. Human rights, at least as modelled in the Universal Declaration, is a 'profoundly national and not an international issue'. International action is 'at best an impetus towards support for national action to implement and enforce human rights'. What then is the significance of the UN initiative?

Contributions and Significance

The most important achievement is the moral force that this system is able to exert on the international community, or even the conscience of nation-states. While genocides may continue to happen, still under no circumstances does the international community consider such regimes as 'legitimate'. The yardstick for judging regimes as legitimate comes in a large measure from the acceptance of the idea of human rights.

One of the notable achievements of the UN and its specialised agencies has been in the area of standard setting. The ILO has made significant contribution in the area of setting standards for labour rights. But worker rights and labour initiatives have, at best, remained marginal to the human rights agenda. This brings us to the issue of selective attention of the UN to some sets of rights. The selective focus on individual civil and political rights have already been discussed. The promotion and implementation of social and economic rights is an accepted agenda now. Yet, it suffers from a lack of clarity of norms, lack of enthusiasm amongst states, and the complexity of information exchange required to implement these. The UN has also been late in recognising the significance of minority rights. The acceptance of a third generation of rights, termed as 'solidarity rights'—development, peace, healthy environment and self-determination—has expanded the focus to a large number of poor non-Western countries. The General Assembly in 1986 adopted a declaration on the 'Right to Development'. The difficulty, however, is in terms of determining who the bearer of these rights are and what the corresponding duties are.

Despite an uneven record of success, there is an ever-growing acceptance of the legitimacy of the concept. Most states accept the UN-led regime as legitimate. The net effect of the working of this regime is such that it is strong on declaration and weak on enforcement. It would, perhaps, be stronger if the states that constitute the UN were willing to build a stronger international system.

On the foundations of the Universal Declaration, a number of human rights treaties and regimes have been built. The regional initiatives include the European, inter-American and African regimes. These vary in quality from the strong European regime with powers of binding regional decisions, to the African one with weak norms and enforcement.

NOTES

1. The charter authorised UN enforcement action only in case of any threat to peace, breach of peace, or an act of aggression. Article 2 (7) provides a further restriction when it says that nothing in the charter authorises the UN to intervene in matters that are essentially within the domestic jurisdiction of a state.
2. The Universal Declaration of Human Rights was adopted by the General Assembly with 48 votes in favour, no votes opposing it and eight abstentions. The abstentions came from the six communist states, South Africa and Saudi Arabia.
3. The association of the natural law tradition with Christian theology was another problem that the UDHR steers clear of. It can be considered one of the implications of the world oriented to secularism and other values of the enlightenment project.
4. Reported in the *Guardian*, London, 28 August 1997, and cited in Freeman (1998: 25).
5. On 17 February 2005, Mauritania became the 154th state party.
6. The optional protocols are documents that are part of a treaty, deal essentially with subsidiary matters relating to a treaty. States may sign a treaty, but are at liberty to sign the optional protocol. For instance, the ICCPR has an optional protocol that allows the Human Rights Committee to consider individual complaints on the issue of violation of rights contained in the covenant. At the moment, 104 states have signed the optional protocol. India has ratified the ICCPR, but is not a party to the optional protocol.

BIBLIOGRAPHY

Donnelly, J. (2003). *Universal Human Rights: In Theory and Practice*. Ithaca and London: Cornell University Press.

Freeman, M. (1998). 'Human Rights and Real Cultures: Towards a Dialogue on Asian Values'. *Netherlands Quarterly of Human Rights* 16(1): 25–39.

Freeman, M. (2002). *Human Rights:An Interdisciplinary Approach*. Oxford: Polity.

Kausikan, B. (1993). 'Asia's Different Standards'. *Foreign Policy* 92(Fall): 24–41.

Kedzia, Z. (2003). 'United Nations Mechanism to Promote and Protect Human Rights' in J. Symonides (ed.) *Human Rights: International Protection, Monitoring, Enforcement*. Ashgate-UNESCO Publishing. 3–90.

Kingsbury, D. (1994). *Difference and Tolerance: Human Rights Issues in South-East Asia*. Sydney: UNSW Press.

Roberts, Adam and Benedict Kingsbury (1994). *United Nations, Divided World: The UN's Roles in International Relations*. Oxford: Clarendon Press.

3

Human Rights, Laws and Institutions: The National Context

INTRODUCTION

The previous chapter focused on the principles and operation of the international human rights regime. The key contribution of international action, which began after the Second World War as declarations of intent, has been to set up global norms, strong promotional mechanisms and a range of monitoring activities (although with limited powers) for human rights. The scene and arena of action to guarantee the reach of these rights to individuals, however, are the nation-states. Donnelly notes that the fate of human rights implementation, abridgement, protection, violation, enforcement, denial and enjoyment is largely a matter of national and not international action. 'This implies a further particularity to universal human rights, a national particularity in the way international norms are put into practice'(Donnelly 2003: 173). It is important, therefore, to understand in a concrete way as to what is happening with respect to human rights in the Indian context. What are the specific forms that state action takes? What is the national approach to human rights in India? The present chapter attempts to answer these questions.

The first set of initiatives, in many countries, is legal–constitutional. Most states of the world incorporate a reference to the Universal Declaration in the set of basic or fundamental rights that they extend to their citizens. In addition, there may be specific legislation to guarantee some of these rights in terms of explicit directives to the executive and punishments for violation. The second set, more difficult to specify precisely, yet crucial, is the action of state institutions like the executive and the judiciary. Judicial activism in democratic countries has been the mainstay of relief in individual cases of violation, as also against violation by the states themselves. In addition, many countries now have a variety of national institutions, specifically focused on human rights protection and promotion. Along these two sets of initiatives, the particular national context of realisation of human rights shall be adjudged.

The first section, as part of this endeavour, discusses the provisions of the Indian Constitution in a comparative frame of reference to the promise extended in international declaration and covenants. This section also makes a reference to the overall character of judicial activism in the area of human rights in India, and some laws that are seen as a threat to civil liberties of individuals. The second section gives an overview of the variety of national institutions that seek to protect human rights, and discusses, specifically, the role of the National Human Rights Commission (NHRC) of India.

HUMAN RIGHTS, THE INDIAN CONSTITUTION AND LAWS

The Constitution of India, amongst the longest written documents in the world, contains a 'bill of rights' in the nature of fundamental guarantees to its citizens, and also a set of Directive Principles of State Policy (DPSP) that are to act as a guide to policymaking of the state as well as to expand the rights of citizens in the future. These are the most explicit incorporation of UDHR in the Constitution and the covenants in the Indian system. ICCPR is said to be included in Part III (fundamental rights) and ICESCR in Part IV. (Directive Principles recognise and guarantee State Policy.)

The Indian Constitution is among the first in the world to enlist rights for the protection of the cultural rights of minorities as fundamental.[1] The following paragraphs will look at the character of citizens, guarantees, and also, the distinction between fundamental rights and Directive Principles. Besides, an attempt will be made to see how such distinctions have been interpreted in the light of evolving human rights principles.

The fundamental rights provided in Part III are related to five broad areas of rights. The first set relates to the *right to equality*, and articles 14–18 guarantee equality before law, equal protection by law and equality of opportunity, and prohibits discrimination on the grounds of race, religion, caste, sex and place of birth.[2] In the same vein, protective discrimination is allowed for the advancement of socially and educationally backward classes of citizens, and the schedules castes and scheduled tribes (SC/ST). The second set is the *right to freedom*. Civil and political freedom specified in this section provides the freedom of speech, expression, belief, faith and worship. There is, in addition, freedom to reside[3] and work in any part of the country. Specific right to freedom of religion allows one to practise and propagate the religion of his/her choice. Provision of these rights has been made for a plural nation, with no preference to any single religion.[4]

Article 21 provides the *right to life* guaranteed to all persons: *no person shall be deprived of his life or personal liberty except according to the procedure established by law*. This right provides people with protection against arbitrary detention or arrest, and their rights to legal aid. This has been the area of primary focus and concern for human rights activism in India, and as will be evident in the discussions on the functioning of the NHRC. It continues to be a key area of action, even though the focus of such action has widened over the years. Preventive detention laws, justified as a measure of maintenance of internal security or to protect the threat of terrorism, rob the individual of the normal procedural protection of law. Extraordinary laws as Terrorist and Disruptive Activites Act (TADA), and later Prevention of Terrorist Activities Act (POTA), have been criticised for the alleged severe violation of civil liberties. Another result of such activism has been the expansion of the scope of right to life, which is defined as not merely a procedural right, but a substantive one—a life of human dignity.

The Indian Constitution also recognises certain group rights, that is, cultural and educational rights of minorities. These rights, enumerated in Articles 29–30, allow minorities who are defined on religious or linguistic criteria, the freedom to establish educational institutions of their choice. While no specific obligations are placed on the state in this regard, the state cannot discriminate against such institutions in providing funds. Further, religious instruction is barred in institutions maintained out of state funds. The Supreme Court's intervention, over the years, has expanded the scope of autonomy that minority educational institutions enjoy.

The last and vital set of rights is the *right to judicial remedies*. These allow the citizen to move to the courts in case of violation of fundamental rights. This is the character of justiceability, that is, the right of a citizen to claim a right that is said to distinguish fundamental rights from the Directive Principles of State Policy (DPSP) enshrined in Part IV. Fundamental to the governance of the country, DPSP are in the nature of directives to the country, and an aid to policymaking. They are, in other words, obligations that the state must fulfil, even though it may not be immediately possible to realise these for the citizens in view of the lack of resource and other constraints. The right to work in just and humane conditions, right to living wages, public assistance in cases of unemployment, old age, sickness, right to education, free and compulsory education of all children up to the age of 14, right to a hazard-free environment, and so on are some of the rights provided in this section. Many of these rights are similar to that provided in ICESR (1966).

FUNDAMENTAL RIGHTS AND DIRECTIVE PRINCIPLES: A HUMAN RIGHTS PERSPECTIVE

A legalistic focus on the primacy of either sets of guarantees contained in the Fundamental Rights and the DPSP has now been brought to a close. In accordance with a human rights perspective, a guarantee of many of the fundamental rights is interpreted together with DPSP. In many cases, the courts have now placed obligations on the Indian state to expedite the fulfilment of the promises under DPSP. A good example is the issue of right to food, brought to the forefront in the wake of starvation deaths in Kalahandi and Bolangir districts of Orissa. NHRC took the view that the right to life ensures a life of human dignity, and not merely animal existence. Article 21, a fundamental right, was to be interpreted together with two DPSP articles. Artilce 39(a) requires the state to direct its policy towards right to an adequate means of livelihood and Article 47 specifies the primary responsibility of the state in raising the level of nutrition and standard of living of its people.[5]

On the issue of the right to education, in Mohini Jain (1992) and Unnikrishnan (1993) judgements, the Supreme Court directed the state to fulfil its compulsory obligation of providing free and compulsory education up to the age of 14. An amendment of the Constitution now makes it a fundamental right to be placed in Part IV. The then UN High Commissioner, Mary Robinson, in a workshop for judges on the justiceability of economic, social and cultural rights in South Asia, put the issue succinctly:

> The topic of this workshop is well framed. It does not refer to whether economic, social and cultural rights are justiceable. Instead, the focus is on how best to address them within the justice system. The practical perspective puts aside the jaded debate whether these rights can be considered as 'rights' at all. Similarly, it goes beyond the mistaken and anachronistic discussion as to whether economic, social and cultural rights are of equal standing with civil and political rights.

In fact, it is such a complementary interpretation of the two sets of rights, with rights themselves being redefined with the central focus of ensuring human dignity, that a more inclusive interpretation and action on such issues is now being taken. More of this is evident in the areas of intervention of NHRC, that is elaborated upon in the next section.

NATIONAL INSTITUTIONS FOR HUMAN RIGHTS PROTECTION: THE ROLE OF THE NHRC OF INDIA

International activism around the human rights agenda, in a sense, somewhat obscures the fact that the basic and most effective responsibility for the guarantee of human rights is with the states. This responsibility is explicitly stated in the Charter of the United Nations, in Articles 55 and 56: *All members pledge themselves to take joint and separate action in cooperation with the Organisation for the achievement of universal respect for and observance of human rights and fundamental freedoms*. This has been further emphasised in various international instruments and conferences on human rights.

The states on their part, seek to fulfil this obligation, in a general sense, through its key arms: the executive, the legislature and the judiciary. In addition, it is now commonplace to have specific instruments that promote and protect human rights. As shown in Fig. 3.1, there are now a variety of such institutions that are specifically focused to protect and promote human rights at the national level.

The National Human Rights Commission of India (NHRC) is an example of a general purpose commission set up with the objective of protection and promotion of human rights. Before we come to the description and analysis of the institution, it might be useful to briefly describe some features of the variety of institutions that we have described in Fig. 3.1.

The institution of *ombudsperson*, set up for the first time in Sweden in 1809, was soon adopted by other Scandinavian countries, and exists now in a number of other countries. A single person institution, the specific powers of the ombudsperson vary from country to country. The general role mandated by the Parliament of that country is that of supervising the functioning of government departments, often acting as mediators between individuals who have lodged a complaint and the related government department. His/her powers of persuasion are crucial to the success of the institution. The other institutions are more collegial in character.

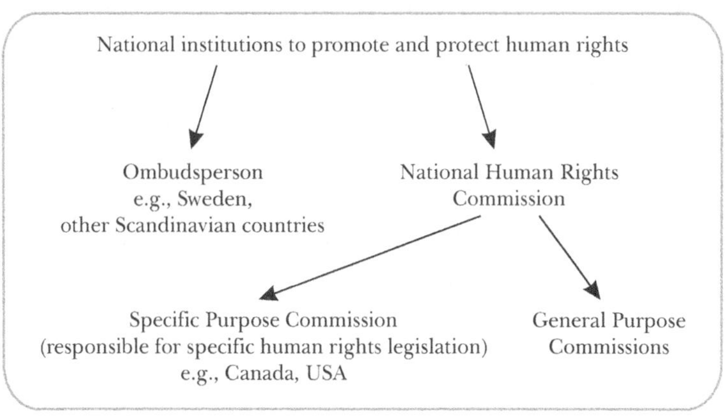

Figure 3.1 Variety of national institutions to promote and protect human rights

National Human Rights Commissions set up by a number of states to protect and monitor human rights are two types of bodies. The first type includes bodies set up to look after specific human rights legislation. These may be located at the federal or provincial levels. The first such institution was set up in Canada, at the provincial level (in Ontario) in 1962, and is responsible mainly for the implementation of anti-discrimination legislation in the province. In the USA, the US Commission on Civil Rights was set up at the federal level by the Congress under the Civil Rights Act of 1957, an anti-discrimination legislation. The members of such commissions may be appointed by the executive or legislature, or both.

The second type of national commissions is general purpose commissions. In recent years, the UN has strongly encouraged the setting up of such national institutions, and has even formulated certain guiding principles—known as the Paris principles—meant to ensure their status. Such national commissions may either be set up by the Constitution, or by law, and although they vary in terms of their specific powers from country to country, they perform a general advisory role to governments. In addition, they act as intermediaries for action in the international field as well.

Background

Set up under the Protection of Human Rights Act of 1993, the NHRC came into effect on 12 October 1993. The first of its kind among South Asian countries, the commission was set up as an autonomous body that seeks to protect and promote human rights. Section 2 (1) (d) of the Act defines human rights as rights relating to life, liberty, equality and dignity of the individual, guaranteed under the Constitution or embodied in the International Covenants on Civil and Political Rights, and the International Covenant on Economic, Social and Cultural Rights adopted by the UN General Assembly on 16 December 1966. The objective of the commission is to protect as well as promote this vision of human rights. To this effect, it can inquire into any acts of human rights violation, intervene in proceedings before a court, visit jails, study national and international treaties on human rights, and make recommendations to the central government for their effective implementation.

Structure and Composition

The commission consists of a chairperson and seven other members. The composition reflects professional and social diversity. The manner of appointment of members, as also their tenure, go a long way in ensuring the

BOX 3.1

The National Human Rights Commission of India

Composition of the NHRC

Chairperson

(A person who has been a chief justice of the Supreme Court)

Seven other members

- One member who is or has been a judge of the Supreme Court of India.
- One member who is or has been a chief justice of any high court.
- Two other members appointed on the basis of their special knowledge or experience in the field of human rights.
- The chairpersons of the National Commission for Scheduled Castes and Scheduled Tribes, National Commission for Minorities, and the National Commission for Women are ex-officio members.

autonomy of the commission. Section 3 (a) of the Act discusses the composition of the commission, as is shown in Box 3.1.

The commission is an autonomous body with the Act specifying the manner of appointment of the chairperson and other members, their tenure and procedure for removal. The chairperson and other members are to be appointed by the President on the recommendation of a committee consisting of the Prime Minister as the chairperson, the speaker of the Lok Sabha, the Home Minister, the Leaders of Opposition in Lok Sabha and Rajya Sabha, and the Deputy Chairman of the Rajya Sabha as members.

The chairperson and other members continue in office for a period of five years from the date on which they assume office, or until their age of 70 years, whichever is earlier. They are barred from reemployment with either the central or state governments after relinquishing office. Further, they cannot be removed from office except in accordance with the stringent procedure for their removal as prescribed in the Act. These clear and emphatic stipulations ensure that the commission remains above the day-to-day tribulations of politics, and is empowered to fearlessly pursue its intervention in a wide range of issues related to human rights violations.

Process and Functions of NHRC

At the time that the NHRC was set up, the reactions to such an institution were mixed. In a review of the decade long working of NHRC, Dayal (2002: 40) notes that these initial reactions could be dubbed more as scepticism than hope.

> While many had an open mind on how the commission would fare and were prepared to withhold judgement, a significant number—and among them

many who were already committed to the promotion and protection of human rights—felt that the statute was fatally flawed, and that the commission would be a 'toothless tiger', that it would function as a 'post office' and as a *Sarkari* body, and that it would, in the final analysis, invariably be chosen to provide the seal of good housekeeping to governmental wrong-doing, rather than to ensure the better protection of human rights in the country. Some went so far as to argue that the establishment of the commission would actually set back the 'movement' for human rights in the country, as the commission would distract the activists from fighting the real fights for rights; while offering them instead a placebo ...

(Dayal 2002: 40)

Over a decade of the working of the commission reveals that NHRC has, in fact, emerged as a nodal point, a vanguard institution at the forefront of the struggle for ensuring human rights. The range of its interventions far exceeds the conventional areas of institutional intervention, such as custodial interrogation, even deaths, to human tragedies, for example, the starvation deaths in Orissa, or the communal riots in Gujarat following the Godhra incident in February 2002. A simple piece of statistics that is often cited as evidence of the significance that this institution has acquired is the data on the number of cases that have been brought to the notice of NHRC every year. Table 3.1 shows that since its inception in 1993,[6] the number of cases has increased ten-fold.

Before we look into the areas, as also the mode of intervention of the NHRC, it might be useful to look at what powers and functions have been envisaged for it under the Act.

TABLE 3.1 Number of cases reported to the NHRC (from1993–94 to 2002–03)

Year	*Cases*
1993–94*	486
1994–95	6987
1995–96	10,195
1996–97	20,514
1997–98	36,800
1998–99	40,723
1999–2000	50,634
2000–01	71,555
2001– 02	69,083
2002–03**	68,779

Notes: *Data for this year covers the period October 1993–March 1994, for other years, it is from April to March.

**Figure reported at the time of compilation of Annual Report 2002–2003.

Source: Annual Reports of the NHRC

Formal Powers of the NHRC

The Act gives wide-ranging powers to NHRC to investigate as well as act in the area of human rights violation. The commission can act on complaints by the aggrieved and affected individuals, or even that of any other person acting on behalf of the affected person. In cases of gross violation of human rights, the commission can act suo moto. As evident in the case of the release of bonded labourers in Punjab (as shown in the box) the commission took notice and a comprehensive range of action—from release to rehabilitation was undertaken on the basis of a news report in *The Indian Express*, on 17 December 1999.

As envisaged in the Act, NHRC is expected to be engaged in a wide range of functions. These are noted by Dayal (2002 :43) to be 'amongst the widest conferred on any national institution in the world, a possible model for others to consider.' Some of the key provisions in the Act, and thereby, functions of NHRC are as follows:

- The capacity to intervene in any proceedings involving any allegation of violation of human rights pending before any court.

BOX 3.2

Release of Bonded Labourers and Their Rehabilitation: Punjab

The commission took suo moto cognizance of a press report which appeared in *The Indian Express*, 17 Dec 1999, titled '84 Bonded Labourers Freed, Narrate Shocking Tales of Torture, Molestation'. It stated that 84 bonded labourers, who were freed from a cold storage construction site, said that they were beaten, given third-degree treatment. The women workers alleged rape and molestation. None of the workers were paid their wages.

The commission directed the DG Police, Punjab, and the SSP, Jallandhar, to send reports to the commission on this article. The labourers stated that they had been working for the last four months and were not given wages as the owner had promised to pay them when they returned to their native places. When the SDM, Shahkot, and SHO, Police, visited the spot, the labourers told them that they did not wish to work, as the owner's behaviour was insulting. A woman labourer, named Saloni stated that one Pappu had beaten her husband and locked him in a room. The Labour Inspector was directed to ensure the payment of wages to the labourers. The labourers were then set free. An FIR was registered under the Bonded Labour System (Abolition) Act, the Indian Penal Code.

The NHRC also directed payment of relief to the workers and issued detailed instructions on their rehabilitation. The rehabilitation measures suggested formation of a cooperative society, securing of land for the labourers by the district administration and employment under Rozgar yojanas.

(*Source:* NHRC Web site (Case No. 663/19/1999–2000, NHRC of India))

- The commission's powers of inquiry— these give it the powers of a civil court, functioning under the Code of Civil Procedure (1908).
- Its vast powers of investigation enable it to utilise the services of any officer, or investigating agency of the central or state government, and also through its own investigative division.

The other functions envisaged for NHRC are in the area of governance as also propagating the idea of human rights. The former includes the task of review of laws in the country (for example, those related to prison administration, or preventive detention laws such as TADA or POTA).

There are wide-ranging questions on the actual work experience of NHRC. Let us look at the working of the NHRC closely.

Working of the NHRC

The working of the NHRC for over a decade now, has gone a long way in allaying the initial fears about the autonomy of the body *vis-à-vis* the government and of the statute being weak, and the emergent commission, therefore, being a powerless body. In fact, the worst fears of the human rights activists, that the commission may weaken the movement in India, have been put to rest by the commission's activist interpretation of its charter. It is its constant endeavour to expand the definition of human rights to cover all aspects of dignity, and ensure this right to the most disadvantaged. The concluding remarks of the Seventh Annual Report (April 1999–March 2000) aptly summarise this endeavour in the following words:

> With each successive year the Commission has widened its area of concern in order to ensure that the most vulnerable do not remain the least protected, the least respected.

Both the commission's method of working and its widening definition of issues of engagement are responsible for this stature. Most significant, however, has been the autonomy of the commission, not only guaranteed in basic design from the Act, but also exhibited in the determination of the commission to remain above the pulls and pressures of majoritarian politics. All these three themes, viz. autonomy of the commission, its method of working, and issues it has engaged with, are discussed in the following sections.

Autonomy of the Commission

It is guaranteed in the basic design by the manner of appointment of the members and their tenure. More significant, however, has been the commission's own determination to exhibit this autonomy in its functioning, even if it involves a determined opposition to the government of the day. Some key interventions of the commission that have gone a long way in building its reputation of autonomy are:

- NHRC opposed Prevention of Terrorism Act (POTA), as also the precursor bill with the same provisions, that is, the Prevention of Terrorism Ordinance (POTO) in 2000. It outlined the threat to citizens' rights inherent in such legislation, and the need for stricter implementation of the existing anti-terrorism laws, rather than a new legislation. Earlier, NHRC had opposed the incumbent government on the continuance of TADA and also sent letters to all the MPs to this effect.
- The most significant intervention of the commission was in the Gujarat riots following the Godhra incident. Taking suo motto cognizance of the communal disturbances in the state, its members visited the troubled state, and in its observations, placed the responsibility for the failure to protect its people on the state government. Even if it was the result of inaction, the onus of accountability for the communal unrest lay with the state government. The commission also gave directions for a payment of reparation to victims, intervened in the issue of facilitating proper filing of FIR, especially in respect of atrocities against women and noted that the compensation for damaged property was often being set at unreasonable and low amounts. It was also seen that many victims were pressurised into withdrawing the cases they had filed, before they could return home.
- On the issue of Dalit oppression, several Dalit human rights groups demanded the inclusion of caste-based oppression at the World Conference against Racism (Durban, August–September, 2001). The government opposed the demand on the ground that the Indian state had provided many protective provisions in the Constitution to prevent atrocities against dalits and other weaker castes. The government objected to internationalising caste oppression at Durban. NHRC, however, took an independent stand and publicly stated that discussing the caste issue at Durban would provide a significant opportunity of discussing the issue openly and courageously, alongside the vexed question of discrimination and inequality as they exist all over the world.

Method of Working

The commission does not take up all the cases brought before it. From the figures available on the number of cases filed before it, since its inception up to 2002–03, almost 50 per cent have been dismissed. Some involved an initial examination of complaint by the commission, and then an issue of specific directions (22.9 per cent of cases). These directions include payment of interim relief to the victims, initiation of departmental proceedings against errant officials who had failed to safeguard human rights or might even have abetted its violation. Certain features with respect to the efficient functioning and method of working are the following:

- In terms of enhancing procedural efficiency, NHRC has computerised its entire case load, and 'fast tracked' certain category of complaints that call for immediate action.
- Equally significant has been NHRC's power to appoint special rapporteurs to assist it in discharging responsibilities. In 1998–99, four special rapporteurs were appointed by it to look at a variety of issues that included bonded labour, child labour, and the situation of hunger in the Kalahandi and Bolangir districts of Orissa.
- It also interacts with external groups and organisations, making itself available for views and suggestions on various human rights issues.
- In summary, it can be said that the method of its working has displayed a focus on speedy delivery of justice, impartiality in dealing with government agencies, and most importantly, a focus on ensuring rights to those on the margins.

These aspects of its working are re-emphasised in the overview of issues of engagement of the NHRC, dealt with in the next section.

Principal Concerns of the Commission

Dayal in his decennial review of the working of the commission, classifies its concerns, into three broad categories.

- First, handling of individual complaints.
- Second, handling of key human rights issues facing the country in the area of civil and political rights, economic, social and cultural rights, and the third generation of rights pertaining to issues of development, survival and group rights.
- The third set of interventions relate to reforms and good governance.

The individual complaints are important as they illustrate the key human rights issues, as also the variety of ways in which their systematic denial occurs. In fact, the case load of NHRC is the heaviest amongst all such institutions of the world. Keeping in mind the wide arena of interventions by the commission, some key interventions in the area demarcated above are placed in Table 3.2.

TABLE 3.2 Key areas of intervention of NHRC, 1993–2003.

Themes	*Action*
Civil and Political Rights	• Letters to Members of Parliament that TADA 1987 should not be renewed. • Also expresses opinion on POTO 2000 and POTA 2001. • Guidelines on custodial death, rape. • Emphasises the need for India to sign the 1984 Convention against torture and other cruel, inhuman and degrading treatment. • Need for police reforms. • Need to rewrite the Indian Prisons Act, 1894.
Economic and Social Rights	• KBK district starvation deaths monitored. • Freedom from starvation is an integral part of the 'right to life'. • Focus on public health and free and compulsory education.
Rights of the Marginalized and Vulnerable	• Rights of women and children, now an important focus area. Sexual harassment at workplace, health rights of women and children, maintenance allowance for divorced women, conditions of women in prison, widows in Vrindavan are some of the issues looked at. • Rights of Dalits, adivasis and denotified tribes. • Pernicious practices such as manual scavenging and bonded labour. • Exchange of views on human rights violation and caste discrimination facilitated at Durban. • Problems of *Musahars* addressed in a special note. • Rights of people affected by natural disasters, viz. Orissa cyclone, Gujarat earthquake, etc. Seeks to ensure that the rights of those affected, especially the most vulnerable, are protected. • Rights of minorities. Considers the protection of this right the most critical test of inclusiveness. Examines many individual complaints of victimisation and discrimination. • Rights of people displaced by mega projects. Intervenes on behalf of those displaced by the Bargi dam. Emphasis on resettlement and rehabilitation of the displaced.

Contd.

Contd.

Rights of the Marginalized and Vulnerable (contd.)	• Rights of the disabled and the elderly. In touch with groups working with the elderly and the disabled; seeks implementation of legislation.
Review of Legislation and Treaties	• Recommends review of existing national legislation in many areas. Also reviews international treaties and conventions, and advises the government on possible steps.

It is evident from the wide areas of intervention of NHRC that from a narrow focus on human rights as civil and political rights, the commission has graduated to implementing a broader and a more inclusive regime, with a core concern for rights of the marginalised and the vulnerable.

Assessment of NHRC

The annual reports of the commission are an exercise in introspection. In a sense, those involved in the working of the institution have the advantage of knowing the impediments in achieving the avowed objectives. These can be classified as:

a) issues pertaining to the relationship of NHRC with the government and other institutions, and
b) those that relate to powers, functions and procedures as outlined in the statute.

In the first category, some of the key issues that have emerged are:

Tabling the Annual Reports of NHRC Before the Parliament

The annual reports of the commission are to be tabled before the Parliament. But there are undue delays in their being placed before it. The Tenth Annual Report for 2002–03 notes that at the time of writing the report, the previous report (Ninth Annual Report for April 2001–March 2002) had not been placed before the Parliament.

State Human Rights Commissions

The Protection of Human Rights Act 1993 envisages the setting up of the State Human Rights Commissions. Being closer to the people of the respective states, they should be able to provide speedier and less expensive redressal of grievances. Some states have indeed implemented this. In many, however, there is a delay in setting these up. In some states, the institution has not been given the financial autonomy, important for its independent functioning.

The key issue that has emerged in the second category is that of the reform of the 1993 Act. The commission has engaged itself in a detailed exercise in this regard (detailed note available as Annexure 1, Annual Report for 1999–2000). The suggestions for the change include the need of including 'paramilitary forces' within the definition of armed forces. The suggestion is intended to include the former in the ambit of NHRC scrutiny, to make the set-up of State Human Rights Commission a compulsory issue, and to set up human rights courts that can work on the basis of the Criminal Procedure Code of 1973. Many other provisions relate to the smooth and focused functioning of the NHRC.

These suggestions for reform remain in the manner of proposals and NHRC newsletters report the urge of the institution to push this issue of reform of the Act.

CONCLUSION

While the working of the institution has helped in pushing the frontiers of action and intervention in the area of human rights, now defined as an integral element of human dignity, the realisation of these rights in our country, still remains an uphill task. The institution is a serious effort in the area of a meaningful democracy and protection of rights, especially for the most disadvantaged and marginalised.

NOTES

1. The international activism in this area has come only in the 1980s, and the guarantees in the Indian Constitution predate such international efforts. For details, see Chapter 4, the section on human rights of minorities.
2. Nariman (2002: 22) notes that the notable omissions in this section on prohibition of discrimination of vulnerable groups are women and children.
3. The only restrictions on this freedom can be said to be the separate set of restrictions applicable to Jammu and Kashmir (J&K), and the restrictions on owning property in tribal areas.
4. The restriction on this freedom, as explained by judgements of the Supreme Court is that this does not include the freedom of religious conversions.
5. Extracts from the proceedings of the Commission, 17 Jan 2003, p. 333, *NHRC Annual Report,* 2002–3.
6. Barring the data on the number of cases for 1993-94. Number of cases in 1994-95 is used as a base for this calculation.

SELECT BIBLIOGRAPHY

Dayal, V. (2002). 'Evolution of the National Human Rights Commission, 1993–2002: A Decennial Review'. *Journal of the NHRC* 1: 40–71.

Donnelly, J. (2003). *Universal Human Rights in Theory and Practice*. Ithaca and London: Cornell University Press.

NHRC (1998–2003). *National Human Rights Commission: Annual Report*. New Delhi: NHRC.

Sinha, M. K. (1998). 'The Role of the National Human Rights Commission of India in the Implementation of Human Rights'. *Netherlands Quarterly of Human Rights* 16(1): 101–106.

4

Human Rights of Marginalised Groups

INTRODUCTION

The promise of universal protection extended by the notion of human rights, as also expressed in the human rights regime over the years, seems to imply the notion of a linear process of extension of these rights to all citizens. Many a time, it is also felt that the very existence and operation of democracy by itself guarantees rights to all. The practical experience, however, has been the persistent exclusion of various groups from attaining the benefits of human rights. The marginalised are among the most vulnerable, and often very poor. They constitute diverse groups. Unorganised workers, Dalits, women and minority groups are some of the most vulnerable that we talk about. The vulnerable, very often, do not have the means or the power to realise their rights, and to report or struggle against its violation. Therefore, a different institutional mechanism, and greater and more specific support, is required for them to realise their rights.

The unorganised workers, even though the most significant part of the Indian workforce, have been unable to avail the protection and benefits extended to workers at large. Working in isolated locations and often at the fringes of the economy, they remain the most vulnerable part of the workforce. Minorities, on the other hand, refer to a smaller number in relation to a *majority* construed on diverse principles such as those of religion, language and ethnicity, among others. They experience exclusion, as human rights are guaranteed generally to citizens who constitute a majority. Persecution of minorities is one of the most violent human rights violations that nation-states have engaged themselves in. Dalit groups,[1] at the margins of the caste hierarchy in India, emphasise their historical exclusion and oppression in an upper-caste dominated Hindu society. While the Dalits constitute a majority in terms of numbers, the caste-based oppression and inequality results into their deprivation of 'equal' guarantee of human rights. In fact, atrocities on Dalits are amongst the most despicable violations of human rights. The most commonly cited example of this is the systematic and persistent exclusion from various public arenas, attack on their dignity, practice of untouchability and violent attacks on them. Similarly, adivasis are denied their individual as well as collective rights over land and other natural resources on account of various discriminatory policies.

The principles on the basis of which these various groups—at the margins of society, economy and the cultural practices of a majority—have been subject to exclusion and persecution, differ. But there is a common thread that runs through them: the violation of human rights, which cannot be redressed without looking at the specific nature of their exclusion. The recognition of 'difference' rather than value-neutral, universal and equal guarantees is the key to developing adequate conceptions of what constitutes human rights for these marginalised groups. The guarantee of human rights to these groups, in practice, is crucial to the ideal of universal guarantee.

The sections that follow will specifically discuss each of these cases of marginalised groups and their human rights. The structure of these focused discussions will follow a common frame of attempting to define the groups, analysing the patterns and principles of their marginalisation, the laws and institutions that attempt to protect human rights for these groups, and the challenges that remain in attaining a more inclusive human rights regime for each of these vulnerable and marginalised groups.

I

HUMAN RIGHTS OF UNORGANISED LABOUR

WHO IS AN UNORGANISED WORKER?

The term *unorganised worker* is frequently used to refer to two types of labour: first that category of labour which works in the unorganised sector, and second, the labour that is unorganised. Expanding further, the first category refers to workers on the basis of the nature of enterprise that they work in, and the second, to workers on the basis of the nature of their work arrangements which are informal and often precarious. Their employment is not permanent; it may often be contractual, and employer–employee relationships are not clearly marked out as they are in the case of the formal sector. As a result, the workers in this sector are unable to reap the benefits of the laws and social security benefits that cover workers in

BOX 4.1

Difficulties in Defining the Unorganized Sector: Second National Commission on Labour

The first difficulty that we came across was in identifying or defining the unorganised sector. Saying that the unorganised sector covers the area that falls outside the purview of the organised sector is not saying much. We looked for a single or primary criterion or characteristic by which the sector could be defined ... it could not be defined on the basis of the nature of work that workers or employees are engaged in, because ... the sector has tribal forest workers as well as home-based, InfoTech and software workers. It cannot be based on the number of employees in an undertaking because it covers agricultural workers, craftsmen, home-based workers, self-employed workers, weavers workers in, cooperatives, as well as workers in small-scale industries where the workforce can be counted on one's fingers. It cannot be based on the level of organisation because some of the enterprises may have very few workers, and even these may be working in a dispersed manner with hardly any organisational link, or interaction with each other, sometimes because of the nature of work, and sometimes because of geographical dispersion ... It would seem that the vocations, employment and conditions of work are so varied and disparate that it is impossible to provide protection and welfare to all workers in all the sub-sectors, with one uniform law, or one uniform system for social security.

(Report of the Second National Commission on Labour 2002, Vol. I:. 596-97)

the formal sector. This is despite the fact that their need for such protection surpasses that of workers in the organised sector, who are often also better organised in terms of trade unions. The difficulty in defining a precise or specific category as unorganised workers and of identifying *who* these workers are has been the starting point of almost all academic endeavours and policy initiatives for this category of workers. This can be read about in Box 4.1, which cites an excerpt from the Second National Commission on Labour (Ministry of Labour, GOI, 2002).

Some notable characteristics of unorganized workers are as follows:

- Their categories of work are many and varied.
- Many such workers, particularly women, may not be recognised as workers at all
- For types of unorganised labour, it is difficult to establish the employer—employee relationship. So it is difficult to place the onus of *employee welfare* as a responsibility of the employer.
- Workers in the unorganized sector, or unorganized workers, generally get low wages.

- Child labour, migrant construction or farm labour fall within this category.
- Workers are not organized in trade unions, and therefore lack collective bargaining power.
- Debt bondage is common. They have little access to credit from institutional sources and, therefore, frequently resort to private moneylenders who charge usurious rates of interest.

Unorganised workers are engaged in a variety of work in the urban as well as the rural areas. To give an idea of this variety, these workers could be involved in activities as diverse as forestry, fishing, mining, *beedi* making, weaving, or even petty trade.[2] Further, they could be either self-employed or paid workers. In terms of numerical strength, they constitute the most significant part of the workforce. Most estimates put the proportion of workers in the organised sector at less than 10 per cent of the total workforce, and those in the unorganised sector at over 90 per cent. Further, most of them work in rural areas are engaged in agriculture, and are the poorest of the poor. Often, these workers remain underemployed or even unemployed for large parts of the year.

Lack of workers' organisation in the unorganised sector results in poor bargaining strength of the unorganised workers. Trade unions find it difficult to access these workers, spread out in various areas of activities and in geographically diverse locations. Also, a high number of them undertake work in rural areas. Cooperative activities are also low. There workers, therefore, have little voice or bargaining power.

In sum, the process of defining who the workers of this sector are begins with describing the nature of the unorganised sector, in comparison and contrast to the organised sector. The issue of difficulty in identifying or defining the unorganised sector as was noted by the Second National Commission on labour (see Box 4.1) is not merely a conceptual one, but also raises complexities when one begins to raise issues of how to organise such workers, or looking for mechanisms to ameliorate their work and life conditions. The term 'unorganised workers' refers to a larger category of self-employed, or even paid workers of the formal sector on unclear employment terms.

India's policy of a mixed economy where the public sector controlled the economy gave rise to a vocal and organised sector of labour, which was subsequently able to negotiate enhanced benefits and securities—something that unorganised labour could not obtain for itself. Even while globalisation has been enhancing the numbers of unorganised labour, there has not been a corresponding increase in setting up of protective mechanisms for the latter. They are therefore left very vulnerable in moments of crisis, as can be seen by suicide of workers in the handloom sector in Andhra Pradesh, or of farmers in Vidarbha.

What Are the Issues Before the Unorganised Labour?

As is evident from the variety of work they engage in, and their dispersed location as workers, it is impossible to talk of a unified set of issues that are applicable to all categories of unorganised workers. It is useful to categorize these issues in three broad areas:

1. Problems that unorganised workers face in terms of life and work-related hardships, across the variety of sectors of their work and activity.
2. Rights of unorganised labour and the difficulties of setting up mechanisms for realising these, and
3. Issues related to their organisation and collective association.

While the issues related to their life and survival are addressed in this section, the institutional mechanisms for protection of rights, as also the problems with respect to their organisation, are detailed in separate sections below. The key survival issues that such workers face are with respect to lack of health safeguards, difficulty in obtaining livelihood, lower wages, insecure contracts and often, no bargaining power.

Survival Issues

The hazardous nature of work that engages unorganized labour in many sectors of activity exposes them to extremely vulnerable conditions of life and existence. In the absence of provisions for looking after their health and working conditions, and insuring their lives against risks, they survive despite the odds.

The mining industry is one of the best examples of illustrating the survival and health related challenges that they encounter. Three types of mining operations are prevalent in the country. The first two, which include public sector mines (such as Steel Authority of India Limited) and the large private sector metaliferrous and non-metaliferrous mines, are characterized by high level of organized union activity of workers. Provisions for workers' welfare and security are, therefore, largely in place. The third category, small mines and quarries, include large numbers of unorganized workers. As depicted in the film *Kala Patthar*, working conditions in these mines are full of hazards. The risk of mine-flooding, fire, and mine-roof collapse are omnipresent. Equally present are the threat of carbon monoxide poisoning due to lack of oxygen in the mines, fear of loss of limbs in industrial accidents and choking of ventilation in mines leading to unimaginable tragedy and deaths. The most common health hazards faced by them are silicosis—an occupational lung disease caused by the inhalation of crystalline silica dust and tuberculosis, a deadly infectious disease contracted due to unsanitary conditions of living and work.

While workers in the first two categories of mines have the benefit of welfare measures and social security benefits as per law, in the third category, workers are often denied such benefits. Employers circumvent the law on social security in various ways. The employment may be through contractors. As a result, there is no direct employer—employee relationship, and therefore no liability on the employer to provide social security benefits. Workers frequently change contractors who, in turn, frequently change mine employers. This process of frequent change makes it very difficult to track the employer—employee trail, and whether an employee has served the minimum number of employment days, to be eligible for benefits. This poses difficulty in the accrual of and tracking of provident fund.

An interesting example of the vulnerable conditions of existence of workers in the Alang-Sosiya ship-breaking yard near Bhavnagar, at the Gulf of Cambay Coast, is provided by the Report of the National Commission of Labour (2002: 630–632). This ship-breaking yard is Asia's biggest and produces almost 3. 5 million tons of steel annually, close to the production of TATA Steel. Interestingly, health and welfare aspects of the workers are looked at by the voluntary actions of the industry as also by the government. When members of the Commission visited some of these facilities, this is what they observed:

Workers at the Along-Sosiya Ship-breaking Industry, Bhavnagar, Gujarat

We visited some of the dormitories of the workers and found that they were congested, ill-lit and ill-ventilated ... Presently, the number of baths, latrines etc. work out to roughly one per 400 plus workforce ...

(Report of the National Commission of Labour 2002: 632)

Similar is the condition of health and welfare of construction workers. In this sector, migrant labour is involved, with very frequent shifting of the site of work. Since workers are recruited on a contract, very often, when work is lean, wages are deducted; they are not even compensated for overtime work. They dwell in temporary sheds at worksites, with no facilities for latrine, urinal, washroom, or first aid. Men and women relieve themselves wherever they find it suitable. Women workers are doubly harassed, with lower wages, child care to be combined with work, and the distress of having to cope with unsanitary conditions. What are the options for escaping these hardships and of protection from vulnerabilities?

The answer to this may be had by beginning with an overview of what the rights of workers are in the international regime of rights, as also how the Indian state has endeavoured, in a progressive way, to protect the rights of the marginalized.

International Efforts

The issue of rights of the unorganised workers belongs to the gamut of social and economic rights. International activism for their rights is credited largely to the International Labour Organisation (ILO), an agency of the United Nations, and a tripartite body representing workers, employers and governments. The Universal Declaration of Human Rights (UDHR) included a reference to the right to work and to form trade unions (Article 23). Worldwide attention was drawn towards the issue in the early 1970s when ILO initiated efforts to study the unorganised sector through its World Employment Programme Missions in Africa.

Through conventions and recommendation, ILO facilitates basic minimum standard setting for labour rights.[3] These include:

- Freedom of association
- Right to organise
- Right to collective bargaining
- Abolition of forced labour
- Equality of opportunity and treatment

Until recently, the rights of workers were largely emphasised from a 'legal' perspective, that is, legal rights of workers in the workplace. This conventional thinking of ILO privileged the rights of organised workers and precluded the building up of a firm focus on unorganised workers. But a shift towards human rights–based perspective, where the focus is more on social ethics rather than a legal realisation of rights alone has widened the scope of thinking on rights and work. Nayyar (2003: 9–13) notes that their realisation requires greater public action in the economic and political sphere. The concept of 'decent work' articulated by ILO and a notion which the UN thinking seems to be converging represents such a fundamental departure. It extends beyond the formal labour market to encompass workers in the unorganised sector, the self-employed and home workers. It is consistent with the emergent thinking that views development as fulfilment of basic human needs.[4]

National Efforts

Plans are afoot for a proposed bill assuring social security for workers in the unorganised sector. The existing structure of protection of workers in the unorganised sector comes from the general citizens' rights guaranteed by the Constitution, but more specifically, the labour laws enacted from the 1920s onwards have protected the rights of the unorganised workers. The Indian Constitution and fundamental freedoms guaranteed to its citizens provide a broad structure of labour protection in the organised as well as the unorganised sector. This includes the freedom to choose a profession of one's choice, equal pay for equal work and absence of discrimination. Besides, there is a movement now to guarantee the right to work for every citizen and a draft bill is in circulation.

Beyond these fundamental freedoms, there are specific labour laws that, in principle, are applicable to the unorganised sector also. These laws are intended to provide work–right protection and social security. Jhabvala classifies these laws enacted from the 1920s till the present, in terms of time periods, and draws out their differing focus over time. A select set of legislation is detailed in Table 4.1.

The first set of labour laws, enacted in the early days of industrialisation in India, protects the basic rights of workers, mainly in industries, and also provides the legal framework in which collective organisation of workers can form and operate. Enacted from the late 1920s till the 1960s, these laws include, among others, the Factories Act, Mines Act, Workmen's Compensation Act of 1923, The Minimum Wages Act of 1948, The Trade Union Act of 1946 (See Table 4.1 for an overview of these laws), and such others.

Legislative attempts in the 1960s and the 1970s sought to expand such protection to workers in non-industrial sectors, and expand the definition of *workplace* to include work done at locations beyond the immediate supervision of the employer such as home-based work. This implied recognition of the need for protection to workers in activities or locations where clear-cut employer–employee relationships did not exist. Further, the ambit of protection was extended to workers employed through contractors, and not directly in the production chain. Examples are the *Interstate Migrant Act of 1979*, *The Contract Labour (Regulation and Abolition) Act of 1970*, and the *Bonded Labour System (Abolition) Act of 1976*, and such others. (See Table 4.1 for an overview of these laws.) Some legislation also refer to workers in specific work areas, such as the *Building and Construction Workers Act*, *Beedi and Cigar Workers Act*, and so on.

Till almost the 1970s, the main concern of such legislation was to expand the sphere of security for labour. From the perspective of the

TABLE 4.1 Overview of select labour laws in India

	Name	*Objective*	*Implementation Issues*
Phase I: 1920–60	Factories Act		
	Mines Act		
	Workmen's Compensation Act, 1923	Compensation of injury by accident to workmen by employers	• To claim compensation, existence of employer–employee relationship is a must • Amendment in 2000 enables casual workers to claim compensation as well
	Trade Union Act, 1926	• Provides for registration of trade unions (TU) • Confers immunity to leaders of registered TUs from punishment for actions done by them with respect to trade disputes	• Amended in 2001. Leaders of TUs cannot be 'external'; must be employed in trade for which the TU is registered
	Minimum Wages Aims Act, 1948	Aims to fix and review the minimum rates of wage for scheduled employment. These may be time rate/piece rate	• Key legislation for securing the rights of the unorganised labour • Complaints for non-payment of minimum wage made to labour commissioner • Proved difficult to enforce, specially in the agricultural sector
Phase II: 1960–70	Contract Labour (Regulation and Abolition) Act, 1970	Regulates the employment of contract labour and specifies obligations of the principal employer and contractor towards workers	• Contract labour covered under the law for the first time • The aim was to finally abolish contract labour • But employers now find ways to obviate the law by sub-contracting
	Bonded Labour System (Abolition) Act, 1976		The authority for enforcement lies with the District Magistrate. Struggles by activist groups have led to strong attacks on the system; for turning a blind eye to the

Contd.

Contd.

		problem and for the NHRC report having taken action on a number of cases of bonded labour
Interstate Migrant Workmen Act, 1979	• Regulates the employment of workers from any particular state, being taken to another for employment by a contractor • Contractor must take a licence before doing so and must fulfil his obligations towards wage and welfare of workers	• Covers vulnerable labourers, generally under the employment of contractors, and bestows specific obligations on the contractors • But Migrant workers without a contractor not protected • Collision with the police and rail authorities makes it difficult to detect movement of migrant workers.

unorganised workforce, the main problems that arose were with respect to its inclusion within the ambit of protection provided by such legislation. The main thrust of security provided by such laws was towards workers in the organised sector, wherein a clear-cut employer–employee relationship did exist; for workers in the unorganised sector, it was difficult to identify such a clear-cut relationship; also, problems of enforcement of these laws were rampant.

Globally, a shift in economic ideologies in the 1980s, more so in the 1990s, led to an emphasis on growth-oriented rather than security-oriented policies for labour. . In terms of thinking on labour, these translated into:

- Evolving policies that facilitated easy hire and fire of labour,
- Allowing firms to operate in flexible ways, and
- Competing internationally.

Discussions on *exit policy* are part of such a thinking. The changes in this period were more in terms of facilitating easy closure of non-profitable firms, redefining of SSIs and reservations for them. No new laws have been enacted, nor have the existing laws been amended. The new perspective on labour was, thus, fraught with the intention of adopting labour firing policies. The general climate has been such that strikes have been more difficult, and executive orders and policy changes have only contributed in easy closure of industries. Since globalisation-related changes have increased the amount of activity through casual contractual activities, the need for social security for such workers becomes important. Accordingly, the Second National Commission on Labour was asked to prepare the blueprint of an 'umbrella legislation' in this regard.

An Umbrella Legislation for Protecting Unorganised Workers

Issues related to social security of unorganised workers acquired centrestage with the setting up of the Second National Commission on Labour. The two key tasks that the commission was entrusted with were:

1. Rationalisation of laws for workers in the organised sector, and
2. To develop an *umbrella* legislation for ensuring minimum protection to workers in the unorganised sector.

Its report, submitted in 2002, included the prototype of a draft bill in this regard. The objective of this act was defined as the 'recognition, promotion and protection of the livelihood of the unorganised sector workers'. This bill noted its difference from the earlier legislation that defined workers narrowly, that is, in terms of industries alone. The new emphasis was on recognition of all types of workers regardless of industry, occupation or work status. The essence was the 'removal of poverty of the working population'. The government's obligations were to be in the area of minimum wages, social security, health, old age and welfare. Reciprocal obligations such as minimum age limit for workers were also envisaged on the workers. While it has been through many consultative procedures, it is still a bill and not an act. Meanwhile, the new Congress government (that come to power in 2004) has also set up a new National Commission for Unorganised Labour which is looking into a wide range of issues related to such workers.

ORGANISATION AND THE STRUGGLE OF UNORGANISED WORKERS

Looking at the nature of work that unorganised workers are engaged in, their spatial spread in isolated work locations, rather than in an identified production unit and their sheer powerlessness in negotiating for themselves, poses challenges to their organisation. Clearly, the trade union model of collective bargaining is inadequate to either mobilise all such workers, or even articulate the range of issues that unorganised workers face. In fact, the trade unions have often been charged with ignoring the unorganised workers. The national federations of labour trade unions do not show much interest in workers belonging to the unorganised sector.

The latter constitute less than 10 per cent of the total membership of national federations. So it can be said that conventional labour trade unions have ignored unorganised labour.

New organisational forms, viz., membership-based organisations, like Self Employed Women's Association (SEWA) (See Box 4.2) or tripartite boards such as those for the headload or *mathadi* workers in Maharashtra have appeared as collectives of unorganised workers. The tripartite bodies representing workers, government and the union have been able to get workers their rights (such as minimum guarantee of 12 days work, weekly off, one-day holiday wage) The *mathadi* workers pick up headloads on Mumbai docks, work in a *toli* or group, often belonging to the same village. Since the hours of arrival of ships are unknown, it is difficult to predict the volume or time of work.

CONCLUSION

It is clear that unorganised workers are the most valueable group, require greater protection, but also face immense challenges in organising for

BOX 4.2

Self Employed Women's Association (SEWA) as an Organisational Model

SEWA was founded in 1972 as a trade union of self-employed women. Its predecessor organisation was the Textile Labour Association that carried forward Gandhi's ideals. The main objective of SEWA is to ensure full employment to self-employed women workers and to make them self-reliant. Full employment means work security, income security, food security, and social security such as childcare, healthcare, and shelter. Self-reliance refers to the autonomy of decision making for women.

The union is open for membership to self-employed women all over India at a membership fee of Rs. 5. Members from each trade elect a trade council. Parallel to this are the 'trade committees' that discuss problems related to their area, at their monthly meetings. This committee elects the Executive Committee of SEWA.

SEWA encourages women workers to form their own organisations, through which they can access resources as well. These groups are registered as DWACRA groups or co-operatives. Many traditional economic activities such as embroidery, weaving, and so on, have been done by these groups. SEWA has done pioneering work in the area of credit access and mobilisation.

While SEWA is a trade union, it is essentially a movement. In this latter role, it has mobilised women workers on the issue of minimum wages, food security campaign and water campaign amongst many others.

collective action. Apart from the support of laws, anti-poverty programmes are also meant to help them. But many groups of workers still do not benefit.

II

HUMAN RIGHTS OF MARGINALISED GROUPS: MINORITIES

The term *minority* is conceptualised in contrast to the notion of a majority. The *majority* can be construed on the basis of numerical strength; a political majority, for instance, may be achieved on the basis of numbers. More than such neutral determinants of a majority or minority are ascriptive identities such as membership of a religious or ethnic group, or linguistic differences. So apart from the notion of smaller numbers, the term minority also implies association with an identity. Liberal political philosophy was built on the assumption of dissolution of traditional communities, that is, members as citizens would leave behind them the identities based on principles of community, and the only valid decisions that would hold would be those of a political majority. As seen in the philosophy of Locke, the minorities were simply citizens who had been outnumbered by a majority. There were no specific interests that they had, and the only guarantee of rights was the protection of natural rights to citizens. In other words, minorities did not exist.

In actual practice, however, the working of liberal democracies, as also other political forms in modern times, witnessed the claims of rights from groups based on nationality, religion, ethnicity, language, and so on. Apart from the claims of a majoritarian bias in the constitutions of many nation-states, there was also the more serious issue of violent persecution of minorities by the majority. The need for specific guarantees for minority rights in liberal democracies was evident. However, the issue that still remains unresolved is the principle on which such rights are to be granted—are these to be construed as individual or as group rights? What is the appropriate sphere of rights of the individual and the group? Further, how are these to be related to human rights principles? Some answers are to be found in the debates between liberal democratic principles and multiculturalism. The issues, however, remain far from being adequately resolved.

Freeman (2002: 116–21) reviews some of the main arguments of this debate, and highlights as to how these accommodate with human rights principles. These arguments help us to understand how operational principles of ensuring inclusive human rights evolve. Kymlicka (1995) suggests that the working of multicultural societies is such that the state necessarily favours certain cultures over others. One language for instance may be an official language, leaving the claims of other languages behind. Such injustices raise the issue of minority rights. Some protection of minority cultures does come from the extension of group rights to communities. But, quite often, the groups themselves are oppressive on their members and deny them their basic rights. On the other hand, Kymlicka supports minority rights only for minorities that are liberal. In such a minority, individuals are free to question the power of the groups, their cultural practices and make individual choices. Human rights principles, however, are considered inadequate by him to resolve the issue of minority rights. For instance, such principles can give no answer to the question of what the official language of a state should be. Minority rights may be violated without a specific violation of human rights. Freeman notes that a different position is that of liberal political philosopher, Brian Barry, who defends liberal democracy and its treatment of all citizens as equals. Institutionalisation of cultural differences makes the minorities more vulnerable, whereas participation in common institutions creates solidarity. In this view, minority rights undermine both individual rights and citizen's rights. Some other arguments emphasise the need for cultural recognition as a basic human need, and also the need for intercultural dialogue. It is unclear, however, how this translates into operational principles of cultural recognition.

Even if minority rights are granted, the question that further arises is as to whether the group or the individual is the bearer of these rights. The individual rights of minority group members may be compatible to human rights, but collective rights may not be compatible to human rights. On this issue, Donnelly argues that while collective human rights are necessary for human dignity and, therefore, compatible with human rights, there are, in fact, no collective human rights. The preservation of cultural rights of a group is valuable, but if the group is violating human rights (such as honour killings of women), it is the individual human rights that take precedence.

The issues find further illustration when it is seen how minority rights are defined in the Indian context. The main criteria on which minorities have been identified in India are on the lines of religion. The Constituent Assembly identified minorities, particularly religious minorities on a national scale. Only those communities that were minorities at the national level were considered for safeguards. Thus, Sikhs, Muslims or Christians were a minority wherever they lived. This view of the Constituent Assembly (incorporated in the Indian Constitution) was overturned by an eleven-judge bench of the Supreme court in the minorities case in

2002. It upheld the view that minorities are to be determined on a statewise basis. Now, Sikhs in Punjab, Christians in the Northeast are not a minority any more. The arguments in the two sections that follow talk about the complex nature of relationship between human rights and minority rights in the international context and in the Indian context.

HUMAN RIGHTS AND MINORITY RIGHTS IN THE UN

The relationship between the two types of rights, that is, human rights and minority right, is described by Freeman as 'complex and problematic', even though it is assumed that minority rights belong to the field of human rights (Freeman 2002: 114) UDHR did not mention minority rights. The prior experience of the League of Nations protection provided an element of caution. Not only was the effort considered a failure, it was also seen as providing a justification to the Nazi aggression. UDHR was drafted on a firm assumption of individual rights. Its specific clauses on the prohibition of discrimination and the freedom to practice one's own religion were considered an adequate protection of minority rights.

The first explicit reference to minority rights was made in the International Covenant on Civil and Political Rights (ICCPR) Minorities were defined on ethnic, religious and linguistic grounds. A statement was made wherein states where such minorities existed, 'persons', that is, individuals belonging to such groups were to be given the right to enjoy their own culture, to profess and practice their own religion, or to use their own language. While this was a step forward, two key sets of problems remained with minority rights so defined, and the obligation on the states. The rights were those of *persons* and not of groups, so the existence of collective rights were not even recognised at this stage. More important, the existence of these rights was dependent on states recognising that such minorities did exist within their boundaries. If they refused to acknowledge their existence, obligations on the states ceased to exist. This was, therefore, an inadequate basis for ensuring the protection of minorities from persecution within nation-states.

It was only in December 1992 that the UN adopted a Declaration on the Rights of Persons belonging to national, ethnic, religious and linguistic minorities. This went a step further than the earlier statement in the ICCPR. It imposed an obligation on the state to encourage conditions for the promotion of minority identities based on 'national or ethnic, cultural, religious or linguistic basis. This brings minority rights firmly on the agenda of the international human rights regime. These rights are still considered rights of the individual than of the group, and it is unclear how the issue of transgression/violation of rights of the individual by the group is to be resolved.

MINORITY RIGHTS IN INDIA

Minority Rights in the Indian Constitution

As mentioned earlier, minorities in India are generally defined in terms of religion at the national level. Rights extended to minorities are of two kinds. The first set comprises the general guarantees to all citizens in the fundamental rights contained in the Articles 25–26. These allow citizens the freedom to practise and propagate their own religion.[5] Besides, there is also a bar on discrimination on the grounds of race, religion, caste or sex. These rights, however, are not specifically minority rights, but those guaranteed to all citizens. The second set of rights is specific to the minorities. The Indian Constitution also guarantees cultural and educational rights of minorities as a fundamental right; in fact, the first in the world to do so. In the Constituent Assembly, the sub-committee on fundamental rights of citizens and minorities also discussed political rights of representation for minorities. These were eventually not taken up.[6] The discussions in the Constituent Assembly saw two contrasting arguments being articulated:

1. A firm need for minority rights as a guarantee against minority fears, in contrast to the arguments in favour of citizen's rights, and
2. Right to non-discrimination.

The latter arguments were put forward by Rajkumari Amrit Kaur, G. B. Pant, A. K. Aiyyar and V. B. Patel. Pant's arguments in favour of citizen's rights are often cited in this regard:

> . . . the individual citizen who is really the backbone of the state should not be lost in that indiscriminate body known as the community. In a new nation-state, the citizen should not be identified on the basis of extrapolitical identities such as religion or caste.

The situation of tense communal animosities in which the Constituent Assembly worked, and also the representation of interests in this body on the basis of religion, meant that the arguments in favour of minority rights were strong. In addition, there was also the principled belief that minority rights would help preserve the cultural diversity in India. Group rights were, thus, accorded to protect the culture of minorities. Besides, personal laws of all communities were retained and these were understood to be outside the purview of fundamental rights.

Minority Rights in the Working of Indian Democracy

Prior to discussing the issue of minority rights and human rights in actual working of Indian democracy, it might be useful to refer to some of the tensions that have arisen in the interpretation of minority rights as group rights, and human rights as individual citizen's right such as equality. We made a mention of this uneasy and unsettled relationship in our discussions on defining minorities, and minority rights in the framework of liberal democracy in Section I. Box 4.3 makes a mention of the contradictions that have emerged in the enactment of a Uniform Civil Code for all citizens and the retention of personal laws based on religion specific to each community. After the Shah Bano judgement in 1985 (See Box 4.3), the Supreme Court on many occasions expressed distress over the government's inability to enact a common civil code to end discrimination between communities, especially gender discrimination in the name of according religious freedom.

BOX 4.3

The Issue of the Uniform Civil Code: Personal Laws and the Judiciary

The Indian Constitution is ambiguous on the issue of personal laws. Constituent Assembly debates have arguments both in favour of community- based personal laws, as also for uniform civil laws for all citizens. The emphasis on protection of minority interests led to personal laws being retained, and the future goal of having a Uniform Civil Code was included as a Directive Principle. Judicial pronouncements have been important in determining the future direction of this debate.

In 1954, in the State of Bombay vs Appa Mali case, it was decided that personal laws were not void even if they conflicted with the fundamental rights of citizens. Religious denominations had autonomy and personal laws were, in a sense, recognised as extraconstitutional, but valid, laws. This position was overturned in the Shah Bano case judgement of 1985. In 1978, a 65-year-old Shah Bano demanded alimony from her husband who had abandoned her after over 40 years of marriage. The Supreme Court, years later, upheld her claim to maintenance. It also ruled that Section 125 of the Criminal Procedure Code overrides the Muslim Personal Law in matters of divorce. The court also emphasised the duty of the State to enact a Uniform Civil Code for all citizens.

There were protests against this judgement by the Muslim community, and the then Congress government inverted the court directive by enacting the Muslim Women's Protection Bill. The right of a Muslim woman divorcee to maintenance was denied by the bill. The bill was opposed by women's groups demanding equal rights and state protection against discrimination based on gender.

(*Source:* Sanghamitra, 2004)

Laws and Institutions in the Protection of Minority Rights

Some of the key threats to minority rights, or even the survival of minorities witnessed in recent times, have been violent attacks on minorities; the most shameful example of which is the murder of the Christian missionary Graham Staines and his two minor sons in an Orissa village in 1999. Massey lists several cases of violation of the religious rights of minorities that range from humiliation of Christian priests to violent attacks, such as that on Staines. NHRC took note of the Staines episode in its Annual Report for 1998–99, and it also reviewed the nature of complaints it had received in this regard. It observed that these were not isolated incidents. Across the states of Orissa, Gujarat, Madhya Pradesh and Bihar, there had been violent attacks on Christians, recurrent in nature and threatening the plural nature of our society. The commission was also in frequent touch with the chief secretaries and director generals of police of the respective states. It also initiated a comprehensive process of review of arrangements for protection of minorities in all countries (NHRC Annual Report 1999–2000: 134–35)

The other major area of human rights of minorities has come from the violent attacks on the minority community through communal rioting, such as that in Gujarat in the aftermath of the Godhra incident. As discussed in Chapter 3, NHRC took suo moto cognizance and visited Gujarat. Its detailed observations made a serious note of the inaction of the state government in protecting minority rights.

The National Commission for Minorities (NCM) set up as a statutory body in 1993, under the National Commission for Minorities Act, is intended to safeguard and ensure implementation of the Constitutional provisions, various state and central government laws, administrative policies and schemes with respect to minorities. Among the issues and complaints that the commission has considered in recent years are those of violent attacks on members of the minority community, protection of *waqf* property from encroachment, grant of minority status to Kashmiri pandits and extension of welfare benefits to minorities.

The key institutional linkage between minority rights and human rights implementation comes from the relationship between NCM and NHRC. The chairperson of NCM is a member of NHRC. It is to ensure that minority rights representation is ensured in the very composition of the apex human rights protection body of India. In a reciprocal arrangement, on many occasions, NHRC has also added the weight of its own opinion to issues that are brought up before it by the Minority Rights Commission. In its working, NHRC takes the challenge of protection of minority rights as a supreme test of its inclusive interpretation of human rights. What remains unresolved is whether the rights that it protects are individual rights of members of the minority community or group rights. It seems to be that while NHRC recognises and protects group rights, the focus is essentially on the individual human rights of the minorities.

The more recent challenges to minority rights, which have emphasised a clear link between these and human rights, have come in the wake of targetting of minorities for electoral gains, and targetting communities in the wake of terrorist violence.

III

HUMAN RIGHTS OF MARGINALISED GROUPS: DALITS

Dalit Identity and the Struggle for Rights

Amongst the most important political developments in India in recent times is the coming to the forefront of a mature and challenging struggle for Dalit identity and rights.

Who is a *Dalit*? The word, in use since the 1960s, especially amongst Marathi-speaking literary writers, neo-Buddhists by persuasion, is of a relatively recent vintage. Simply put, it refers to the poor, and as Shah (2001) claims, to oppressed. In a narrow sense, the term finds meaning with reference to the caste-based Hindu society. Those at the bottom of the caste hierarchy, almost outside its pale and treated as 'untouchables', are referred to by this term. However, if the principle of exploitation is applied, all the socially, politically and economically oppressed sections of the Indian society are Dalits. This latter formulation makes it akin to a *class* -like formulation, though the existence of social practice of discrimination makes Dalit exploitation more thorough. Historically, many terms have been used to describe this social class—*mlecchas*, *candala*, *antyaja*, *achuta*, *harijan*, and depressed classes are some such terms. Though there is no firm historical evidence on the origins of this system, by the time the classic texts of Hindus—the *Manusmriti* and the *Arthasastra*—were written, the caste system seems to have taken its rigid form. The principle of purity and pollution has been crucial in governing the relations between the higher and the lower castes.

In actual practice, a wide variety of regional groups are included as Dalits, and not all of them discriminated as untouchables. The administrative term used almost interchangeably is that of the Scheduled Castes, and in our discussion on laws and institutions for the protection of Dalit rights we will in fact refer to scheduled castes as Dalits.

Dr Bhimrao Ambedkar, whose philosophy is crucial to the Dalit struggles and conceptual categories, did not himself use the term. His main criticism was that of the caste system, a system of *graded inequality*, regulating all spheres of life—spiritual, moral and legal. Brahminism and capitalism were identified as the two sources of inequality in our society. A change of social order was not possible within Hinduism. It required a rejection of caste and Hinduism. In this, his stand differed from that of Gandhi. For the latter, the abolition of untouchability was an important part of the agenda of social change. The primary instrument of such change for Gandhi was the method of persuasion of the upper castes for a change of heart.

Two issues central to the issue of Dalits moving centrestage are that of:

1. Reservations in public sector employment, and
2. The politics of vote banks.

While the two issues are significant in terms of increased political visibility and participation in modern employment, the current emphasis on *Dalit identity* goes beyond just these issues. It also moves beyond the framework of caste, that is, the Dalit is not a caste, even though it builds up on the anti-caste ideology. It is a positive identity of the oppressed people. It rests on firm analyses about the nature of the Indian state, civil society and democracy. Further, it seeks to draw alliances with other exploited people and draw analogies with other forms of social exploitation. Notable in this respect are the conceptual attempts at a definition in the background of the World Conference Against Racism (WCAR) at Durban and the Bhopal conference.[7] At Durban, the attempt was to explain caste discriminations as akin to racial disparities. It was criticised for theoretically confusing caste with race, and politically attempting to internationalise the issue. The Bhopal document attempts to project an *inclusive* identity for Dalits, which includes adivasis among the category of Dalits.

As Gopal Guru (1997) aptly puts it, 'Dalit identity not merely expresses who dalits are, but also conveys their aspirations, struggle for change and revolution. ' It relates to the suppression of culture, way of life, value system, and more importantly, the denial of dignity. So, the category is not merely an expression of caste, but a symbol of change.

LAWS AND INSTITUTIONS PROTECTING THE DALIT RIGHTS

Constitutional provisions envisage an active intervention by the state in protecting Dalit rights and transforming an inequitable social order. The

Preamble affirms that the notion of social justice is to be a cornerstone of the Indian nation. Citizen's rights elaborated in Part III, Articles 14–16 assure the right to equality and absence of discrimination. Article 17 specifically prescribes the abolition of untouchability as a fundamental freedom of the Indian citizen. Besides, protective discrimination for scheduled castes and scheduled tribes is not considered a violation of either the principles of equality or the rights against discrimination. The law provides for such affirmative action as reservations in political representation, and also in jobs for those listed as scheduled castes in Article 341 of the Constitution.

Since the Constitution does not define untouchability, laws to this effect were put in place in the early days of the Republic, viz., The Untouchability Offences Act, 1955. This was later renamed as the Protection of Civil Rights Act in 1976. The Act enumerates the places where untouchability is practised and the specific practices that constitute this discriminatory act. The list is a reminder of the pervasive nature of this practice. Restaurants, temples, bathing *ghats*, *musafirkhana*, burial grounds and places of public entertainment are among the many places listed where access cannot be denied on the basis of caste. Unlawful compulsory labour is also a part of untouchability. Punishment for committing the offence, as also the provision of special courts for trial, is provided for in the Act.

The Scheduled Castes and Scheduled Tribe (Prevention of Atrocities Act), enacted in 1989, is perhaps a sad reflection of the state of discriminatory practices with respect to these groups, and the need for stronger legal measures. Scholars note the changed (heightened) nature of atrocities against Dalits, in the face of increased consciousness amongst them and stronger movements for their rights. The Act lists out the punishable atrocities and raises the severity of punishment. Some of the atrocities listed are reflective of the heinous ways in which the Dalit dignity is violated:

- Forcing a member of the SC/ST to drink or eat any non-edible or obnoxious substance.
- Dumping excretion, waste matter, carcass in his premises or neighbourhood.
- Forcible removal of clothes from the person or parading him naked with a painted face violative of the dignity of the individual.
- Wrongful dispossession of land/premises.
- Forcing/intimidating a member not to vote/vote for a particular candidate alone

Apart from enhancing the severity of punishment, special courts are provided for speedy trials. The rules accompanying the Act provide for a range of preventive and protection oriented measures like provision for legal aid from a panel of competent lawyers, rules directing officers-in-charge of police stations to help file FIRs, SC/ST protection cells at police headquarters under the charge of an IG. The state governments have been entrusted with the task of providing provisions in their budget for relief and rehabilitation facilities to the victims.

DALIT RIGHTS AS HUMAN RIGHTS

The Nature of Dalit Oppression: Human Rights as Individual or Group Rights

It is proper to look at the nature of Dalit oppression before we look at the issue of Dalit rights and human rights. The nature of this oppression, in essence, is one of the worst forms of violation of human dignity. It foregrounds caste as a system of oppression. An excerpt from Prakash Louis' *Dalits and Durban Discourse*, citing examples of violence on dalits, is indeed shocking.[8]

While Box 4.4 includes examples of attacks on Dalit individuals as well as groups, consider these examples (reproduced from Hargopal 2002: 155) where Dalits are attacked as a group:

- 1977: Belchi (Bihar), 11 Dalits were killed
- 1978: Chainpur (Gaya), 2 Dalits were killed

BOX 4.4

Atrocities on Dalits: A Violation of Human Dignity

A dalit woman was stripped naked and beaten to death by two upper backward caste men in Negla village in Agra district. This woman made the mistake of crossing the path of Virendra Pal and Vijay Pal, carrying an empty pot. Six persons belonging to the Dalit community in Barabanki district, barely 22 kms from Lucknow- the capital of Uttar Pradesh- were subjected to a brutal acid attack on 24 October 2000. The dominant caste *thakurs*, who are also the landed gentry of this area, carried out this barbarous assault because they were infuriated by the failure to procure a tender for fishing rights in a nearby pond. The Dalits who dared to challenge the hegemony and monopoly of the thakurs were 'taught the historical lesson'. Similarly, in Hasanpur of Varanasi district, five Dalits were beaten to death by thakurs because one of them defied the dictates of Rajputs and filed an FIR against the criminal assault by a Rajput of the village. This enraged the dominant caste Rajputs and they took law into their own hands against the erring untouchables of the village.

(*Source:* Louis 2001)

- 1980: Pipra (Bihar), 14 Dalits were killed
- 1983: Vijaynagar (Rajasthan), 3 Dalit families were attacked, and 2 Dalit women were gangraped
- 1984: Bichgaon (Rajasthan), 7 Dalits, including 2 women were massacred
- 1986: Golana (Gujarat), 4 Dalits were killed, and 20 injured
- 1988: Nonki-Nagwa (Bihar), 19 Dalits were killed

Clearly, the issue is more than an individualised attacks, or isolated incidents of mass violence. The discussion foregrounds caste and confirms systemic oppression. Scholars and activists consider such violence, emanating from an imagined threat to the perpetrators of violence as central to the Dalit discourse. Humiliation and anger, caused by such atrocities are, therefore, central to articulating the identity of the oppressed.

Further, such atrocities are characterised as lying somewhere between individual torture and genocide, the latter seen as an act of erasing a collective identity. The issue of human rights for Dalits, therefore, is more than a violation of individual civil liberties; it does involve the notion of a collective. Dalit intellectuals and activists now emphasise on the group nature of such rights. Gopal Guru (1997) attempts to conceptualise these experiences and relate the Dalit discourse to that of human rights. He lays emphasis on the need to 'broaden the definition of human rights through the inclusion of Dalit rights', and for the latter to 'acquire space in public discourse'. Human rights are denied to Dalits because of their group character. What starts off as an individual attack on a Dalit, is merely a spark. It finds its logical end in a 'package deal violence', that is, mass violence against Dalits. Hargopal (2002 :158) carries the argument further and concludes that 'the Dalit perspective on human rights of Dalits is different because of its group character, as against the legalistic, individualistic approach taken by the Indian state towards human rights of Dalits'.

A firm critique of the operation of civil society and public institutions is put forward by Dalits, the complaint being that of a structured bias in favour of the twice born. Institutions such as universities, research organisations and media are seen as preserves of the upper caste, and another mode of existence of caste society. Chapter 2 of the Bhopal declaration contains a long discussion of how the reformist agenda of the state with respect to achieving social equality has constantly been thwarted by this civil society and these public institutions. The state is looked upon as an agency of transformation and a guarantor against caste discrimination. The challenge to such a strategy of reliance on the state comes from the context of global economic developments, where the state is in fact fast withdrawing from many sectors of activity.

State guarantees of Dalit human rights reflect a certain evolutionary perspective of thinking on this issue—from the Untouchability Offences Act in 1955 to its amendment in 1976 as the Civil Rights Protection Act, and in 1989 as the Prevention of Atrocities Act. This evolution points towards understanding atrocities as central to the issue.

NHRC interventions have included looking into individual complaints of atrocities. There is a conceptual recognition of the group dimension of the inequality as well. Most notable has been the proactive stand of the commission in taking the issue to Durban. NHRC noted in its Annual Report (2001–2002) that 'the debate whether race and caste are coterminus, or similar forms of discrimination is not the essence of the matter', 'it is not so much the nomenclature that is the cause of concern, but the fact of its *(caste discrimination)* persistence is' (p. 103; emphasis mine). Contrary to the opposition to taking the issue to Durban from many quarters, which included academics as well as government departments, NHRC concluded that the conference provided a singular opportunity to 'deal openly and courageously with all issues of discrimination and inequality, as they exist all over the world, in all their variety ...' (p. 103). Such recognition is, perhaps, only the first step. There is still a long process of engagement and struggle before the guarantee of human rights for Dalits prevents atrocities and translates into a pursuit for dignity itself.

IV

HUMAN RIGHTS OF MARGINALISED GROUPS: ADIVASIS

The Problem of Defining Adivasis

The term *adivasi* is used for a certain category of people, in contrast to a dominant majority, and is distinct from the term *minority* that we have discussed in Section II. In meaning, it may be taken as the Hindi term for indigenous people, now widely used in the international arena to describe original inhabitants, who claim to have been colonised. In the context of America, it refers to those who were the original inhabitants prior to their colonisation by Europeans. Taken out of the European context, the term *indigenous* ceases to have this specific meaning. So, an important starting point in understanding the concept is the absence of a specific, commonly agreed-upon meaning.

In India, the term adivasis has been widely used by social workers, missionaries and academics, almost interchangeably with the term tribe. The use of the term was initiated by the British in India. Its attempt to understand Indian people in terms of the dominant race–religion framework of the West meant that groups that could not fit in the caste–religion framework of Hinduism were described as *tribes*. The 1901 census described tribes as practising Animism as a form of worship. However, this was not the distinguishing mark by which tribes were to be identified. One of the key arguments put forward was that they were outside the pale of Hindu caste society. Sociological research, especially by N. K. Bose and G. S. Ghurye, illustrated the continuum between tribes and caste, rather than a dichotomy. The other criteria put forward to identify tribes include their location in remote hilly regions and forests, close relationship with nature, rudimentary use of technology, and so on.

In fact, adivasis may exist in various of stages of development. From the Sentinelis of Andaman and Nicobar islands who have no contact with the outside world, the Jenu Kurubas of Karnataka who are still honey-collectors, to shifting cultivators in the Northeast, and settled agricultural people in many parts of India, the variety is evident. Sharma states that each of these stages from hunting to settled cultivation represents a life complete in itself, in complete harmony with nature. The command over the habitat by a community is a natural right respected by all within the community and acknowledged by those outside as well.

A key aspect of their identity in the Indian context has been the administrative act of their inclusion in the list of Scheduled Tribes (ST) listed in Schedules V and VI of the Indian Constitution. The extension of special administrative protection and reservation in jobs on the basis of such listing imply that the demands for inclusion in this list have gone up. Simultaneously, there are also complaints about improper exclusion due to inadequacies in the listing procedure. Some of the most commonly cited examples are those of *gonds* and *kols* in Sonebhadra and Mirzapur.[9]

In addition, there are the denotified tribes (DNTs), classified as criminal tribes during British rule, and thought to engage in criminal professions such as loot, dacoity, and so on, for a living. These groups were denotified from this list in 1952, and unlike the STs they are not categorised as a class under the Constitution. Some are included in the state lists, but there is no uniformity in this regard. For example, the *Phanse Pardhis* are included as STs in Maharashtra, but similar groups such as the *Gaon Pardhis*, *Haran Shikaris* are listed as *Vimukta Jati* and Nomadic Tribes in the same state.

HUMAN RIGHTS AND RIGHTS OF INDIGENOUS COMMUNITIES IN THE UN

The rights envisaged in UDHR were seen to be largely individualistic. The special reference to rights of indigenous people was included in the

International Labour Organisation (ILO) convention no. 107, in 1954, about indigenous tribal, and semi-tribal people in independent countries. The primary emphasis was on the assimilation of these people into the mainstream. Some of the important features of the convention are acceptance of community as basic unit, and the command of the community over its habitat. The convention takes exception to involuntary displacement of indigenous people from their habitat. India is a signatory to the convention, even though the official policies of the country do not encourage assimilation of such population into the mainstream. A later convention of the ILO, no. 169, adopted in 1989, asserts the issue of identity of tribal communities and their right to self-determination, in stark contrast to the earlier emphasis on assimilation. This latter position, accepted by the UN, emphasises on the 'need right' and 'power right' for this category of people, that is, marginalised and dispossessed from their livelihood, and now increasingly vulnerable to the loss of their identity.

India is not a signatory to this convention because of the contested issue of determining who an original resident of a place is, and also the political implications of accepting self-determination as a principle.

ADIVASI RIGHTS IN INDIA

While fundamental rights in India provide general guarantees of equality, non-discrimination and freedom of faith/belief, the specific protection to STs, and the guarantee of a special form of administration comes from Schedule V and VI of the Constitution. The roots of these special provisions are traced back to the colonial rule, when many of the tribal areas were declared as non-regulation areas. The Government of India Act of 1935 designated tribal dominated areas as 'excluded' and 'partially excluded', and ordinary laws of the centre or provinces did not automatically extend to these areas. The special provisions so enshrined in the Indian Constitution acknowledged the socio-economic complexities of administering tribal groups and the regional diversity that their spread entailed. Article 342 provides for statewise schedules for groups or tribal areas. [10] These are notified by the President, and at present, almost 350 tribal communities and sub-groups have been listed as STs. The 'tribal areas' in the states of Assam, Meghalaya, Tripura and Mizoram, and 'scheduled areas' for other states are governed by the special provisions in the VIth and the Vth Schedule, respectively.

Rights extended to such groups are in three key areas:

1. Special administrative provisions of which we have made a note above,

2. Reservations in political representation, and
3. Reservations in educational institutions and public professions.

In addition, a number of welfare schemes have been put in place, especially the development policies initiated in the 1970s. Of these, we first discuss the special administrative provisions and the welfare policies.

Among the key features of these special provisions are the establishment of an autonomous district council (VIth Schedule) with wide ranging powers. The area of jurisdiction of such councils extends to management of land, water resources, forests (except reserve forests), *jhum* cultivation and social customs. No state legislature laws are applicable to the councils, unless the councils direct so. In the case of scheduled areas, the Governor has special responsibilities of administration. In consultation with the 'Tribes Advisory Council', he can make special regulations prohibiting the transfer and sale of land and moneylending. The financial requirements for bringing the level of development in these areas at par with the rest of the state are not voted upon by the state legislature, but 'charged' upon the Consolidated Fund of India. The working of these constitutional safeguards and other legal provisions are to be monitored by the National Commission for Scheduled Castes and Scheduled Tribes.[11] The Commission also investigates individual complaints.

Development Policies

A special strategy for the development of these demarcated areas and groups emerged in the 1970s; this was the Tribal Sub-plan (TSP) strategy of assistance. The Centre extended its assistance to this by way of Special Central Assistance (SCA), and centrally sponsored schemes (CSS)

Political reservations in seats in state legislature and the Parliament, and now also the Panchayats, is also a Constitutional mandate. Initially provided for 10 years, the reservation of seats in state and central legislature has been extended every 10 years. Similarly, reservation of seats in educational institutions and for jobs under the state and central government has also been provided for. Whether such reservations have resulted in meaningful political participation and empowerment, as also in the modern professions, is a question we will subsequently take up in the discussion on human rights issues for the adivasis.

THE STATUS OF HUMAN RIGHTS FOR ADIVASIS

One area where community-based rights have been crucial to the conception of human rights is with respect to the rights of adivasis. The core interventions of the judiciary, NHRC and the activists have focussed on the guarantee of collective identity and rights. In fact, one of the key challenges in ensuring adivasi rights is striking a balance between the individualistic frame within which all modern legal systems are structured, and the completely different rationale of community based ownership and resource use in the adivasi system.

Some of the key areas of intervention by the judiciary and NHRC are on the issues of land, forced labour and displacement by mega projects. A few examples are listed hereunder:

- The most important issue is that of land. In the Samatha case (1997), the Supreme Court made an emphatic statement about the significance of land as 'their most important natural and valuable asset, and imperishable endowment from which the tribals derive their sustenance, social status, economic and social equality, permanent place of abode, work and living'.[12] The two ILO conventions mentioned above (nos. 107 and 169) also instruct the state to recognise both individual and community ownership. The practical problem that comes up is the inadequacy of the legal system /lack of clarity about community ownership. Such rights are recognised only in some small pockets, for instance, the Munda areas in Khunti, Jharkhand. In most places, it is the individual rights through *pattas* that are accepted. Even more challenging is to accommodate the rights over land of shifting cultivators. In actual practice, the adivasis face the challenge of large scale alienation of land, either through making use of loopholes in existing laws, or by way of displacement through mega development projects.
- Forced or bonded labour is another issue where comprehensive and stringent laws have been enacted for its abolition. Bondage is still rampant in many parts, especially in kilns and quarries, and adivasi human rights are violated on account of forced labour extracted by powerful musclemen, or in the name of fulfilling debt obligations. NHRC has focussed on the release and rehabilitation of those freed.
- One persistent issue is that of vital omissions in listing groups in the Schedules, despite the Parliament's resolve in 1976 to do so at the earliest. Problems of listing are rampant in areas that were erstwhile princely states, in large parts of central India where, according to Sharma, extensive tribal tracts have been excluded. In Kerala and Karnataka, no areas have been listed in the schedule, and tribal pockets in these states are noted to be pockets of extreme backwardness. The issue here is that the omitted groups are simply denied even the Constitutional guarantee of human rights.

- Laws miss out the nuances of patterns of resource use by communities that are in a pre-agricultural stage such as hunting, gathering or pastoral activity. The most noted conflict is with shifting cultivation, which is looked down upon as devastation of resources, and is recognised only in VIth Schedule.
- Many routine beneficiary schemes, such as those for environment and wildlife protection, miss out the nuances of command over natural resources as an integral part of the adivasi life. Often, they are denied access in the name of some or the other welfare scheme, and may even be forced out of their habitat.
- Denotified tribes are still looked upon by the police and administration as criminals, and there have been many areas where NHRC has intervened.

Adivasis as a group are specially vulnerable to the threats of commericialisation and globalisation. These twin processes threaten their intrinsic relationship with land and community living. They face great threats to their simple principles of life.

NOTES

1. Dalit groups means caste groups that have been traditionally discriminated in terms of role and status in society. The Constitution of India specifies it with reference to schedule castes and schedule tribes. The various volumes of the NHRC Annual Reports highlight the variety and persistence of violence perpetrated on Delits.
2. The First National Commission on Labour, chaired by Justice Gajendra Gadkar listed an illustrative category of work that unorganised labour was engaged in. This included contract labour including construction worker, casual labour, labour employed in small-scale industry, handloom and powerloom workers, *beedi* and cigar workers, employees in shops and commercial establishments, sweepers and scavengers, workers in tanneries, tribal labour, and other unprotected labour. Efforts by SEWA led to the inclusion of self-employed women in this category. (Report of Second National Commission on Labour, p. 597.)
3. The ILO conventions are international treaties that have to be ratified by individual countries. India has ratified ILO conventions related to discrimination and forced labour, but not those related to child labour or trade unions. The latter are addressed by the Constitution and other specific laws.
4. In keeping with its origins, the initial focus of the ILO was on workers in the formal sector alone. The concept of 'decent work' is taken from ILO (1999), Report of the Director General, International Labour Conference, 87th Session, 1999, ILO office Geneva.

5. Various Supreme Court judgements clarify that conversion is not a part of this freedom to propagate one's religion. Landmark judgement is given in the Stanislaus case.
6. For a detailed discussion on minority rights in the Constituent Assembly and the process of defining a minority, see Chapter 4 'Minority Rights and Religious Communities', pp. 78–114 in Mahajan (2001). For details on minority demands for representation in the form of proportional representation, or for reserved seats, see Jha (2003).
7. The World Conference Against Racism, Racial Discrimination, Xenophobia and Related Intolerance was held in Durban between 31 August and 8 September, 2001, at the initiative of the UN. The Bhopal Conference for Dalits was held at the initiative of the then Chief Minister Digvijay Singh, 12–13 January 2002.
8. As cited in Visvanathan (2001), p. 3123
9. These were earlier listed as tribes, and their areas demarcated as non-regulation areas, but later left out. See Sharma (2002), p. 96.
10. The operation of state-wise listing is different from the national listing of minorities, and implies that groups listed as scheduled tribes in one state, may not be so listed in another. These often lead to political protests. An example is that of the *kaccha* Nagas in Manipur. In Nagaland, these are STs, not so in Manipur.
11. Now bifurcated as two separate Commissions, so a separate Commission on scheduled tribes is to look after these responsibilities.
12. As cited in Sharma: 2002, p 112.

BIBLIOGRAPHY

Bokil, M. (2002). 'De-notified and Nomadic Tribes: A Perspective'. *Economic and Political Weekly*. 37(2): 148–54.

Dhavan, Rajeev (2002). 'The Minorities Case'. *The Hindu*, 15 Nov. New Delhi.

Dutt, Rudar (ed.) (1997). *Organising the Unorganised Workers*. Delhi: Vikas.

Guru, G. (1997). 'Human Rights and *Dalits*: An Inquiry into the Human Rights Discourse in India'. *Indian Journal of Human Rights*.

Hargopal, G. (2002). 'Rights of *Dalits*: Law and Reality'. *Journal of the NHRC*. 1:133–59.

Jha, S. (2003). 'Rights versus Representation: Defending Minority Interests in the Constituent Assembly'. *Economic and Political Weekl.*, 38(16) 19–25 April: 1579–83.

Jhabvala, R. (2003). 'New Forms of Worker's Organisations: Towards a System of Representation and Voice'. *Indian Journal of Labour Economics*. 46(2) April–June: 203–218.

Jhabvala, R. (2005). 'Unorganised Workers Bill: In Aid of the Informal Worker'. *Economic and Political Weekly* XL(22 and 23) (May 28–June 4): 2227–31.

Kymlicka, Will (ed.) (1995). *The Rights of Minority Cultures.* NY: OUP.

Ministry of Labour (2002). Report of the National Commission on Labour, Vols I and II. New Delhi: Government of India.

Louis, Prakash (2001). 'Casteism is More Horrendous than Racism: Durban and Dalit Discourse'. New Delhi: Indian Social Science Institute.

Mahajan, G. (2001). *Identities and Rights: Aspects of Liberal Democracy in India.* New Delhi: Oxford University Press.

Massey, J. (2003). *Minorities and Religious Freedom in a Democracy.* New Delhi: Manohar.

Nayak, N. (2005). 'Social Security for the Unorganised Sector'. *Economic and Political Weekly.* XL(22–23): 2231–33.

Nayyar, D. (2003). 'Work, Livelihoods and Rights.' *Indian Journal of Labour Economics.* 46 (1): 3–14.

Nigam, A. (2002). 'In Search of a Bourgeoisie: *Dalit* Politics Enters a New Phase'. *Economic and Political Weekly.* 37 (13) 30 March.

Padhy, S. (2004). 'Secularism and Justice: A Review of Indian Supreme Court Judgements'. *Economic and Political Weekly*. 39(46 and 47) 20 Nov: 5027–32.

Government of Madhya Pradesh (2002). Report of the Task Force on Workers in the Unorganised Sector.

Shah, G. (ed.) (2001). *Cultural Subordination and the Dalit Challenge:Dalit Identity and Politics*. New Delhi: Sage.

Sharma, B. D. (2002). 'Rights of Tribals.' *Journal of the NHRC.* 1: 79–132.

Thorat, S. (2000). 'Human Rights of Ex-Untouchables in India: Violations and Rights Enforcement.' *Indian Journal of Human Rights.* 4(1 and 2).

Indira Gandhi National Open University (IGNOU) (ed.) *Organising the Unorganised.* New Delhi: IGNOU.

Xaxa, V. (1999). 'Tribes as Indigenous People of India.' *Economic and Political Weekly.* 34(51) 18-24 Dec: 3589–95.

——— (2001). 'Protective Discrimination: Why Scheduled Tribes lag behind Scheduled Castes?' *Economic and Political Weekly.* 29 (21 July): 2765–72.

5

Human Rights Movement in India

INTRODUCTION

Human rights movement in India, today, can be said to encompass a variety of groups and institutions that struggle for the rights of the marginalised. It began with a core focus on civil liberties and insistence on the application of the rule of law by state and its machinery. It especially pointed to the use of violence in dealing with those struggling for the traditionally oppressed. Moving further, the movement today includes a variety of struggles, it is indeed a 'rainbow coalition' of social movements on issues of natural resource management and livelihood, multicultural identities, gender issues and opposition to communalism among others. While the initial momentum to the movement was provided by the struggle against British colonialism, the context changed after independence. Colonial rulers were no longer the target, and a government of the Indian people was in power.

After independence, political events such as the Naxal uprisings and the imposition of Emergency provided a context for the movement for rights to grow. In both cases, the Indian state was involved in curtailing and violating the rights of its own citizens, and in the use of violence. The focus of the rights movement was essentially on struggling for civil rights of individual citizens. The late 1960s witnessed the killing of Naxals, encounter killings without resorting to the appropriate process of law by state police mainly in the hotbeds of Naxal uprising in West Bengal and Andhra Pradesh. The imposition of nationwide Emergency in 1974 clamped down on the fundamental rights of citizens. It amounted to curbing the press, illegal detention of the opposition, arbitrary arrests and police violence. The civil liberty and democratic rights groups protested against these draconian measures of the state.

Over time, while the core focus of human rights remains on civil rights, the answer to the question as to *what is included in human rights* is a more inclusive and expanded list. There is a more holistic understanding of rights as not merely individual entitlements, but also that which comes to them by the virtue of collective and gendered identities. The bearer of some of these rights need not be strictly an individual, it can also be a group. This broader understanding of rights inspires a large number of groups across the country to take up the case of human rights on the variety of issues mentioned in the preceding paragraph. These groups and activists occasionally join hands to fight against issues that pertain to gross violation of human rights, such as the recent communal riots in Gujarat or the Bhopal Gas Tragedy. Civil liberty and democratic rights groups, women's, dalit's and other groups struggling on various issues of survival, are amongst those included in the ambit of a 'human rights movement'.

Occasionally, on issues of gross violation of human rights, national level coalitions across these groups are built up. Presence of more effective means of communication has facilitated networks, alliances and frequent interactions amongst these groups.

All these groups that struggle for human rights are in a certain sense the product of 'oppositional politics', that is, they oppose the transgression or violation of citizens' rights by the state, as we have just discussed in the case of the struggle against British rule prior to independence, or against the Indian state during the imposition of Emergency. Now, opposition to the dominant paradigms of development and structures of social domination that violate rights of individuals or collectives, are also considered integral to the struggle for rights. The groups are small in size and numbers; yet, they often face violent attacks—from the state as well as the majority parties in power. This capacity to oppose the 'dominant' social, political or state power means that their presence is absolutely crucial to the working of democracies.

Human rights groups provide a way of mobilising people on issues that are not mainstream. They are voices of the oppressed and the minorities. Very often, the agenda that they spearhead through long periods of struggle, gets adopted by the state as legislation, especially when new parties, alliances or groups come to power, or when those in power have to concede to determined struggles. The adoption of reservation for women in Panchayati Raj, or repealing of Draconian laws such as TADA are a few examples of this type of state action in response to the pressure from the rights movement. In many states, the People's Union for Democratic Rights (PUDR), People's Union for Civil Liberties (PUCL) and many other groups continue to struggle against extraordinary powers of the state that arise from laws such as the Chhattisgarh Special Public Security Act, or MCOCA in Maharashtra. State functionaries often argue that such special or extraordinary laws have been put in place to secure the rights of citizens from the disruptive activities of terrorists or communal violence. Inquiries by human rights groups reveal the misuse of these extraordinary laws to get rid of opponents by putting them in jail on frivolous charges, and curtailing the rights of the latter. Inquiries by five leading human rights organisations into the *Selwa Judum* movement in Dantewada district of Chhattisgarh found that it was a state-sponsored movement. Such oppositional politics therefore has a constructive role in democracies.

In this chapter, we look at the origins and functioning of some of the civil liberties and democratic rights groups in India. Some of the other issues and struggles of the marginalised that comprise the holistic agenda of the human rights movement in India, those of unorganised workers, Dalits, adivasis and minorities, have been already discussed in Chapter 4. Many issues of rights related to gender and environment are discussed in detail in Sections II and III of the book. In a sense, the focus of this chapter on groups articulating civil and political rights may be criticised on two grounds. First, that it reflects the divide between civil and political rights on one hand, and social, cultural and economic rights on the other. Second, that it is premised upon the preoccupation of human rights agenda with civil and political rights that accords a specific and exclusive meaning to human rights. This criticism is valid in part. The struggle for human rights is for more than just civil liberties of citizens, enshrined in the Constitution. However, the specific colonial context of violation of citizens rights, and the struggle to attain these rights, within which the human rights movement in India originated, and citizen rights violation even in independent India, makes it important for us to look at the civil liberty groups. The democratic rights groups subscribe to a more political understanding of rights and place the issue of equality at the centre of their understanding of rights.

In this chapter, we review the evolution of the movement while opposing British colonialism, and after independence, in opposing or putting pressure on the Indian state. The main focus is on the working of these groups, the issues they articulate, the strategies adopted, the contest between different groups over the appropriate concept of rights—civil liberties or democratic rights, and the challenges that these groups face, especially in associating with other mass organisations, as also in articulating new issues. Crudely speaking, the rights enshrined in the Constitution constitute the ambit of civil liberties, as we have already noted before. The democratic rights, in the framework of the Constituion, imply a more political meaning of human rights with the issue of equality at the centre. Movements for survival, natural resource management, gender and caste, amongst others, bring out the manifold ways in which domination takes place. They, thereby, engage with and continually expand the notion of rights

EVOLUTION OF HUMAN RIGHTS MOVEMENT IN INDIA

Human rights are the product of movements and struggles, of *opposition*, as we have noted. In this sense, these rights are very much the product of politics, not above politics. The struggle for these rights and their evolution in India, has taken a path different from that in the West. This difference of context has had its implications on the concept of human rights as well. In the West, the renaissance movement with its focus on the individual, and the industrial revolution provided the context for the development of struggle for citizen's rights. This was, therefore, the struggle for individual rights. It, also, aimed at locating the appropriate sphere of action for the state and the individual, a public and a private domain, respectively, for the two different actors. The freedoms of the citizens were to be respected and protected from arbitrary encroachment by state action. Some of the typical rights and freedoms of citizens were the rights to life, equality, freedom of thought and expression, and political participation—the right to vote was initially a restricted right, not available to all citizens. Women, even in Western countries, obtained this right only in the early twentieth century.

HUMAN RIGHTS AND BRITISH INDIA

Denial of such rights to the colonial subjects provided the starting point for the struggle of individual rights in India. European and British citizens were not treated equally before the British judicial system. The Jallianwala Bagh tragedy is a cruel but important example of how even a peaceful assembly of Indian people, in a closed park, was fired upon by the British. General Dyer, the British police official who ordered the firing, could not be tried or penalised before law for his action on Indians. Needless to say, such action anywhere in the West would have been tantamount to genocide, and appropriate trials would have been conducted for the perpetrators of the crime. The colonial rule, thus, provided the context for the growth of a consciousness for rights of Indians. As we have noted in the case of Jallianwala Bagh tragedy, by its very nature, the colonial rule meted out differential treatment to its *subjects*. Racial and colonial prejudice denied equality of treatment before the eyes of law for colonial subjects, and this denial provided an important rallying point for nationalists.

Another example of the prejudiced action of the British was the Rowlatt Act of 1919 that extended wartime restriction on civil rights in normal times, and advocated separate courts and trial procedures for colonial subjects, that is, Indians. This was widely considered a way of placating the white public opinion.

The demand for equal treatment in matters of civil service employment, equal treatment before law or the right of Indian judges to try Europeans were the early expressions of the demand for civil rights. The Indian National Congress (INC) further articulated this demand for rights from time to time, and the charter of basic civil and political rights gradually emerged. These included social and economic rights. The most significant of these efforts was the Nehru Committee Report, adopted by an All Parties Conference, in 1928, opposing the all white Simon Commission. The report devoted a section to fundamental rights. Within the Congress party, specific consciousness for human rights developed with the emergence of a civil liberties group formed in 1936. The Indian Civil Liberties Union (ICLU) was established in 1936 with the efforts of Jawahar Lal Nehru. At its inaugural session in Bombay in August, Nehru is noted to have said that 'the idea of civil liberties is to have the right to oppose the state'.[1] The significance of ICLU can be estimated from the fact that at its inaugural session, Rabindra Nath Tagore was the President and Sarojini Naidu the working President. In its working, ICLU brought up the issue of harassment of political prisoners and violation of citizens rights not only in British India, but also in the princely states. Dutta (2000: 279) notes that 'as a result of the ICLU's campaigns, a considerable consciousness about civil rights was created within the major party of the national movement, the Congress'. The significance of the rights agenda for the Congress is evident from the fact that when provincial governments were formed in 1937, and the Congress was the ruling party in many states, circulars were sent instructing preservation of civil rights. Needless to say, the rights agenda was significant within the Congress when it was not involved in a mass mobilisation against the British. Amongst the most notable achievement of this group was the legal defence of nationalist leaders, jailed by the British, and charged of sedition.

The outbreak of the Second World War meant that the draconian arm of the colonial state was extended and civil liberties of colonial citizens curtailed. The resumption of mass movement activity, opposing the British, by the Congress in the form of the Quit India Movement meant that for the moment, activities related to civil liberties had taken a backseat. Many important leaders were in jail and workers lost interest. ICLU's momentum dwindled slowly.

INDEPENDENCE AND THE CIVIL LIBERTIES MOVEMENT

With independence, the situation changed. No longer was the rule by a *foreign power* the rallying point for opposing denial of human rights. In fact, those who struggled against the British rule were themselves in power.

Did this mean the end of struggle for human rights? It was not so, as in independent India, opposition to majoritarian party politics and use of violence by the state, violating the rule of the law of the land, provided the ground for a resurgence of the human rights movement. Initially, it was the ban on the Communist Party at the instance of the Congress that was then in power, that provided the impetus to the civil liberty groups. Later, it was the Naxals, who being opposed by the communists in West Bengal, were instrumental in setting up the civil liberty groups. At the time of Emergency, a broad alliance of people and groups cutting across different political ideologies was formed to oppose the authoritarianism of the ruling parties.

Two sets of developments influenced the human rights movement in independent India. They were:

1. the debates within the Constituent Assembly on fundamental rights of citizens, and
2. the development of the communist movement in various parts of the country, notably in Andhra Pradesh and West Bengal.

The charter of rights considered by the Constituent Assembly included civil, political, social and economic rights. The conception of citizens' rights outlined in the Constitution, included individual and group rights. A brief mention of this is made in the introductory part of this chapter.

In West Bengal, state repression of the communist movement led to the Civil Liberties Committee (CLC), set up in 1948, with individuals such as Meghnad Saha and N. C. Chatterjee. With the lifting of the ban on the Communist Party and the release of their cadres, enthusiasm for CLC, like ICLU, waned. Dutta (2000: 279) notes that due to the awareness building exercise of the two organisations, the Constituent Assembly witnessed long and lively debates on fundamental rights.

The Naxalite movements in Andhra Pradesh and West Bengal in the late 1960s and the early 1970s led to the rise of civil rights groups in these two states. In West Bengal, it was the Communist Party in power which was accused of persecuting the Naxals. The Association for the Protection of Democratic Rights was formed in Calcutta in 1972. The Andhra Pradesh Civil Liberties Committee (APCLC) was formed in 1974. The direct identification of these groups with ultra left politics and their use of violence to counter state repression meant that civil liberty activists were now exposed to, and at times, tortured by, the aggressive hands of the ruling party and the state.

The imposition of Emergency in 1974 provided the opportune moment for the launch of all India scale organisations. Kothari (1991: 85) notes that the imposition of national Emergency represents a watershed in the history of post-colonial India. It was in this period, says Kothari, that the civil rights movement developed a wider organisational base and grew more visible. Jayprakash Narayan, popularly known as JP, led the movement called People's Union for Civil Liberties and Democratic Rights (PUCLDR) against the authoritarianism of the Emergency. It saw the coming together of people with different political ideologies and professions in defence of civil and political liberties. Apart from this, there were many state-level groups with which PUCLDR often worked in collaboration. Imposition of curbs on citizen's freedoms, the press, assumption of draconian powers by the state, and arrests of civilians on a large scale, were the issues around which mobilisation took place. The situation at this time was hardly appropriate for moving the courts in matters of citizen's rights. The authoritarian state resorted to a cracking down on civil rights activists in a major way.

With the fall of Indira Gandhi's regime and lifting of the Emergency, the political scenario changed. Many of those who had struggled against the Emergency were now in power. Relationship of many of PUCLDR activists with the Janata Party, now in power, were strong. The issue of rights violation by the state and party in power still remained, and now it posed a dilemma. A radical group emphasised that understanding human rights as mere civil liberties was not enough. There were, however differences of opinion regarding the concept of rights and the means to achieve them. The result was a split in October 1980. PUCLDR split into the People's Union for Civil Liberties (PUCL) and the People's Union for Democratic Rights (PUDR). Civil liberties or democratic rights formed the core of the difference, and at the heart of it, lay a contest over the concept of human rights. The details of this contest over meanings, is briefly taken up in the next section.

Dutta (2000: 283) notes that these debates and differences were not merely a 'war of categories', nor were they restricted to the PUCL and PUDR. Those who subscribed to the meaning of human rights as democratic rights were opposed to the sectarianism and legalism of PUCL. Apart from PUDR, many other regional formations such as the CPDR in Bombay, the Naga People's Movement for Human Rights, APCLC in Andhra Pradesh, and APDR in West Bengal, are strongly associated with opposing rights violations since the 1980s. He further notes that debate on the meaning of democratic rights happened in West Bengal as well. Within APDR, there were objections on the use of the nomenclature 'protection of democratic rights'. The question asked was whether democratic rights existed at all in India, and if they did not, how could they be protected? A splinter group called Association for the Establishment of Democratic Rights was formed; it was short-lived as a body.

Human Rights as Civil Liberties or Democratic Rights: Contest Over Meanings

As stated earlier, the difference between human rights and democratic rights is not merely a war of categories. Rather, it is also a strong debate on the meaning of rights themselves. It is, in this sense, an essential part of the struggle for human rights in India, with ramifications for the rights discourse internationally. Those who interpret rights as civil liberties accord significance to those rights guaranteed in law and the Constitution. The voices in support of rights as democratic rights, in turn, attach significance to struggle and opposition to domination and oppression, as the centre of defining rights. In this sense, legally guaranteed rights are not the only rights. K. Balagopal (1997: 87) notes that while it is not enough for human rights movement to speak only about legally guaranteed rights, the two need to be seen in a continuum. According to him,

> Every right traverses a path in which it is a desire hopefully sought for at one stage, a politically asserted demand at another, and a legally guaranteed right at the last, . . . Thus, every legal right was a political demand once upon a time, and every political demand hopes to get statutory recognition at some time in future. The two are not superior or inferior rights, but two stages of a process.

A second set of arguments seeks to distinguish civil liberties from democratic rights. It extends democratic rights to mean the rights of groups and collectives as well. For example, the Naga people's struggle is a struggle for collective identities. The struggle against oppression of the landlords in Bihar or Andhra Pradesh is a collective struggle of the landless poor. With survival rights being added on to the agenda, such as displacement by dams, rights of collectives gain even greater significance. However, even here, there is a sense of mutuality in the two conceptions of rights. Some of these issues can be taken to courts as violation of entitlements; the challenge is how the legal system and the state institutions grant recognition to the rights of collectives.

WORKING OF HUMAN RIGHTS GROUPS

Many significant achievements, in terms of establishing, securing and protecting a vast range of rights, are credited to human rights groups. One of the main functions has been the robust opposition to the transgressions of the rule of law by state instruments such as fake encounters, police torture and other brutalities. Violation of citizens' rights by the army in the Northeast and Kashmir has also been raised. In addition, other issues of social oppression, where the source of oppression is not the state, but social structures, like bonded labour, caste oppression and killings by landlords, and collaborating with Dalit groups for rights protection have also been taken up. The groups have used the media and courts to build a consciousness for, and secure rights, through legal means.

In cases of gross human rights violations such as communal riots, investigations have been conducted and reports released. Two of the famous reports are that on the anti-Sikh riots in Delhi in 1984 titled *Who Are the Guilty?* and on the Gujarat riots that followed the Godhra incident titled *Maro Kapo Balo*. The human rights groups often collaborate amongst each other, or support independent action groups in the event of a major crisis and/or relief work. These groups differ on the methods of working. They debate upon whether legal means are the only appropriate means to struggle for rights, and whether violence should be used to secure rights or for opposing state violence.

CHALLENGES AND FUTURE DIRECTIONS

A large number of human rights groups operate in various parts of the country. But they come forward to form a national alliance on a number of issues. The struggle of Bhopal Gas victims is one such example where medical practitioners, scientists, environmentalists and other rights activists stood together. The international activism for human rights is also significant. At the national level, the setting up of the National Human Rights Commission (NHRC) seems to be the appropriate institutional support mechanism for rights protection. Where does the movement stand amidst these developments? Commentators note that despite the proliferation of groups, there is no significant imprisonment in the number of cases pertaining to the violation of rights.

The groups also face many challenges in their working. Linking up with other mass movements and political parties, and responding to new issues that threaten life and livelihoods are some of the crucial challenges/tasks before the movement.

One of the most common state responses is the use of physical repression on human rights activists. The use of physical violence has deeper consequences. Often, groups need to work undercover so that they do not invite the state's wrath. This method of working, in turn has its consequences. These are basically in the nature of splits in the groups mainly over the future course of action, and the sacrificing of internal democracy within the group. Over time, the views of members crystallise. This also raises the related issue of the use of violence by these groups. Should state violence be responded to by counter-violence of the groups? Or, should the path of liberal constitutionalism still be followed, even when the state has indulged in gross violation of rule of law?

Liberal constitutionalism itself has its limitations. The process is long drawn and tedious. At times, so severe is the transgression of rights by the state that liberal constitutional methods such as appeal to courts of law seem like a futile exercise. Also, court cases seldom create the ground for mass involvement, and seem more like isolated activities. The common man may or may not take interest in the outcome of legal battles fought over a period of time.

Sethi (1991: 76) notes that far more challenging than physical repression is social repression. Growing communalism and extremist violence has led to the polarisation of opinion in society. The media also reflects such polarised opinion, rather than acting as a watchdog of democracy. Often, there is a feeling among people that it is the state which is under attack. Increasing terrorist attacks on public places, such as markets, cinema halls, means of public transport or places of worship, evoke a feeling of fear in the people and, therefore, justify in their minds the need for a strong state. Under such circumstances, civil liberties and human rights groups are seen as attacking the state!

Kothari (1991: 20–21) sums up in the following words:

> . . . increasingly the relevance of human rights activists and organisations is reduced to holding protest meetings and rallies, and to registering and fighting court cases . . . nothing much comes out of writs and petitions anyway. This has made the human rights movement even more segmented and specialised—reducing it to lawyers and orators—and given the pillar-to-post nature of the running that is involved, has produced a growing state of exhaustion and shrinkage in its composition and character.

Another set of challenges has been thrown up with respect to linkage of human rights groups with political parties. There are multiple facets to this issue. Though these groups have a non-party political standing, its members have generally been associated with opposition parties, and have actively opposed ruling party members. The human rights platform, therefore, has been used, or is likely to be used, as a party platform. This entails a compromise on autonomy, and there are counter-charges that such groups raise 'political' issues and not strictly human rights issues. In the early days after independence, when the Communist Party was banned and its members grouped under the Civil Liberties Committee (CLC), critics pointed out that CLC was merely interested in fighting the legal battles of jailed communist cadres and not strictly involved in the struggle for civil liberties. There was a grain of truth in this criticism; as noted above, the

CLC dwindled once its cadres were released and the ban on the Communist Party was lifted.

Links with political parties also expose human rights groups to attacks from the parties they oppose. In West Bengal, difference between the Communist Party and the Naxal groups led to violent attacks on civil liberty activists for being Naxal sympathisers. How far can these groups remain completely independent of political party linkages? One compulsion that human rights groups face is the need to enhance their legitimacy in popular consciousness, and this, in turn, may require linking up with other mass organisations that include political parties.

Critical reviews of human rights movements in India by Kothari and Sethi, note that not all limitations of the movement are on account of state repression. Nor are the challenges limited to majority parties in power. Rather many of the challenges relate to the internal structure of the groups and the differences between them. A further set of challenges arise in responding to new issues of development, environment, survival rights, and gender and community rights.

There are limits to voluntarism, which is the basis on which activists of the groups are mobilised. The volunteers often lose interest or drop out over a period of time, tired of the intense efforts in mobilising against rights violation in isolated locations, working in remote habitation, or simply with the disappointment and inability to get adequate state cover.

Again, there are differences between the human rights groups on the justification of using violence. State violence is justified as a *pursuit* of law and order, and citizen's violent response to it is often dubbed as a *threat* to law and order, and the groups or individuals engaged in it are portrayed as terrorists. Some groups eschew violence, and believe in moving to courts; other groups justify violent retaliation to state repression. This is not a watertight compartment as, very often, the groups join hands; jailed activists of the People's War Group (PWG) are often defended in court by lawyers and civil liberty activists of the Andhra Pradesh Civil Liberties Committee. The PWG upholds violence as a means to achieve citizen's rights, whereas the A PCLC does not.

A more significant set of challenges emerge from the new issues that face the movement. Protecting the rights of those displaced by development projects places the groups in a corner. They are often portrayed as anti-modernist and anti-development; a portrayal that influences the way people perceive these groups to be. If Medha Patkar opposes big dams because they displace people living there for centuries, she is often perceived as being opossed to economic development. Often in protecting one set of rights, a different set of rights are claimed to be transgressed. For example, protecting the rights of divorced Muslim women exposes the groups to the charge of treading upon community rights. Interventions in communally charged situations have led the groups to be accused of exhibiting a pro-minority bias. These claims and arguments essentially underline the basic understanding of human rights as political; a product of human endeavour and struggle, and of the evolving character of the rights discourse in India. It is in response to, and in engagement with, these challenges that the future directions of the struggle need to be mapped out.

NOTE

1. J. Nehru *Selected Works*, vol. 7, p. 428, cited in Dutta (2000), p. 279.

BIBLIOGRAPHY

Balagopal, K. (1997). 'The Human Rights Movement: Its Context and its Concerns.' *Indian Journal of Human Rights* **1**(1): 82–106.

Dutta, Nilanjan (2000). 'From Subject to Citizen: Towards a History of the Indian Civil Lights Movement' in Michael R. Anderson and Sumit Guha (eds) *Changing Concepts of Rights and Justice in South Asia*. Oxford (Oxford India—SOAS Studies on South Asia Understandings and Perspective Series). 275–288.

Kothari, Rajni (1991). 'Human Rights—A Movement in Search of a Theory' in Smita Kothari and Harsh Sethi (eds) *Rethinking Human Rights: Challenges for Theory and Action*. New York and Delhi: New Horizon Press and Lokayan. 19–29.

Kothari, Smita. (1991). 'The Human Rights Movement in India: A Critical Overview' in Smita Kothari and Harsh Sethi (eds) *Rethinking Human Rights: Challenges for Theory and Action*. New York and Delhi: New Horizon Press and Lokayan.

Kothari, S. and Harsh Sethi (eds) (1991). *Rethinking Human Rights: Challenges for Theory and Action*. New York and Delhi: New Horizons Press and Lokayan.

Sethi, H. (1991). 'Beyond the Fragments: The Civil Rights Groups Today' in Smita Kothari and Harsh Sethi (eds). *Rethinking Human Rights: Challenges for Theory and Action.* New York and Delhi: New Horizon Press and Lokayan.

Section II Gender

6

Patriarchy

As students of social science, we seek to understand our society and its evolution. During the course of this enterprise, we are bound to discover that many of our assumptions about our own society need to be revised, or perhaps we desire a complete transformation of the existing social structures. Thus, some of the supposedly basic structures of our society would come under relentless scrutiny; for example, the institutions of the family, marriage and so on. Many of these questions were not commonly raised even 50 years back; of course there were isolated attempts at a critical evaluation of one of the most fundamental aspects of human life, that is, the relationship between men and women, and how a given society organises the distribution of power, resources and opportunities among them.

Since then, a concerted attempt has been made in this direction. This new effort has meant the formulation and usage of new concepts that were non-existent in social science literature or, if they did exist, they were used in an altogether different sense. Among the plethora of such new terms is 'gender' which is the theme of this section of the book. An understanding of this term, therefore, is absolutely essential, but before that perhaps yet another term that has gained tremendous currency needs to be understood; that term is 'patriarchy'.

Why do we need to define patriarchy? Because we need to understand the way in which power, resources and opportunities are distributed among men and women. Further, we need to understand how this distribution is justified. Most importantly, if we find this to be skewed in favour of men, then how we might want to challenge and change this. In order to do all this, it would be extremely useful to understand what patriarchy means.

Sylvia Walby (1997) defines patriarchy as a system of social structures and practices in which men dominate, oppress and exploit women. When Walby uses the term social structure, she is implying that this system of control, domination and oppression is not biologically determined. This implies that men are not naturally superior to women and, therefore, women are not naturally subordinate to men. The subordination is rather a consequence of a particular kind of social organisation, that is, patriarchy. Of course, this is not to suggest that every individual man is in a dominant position and that every woman in a subordinate one.

The word *patriarchy* is derived from the word '*patriarch*', which means the head of a specific type of male-dominated family, which consisted of women, younger men, children, servants and slaves. Today, it is used more often than not to suggest a social system where women are subordinated to men. Kamala Bhasin (1986) in her book on patriarchy refers, in particular, to south Asian context and how patriarchy manifests itself here. In our context, patriarchy or *pitrasatta* (in Hindi) manifests itself in many ways that include preference of a male child, discrimination against girls in food distribution, burden of household work on girls and women, lack of educational opportunities for girls, restricted mobility for girls and women, wife battering, sexual harassment at workplace, lack of inheritance rights to women and, of course, no control over fertility. Patriarchy is inextricably linked with property and inheritance rights. It is the son who is seen as the rightful heir and it is only through him that a family traces its continuity. Daughters are seen as temporary members of the family who would go away and help other families continue their line. It is this temporary nature of their membership within their natal family that is responsible for denying them rights. Marriage marks a clear break in the status of the daughters within patriarchy, as we see it in our context. Daughters have no rights and are excluded from the membership of their natal families. Dowry, which is characteristic of marriages in this context, is seen as a kind of settlement of whatever claims the daughter might have over her natal family. Henceforth, she is considered to belong to her husband's family, and within the natal family, she can, at best, hope to be welcomed cordially on an occasional visit that she might make. It is the son who would inherit the family name and wealth, and carry it forward, and be responsible for the care of his parents. Having daughters, therefore, is seen as a drain of resources and as serving no purpose, because, after all, she would go away. All the expenditure incurred on her would be merely a waste, for it is not going to benefit her natal family in any way. This is the context for son preference, which is backed by justifications from mythology, literature, cinema and even the hoary scriptures. There are prayers, fasts and other religious activities that supposedly enable couples to have sons and hopefully avoid having daughters. To this list can be added the modern practice of pre-natal diagnostic tests like amniocentesis that is used to get rid of female foetuses. Families would rather invest in these diagnostic rather than have to spend on the upbringing of a daughter who will finally be of no benefit to them and would also have to be given dowry. Despite the test being legally banned in India, statistics have been showing an alarming picture of male to female ratio in our population. Linked to this whole culture of son preference is the discrimination against girls in food distribution. Since sons are seen as the rightful heirs and inheritors of the family, and daughters as a burden and a drain on the resources, the best and most nutritious food is served to the sons and daughters are expected to make do with the little that might be left over. This is also considered to be training for the development of *womanly* virtues like self-effacement and sacrifice that she would need in her husband's house. Moving away from the domestic to the public arena, the whole issue of women's mobility presents a completely different example. The public spaces within patriarchy are seen as rightfully belonging to men and any woman who desires to claim it does so at her own peril. This assumption is behind the justification of instances of women being raped in our cities, for instance, while travelling back home from work after a long day or going out for dinner. Bhasin points out that most women and young girls in south Asia would have experienced one or more of these forms of control.

When we put these fragmented experiences together, we discover a pattern, which is, *the subordination and control of women by men*. This, then, is patriarchy.

This system of control and domination of women by men has an elaborate and sophisticated network of cultural and ideological props, that is, cultural and ideological elements and practices that range from cinema, literature, painting and fashion, to high philosophy and religion—all of which help keep the system of domination intact. The underlying message is that women need to be controlled by men and that women are a part of men's property. As Kamala Bhasin points out, it is premised on the idea that men are superior to women.

Over the last century, gradually but steadily, more and more women have gained access to education, have become a part of the market economy and the wage differences in many sectors has narrowed. There are special provisions to enable women to remain active participants in the workforce and participate in governmental processes. Does all this then signal the end of patriarchy? The answer is that patriarchy far from being a relic of the past, continues, albeit in new forms, and while it might be weakened in some aspects, there are new arenas where it is now in operation. The lesson drawn from this is that patriarchy is not uniform and the history of patriarchy is not the same everywhere. It would be rather misplaced to imagine a uniformity in the structures and practices of patriarchy. Different societies have controlled and oppressed women using different social, economic and cultural practices and structures. Foot binding in China, *sati* in India and, as some would argue, beauty contests in contemporary societies are all manifestations of patriarchy in one way or the other.

ORIGINS OF PATRIARCHY

The most accepted explanation for patriarchy is the traditionalist view that it is based on a natural division between men and women, the latter being weaker and therefore subordinate to men. It is thus justified as being natural. This becomes the basis for a supposed natural division of labour. Men being stronger would be hunters and providers while women being weaker would be nurturers and care givers. Religion, literature, philosophy and every other sphere of life including economic practices and transactions are based on this belief, rendering it immutable and a natural fact of life.

A lot of 'modern' analysis also accepts many of these assumptions on which patriarchy rests; conventional psychology is a very good example. The female, according to Sigmund Freud, envies the complete and whole human body that the male has. Lacking a penis, the female is eternally doomed to feel sexually incomplete and passive. This leads women to feelings of repression and thus makes them vulnerable to hysteria. Critics, especially feminist critics of Freud, have argued that the supposedly objective basis of Freudian psychology is rather suspect, based as it is—actually—on routine male prejudices against women. V. Geetha (2002) in her book *Gender* has an interesting account of the various debates that later psychologists and his own contemporaries had with Freud. Gloria Steinem for instance created a fictional character called Phyllis Freud who was gripped by womb envy and succumbs to 'testyria'. Thus, in the play men are shown as feeling envious of women since they do not possess a womb. By doing this, she wanted to prove that Freud's theorisations made sense only within a patriarchal framework.

Going beyond the assumption of natural division, Marx's comrade and co-author, Fredrick Engels wrote the *Origin of Family, Private Property and the State* as an attempt to explain the beginnings of the system of subordination of women. His analysis led him to conclude that the female sex was defeated with the evolution of private property. The earliest stage of human history was characterised by Engels as savagery, a stage prior to any class or gender divisions. Food gathering and hunting was the main activity and there was no marriage and no notion of private property. Ancestry was, therefore, through women. Thus, for Engels this is a stage in human history prior to patriarchy.

With greater sophistication in tools, men started moving further afield to hunt while women stayed back to mind the children and take care of the homestead. This, to Engels, is the first instance of a sexual division of labour. He characterises this stage as barbarism. However, as agriculture and animal husbandry evolved, settled life became the norm and the earliest forms of property acquisition began in the form of animals and gradually slaves, often female slaves. Men now desired to amass property and pass it on to *their* children. This paved the way for a shift away from ancestry based on mothers to one based on fathers. This meant that women had to be controlled, their sexuality regulated and monitored. In response to this need, patriarchy based on monogamy for women evolved. For, how else would a man be sure that the property he was passing on was to his own children? Control over surplus became a male prerogative and women came to be economically dependent on men. Women were accorded the role of producing heirs to whom the man could pass on the property that he had amassed.

Engels argued that under conditions of capitalism, however, patriarchy plagued only the bourgeois woman and not the working-class woman. The bourgeois woman of Europe in his time stayed at home and did not work outside the family. Thus, he argued, her only function was to produce heir for her husband' s property and, thus, she becomes completely dependent on her husband. In fact, she herself is reduced to being her husband's property.

On the other hand is the working-class woman who, by joining the labour market, has escaped being oppressed, or so Engels thought. He argued that there was no material basis for the oppression of the working class woman, because after all she was part of the labour force and her husband did not own any property. This meant that he had no material basis to oppress the woman because, according to him, oppression of women is linked to ownership of private property. Thus, the conventional Marxist explanation of the origin of patriarchy argues that the primary contradiction in society is based on ownership of property and, hence, on class. Once women become part of the labour force and work towards abolition of private property, patriarchy would disappear.

While feminists have critiqued Engels' explanation of the origin of women's subordination, they acknowledge that it is he who, as Gerda Lerner says, gave historicity to this event. Engels' description of patriarchy demonstrated that far from being an eternal structure that has existed from times immemorial, women's subordination has clear roots in history. Thus, he showed that at a definite time in human history, women's subordination begins and then gradually assumes the status of an eternal, natural fact. Research in anthropology shows that women were far more involved in the development of agriculture than Engels knew to be a fact. If so, then this raises questions about his argument that men got more involved with hunting and agriculture, and women became responsible for childcare and home management. Most feminists today would also not be able to accept Engels' contention that there was no material basis for women's subordination in working-class families.

Radical feminists argue that patriarchy precedes private property. For radical feminists, the fundamental and original contradiction is between sexes and not between classes as Engels argued. They trace this to biological and psychological differences but do not believe that these differences are immutable. Shulamith Firestone, for instance, argues that women are oppressed because of their ability to reproduce. This makes men fear women and in turn leads them to control and subjugate women. Firestone is suggesting that women's ability to give birth is something that men do not have (at least not as yet). This makes certain aspects of women's life appear mysterious and unknowable. It also seems that women have some unknown source of strength and power—which enables them to bear children—not possessed by men. Firestone is arguing that this probably makes women seem remote, powerful and in possession of qualities that the men do not have. There is, thus, the fear that women might employ these powers to dominate men. Hence, in a pre-emptive sort of way, men organise society in such a way as to subordinate women. With advancements in the sphere of fertility and reproductive medicine, Firestone sees liberation for women from the job of reproduction and, thus, the possibility of the end of patriarchy.

Similar to this position is the argument that it is men's control, the determination of women's fertility and conditions of reproduction that give men the power to subordinate women. Thus, it is not simply their biology that does women in but it is, indeed, the way in which men control, value and regulate women's biology that gives rise to patriarchy. Radical feminists often talk about two systems of oppression: the sex class system and the economic class system. They, however, have not theorised the relationship between the two to any great extent. The other point of discomfort with their theory is the proximity that they share with the old-fashioned biological determinism. The latter of course seeks to legitimise women's subordination as being grounded in biology and, hence, natural and eternal.

Socialist feminists have tried to establish the connection between the sex class system and the economic class system. To do this, they have moved away from the confines of the conventional Marxist analysis of patriarchy and looked at the radical feminist perspectives rather creatively. Unlike the radical feminists, they argue that patriarchy is not universal and unchanging. They contend that patriarchy interacts with the given economic system and in conjunction with other important factors, like ideology and culture, creates new and changing patriarchal ethos and practices. Unlike conventional Marxist theory, they do not argue that patriarchy emerged as a consequence of private property and would disappear with its abolition. For socialist feminists, the *relations of production* are as important as the *relations of reproduction*. For the radical feminists it is only the latter that has significance and for the Marxists only the former.

Radical feminists like Shulamith Firestone have argued that the primary class division in society is between women and men, and it is this division that she describes as the relations of procreation that form the basis of society rather than the economic relations of production. This primary class division between men and women is described as the sex class system and the divisions that are a consequence of different economic positions in society are described as the economic class system. However, they do not explain very effectively the relations between the two apart from repeatedly stating that the sex class system forms the basis for every division in society.

Socialist feminists argue that the organisation of procreation (reproduction) is very much a part of the economic foundations of a society. Traditional Marxism did not perceive it this way and this is an important point of departure for the socialist feminist from traditional Marxism. This shift in position is possible only if procreation and sexual labour is also seen as a distinct form of human labour. Following this, it can be argued that procreative and sexual labour like other forms of labour is not biologically determined but is definitely constituted by the forces of change in history. Thus, for socialist feminists, it is not enough to evaluate the relations of production that govern the sphere of production; it is equally important to evaluate and take into account the relations of reproduction that govern the sphere of procreation and sexual labour.

Within the socialist feminist approach itself, there are different ways of looking at the relationship between capitalism and patriarchy. Zillah Eisenstsein argues that the two are so closely linked that they become fused. She argues that patriarchy provides the much needed framework of control and order within which capitalism flourishes. Heidi Hartmann argues that patriarchy benefits all men irrespective of their class because patriarchal relations are crucially located in the expropriation of women's labour by men in the household and paid work in the market. Women's disadvantaged position in wage work makes them vulnerable in matters relating to division of labour within the household. On the other hand, their position and role within the household acts as an obstacle in the context of paid work. Thus, men are able to control and regulate women's labour power, both within the household and the market; control in one arena reinforcing the control in the other.

Maria Mies argues that patriarchy is not a consequence of capitalism, but predates it. Though she accepts that the two are interlinked, she sees capitalism as yet another form; indeed, the latest form of patriarchy. She argues that patriarchy is a world system with its own network of institutions and practices such as family, expropriation of women's labour, and so on.

The lives of women in the industrialised West, she argues, is dependent upon the exploitation of the Third World, specially the women in these countries.

Patriarchy as a concept has been criticised for being essentialist, ahistorical and reductionist, and for being unable to deal with cultural diversities. These three charges are interlinked. To think of all men as oppressors at all times and in a position to control all women is an extremely static and ahistorical approach. This criticism cautions against imagining men as a universal class of oppressors who control and oppress all women, thanks to their being men. This clearly assumes that men control women due to some essential biological characteristics, and if so, then this would be an unalterable fact. Therefore, Sylvia Walby responds by saying that these problems emerge when the definition of patriarchy uses only biology as a tool of analysis. The attempt to privilege either the sex class or the economic class over the other is also problematic. Walby believes that if these two problems can be addressed then the criticisms would no longer be valid. Patriarchy, she contends, needs to be conceptualised as being composed of several internal interrelated structures. Within each of these structures, specific patriarchal practices can be identified. Thus, we might come across empirical instances that reflect not only the effects of patriarchal structures but also of capitalism, and in the Indian context caste and religious structures. The experiences of a woman who belongs to a minority community in India would vary greatly from the experiences of an upper-caste woman who belongs to the majority community, or the life of a poor woman in a slum cluster in a big city in India would be different from that of a woman who lives in one of the fashionable localities of our cities. Thus, patriarchy does not act alone; rather it acts along with other factors like caste, class or religion.

Gerda Lerner has an extremely systematic account of patriarchy, its origins and development. According to her, subordination of women by men begins with men's appropriation of women's sexual and reproductive capacities. (This could take the form of sexual slavery and even abduction.) Control over women's reproductive capacities led to control over their offsprings as well and this became the basis for consolidation of the institution of private property. Soon a legal and state structure emerged to support this patriarchal family. The position of men came to be determined by the control they had over the production process. Women's position was controlled solely by the sexual ties that they had with men. Despite being venerated and worshipped for their fertility, women were systematically excluded from education and skill development.

Patriarchy in Lerner's account is linked with women's biological ability to bear children. There is clearly nothing natural about it in her understanding, and therefore, it can and must be challenged. She is suggesting that just because women happen to bear children, it does not follow automatically that they should therefore be subordinate to men. Lerner is arguing that while it is a fact that women do bear children, their subordination is a social construct. Patriarchy uses this fact to justify and present women's subordination as a natural fact. When something is presented as a natural fact, it suggests that it cannot be changed or challenged for it is in the nature of things. However, when we argue that women's subordination is a social and not a natural fact, we are implying that being such it can be challenged and changed. For social institutions and practices are put together by men and women, and therefore, should the need arise, they should be able to restructure and change it. Maria Mies, for instance, thinks that apart from being unequal and repressive, societies based on patriarchal thought tend to be exploitative not only of other human beings but also of environment. In such societies, the experiences and voices of a big section of their population, that is, women, is not heard and not valued.

Under conditions of patriarchy, women's labour—both within and outside the family—is controlled and expropriated by men. Women may be compelled to work outside the home and their earnings appropriated by their husbands, or else they might be prevented from working outside the house and thus become economically dependent on their husbands. Even when they do work outside the home, they are inevitably pushed into lower paid or intermittent jobs, or else into home based production, which is one of the most exploitative systems. At home, women's tedious, repetitive and endless labour is not seen as work at all. Thus, it is patriarchy that defines women's work and the conditions of their work as well. Patriarchy also makes it difficult for women to own property, since most property is owned by the father and passed on to the son. On the other hand, patriarchy creates the ideology of motherhood and forces women into it. At the same time, it also determines the conditions under which motherhood might be allowed. Only those childbirths that take place under the conditions and frameworks prescribed by patriarchy would be considered legitimate. Thus, patriarchy controls women's reproduction as well.

Sexuality is another aspect of women's lives that is completely regulated by patriarchy. Regulating their dress, behaviour and mobility, it closely monitors expression of sexuality by women. All this is justified by social, cultural and religious codes. Patriarchy evolves a complex legal and moral network to control women's sexuality, and there is, of course, the threat of rape for any woman who 'strays'.

Kamala Bhasin identifies family, religion, media and law as some of the most important pillars of the patriarchal system. Together, they maintain, perpetuate and legitimise patriarchy, making it appear natural, and hence, unchangeable. Families are considered incomplete without the male head of the household. It is within the family that young people learn the roles assigned by society to men and women as well as the 'appropriate' behaviour. Boys learn to control and girls learn to be subservient, and expect to be treated unequally. This helps in the perpetuation of the general order in society based on hierarchy and control. Most religions define morality, truth and goodness from a largely male perspective and most figures of authority within religious establishments are men. Legal frameworks in most countries are completely determined by the interests and the perspectives of men.

Politics (and political institutions) is overwhelmingly controlled by men and practised within a framework determined by men. It is, therefore, not surprising to learn that at no time have women in representative institutions in south Asia been more than ten per cent. Media, very powerfully and cleverly perpetuates stereotypes about men and women. The biases in reporting, portrayal of women as inferior and violence against women—all seem to legitimise patriarchy. With the sophistication of technology and refinement of aesthetics, the messages and images that the media creates becomes irresistible.

Like all systems of power, patriarchy also has a system of honouring and rewarding those whom it oppresses, and occasionally allows some women access to the hallowed interiors of the corridors of power. All this is, of course, done within the framework determined and put together by patriarchy. As Kamala Bhasin puts it, the problem is not with what women *do* or *are*, but it is with *how* they are valued and *who* has the right to assign the value. Women might, indeed, be allowed to make decisions or even be in control, but the framework given to them, is determined by patriarchy. Gerda Lerner compares this to a stage performance where both men and women have equally important roles and the play cannot progress without either. However, the whole stage is set, conceived of and directed by men. They, therefore, have given themselves the most interesting and heroic roles, giving to women only supporting roles. In all this, women have to internalise the message and ideology that seeks their marginalisation. This indoctrination happens at home, at school, in the workplace, and through the legal and political system, and of, course through the media.

Women's 'cooperation' in keeping the system of patriarchy continuing over centuries is one of the most intriguing aspects of the ideology of patriarchy. Uma Chakravarti argues that the 'cooperation' or 'consent' that women seem to exhibit is not really consensual as it is a consensus extracted by various means: denial of access to resources and economic dependence on men. Women who dare to question or challenge the practices of patriarchy could be threatened with dire consequences like being turned out of the house. Often, such women are forcibly sent into mental asylums on the charge of being mad. Privileges and honours come the way of 'consenting' women. Such women are honoured and considered respectable. Those who do not, are denounced as deviant.

Benevolent paternalism is a very important part of patriarchy. This means that women who have obeyed the rules and live within the framework prescribed by patriarchy would be accorded certain rights and privileges, and of course, security. This results in a situation where women might be seen actively collaborating in the perpetuation of patriarchal ideologies and practices. Women in this system of power need to constantly bargain and renegotiate their own positions. In this process, they might often do so at the cost of other women. Kamala Bhasin quotes a rural woman whose understanding of the working of patriarchy is remarkable. She compares women to satellites, who having no light of their own have to compete with one another to ensure that the sun shines effectively on them. This makes it rather difficult for women to support and assist each other, and perhaps explains why women are actively involved in the mistreatment of their daughters and daughters-in-law.

PATRIARCHY AND ITS IMPACT ON MEN

Men under conditions of patriarchy enjoy certain privileges, powers and rights by virtue of simply being men. While lower class men might be powerless vis-à-vis the upper class men, they no doubt have absolute power over their women. However, just as women are expected to perform certain roles and behave in a certain way, men too are in a sense trapped by the stereotypes that patriarchy sets up for them. Any activity or emotion that is generally associated with womanliness is taboo for men. Any man who enjoys cooking at home, or stays at home to take care of the child while his partner works outside the house, or a man who enjoys embroidery and housework would all be a rarity. Manliness is defined, as the exact opposite of what a woman should be like. Hence, for the picture of womanliness to be complete, it is essential that men, too, be slotted in a particular way. Many men have begun to realise this and are making an earnest attempt to breakaway from these stereotypes. Any deviation from this is ridiculed and effective genuine choices are denied to men as well. But the difference is that lack of choices in the case of women lead to their marginalisation and subordination as a group; in the case of men that is not true.

THE FUTURE OF PATRIARCHY

We live in times when there is much greater awareness of women's oppression accompanied by many efforts to fight it. Many more women have access to education and are part of the workforce. Also, some women are in powerful political and administrative positions. Equally true are the facts about increasing violence against women; and in our context, for instance, the rapidly spreading practice of dowry, and even killing of infant girls. Michael Mann has argued that patriarchy no longer exists but what exists is gender inequality. Of course, his context is the West, more specifically the UK. His conclusion is based on the changed conditions wherein male-headed households is no longer the norm and where a clear demarcation between the public and the private exists. Since these conditions do no longer hold, he proclaims the end of patriarchy. Sylvia Walby finds this analytical framework weak and instead suggests that the key element in our understanding of patriarchy is not the prevalence of male-headed households as much as it is a systematically structured gender inequality.

Walby makes a distinction between public and private patriarchy at least in the West. Put very simply, public patriarchy is based on structures other than the household. Public patriarchy is characterised by women having access to both public and private arenas, but being subordinated in both the realms. The household continues to be a site of patriarchal oppression but it is no longer the main or exclusive arena where women are present. The central feature of subordination in the private form of patriarchy is the complete exclusion of women from the public. Of course, the relations outside the household are crucial in shaping and upholding patriarchy, but women's experiences are privatised, and the beneficiaries in the most immediate sense of this patriarchy are also located within the private sphere.

On the contrary, in the public form of patriarchy, although women are exploited at all levels, they are not excluded from any sphere, and all structures are open to them. Walby describes this as a movement away from individual to a more collective form of appropriation of women. (It is indeed appropriation and not exploitation.) The trend has been to move away from exclusionist to a more segregationist and subordinating strategies. Thus, women are no longer debarred from paid work, and their presence is accepted; only that they are segregated in the lowliest paid jobs. The needs of an expanding economy combined with powerful feminist movements have brought about many changes, but they do not necessarily signal the *end* of patriarchy as much as they suggest a change in the *form* of patriarchy.

In this context, it is clear that one of the most important tasks for feminist scholarship is to outline the various forms and situations in which patriarchy appears in different regions and periods. Hence, many scholars prefer to use the term patriarchies. This enables us to establish the linkages between patriarchy and other structures such as race, class, caste, state and ideologies. Subordination of women might be a feature that characterises most societies, but the extent and the exact form of this subordination varies, determined by the social and cultural environment in which women are placed. Hence, it is important to look at the linkages between gender and culture.

POINTS FOR DISCUSSION

- Do you think your experiences in school and college have reinforced patriarchy? Looking back, can you recount some of the specific ways in which our school and university system might be reinforcing patriarchy?
- It is very difficult to look at one's own family objectively, but do you find any of the assumptions discussed in this chapter working within your immediate context?

REFERENCES

Walby, Sylvia (1997). *Theorizing Patriarchy*. Oxford: Basil Blackwell.

Bhasin, Kamala (1986). *What Is Patriarchy?* New Delhi: Kali for Women.

Geetha, V. (2002). *Gender*. Kolkata: Stree.

7

Gender, Culture and History

In the last chapter, we discussed the material basis of patriarchy, but economic exploitation is only one of the many dimensions of patriarchy. Cultural oppression is far more difficult to understand and theorise. Under colonialism, for example, India experienced a kind of cultural oppression. Indian language and literature, philosophy and art, dress and food, and indeed, all manner of indigenous knowledge systems like medicine, aesthetics or performing arts were considered to be inferior. European system of learning and knowledge were presented as the yardstick against which all other systems were to be evaluated. On the basis of this evaluation, it was declared that the Indian systems were rather suspect and could not be defined as knowledge at all. The parameters for evaluation were European and it was no wonder that the Indian systems of learning and knowledge were rather inadequate. This idea was at the heart of the cultural disempowerment that the Indian people experienced. The British by virtue of being in a dominant position became the arbiters of good taste, refinement, knowledge, learning and aesthetics. Patriarchy in a similar way has systematically disemponered women and their experiences. Uma Chakravarti (2003) in her book *Gendering Caste*, very rightly observes that far more dehumanising than economic oppression has been the cultural oppression experienced by the lower castes in India, especially the women of the lower castes. Those who dominate and control the economy and the material basis of life, also begin to dominate and control the means of producing symbols and their representation. Every culture thrives on the production of these symbols and their appropriate representation. In the context of caste in India, Chakravarti has argued that it is such a symbolic hegemony that allows the oppressor to control the very standards by which their rule is evaluated. In the process, the vision and perspective of the oppressed is completely obliterated, dismissed and ridiculed. The control by the upper caste over all systems of learning and knowledge has meant that they have decided what constitutes legitimate art, music, dance, theatre, philosophy, science, and so on. Lower-caste knowledge of say farming and irrigation and other agricultural practices or their understanding of animals was seen as not worthy of being defined as knowledge at all. The upper castes define, regulate and evaluate learning, knowledge, philosophy and arts. All other attempts at artistic expression, for instance, would at best be patronisingly tolerated as 'folk'. This implied the lack of standards of high art and learning that imbued the cultural expression of the upper caste. In more intolerant instances, alternatives forms of expression would be condemned as sinister and evil.

The relationship between gender and culture under conditions of patriarchy follows a similar pattern. Patriarchy seems to deny women subjectivity, and thereby, dignity and personhood. Historically, women's perspectives have not been heard or represented. They have not had the power to become producers of cultural symbols. Of course, women, like all oppressed groups, have tried to create their own worlds in which they have a measure of power that they use to reinterpret the world around them. Lacking in subjectivity has implied that women are seldom seen as actively involved in the creation of anything meaningful. Their experiences and expressions are considered not worth recording, nor are they considered legitimate. Women, thus, have to learn to fit their experiences and expressions into the framework provided by patriarchy or run the risk of being ridiculed, dismissed or even threatened.

While culture is a significant aspect of feminist historiography, it needs to be clarified that feminist historiography does not subscribe to the idea that women are simply framed by a context; rather the approach calls for a significant reorientation suggesting that gender differences are both, structuring and structured by, the wide network of social relations.

Kumkum Sangari and Sudesh Vaid in their book *Recasting Women* contend that in order to understand the cultural history of women, it is important to see this aspect as being crucially linked with class, and in our context, with colonial economic considerations. Sangari and Vaid do admit that there might be no neat fit between ideological constructs and assumptions, and the ordering of social relations. The fact, however, is that the network of ideas, traditions and symbols intrude upon the labour process; some in a causative way while others serve the purpose of legitimisation. It is obvious that caste and class differences create different patriarchies. The lives of women in India, Sangari and Vaid point out, exist at the interface between caste and class inequality. This is so because management and control of female sexuality is the most important mechanism of controlling women, and maintaining and reproducing social inequality.

CULTURE AND THE CONSTRUCTION OF MASCULINE AND FEMININE

Ideas about what is masculine and what is feminine influence all aspects of social relations. It is through these ideas that gender is represented, and it is thus that a particular culture gets its specific notions about what is masculine and what is feminine. The conventional explanation for these differences turns to biology, differences in the structure of the body, hormones, muscles and genes. The social consequences of these biological differences are what interest theorists of gender. All historical explanations of gender, as V. Geetha has suggested, are agreed upon one fact that notions of masculinity and femininity are not eternal. Instead, they have been elaborated, interpreted, institutionalised and made to appear eternal, the purpose being the justification of subordination of women.

Sylvia Walby (1990) identifies three broad approaches to the understanding of gendered subjectivity—socialisation theory, neo-Freudian psychoanalytic theory and discourse analysis. Socialisation theory argues that masculine and feminine identities are the consequence of a process of socialisation that starts in childhood. This framework defines masculinity as behaviour characterised by assertiveness, and being action-oriented and lively, whereas femininity is conceived as being passive, cooperative and gentle. This approach contends that training in one or the other set of gender attributes starts right at birth, for example, when babies are dressed in pink or blue. Toys, activities, language, levels of boisterousness, television programmes and reading material are carefully chosen and monitored to suit the gender. Girls are encouraged to play with kitchen sets and boys with guns in preparation for their roles in adulthood. The media further reinforces these ideas through its images of women as sexually attractive and glamorous and hence popular; the men are portrayed as successful and powerful individuals. This approach is concerned with the creation of stereotypes in the field of education as well where it is assumed, for instance, that boys would be better suited for the pursuit of science and technology. This reinforces the sexual division of labour with more girls opting for arts and other related streams. This approach holds institutions such as the family, media, and indeed, education guilty for the creation and perpetuation of masculine and feminine subjects.

There is no doubt that this theory is a fitting response to the biological theories that seek to argue that gender differences are an attribute of nature. Through a considerable amount of research, these theorists have been able to demonstrate that it is through a variety of social and sociopsychological processes that girls and boys acquire gendered subjectivity. These theories are, however, limited by their inability to explain how these ideas of what constitutes masculine and feminine in a particular culture get created. Thus, Walby describes socialisation theories as being theories of acquisition of gender and not of its construction, because it does not explain where the content of these notions comes from. In this framework, men and women are seen as being relatively passive in their acquisition of gender identity. As Walby says people are, after all, not 'cultural dopes' and they are more involved in this enterprise than this theory would give space for.

If both masculine and feminine are roles that every culture expects people to fit into, then what really is the problem? Because, after all, even men are being slotted. This observation would not arise if the socialisation theorists could make clear the linkages between masculinity and power, which not all of them do. The other big limitation that this approach suffers from is its inability to deal with variations in the content of gender identity mediated by class, ethnicity, race or caste. As discussed earlier, gender cannot be the only and complete description of conflict in society. Gender does get reinforced by other structures like race, caste or ethnicity. For instance, the experiences of lower-middle-class South Asian women would be obviously very different from that of upper class white women.

In Walby's opinion, this approach is severely limited by its inability to realise that gendered culture does not inhabit the specialised places of media, family or education, but is rather constructed in all areas of social life. For example, small cars are considered to be feminine and four wheel drives masculine. Certain soaps are considered masculine and others feminine; the list could go on and on!

Despite being discredited by most feminists, an attempt has been made by Nancy Chodorow, Juliet Mitchell and some other feminists to rescue certain aspects of Freud's work to understand the process of creation of gendered subjectivity. This framework is described as the neo-Freudian psychoanalytic theory. Chodorow argues that motherhood is the key to our understanding of gender differentiation and of the subordination of women. She values motherhood highly and thinks of it as a rewarding and rich experience, but she points out that it also becomes a trap for adult women—a trap that is not highly valued or rewarded by contemporary society. Girl children, she argues, identify with their mothers and prepare for their future role as mothers; boys, on the other hand, have to forcibly break away from their mothers preparing for a different role in life. This creates in boys the basis for a less nurturing personality. This, for Chodorow, is the basis for gender differentiation. Her solution is very creative and interesting in that she recommends mothering roles for men as well. In her analysis, however, there is no explanation of the social processes that generate such low regard for motherhood.

Juliet Mitchell argues that women's oppression in most cultures is a consequence of the deeply entrenched patriarchal ideology in people's psyche. Across generations, human beings carry memories of patriarchal beliefs and practices. While capitalism does reinforce patriarchy, the latter has its own logic based in culture. Following Freud, Mitchell refers to this as the unconscious. Thus, her prescription is to fight patriarchy on its own terms and not simply as a derivative of capitalism.

Psychoanalytic theories seem to be arguing that unseen processes entrenched in the psyche passed from one generation to another are the basis on which gendered identities are created. While this is a valuable insight, this position seems unable to account for the differences in notions of femininity and masculinity when mediated by social processes and categories . The charge is then of being ahistorical and essentialist.

Discourse analysts see the ideological constructs of patriarchy as being crucial to women's subordination. To understand this, they have analysed language and its use, religion, mythology, cinema and literature as sites of patriarchal discourse. This approach, while providing us with a provocative and insightful framework, has been criticised for its underestimation of economic and political institutions and an exaggerated preoccupation with the world of ideas and their role in creating gendered subjectivity.

Walby argues that gendered subjectivity is created everywhere. In other words, there is no privileged site for the creation of gendered subjectivity, neither early childhood nor sexuality. Thus, she argues that changing gender relations in all sites is the basis for the generation of new norms of femininities and masculinities. It is the struggles over these norms that contribute to our understanding of change.

CHANGES IN FEMININITIES AND MASCULINITIES

While there have been important changes in what is considered masculine or feminine, the fact is that dichotomy still persists. Sylvia Walby's interesting argument is that the notion of femininity is no longer limited to domestic sphere and is today located in a far wider arena. In modern industrial societies, domesticity is no longer seen as the central feature of femininity. Masculinity is less determined by the possession of a dependent wife than it is by the ability to bring in a decent wage. Interestingly, paid work is no longer seen as being antithetical to femininity, but the particular sort of work continues to be a determining factor. Highly technical or very powerful work creates problems for the construction of femininity. Women in such positions can redeem themselves as being feminine if they can establish themselves as happily married women and still better as mothers. Some areas of work such as clerical, secretarial assistance, nursing and so on have undergone a transformation and are perceived as feminine. Today, at least among the middle classes, it is particular sorts of work that are imbued with more ability to bestow masculinity upon its doer than others. Thus, Walby concludes that waged work is no longer an important signifier of masculinity.

Walby then suggests that rather than containment within the domestic sphere being the key to femininity, today, it is sexual attractiveness to men, which is the most important signifier of femininity. While her approach reflects the changes in the West, there are similarities discernable in the experiences of middle-class women in India. It is not just young women who are being defined thus, but even little girls and older women are subjected to this kind of definition. The issue of sexuality does generate a lot of differences. Some theorists of sexuality would like to see the display of women's sexuality as a sign of their resistance while others see it as yet another instance of incorporation into a patriarchal system. Some, of course, see it as simultaneously being both. Fundamentally, though, there is no disputing the fact, as V. Geetha argues, that notions of sexual appeal and beauty are a product of ideas, and opinion, entertained and expressed by men about women. Measures of beauty, she goes on to say, were outlined and framed by the brushes, chisels and pens of men.

How did women become objects for men's imagination, poetry, art and aesthetics? V. Geetha contends that it is, perhaps, a consequence of the power that they wielded over women as fathers, husbands and rulers. Their exclusive access to education and the arts gave them this privilege of defining and expressing their ideas of beauty, grandeur and perfection. This, she denotes as male gaze, that is, the arbiter of all standards in society—not just economic and political, but even cultural and aesthetic.

Women by virtue of being powerless have systematically found themselves in positions that did not permit them to express themselves. This, perhaps, explains why there have been such few women writers, poets or musicians. The norms established by patriarchy appear to be universal. It established its way of seeing things as natural to human beings.

Today, in India for instance, the fashion industry, the glamour and celebrity press, and of course, cinema in a sense represent and embody what V. Geetha characterises as the male gaze. The entire beauty and cosmetic industry, for instance, defines a beautiful woman, and urges all women to approximate those rather impossible standards. No woman is perfect. Even beauty queens need to enhance their appearance with the aid of not only various cosmetics but also plastic surgery.

Education is an interesting arena for observers of changes in the definition of masculinity and femininity. While traditionally women were kept out of education, today, that is no longer the case. Today, education exhibits segregation, with boys dominating maths, physics, engineering and technology. Walby concludes her discussion of gender and culture by saying that we seem to have moved away from justification of difference (in the context of the ideology of masculinities and femininities) to a dissimulative approach that denies the extent of the inequality. This is typical of a dissimulative approach that attempts to disguise the truth. Hence, it deliberately denies the inequality and pretends not to be able to see it. There might be a grudging acceptance of the fact that in the past, women were loudly and proudly kept out of certain spheres of life. This would be followed by the claim that today there are no barriers preventing women but the facts prove that this is far from the truth. What, then, are the barriers that hold women back?

CULTURE, CUSTOM AND RELIGION

Vasudha Dhagamwar in her essay titled 'Obstacles to Empowerment of Women' argues that social pressures and perceptions hold women back. She argues that culture, custom and religion are intertwined in India. Answers to questions like why can't a girl go out late at night for a stroll or plough the field might be answered with 'it is not done amongst us'. Faced with this answer, it is very difficult to challenge such beliefs and practices that, in a certain sense, form the foundation of the identity of specific communities. For most women in India, despite the fact that the identity of being a secular citizen is available, it is the identity conferred upon them by their families that is the most significant and abiding. This identity is controlled and created by putting together elements from culture, custom and religion—elements that determine what it means to be a woman (or a man), and what are the appropriate roles, activities and aspirations for the woman so defined.

In order to establish the linkages between cultural practices and patriarchy, we could turn to Uma Chakravarti's insightful analysis of the relationship between gender and caste in India. Chakravarti quotes Nur Yalman, an anthropologist who described the caste system as central to the Hindu social organisation. Its closed nature helps preserve land, women and ritual quality within. These three are seen as structurally linked, and to preserve this linkage female sexuality needs strict regulation. Purity of the caste, which is crucial for determining inheritance, is thus contingent upon guarding women. Brahminical patriarchy wove together an ideological web of beliefs, festivals, rituals and symbols. All of these reinforced the subservience of women to men, and of lower caste to upper caste. The upper-caste woman is seen as the gateway—literally, the point of entrance into the caste system. So, it was absolutely crucial to regulate her sexuality. This required her compliance, which was created through the powerful ideology of *pativratadharma* and *stridharma*.

In order to justify this control and regulation of women and their sexuality, various myths and stories were invoked. The *Mahabharata*, the *Satapatha Brahmana* or the *Ramayana* are full of accounts of the essentially sinful, greedy and treacherous nature of women. This belief becomes the justification for the control and surveillance of women whose sexuality was exaggerated and portrayed as uncontrolled. The next argument in this ideological web is the supposed contradiction between the innate nature of women (*strisvabhava)* and their basic duty in life (*stridharma*). The innate nature of women, governed as it is by uncontrolled sexuality, is thus in conflict with their duty of fidelity towards their husbands. Chakravarti argues that the entire idea and practice of *pativratadharma* comes up in this context. Wifely codes were internalised by women based upon the notions of an ideal wife created by the ideologues of the society. So successful were they in their attempts that upper-caste wives began to think of chastity and wifely fidelity as the greatest possible expression of their selfhood. Chakravarti believes that the *pativrata* concept is truly a masterstroke of the genius of the Hindu normative order expressed in its cultural values for women. Thus, upper-caste Hindu women derive their ideas of ideal womanhood and wifehood from a network of myths, stories and legends that have a rather unflattering construction of the innate nature of women. The stories and legends teach and guide her to overcome this innate sinfulness and approach the ideal of wifely fidelity.

The cultural institutions and beliefs surrounding the ideology of *pativrata* are described by Uma Chakravarti as one of the most successful ideologies constructed by any patriarchal system, because it resulted in a system in which the women themselves controlled and regulated their own sexuality in the belief that by doing so, they would gain power and respect. A woman who worships her husband as a veritable God is thought to be automatically protected and her chastity guarded. This would bestow powers on her, enabling her to protect herself; not even the evil Ravana could overcome the chaste Sita in the *Ramayana*, thanks to Sita's own powers of chastity and fidelity. Other chaste women in other tales have been able to bring back their dead husbands to life (Sati Savitri) or stay the motion of the Sun (Arundhati).

For the errant woman, there were accounts of women who strayed, if only in thought and that too momentarily, that would have a restraining effect. Stories that justified sons beheading their mothers for the sin of infidelity even in thought consolidated these ideas. (Renuka's head is fell by her son Parasurama as she happens to see a flying gandharva and is struck by his handsome features.) Thus, patriarchy came to be completely naturalised through the aid of a variety of beliefs, customs, legends and festivals. These became an inseparable part of the cultural experiences of upper-caste women.

Following self-regulation, it was the husband who was enjoined to protect and guard his wife and thus the purity of his progeny and caste. Use of force was justified in this regard, and the extended kinsmen also had a role to play in regulating the woman's sexuality. If all this failed, then, of course, the king and the law would intervene. Transgressions by upper-caste women were not unknown but sex with lower-caste men was one of the greatest threats, since it challenged both patriarchy and the caste structure. The law when it intervened was, thus, upholding the authority of both a caste/class state and a particular patriarchal order.

The relationship between caste and gender gives us an insight into the nature of the powerful interaction between the two categories. Some of the most fundamental beliefs and practices of upper-caste society in India are derived out of the notions of Brahminical patriarchy. The cultural ethos and matrix of their lives is inseparable from a particular notion of women and their sexuality. This is only one example, and it would yield even more startling insights, if we were to see how these ideas have adapted and yet survived.

For instance, we could turn to Uma Chakravarti's examination of the students' agitation in the early 1990s against the government's proposal to implement the Mandal Commission's recommendations to extend reservations in government service and educational institutions to members of the Other Backward Castes (OBC). Upper-caste male students from the University of Delhi protested and went on a rampage through the streets of the city. Ironically, the women students (who were obviously upper caste) protested, too. They, however, did so on behalf of their potential husbands, carrying placards that read 'we do not want unemployed husbands'. Clearly they could not even dream of the possibility of marrying employed men from the OBCs. This is an example of the internalisation of one of the central beliefs of Brahminical patriarchy—the belief of restricting marriages to within the caste or subcaste in order to preserve the caste purity. The linkages between cultural beliefs and ideals with a particular construction of gender are indisputable, but each culture would have its historic specificity, and hence, a unique way in which it expresses these notions. Here, we have attempted to establish linkages between caste and gender.

POINTS FOR DISCUSSION

- The connection between food, fasting and chastity might be an interesting point for discussion. Festivals celebrating the wife's devotion to her husband often expect her to observe a rigorous fast.
- In the totally different context of widowhood, the food permitted and the food prohibited for widows might be another point for discussion.
- Any recent film could be discussed in the light of the two chapters that you have read so far.

REFERENCES

Chakravarti, Uma (2003). *Gendering Caste: Through a Feminist Lens*. Kolkota: Stree.

Walby, Sylvia (1990). *Theorizing Patriarchy*. Oxford: Basil Blackwell.

8

Women and Development

The concept of development has been at the centre of many political and academic divides. There is clearly no one accepted definition. The responses to the idea range from enthusiasm and the desire to proselytise, on one hand, to an almost fanatical opposition and a messianic faith in alternatives, on the other. While some of the theories of development focused on growth, others paid greater attention to the distributive aspect. Still others, like the Gandhians for example, are so sceptical of the whole project that they have argued that it is focused too narrowly upon material prosperity and abundance. Unlimited pursuit of wealth and material abundance, they have argued, leads to alienation and violence within the human society and towards nature. Yet others believed that being within the world capitalist system, inequalities of wealth and power would remain a constant feature.

But there was a general consensus in the post–Second World War world that the West had successfully moved forward with development, and the newly independent countries would do well to emulate this path, and build their societies and nations along similar lines. Being fragile, these new nations were advised to follow the path of development—political and economic that had been tried and tested by the West. It was hoped that this would bring in not only material prosperity but also stability, besides freeing the traditionally oppressed sections of these 'backward' societies by integrating them with the modern and 'egalitarian' market forces.

Naila Kabeer argues that much of the development discourse was based on a particular vision of society, economy and the individual. The 'modern man' (who makes up the modern economy) is supposedly endowed with a systematic will determined by rationality. This, in turn, enables him to make free and independent choices. Such a man would display all the qualities essential for a modern market economy to function, that is, risk taking, dynamism and competitive behaviour. Such a man would be the basis of modernisation and development. This description seeks to portray the modern man as the universal man, while in reality this is the man in a specific historical context. A big and important question, however, remains unanswered, 'what is the modern woman like?'

While most theorists of development did not even think about this issue, some who did, pronounced very happy results for women. They argued that with primordial ties weakening and the market becoming a great leveller, women would finally be able to seek their own space. With production shifting out of the family sphere, clear division of labour within the family would now be possible. Women, given their special procreative role could now focus only on duties related to domestic labour. At the same time, they could explore possibilities that the market offered, provided it did not clash with their natural calling as homemakers. The market, characterised as a universal space, would not discriminate against anyone on the basis of ascriptive categories, for it recognised only individuals. Even if women chose not to enter the market, it was argued that the egalitarian and universal values upon which the market was based, would undermine traditional family and authority structures. It was even suggested that the market would finally liberate women and help them discover their personhood by giving them a chance to exercise their rationality.

WOMEN IN DEVELOPMENT (WID)

Welfare and efficiency are the two ends of the spectrum of the discourse on development and women. Of course, something like the empowerment approach is not even acknowledged by most official development thinktanks and agencies. One of the outstanding successes of the WID approach has been to force a shift in official development thinking from welfare to efficiency. The empowerment approach broadly refers to the idea that women should no longer see development as a way of ameliorating their lives but rather as a means through which they can take charge of their lives and initiate meaningful changes.

By the 1970s, it was becoming apparent that none of the promises made to women by defenders of the development discourse were fulfilled. Women in the Third World were not given access to the new technologies or the new productive opportunities. The market, Kabeer argues, did not liberate women from the drudgery of the domestic sphere. The consequences of the supposedly universal market were still not gender-neutral. This was a result of rather sex-specific ways in which women had been brought in. Women in the Third World continued to be addressed basically as occupants of domestic space whose primary role was nurturing and caring. Thus, all the development policies were targeted at the men, and the women constituted the residual section and were relegated into the marginal welfare sector. Kabeer argues that in doing this, a distinction was made by policymakers in the West between mainstream development resources that needed to be directed towards the markets, and the residual resources were transferred through development planning via welfare measures to the marginal and the vulnerable groups, to the Third World as a whole, and to women more specifically.

Dissatisfied with the existing methods, a new way of looking at women in the context of development slowly began to take shape. This new approach came to be referred to as the Women In Development or WID. While the WID approach is a fundamental departure from the conventional development paradigm, it remains within the liberal–individualist framework. Kabeer argues that WID did not mount a critique on the existing development approach; rather it sought to integrate women into it. The WID approach was basically critical of the fact that women had not benefited from development. The WID perspective saw the market as the saviour. However, they contend that planners, governments, and sometimes women themselves, failed to integrate women with the market because of irrational prejudices and discriminatory attitudes. Hence, WID prescribed to women greater and better access to—and integration with—the market. One of the best representatives of this argument has been Boserup's *Women's Role in Economic Development*.

Boserup with her pioneering study laid down the foundations of the WID approach when she argued that variations across sex roles in cultures were the key variables for explaining differences in the status of women across the world. In other words, where women were confined to only reproductive labour, their status is likely to be lower than in societies where they are part of farming and other productive activities. Boserup condemned the attitude of planners who see women as secondary earners. She criticised the existing approach that focused only on training housewives into becoming more efficient housewives and did not impart any professional training to women that would have enabled them to integrate better within the market. Therefore, Boserup made strong recommendations for better designed education for women that would improve their competitiveness and productivity. This approach criticised planners for completely ignoring work that is done within the domestic sphere. This approach insisted that work that is unpaid—subsistence work and childcare—and work in the informal sector should also be accounted.

The question that the WID approach needs to ask—but does not ask—is whether women were kept out of the market only as a result of misinformation and prejudiced thinking, or was it a consequence of deeper institutionalised structures? Did the development process in the Third World bypass women only because of irrational thinking about women? And, of course, can the market bring deliverance?

Some studies argued that planners, because of their prejudices, were not able to go beyond offering special projects to women. Women were consistently seen as illogical and irrational, and hence were not offered an entry into the market that operated on the basis of logic and rationality. Women were invited to enter residual welfare efforts only when growth that remained the overriding aim of the development initiative had been achieved. Needless to add, these efforts would be the first to be axed in times of austerity. Women entered these projects without any agency, and as mere clients. On the contrary, the WID approach cannot hide its enthusiasm for—and confidence in—the ability of the market to work as a great leveller and as a catalyst for ushering in equality. The approach agued that although women are rational economic agents, they are severely constrained by faulty and prejudiced planning processes.

WID: A CRITIQUE

Boserup has argued for a shift in the orientation of development initiatives from 'welfare for women' to 'equality for women'. The development process, it was argued, was adversely impacted because of women's absence. Development needed women and keeping women out of it in the Third World would be a costly mistake. This argument finally clinched the issue for the WID advocates. The development agencies understood the need for efficiency and were thus persuaded to review their policies. The arguments of WID came to imbue the policies of national and international development thinking.

Of course, today, this stress on efficiency in the context of neo-liberal interpretations of efficiency have produced results that WID advocates might not be comfortable with. Structural adjustment programmes in many Third World countries have forced a cutback in public expenditure. Neo-liberal economics and the WID focus on women's role as economic agents have created a gender trap for women. Compelled to be part of the market in order to ameliorate their life chances, women are increasingly becoming part of the market in the Third World. However, with less purchasing power, they find themselves unable to pay for the services that would reduce their domestic labour. Without being able to purchase these services they find it difficult to enter the market and improve their purchasing power. Within the WID approach, there seems to be no escape route for women caught in this trap.

The WID approach has several inadequacies, but there is no denying that it ushered in a new way of looking at women in the context of development. Old stereotypes were challenged and most governments were obliged to set up some kind of machinery for the advancement of women. Thus, WID has scored many victories, albeit largely of a symbolic nature.

Naila Kabeer in her book *Reversed Realities* writes that the WID approach may actually be described as liberal feminism writ global. Thus, all the limitations of liberal feminism are bound to haunt WID. It shares with liberal feminism its enthusiasm for universal notions of human beings. Following the best liberal traditions, it is committed to ideas of universalism, egalitarianism and individualism. In this paradigm, all individuals are considered to be equal by virtue of the fact that they possess rationality. Rationality is to be used for making free and independent choices. It is thus that individuality is affirmed and the individual experiences autonomy. All of this is possible only within a market system and the WID approach argues that it is irrational and unfair to keep women out of it, since women, too, are individuals endowed with rationality that needs to be expressed through the act of making free and autonomous choices. This, the advocates of this approach believe, would be possible only through the market and not if women are relegated to the domestic sphere alone. The approach argued that the development discourse till now has constrained this ability severely and thus prevented women from expressing their individuality. This is a grave crime in the liberal universe. Thus, they argued for similar opportunities to be given to women, for, after all, both women and men are individuals possessing rationality.

In doing this, the WID approach sought to move away from the traditional theories that justified social and other inequalities among men and women on the basis of biological differences. It, however, glossed over these differences and was guilty in the end of being indifferent, as Alison Jagger has argued, to the social consequences of biology.

Typically, liberal feminism seeks to focus on the mind rather than the body. Liberal philosophies tend to devalue the labour and time devoted to the fulfilment of biological needs. In this scheme, time spent on cooking, cleaning, nurturing children and caring for the old and the infirm would simply be seen as part of the domestic sphere *governed by instincts*, and thus, closer to nature rather than being part of the social structure. Historically, in most societies, women have been assigned these tasks. These are seen as part of the natural role that women have as care givers, and thus, it is not seen as labour. As opposed to this, the public sphere is supposedly *governed by rationality*. The WID approach accepted this dichotomy and hence did not direct any resources into the private and domestic realm, since this is conceived of as part of nature and hence not amenable to policy intervention of any kind. Policy initiatives have to be directed at restructuring the public sphere. Women need to be made a part of this sphere. In arguing this way, WID overlooked the need for restructuring of the private sphere. Obviously, the approach did not see the interconnection between the private and the public sphere. It has failed to recognise that the limitations that women face in the public sphere are intrinsically related to their roles within the private sphere. This approach expected changes in the public sphere without reviewing the private sphere. This is one of the most important shortcomings of the WID approach.

Yet another criticism made by Kabeer against the WID approach is that it overlooks the implications of gender division of labour for how women and men perceive their needs and interests, and even their ability to act as rational economic agents capable of maximising their goals. It has often castigated planners and policy formulators for biased provision of incentives that results in men and women responding to the same economic initiatives very differently. Kabeer suggests that the answer to this problem might actually be found in the gendered construction of rationality and agency itself. Men can behave like disembodied rational agents because they have women to take care of all their bodily needs, and because of this, women experience a complete identification with the bodily sphere. Hence, despite similar opportunities and avenues that the market might provide to both men and women, the latter seem unable to make full use of it. This is most definitely not a result of irrational and incompetent policies but rather a consequence of the specific way in which relations between men and women are structured. The WID worldview failed to consider the question of male power as a property of gender relations, and reduced it simply to a set of ill informed prejudices.

Thus, Kabeer holds the mind–body dualism within the liberal paradigm to be responsible for the WID influenced policies' exclusive focus on the sphere of production and complete oversight of the sphere of reproduction. In a context, where men dominate the former sphere and women almost exclusively inhabit the latter, such policies could not make any substantial difference. In fact, very often they ended up reinforcing the status quo for women.

Kabeer examines the WID approach's celebration of women's potential as producers. This approach argues that women's absence from the market leads to grave inefficiency in the allocation of resources. This argument comes from the realisation that the market did not value women's reproductive role and related activities. WID sought to establish that women could be as good as men in the market, but there was no reciprocal attempt to establish that men, too, could be competent in the sphere of nurturing and care giving activities.

On the basis of the critique of WID offered by Kabeer, we can conclude that WID recognised women as agents and not as mere recipients of development. However, the understanding of their agency was premised on an incomplete and rather truncated view of the lives of women. The WID approach failed to integrate the role of production and reproduction in the lives of women.

WID came in for criticism from the Third World women's groups. They were disappointed by the fact that the WID approach did not take a critical look at the issue of political and economic structures within which women were located. Thus, the structural inequalities of the development process itself were never addressed. It was only ill informed planning that came in for criticism. The recommendation made by Boserup and other WID advocates was to open up educational and training opportunities for women in the Third World. This suggestion was based on their basic evaluation of the modernisation process as positive. This and other similar suggestions came in for increasing criticism from the Third World writers and activists who likened this to 'treating cancer with band aid'.

Further, within the WID perspective there was no acknowledgement of the basically unequal world order. Hence, the realisation that any development initiative in this context would only lead to reinforcement of the existing inequalities was absent. Critics pointed out that international development programmes routinely further the interests of powerful imperialist states that were part of these donor agencies and did nothing by way of alleviating the sufferings of the poor in the Third World.

DAWN, a network of activists, policymakers and researchers from the Third World, observed that women from the Third World were caught between their reluctance to separate the struggle against women's subordination from other struggles against poverty, neo-colonialism and racism, on one hand, and their unwillingness to postpone the struggle against women's subordination to some distant future, on the other. DAWN also drew attention to the fact that even within the first world, voices of racially and ethnically marginalised women was hardly ever heard, and hence, this predicament was not unique to the Third World.

In this context, we could turn to the criticism of the WID approach made by the dependency feminists. They saw sexual inequalities as part of a larger system of inequality essential for the capitalist process of accumulation to succeed. They denounced the development paradigm itself as ideologically loaded, and for suggesting that a progressive and inevitable improvement awaited all peoples who followed the prescribed path. These scholars sought to make systematic linkages between unequal structures at the international, national and household levels. One of their most forceful arguments has been that women's domestic labour, far from being isolated within the private sphere, is actually the basis for the subsidisation of the process of capital accumulation. The Women and Development approach (WAD), while providing a sharp critique of the development perspective, continued like the standard marxist approaches to privilege class contradictions over all others.

Disagreement with this privileging of class over gender but general agreement with the dependency approach led a group of German feminists led by Maria Mies to argue that men as well as capital benefited from women's relegation to unpaid subsistence work. They argued that women's position in contemporary society is a consequence of a long and established system of men's domination over women, nature and colonies. Within this approach, then, there can be no sympathy for the WID paradigm, for they see the discourse on development as an extension of what has been described as capitalist patriarchy. Mies and others see this is as a result of the relentless march of patriarchy in history, capitalism being only its latest manifestation.

Her suggestion, therefore, is to create an alternative society based on feminist understanding of labour where human beings would have a relationship with nature that is direct, sensuous and unmediated by technology. It would also require rejection of all forms of control by the state and by males over the reproductive capacities of women, and finally men's participation in nurturing and subsistence work so that they, too, can experience the unity of mind and body. Such a strategy requires global changes premised upon global solidarity among women, which at the moment is a dream that few would even dare to admit to. This approach, as Jackson and Pearson (1998) have shown, does not ground women in the concrete context of economic, social and political relations, and is based rather on a free floating naturalistic perspective which tends to equates women's realities with natural futures.

GENDER ANALYSIS IN DEVELOPMENT (GAD): BEYOND WID AND WAD

Development policy has experienced many changes from the 1970s to the contemporary times. In the 1970s, the focus was on the ability of state agencies to bring about transformation. From the 1980s, there has been much rethinking and the WID perspective, while being appreciated for its insistence on incorporating women into the development process, is no longer acceptable, primarily because of its inability to address the basically unequal gender relations that inhibit the success of any programme. The new position which came to be called Gender Analysis in Development (GAD) insisted on the need to start-off from a feminist position examining the structure of subordination of women in a specific societal context, thereby avoiding the trap of universalism or essentialism. This approach was informed by a feminist understanding of key institutions like the family, the market and the economy.

From the 1980s, we discern a shift away from the state and an increasing enthusiasm for non-governmental organisations. The need for greater participation in the development processes was celebrated by people who would be beneficiaries of the process. Yet another criticism that was made of conventional wisdom on development and women was the tendency of 'white men saving brown women from brown men', as Gayatri Chakravarti Spivak put it. In other words, the perception of the beneficiaries has become rather belatedly central to the development discourse. The GAD approach for a while seemed to be able to satisfy all expectations.

The GAD approach implies analysing the forms and links that gender relations take, and the links between them and other wider relations in society. Lise Østergaard votes for this approach in her book, *Gender and Development*, for she believes that this approach makes it possible to distinguish the biologically founded sexual differences between men and women from the culturally determined roles assigned to them in different societies. She believes that the concept of WID is concrete and could lead to marginalising women as a species with inherited handicaps, whereas GAD is abstract and opens up for the realisation of women's productive potentials in development. In the WID approach, feminists were quick to realise that the parameters were already given by the patriarchal structures and principles of development, but a shift in the argument to GAD implied that there would be no givens and women could fashion their own understanding of development based on their needs. The Institute of Development Studies at the University of Sussex has been at the forefront of developing this new approach, and has pioneered much of the theoretical and conceptual research in this field. Anne Whitehead from this institute defined the concept of gender. It was clear from their analysis that no study of women and development would start from the point of view that the problem is women; rather it has to acknowledge that the problem is specifically the relations between men and women. These relations are often not harmonious, and these conflicts have a bearing on development and need to be analysed and studied.

It is, indeed, a measure of the success of the GAD approach that today, almost all international agencies and governments have accepted the need for gender awareness. This awareness is incorporated into all phases of the project cycle—from the identification of a development project, budget allocation and operation, and of course, the recruitment of appropriately trained staff. Collection of data relevant to gender concerns on a consistent basis and documentation is also accepted as being vital for the success of this approach.

In the 1990s, 'mainstreaming' has become the dominant theme in GAD. Mainstreaming involves setting up procedures and mechanisms within organisations, particularly government and public institutions to take account of gender issues at all stages of policymaking, programme designing and implementation. This has not been without its critics. Sally Baden and Anne Marie Goetz have argued that there has been a tendency to strip the relational content of gender based on power and ideology, and to use it merely in a reductionist way. They warn against the danger of delinking the investigations of gender issues from a feminist transformatory project. They go on to point out that quantitative expertise of male economists on gender is fast gaining ground as the discourse becomes more technocratic, and the qualitative feminist research on similar themes runs the risk of being devalued.

The feminists of the developing countries are deeply suspicious of this attempt at mainstreaming. They have argued that this leads to gender becoming comfortably 'institutionalised'. It is reduced to a mere descriptive category losing its ability to be employed as the platform from which to raise questions about power.

Within the GAD approach there is, thus, an acceptance that the problem is not just women but the nature of the relationship between women and men, leading to the subordination of women. Thus, today in Jackson and Pearson's opinion, there is an increasing acceptance of the desirability of accepting gender as a development goal of agencies and policy makers fusing within development policy, planning and research; this, as a consequence of the shift from the WID approach to the GAD approach. This shift in the approach would be viable only if it simultaneously engages with the dynamics of accumulation, globalisation and polarisation in their totality, and not in a piecemeal and reactive way. The failure to do so could lead to unexamined positions that become part of the received wisdom within the gender and development theme. For instance, wage employment was seen as the best method of dissolving gender asymmetries. Such an analysis needs to be nuanced in the context where the majority of the women are being drawn into semi-skilled labour of an exploitative nature. Such employment can hardly be expected to develop women's consciousness; on the contrary, this kind of employment turns out to be quite inimical to women's interests. The conflation of employment with empowerment is, thus, rather simplistic.

Padmini Swaminathan criticises the ulterior motives—both at the national and international level—that seem to be guiding women's education and employment programmes. The standard wisdom has been that education plays a key role in changing women's status and behaviour. It is credited with bringing down fertility rates, and thereby, controlling populations. As argued famously by Amartya Sen, it is assumed that processes like education and employment would generate greater agency for women, leading to their well-being and help them to take reasoned decisions about matters like fertility among a range of other possibilities. On the contrary, falling fertility rates could be linked to the logic of the male dominated family system, in which low fertility is seen as economically rational, and thus, not necessarily a consequence of increased female autonomy which is itself supposed to be a consequence of women's education.

Swaminathan is arguing that women's education and employment policies are often framed by the desire to control fertility, and thereby, population; and in the process, facilitate a cutback on community health projects. Educating women, it is argued, brings down infant mortality, thus compensating for the absence of medical facilities. The point that she wishes to make is that it is economic and demographic concerns rather than any concern for the enhancement of women's autonomy that guide these efforts. Swaminathan accepts that education and employment may bring about change, but she argues it has to be placed in the context of a whole range of information regarding the increasing 'violence of development' directed against women.

Swaminathan, in her study of increased work participation rates of women in certain districts of Tamil Nadu in South India, has demonstrated that this is rather disconcertingly related to a high percentage of female children and adolescents who are not attending schools. Thus, a high WPR (work participation rate) for women is not automatically a cause for celebration. We need to place this data in the context of the specific ways in which relations between women and men are constituted within a particular economic and political framework. The plea therefore is to go beyond social and demographic indicators, and try and understand the motivations behind the change and how it affects women and their relationship with men and other structures in society.

In the context of globalisation, thus, efficiency is valued above everything else. Poor women, especially in the Third World countries, are seen as efficient managers of limited resources, and hence, good subjects for governance. This is the reason for global agencies' and lending bodies' willingness to align with women. The nation-state—worryingly for women, especially in the Third World societies—is no longer the most important economic actor. The pride in the nationalist market has been replaced by the frenzied worshipping at the altar of global consumerism. This encourages unbridled individualism. Lure of the global market, focus on efficiency above everything else and marginalisation of the nation-state are, indeed, very challenging issues in the context of the debate on women and development in India. In a surprising turn of events, international aid and 'development' agencies have incorporated a concern and commitment to 'grassroots' and to gender in particular. They look at women as ideal subjects amenable to efficient governance.

Thus, despite promising to focus on unequal relations of power between men and women, the term gender has within the GAD approach also been employed in a rather simplistic way. It has failed to address the issues of power, conflict and larger social, cultural and political features that control women's lives. This lacuna has led grassroots level activists to mount a strong critique of the GAD framework. Cecile Jackson has suggested that the instrumental interest in women as the means to achieve development objectives, for instance poverty reduction, may ultimately undermine GAD. GAD stresses on the poverty of women as the primary justification for development initiatives designed to improve the position of women. Gender, it seems, has fallen into the poverty trap. Jackson and many others are, today, arguing that poverty cannot serve as a proxy for the subordination of women. In other words, anti-poverty programmes cannot automatically be expected to improve the subordinate position of women. In fact, in the context of subordination of women, such programmes might produce results that are rather alarming. Assimilation of gender into the standard development practices and policy formulation has reduced gender to a variant of poverty problems. Such an instrumentalist approach characterises the understanding of major development agencies. The justification for paying attention to gender is the belief that this, in turn, would facilitate other development objectives rather than being an end in itself. Gender concerns are brought on board because they are understood to be consistent with other development concerns, like poverty reduction. For all this, woman are seen as offering good and effective means.

Projects such as the Grameen Bank in Bangladesh have often been cited as a successful example of tackling gender and poverty in an effective and synergistic manner. Goetz, however, in her study of this project has concluded that although the loans are disbursed to women, they are of limited use to women because the loans enter a gendered space—the society and the household—where women, being subordinate, lose control of the loans.

Gender can be rescued from the poverty trap only by recognising the need for poverty-independent gender analysis. Jackson has explained this to mean the recognition that anti-poverty policies are not necessarily appropriate for tackling gender issues since the subordination of women is not caused by poverty alone. In not doing this, GAD would be unable to focus on non-poor women. It has to be reiterated that women who are not poor also face a number of problems that are a consequence of their subordinate position in society.

BOX 8.1

A Short History of Grameen Bank

The origin of Grameen Bank can be traced back to 1976 when Professor Muhammad Yunus, Head of the Rural Economics Program at the University of Chittagong, launched an action research project to examine the possibility of designing a credit delivery system to provide banking services targeted at the rural poor. The objectives were to extend banking facilities to poor men and women, eliminate the exploitation of the poor by moneylenders, create opportunities for self-employment for the vast multitude of unemployed people in rural Bangladesh, and bring the disadvantaged, mostly the women from the poorest households, into an organisational format that they could understand and manage, thereby freeing them from the trap of low income, low savings and low investment, and move them towards more savings by injecting credit and generating more savings. The rural poor, whom it serves, own the Grameen Bank today. Borrowers of the Bank own 90 per cent of its shares, while the remaining 10 per cent is owned by the government. Today, the bank reaches out to five million borrowers in Bangladesh without any collateral. At Grameen Bank, credit is a cost-effective weapon to fight poverty and it serves as a catalyst in the overall socio-economic development. Microcredit is the extension of small loans to entrepreneurs too poor to qualify for traditional bank loans. It has proven to be an effective and popular measure in the ongoing struggle against poverty.

CONCLUSION

Economic growth could be useful for human societies if it can transcend the obsession with statistical growth indicators to embrace issues like health and well-being. Unfortunately, it seems that we need to make a choice between development guided entirely by market rationality on one hand, and guided by commitment to human well-being on the other. In the latter approach, Naila Kabeer points out that activities geared towards assuring health and well-being for all would be seen as productive, regardless of whether such activities are going on within the personalised space of the family, the commercialised context of the market or the bureaucratised context of state production. Markets would not be the only source of 'value'. Such an approach, Kabeer suggests, would promote both gender and class equity. According to this approach, poor women could be the key actors in the development process by the virtue of their contribution to human survival and well-being. Of course, the adoption of such an approach requires a complete change in perspective; in fact, more than change it requires a reversal of priorities. Unlike in the 1980s, when there was total distrust of the state, and neo-liberal agendas controlled all efforts, today, there is an increased interest in the human development aspect of development.

This, Kabeer argues, is a far more hospitable context for a reversal of priorities than the earlier neo-liberal one. In such a context, the need is to fight for policies that go beyond the market, and make room for policy approaches designed to equalise access to market opportunities as well as to welfare provisions, thus enabling the social management of the market.

As described by Kabeer, a different notion of gender equity is possible within this reversed hierarchy; a notion grounded in the interdependence of people, resources and activities. It is hoped that this would lead to a revision of the false dichotomy between welfare and efficiency. In the predominant discourse, recipients of state welfare are seen as failed citizens passively living off the state's resources. On the contrary, if care giving and nurturing activities are valued as much as the production of material resources, then the provision of welfare services would not be seen as wasteful expenditure but as complementary to development goals. Such an approach would free women to pursue goals and options rather than impose a predetermined set of life choices upon them. Gender equity would require that welfare be seen as complementary to the idea of efficiency and not as opposed to it.

An approach based on equality of opportunity would not suffice because all opportunities are institutionalised into structures that have evolved in a gendered way. The typical economic agent is assumed to be unencumbered by bodies, families and sexual identities. The issues related with sexual harassment at the workplace, separate toilets, facilities for breastfeeding, and so on, surface only when women join the workforce. These might require the creation of special provisions for women, which is not in keeping with the abstract economic agent that much of the thinking on growth and development has worked with. Thus, arguments for gender equity to go beyond equal opportunity require the transformation of basic rules, hierarchies and practices of public institutions. The conventional development paradigm assumes equal, free and rational individuals as engaged in economic processes. Feminist evaluation of these approaches remind us that individuals are not abstract but are grounded in a gendered society, and the political and economic structures of the society would also be gendered. Development, therefore, cannot be understood in a gender-neutral way; indeed, such an attempt would reinforce the existing inequalities.

In this context, thus, any discussion of women's political participation becomes a rather contentious issue. The question, that must be asked, is why are women being encouraged to take part in active politics? Is it because they are seen as safe and manageable, as agents who would effectively translate the economic goals of a particular regime into reality? On the other hand, there is an understanding that women have for long been marginalised in society and their voices have not been heard. Women need to challenge this marginalisation and this calls for more involvement and participation in politics. This would hopefully challenge the existing power structures that keep out the women and their interests.

POINTS FOR DISCUSSION

- The human development reports can be an interesting take-off point for further discussions in the light of this chapter.
- Eco-feminist evaluation of the development paradigm and its limitation could be the topic of yet another stimulating discussion.

SELECT BIBLIOGRAPHY

Jackson, Cecile and Ruth Pearson (eds) (1998). *Feminist Visions of Development*. London: Routledge.

Jagger, Alison (1983). *Feminist Politics and Human Nature*. Lanham, MD and London, UK: Rowman and Littlefield.

Kapadia, Karin (ed.) (2002). *The Violence of Development*. New Delhi: Kali for Women.

Moghadam, Valentine M. (ed.) (1996). *Patriarchy and Economic Development*. Oxford: Clarendon Press.

Østergaard, Lise (ed.) (1992). *Gender and Development*. London: Routledge.

Saunders, Kriemild (ed.) (2002). *Feminist Post-Development Thought*. London: Zed Books.

9

The Issue of Women's Political Participation and Representation in India

PARTICIPATION AND REPRESENTATION: SOME THEORETICAL ISSUES

Participation and representation are both words that are central to the vocabulary of modern democratic politics. They, however, have a long history and did not have the nearly universal connotation that they have today. Most political systems today claim to make both participation and representation possible. And interestingly, most of them have also to contend with groups and interests that protest their non-representation and their inability to participate. Any credible democracy, today, would immediately respond to these demands and try to remedy the situation. The methods vary, but are an acknowledgement of the fact that in order to be taken seriously as a democracy it is important to ensure participation and representation to the widest possible groups.

The idea of representation goes a long way back in time; indeed, to one of the earliest liberals in the seventeenth century who argued for limited governments based on the principle of representation. This was none other than the English philosopher John Locke. Of course, when he talked about representation, he had in mind only property-owning men. In Locke's understanding it was only men who were individuals, for he believed that women were naturally born into subjection. Hence, just as the commonwealth commanded obedience of all individuals who consented to its sovereign power, women would consent to the power of their husbands within the family. Thus, it was clear that the concept of individuality did not extend to women and was limited only to men. Therefore, the questions of representation and participation were dealt within the liberal framework with complete disregard to women and their needs.

The Greeks were perhaps the earliest people to talk about democracy, but in their scheme there was no place for either slaves or women; both were the property of the adult Greek male citizen. Many centuries later, when talk of democracy was revived, albeit in a different context, liberals could talk very easily about the connections between ideas of equality and democracy, and yet not see the contradiction in their practice that kept women firmly out of this space. The obvious implication was that women were not equal and that they did not possess rationality. So, while liberals rejected the idea of a sovereign monarch, the husband's sovereignty over the wife was accepted as natural.

It was only by the nineteenth century that women in Europe started organising themselves and fighting for an extension of democratic rights. For a long time, the entire discourse of democracy was conducted as though women were absent. This oversight was not even noticed by most. Still others would justify this absence on grounds of women's general unworthiness. The task then is rather challenging for those who take the universal claims of democracy seriously. As Anne Phillips (1991) says, old concepts need to be rethought and politics itself needs to be reconceptualised without the blind spots of gender and democracy.

Karl Marx, while appreciating the universal claims of liberal democracy based on individualism and egalitarianism, has in a different context, been critical of its limitations. The proletariat in the capitalist society, he pointed out, was not part of the democratic institutions supposedly based on universal principles of participation and representation. He argued that this limited its democratic credentials. He believed that the proletariat, as bearers of new values would bring in a new perspective, and thereby transform politics. Anne Phillips finds a similar argument within feminism about the need for women's participation and representation, while also protesting the injustice of silencing such a big group within society.

Feminism has undoubtedly challenged the Marxist claims of class being the primary contradiction in society. Simultaneously, the Enlightenment credo of Universalism and Humanism has also come under scrutiny. The principle of certainity on which eighteenth and nineteenth century European thinking was based seems rather naïve in the current context. Heterogeneity and difference are the new ideas that have powerfully challenged the enlightenment ideas of Universalism and Humanism. The idea of the disembodied individual who is central to the liberal theory has come in for particular criticism. Liberal philosophy is based on the idea of abstract individuals who are equal irrespective of identities like sex, caste or race. On the contrary, a new conception of individuality that is not unitary, but embodied and sexually differentiated has become more acceptable.

These new ideas see the conventional assumptions of the non-gendered, abstract citizenship on which modern ideas of democracy, participation and representation are based, as privileging the male. By ignoring gender, conventional structures and practices of democracy have reinforced the predominance of the historically dominant group—men—in society. This is possible because of a supposed dichotomy between the public and the private. Politics is identified with the public sphere occupied by men while women occupy the private sphere, which is out of bounds for politics. Politics based on this dichotomy can never be truly participatory or representative, for it would keep women and their specific concerns and interests out, identified as they are with the private sphere. Anne Phillips has persuasively argued for the need for developing representative mechanism that explicitly acknowledge gender differences and gender inequality, and thus, ensure a new proportionality between the two sexes in those arenas within which political decisions are made. She simultaneously argues for the reordering of relationships between public and private spheres. Underlying these suggestions is her hope that this would finally create a world where the public and the private would no longer be divided on a gendered basis, a world where men and women would be equally responsible in both the spheres.

Liberal democracy finds any suggestions of affirming differences among individuals a difficult enterprise, because it is based on the fundamental principle of equality of all individuals on the basis of rationality that guides them in the making of independent choices. Within this framework, it is inconvenient to think of groups of people with similar interests, let alone translate this idea into institutionalised practice. On the other hand, there is the realisation that no democracy can conduct itself based on the pretence that the major and continuing divisions in society do not exist. Yet, despite this recognition, Anne Phillips for instance, feels that democracy is lessened if it treats people only in their identities as women or men, Dalit or upper caste, Hindu or Muslim, and so on. However, in this context, it needs to be pointed out that in postcolonial societies of Asia and Africa, the idea of democracy itself emerged in the context of anti-colonial struggles based not on the individual but on group identities such as religion, caste or ethnic groups.

Today, most liberal democracies have evolved a system of government based on universal adult franchise with periodic elections in the hope that those elected would represent the interests of the electorate. The claim of being the representative has been challenged for being rather limited and not fully accountable; after all, elections take place only every four or five years. By the 1960s, both in Europe and in America, there was a considerable amount of rethinking about the democratic claims of the existing liberal democracies based on the idea of representation. In many of these societies, this was a time to review some of their most fundamental institutions, like family, sexuality, race relations, and so on. It was felt that participation in a fuller manner was essential to boost the democratic claims of the existing systems of government; representation came to be seen in Anne Phillips words as a 'pretty dubious affair'. The alternative that was being offered was increased participation by people and not just the passive act of voting. They advocated popular control in everyday life. This version of democracy has been described as participatory democracy and is based on the idea that democracy should guide every aspect of our lives and not just the formal institutions of the state; thus, enabling people to take part in decision making at all levels. This would obviously challenge the existing dichotomy between the public and the private.

Most liberal democracies, however, when they talk of participation, do not mean it in the above sense; they are rather referring to the safer and more manageable alternative of representation. Liberal democracies have trouble even with the idea of representation that is far less threatening that participation. For instance, as Anne Phillips observes, most liberal democracies have remained resistant to any substantial representation of women and even in Western democracies the numbers of women in the representative bodies remains rather low. This is true of India as well.

In most democracies, women have enjoyed at least formal political equality for some time now. Of course, even this was the result of fierce struggles. They have the rights to vote as well to be elected. Despite this, the actual number of women participating in politics is very low. Here, it should be mentioned that there is an opinion that holds that it is futile to hope for anything different till time when the social and sexual relations in society change.

Women's under-representation in politics is worrying, especially when liberal democracy makes such a neat correlation between democracy and representation. Those who have been arguing for a greater degree of representation by including hitherto ignored groups are often asked to look at the absurdity of their position. They argue that representative democracy cannot produce a perfect reflection of society, of all the groups and interest within it. This ignores the fact that obstacles in the way of being elected are as unfair as the denial of the right to vote.

Explanations for women's relative invisibility in politics are many. Women are socialised into considering politics as an activity that is alien to them. Then, of course, there is the very obvious fact of women singularly tied down by the responsibilities of home management and care for the children and the old. This makes it rather difficult for them to be committed to a fulltime career in politics. The hostile attention from the media and the locker room camaraderie shared by men in politics act as further obstacles. In many Nordic countries interestingly, this issue has been resolved; but in the United Kingdom (UK), the United States of America (USA) and France, this issue continues to be debated. In our own country, this is a far from resolved issue.

PARTICIPATION AND REPRESENTATION IN POLITICS IN INDIA

Leela Kasturi in her paper 'Indian Women in the Political Process' has evaluated the history of Indian women's involvement with politics since independence up till contemporary times. She refers to a UNESCO seminar on 'Participation of Women in Political Life', where women activists and researchers defined politics to include all social relations based on power, and where this power is used to control and regulate people's behaviour, beliefs and attitudes and, of course, to control and regulate resources. Thus, it is based on an understanding of politics that includes every kind of issue, including those of everyday life, and indeed, of survival itself. Collective action by the powerless, challenging those in power is the stuff of politics. Women have always participated in such actions, but their participation has mostly gone unrecorded.

By the late nineteenth century, social reform movements were beginning to show effect, and the presence of women in the public sphere was increasing. Around the same time, women began to get involved in the nationalist campaign, although they met with stiff resistance from men. In the 1889 session of the Congress party, women delegates made their presence felt. It was at this session of the Indian National Congress (INC) that, perhaps, a woman spoke for the first time. The disappointing fact, however, is that the woman who spoke merely presented the vote of thanks! But this was an important beginning. By early twentieth century, active steps were being taken by many nationalist groups, especially in Bengal, to woo women. Middle-class nationalist women formed support groups for the movement and often contributed their jewellery. Women's education came to be focused upon, especially in the context of their role and responsibilities as mothers. By the 1920s, attention gradually shifted towards the nationalist movement and a few all India women's organisations were set up around this time. By the 1920s, there were two clearly identifiable streams of thought on the issue of women and their participation in political life. The first position emerged from the traditional position that women in their role as mothers have a very crucial role to play in the context of nation building, and hence, their rights must be recognised to strengthen their position in society. The other view was that women like men had capacities, needs and desires that need to be fulfilled and this requires them to have rights. The 1920s also saw a recognition of women as workers and their special problems. Among a plethora of organisations and groups that were set up around this time, the All India Women's Conference in 1926 remains most significant. It continues to this day and has its headquarters in New Delhi, but is far removed from concerns of the contemporary feminist movement of India. By this time, the Gandhian movement was gaining momentum, and the Gandhian idea of self-help appealed to the women's movement that was gaining ground.

Meanwhile, the nationalist movement was gaining in strength and there was some confusion amongst the activist women regarding the reconciliation of need for social reform, on one hand, and the nationalist agenda, on the other. While women joined the salt Satyagraha and the civil disobedience movement in large numbers, there was always the unfinished task of fighting for women's education, health and rights within the family, and so on. It seemed often that focussing on one could derail them from their pursuit of the other.

By the 1920s, however, there was a realisation that the two are inextricably linked to one another. Women responded to Gandhi's call for civil disobedience very enthusiastically. Madhu Kishwar has seen this as a consequence of Gandhi's attempt to give women a new dignity and confidence that transformed them from passive objects to active agents of change and reform. Gandhi undoubtedly legitimised women's participation in public activities, but this extension was based on traditional upper-caste Hindu patriarchy and its conceptions of womanhood and womanly virtues. Radha Kumar suggests that he always took care to limit the role women would play in politics rather than allow for its extension. Kumar makes an interesting argument when she says that Gandhi turned the private area of the family into a public domain by making it a site for social change. On the other hand, he clearly disapproved of any further expansion of women's role. For instance, in the Swadeshi movement he emphasised the woman's duty to spin the charkha at home and ensure that she and her children dressed in Khadi. Thus, the nationalist woman was confined to the house.

Women in pre-independence India thus participated in both the national and women's movements. Elite women (the earliest presidents of the All India Women's Conference, for instance, were mostly Maharanis from the royal families) campaigned for legislative actions regarding women's education, political rights, marriage and property. Simultaneously, they focused upon the socio-economic reasons for the subordination of women. For instance, the rights of women workers, especially the question of their wages, health and sanitation facilities for women, and the lack of maternity benefits. They also engaged in welfare activities. Many of them were committed to the idea of equality and never let it go out of their agenda. They were, thus, not satisfied with the call for women's upliftment. In fact, as early as 1931, the Congress party at its Karachi session committed itself to a vision of Indian citizenship based on equality irrespective of caste, creed and sex.

Many years before independence, in 1939, Jawaharlal Nehru, as the Chairman of the National Planning Committee, appointed several sub-committees. One of the sub-committees examined women's role in a planned economy. Among the plethora of issues discussed in the report was the issue of women's presence in employment. One of the suggestions made was to have a certain amount of reservations to favour women. This suggestion was turned down by the sub-committee, not just in the context of employment, but as a principle itself. This opposition, therefore, extended to the principle of reservation in the electoral process also. This rejection was based on the idea that women and men should be given equal opportunities and should, therefore, compete on equal terms. It was hoped that with independence, legislations based on equal opportunities and freedoms to men and women would go a long way in addressing the issue of marginalisation of women in the public arena.

The twentieth century witnessed a remarkable challenge to the traditional role and image of the Indian woman in the wake of the national movement. The first stage of women's movement, thus, fought for equality and equal opportunity for women as individuals. The belief rested on the assumption that with equal opportunities, women would be able to overcome their subordination.

After nearly two decades of independence, in the 1970s, it was time for stocktaking and the Committee on the Status of Women in India (CSWI) discovered that the development process over two decades had, instead of improving women's lives, become one of the primary reasons for accentuating inequality. Adverse sex ratio, school enrolment figures and women's legal position—all pointed to a worsening of women's position and thus many of the women who had been opposed to special provisions for women began to rethink. One of the most important realisations has been the need for collaborating gender-specific movements with other social and political movements. In the 1980s the strengthening of backward caste politics in north India and the response to it in the form communalism added new dimension to the issues being raised by women's groups.

Leela Kasturi's survey of women's participation in the political process in India suggests that women have been associated to a greater extent with political processes in the wider society and less with the formal political system, and hence, with the government.

Post independence, it was clear that these expectations had not been fulfilled. Women remained conspicuous by their absence in the realm of decision making in formal politics. The Indian state and the development strategy that it was committed to, in Kasturi's words, jettisoned the entire gender question. Patriarchy was not challenged in any way; on the contrary, it was reinforced by the new pattern of development. This is the context in which the demand for women's reservation ought to be discussed.

THE QUESTION OF RESERVATIONS FOR WOMEN IN INDIA

The issue of reservations for women is not new in India. The Constituent Assembly, faced with this demand, decided against it in the belief that parliamentary democracy in independent India would automatically redress the issue. There was also the fear that any such special provisions might lead to an underestimation of the strength of Indian women and their ability to compete with men as equals. The Committee on the Status of Women in India presented its report in 1974 in the background of the realisation that women's expectations at independence had been belied. This Committee did admit that women were not present in sufficient numbers in the elected and representative bodies.

The issue of reservations generated debates within the committee. Those opposed to the idea of reservation for women held that the principle of equality enshrined in the Constitution made the demand for reservations redundant. The fact that women are not a homogenous group would also make any such reservation difficult. Those opposed to reservations for women feared that the introduction of any such provision would lead to similar demands from other quarters as well, thus threatening national integration. Those who supported the idea of reservations for women believed that more women in the elected bodies would change the direction and issues being debated in the parliament. Supporters of reservation for women argued that the presence of women in Parliament would enable them to work as an organised lobby and in the context of political parties that are deeply entrenched in patriarchy, reservations for women is the only way of ensuring their political presence. In the end, the committee decided against the idea of reservations for women in legislature.

Towards the end of the 1980s, this issue was brought to centrestage when the National Perspective Plan recommended a 30 per cent reservation of seats for women in Panchayats and Zila Parishads. The 73rd and 74th Constitutional Amendments in 1993 finally provided for one-third reservations for women in these bodies. This was greeted with great deal of enthusiasm by women's groups who by 1996 started actively campaigning for reservations for women in the Parliament and state assemblies. Three attempts were made to pass the bill in Parliament in 1996 by the United Front government that had included the issue of reservation for women as part of its common minimum programme, in 1998 by the BJP government and yet again in 1999 only to be hotly debated and finally dumped.

It is interesting to point out that women's groups from the pre-independence period up till the 1970s steered clear of making demands for reservations for women in Parliament and state assemblies. Vina Mazumdar and others, who were members of the CSWI, described themselves as 'daughters of independence' and reasoned that in the context of an egalitarian Constitution and a democratic political framework, special provisions of any kind would be uncalled for. By the 1980s, these groups had revised their position. As Nivedita Menon says, they realised that abstract citizenship was merely a cover for privilege; differences are politically significant and need to be acknowledged.

In the post–1980s India, the whole issue of reservations for women was argued for and against vehemently. While many of the arguments are familiar, the context is completely different. The growing strength and mobilisation of Dalit and backward-caste politics, on one hand, and majoritarian politics, on the other, have added a new dimension to the debate on reservations in general and for women in particular. It is in this context that Nivedita Menon has identified feminist or at least pro-women arguments for and against reservations, as well as caste-based arguments for and against reservations.

The feminist argument for reservations contends that such a step would enable the formal equality granted by the Constitution to be more substantive. The pro-women argument against reservation is attributed to Madhu Kishwar and Gail Omvedt who have expressed the fear that reservations for women would lead to the 'biwi-beti brigade' dominating Parliamentary and assembly seats reserved for women. In other words, they fear that women from privileged backgrounds would corner the benefits of reservation for women.

Both Kishwar and Omvedt would admit without any hesitation that democracy in India has largely excluded women and steps need to be taken to change this exclusion. Therefore, Menon describes their position as pro-women opponents of the WRB. They do not agree with the current proposal for reservations for women, and have made their own suggestions for alternatives. Omvedt has suggested a long-term overhauling of the electoral process itself, wherein each voter would have three votes, at least one of which should be cast for a woman candidate. Kishwar has argued rather unconvincingly that reservations for women are redundant in the Indian context where the culture is disapproving of any disrespect shown to women. Her alternative proposal is based on the Election Commission ensuring that all political parties field a certain number of women candidates. The Left parties have criticised this proposal as a 'compromise formula' because this would only ensure that women get tickets and not ensure their presence in Parliament. The stronger objection is made on the grounds that an unaccountable body like the Election Commission cannot be given policing powers.

Caste-based opposition to the current form of WRB is the next argument that Nivedita Menon takes up. She attributes this opposition to the politics of identity, in this case based on caste. Problems with the present form of the WRB arise out of the undifferentiated category of employed women. Dalit and backward-caste leaders have pointed out that the bill, as it stands, does not acknowledge the fact that women from Dalit and backward castes are oppressed not only because of their gender but also because of their caste.

Uma Bharati is perhaps the only one from the BJP who has consistently supported the idea of reservations, but has against her party's standpoint argued for a quota for Dalit and backward caste women within the quota reserved for women. In keeping with her party's general orientation, she, even while admitting the backwardness of the Muslim community, refrains from accepting the suggestion for reservations for Muslims. In her opinion, this would go against the secular ethos of the Constitution that does allow for caste based reservations. She would, however, be prepared to accept reservations for the backward castes among the Muslims. Thus, Bharati by accepting the pre-eminence of caste identity does create an awkward moment for her party that is committed to a homogenised Hindu identity. Menon contends that it is the fear of strengthening caste identity at the cost of the homogenised Hindu identity that is the reason for the half-hearted support extended by parties like the BJP to the WRB. Not surprisingly, backward caste leaders have described the bill as yet another attempt by upper-caste groups to stem the growing tide of Dalit and backward caste men in politics.

Menon contrasts this position with those who make a defence of abstract citizenship, and hence, oppose any kind of reservations. Such a position sees the assertion of identity politics as backward and medieval. Abstract, unencumbered individuals define modernity for them. Menon argues that this support for abstract citizenship actually represents interests similar to those positions that while supporting reservations for women oppose caste-based reservations for women. Sushma Swaraj, for instance, from the BJP is a vocal supporter of the WRB but is equally vehement in her opposition to the idea of caste based quota within this. Both, the BJP and the Congress, would share this perspective.

Menon questions the basis of this acceptance of 'women' by upper-caste political interests. How come, she wonders, the category of 'women' is not seen as a threat to social order? Perhaps, she says, this can be attributed to the domestication of the category of gender, and the co-optation of gender concerns and analysis into the mainframe of Indian politics. This also coincides with the loss of radicalism of the once highly militant and visible autonomous women's movement, that by the end of the 1980s had become dependent on government funding. Dependence on government funding meant that many-a-compromise had to be made on the radical positions that the movement had adopted. Another reason for acknowledging gender concerns is directly related to the change in the development discourse that argued that it was quite a shame to waste women's resources, and therefore, the suggestion that gender should be 'mainstreamed'. For better governance, women's empowerment became the favoured strategy. From such a perspective, the WRB in its present form minus the demand for a quota within it for Dalit and backward caste women would make perfect sense and can be enthusiastically defended.

In August 2005, a new draft of the bill that proposes to increase the number of seats for women in the Lok Sabha without affecting the old seating arrangements was discussed without any success. The new draft proposal suggested an increase in the number of Lok Sabha seats from 545 to 900 and increase in number of seats in the Rajya Sabha as well, 9000 members in both Legislative Council and Legislative Assembly instead of 6000, and 33 per cent of the newly created seats to be reserved for women. However, consensus eluded the bill, with the major opposition coming from the Samajwadi Party and the Rashtriya Janata Dal. The former made three points: it should be mandatory for parties to give ten per cent of their tickets to women; if inadequacy of representation is the issue, reservation should be extended to Muslim women as well besides the 33 per cent reservation for women, and 22.5 per cent reservation for SC and ST. Thus, the total reservation would exceed 55 per cent and they pointed out that this would be unfair to other sections of the population. Thus, it is a fact that the Women's Reservation Bill providing 33 per cent reservation for women in the Lok Sabha and state legislatures has been a non-starter through seven Lok Sabhas, from 1996 onwards. Successive governments have placed it on the floor of the house, only to have it shelved.

Thus, feminists who support the WRB need to rethink their stand; especially in the context of the realisation that 'women' as a natural category does not exist prior to political mobilisation. Anne Phillips has argued for reservations on the grounds that because women are present in the population, they ought to be present in the elected and representative bodies as well. Nivedita Menon's response to this argument is that identities do not exist prior to a particular ideology and mobilisation that sees it as an identity. To assume that 'women' exist in society independent of political forces and concerns is rather difficult to accept. Different political configurations would produce different identities. After all, gender is one of the ways in which people might be mobilised, other than race, caste, religion, and so on. Menon is arguing that 'women' is not an intractable biological category; rather it is produced by political mobilisation.

Besides, in a context like ours, the category 'women' has to be, as Menon points out, located within a grid of other identities such as religion, language or caste. Therefore, she argues that feminist politics should support the idea of quota within quota, for, after all, women are not just women but are defined by various other identities such as caste. Not acknowledging this and pretending that 'women' exist as a readily available category for feminist mobilisation is, therefore, not a helpful position. If so, then while supporting reservations for women, it would only be correct for feminists to extend this support to other similarly marginalised groups within society.

POINTS FOR DISCUSSION

- Does the practice of reservation in representative bodies challenge the basic principles of liberal democracy?
- The performance of women sarpanches and members in the various Panchayat bodies would be an interesting point for discussion.

REFERENCES

Kasturi, Leela (1996). 'Development, Patriarchy and Politics: Indian Women in the Political Process, 1947–1992', in Valentine M. Moghadam (ed.) *Patriarchy and Economic Development*. Oxford: Clarendon Press, 99–143.

Menon, Nivedita (2004). *Recovering Subversion*. New Delhi: Permanent Black.

Phillips, Anne (1991). *Engendering Democracy*. Cambridge: Polity Press.

10

Laws, Institutions and Women's Rights in India

FEMINISM AND LAW: AN INTRODUCTION

Over the last two decades of the twentieth century, 'feminist legal theory' or 'feminist jurisprudence' has been a growing discipline. This is more in the West, although it has found a following in our country as well. Engagement with law by women's groups, however, predates the development of this discipline.

The earliest women's struggles in the West were for securing the right to vote, to own property as married women (yes to own property and not inherit) and to gain legal access to birth control. By the 1970s, there were many women in the legal profession in the West and many of them grappled with the specific relationship of gender and law. They challenged in the courts of law as well as in the legislatures the assumptions underlying many laws. These assumptions were based on the ideas of female dependence and unsuitability of women for certain jobs, and so on. Katharine T. Bartlett and Rosanne Kennedy in the introduction to their book, *Feminist Legal Theory* observed that by the end of the 1980s, these victories although significant, were beginning to lose their sharpness, especially in the wake of the defeat of the Equal Rights Amendment Act (in the USA), the retrenchment of abortion rights, and the increased incidence of violence against women. It became rather clear that laws could not be depended upon to eliminate sexual subordination. Feminists have today moved away from an uncritical commitment to the efficacy of law as an instrument for bringing about change in society. While the struggle for bringing about appropriate legal changes would continue, law alone would not be depended upon to bring changes. Merely changing laws do not result in any considerable improvement in women's lives and conditions. This has compelled feminist scholars both in the West and in India to rethink their engagement with law.

This is not to deny that laws have helped, and yet constrained feminist agendas. After all, in modern democracies, the law's guarantee of equality on one hand, has enabled women to articulate differences in the law's treatment of men and women, on the other. The constraints, Bartlett and Kennedy attribute to law's respect for precedent, thus making it conservative, and also its insistence upon arguments that are rational and coherent. The latter is a rather difficult situation because standards of what is rational reflect the interests of those who hold power. It has also been observed that law has a limited capacity to act as a tool of reform because it is unable to transform the social structures, ideologies and divisions of labour within the household. In other words, laws might be gender neutral but the division of labour within the family or roles ordained for men and women by society have not changed. Under these circumstances, law would have only a limited capacity to act as a tool for bringing about reform.

Does that mean that laws are of no significance for women? The answer is rather complicated. Bartlett and Kennedy argue that laws are significant because laws represent power and make options available. Indeed, legal reforms create as well as resolve problems for feminism. Nivedita Menon demonstrates the nature of these challenges in her book, *Recovering Subversion—Feminist Politics Beyond Law*.

Linda Lacey divides feminist legal theory into three approaches—liberal feminism, cultural feminism and radical feminism. Liberal feminists have traditionally appealed to legal intervention and have displayed great faith in the ability of laws to bring about changes in women's lives. Liberal feminists work within the liberal paradigm and hope for complete formal equality between men and women. Such a philosophy is based on the division between the public and the private, and the understanding that the individual is sovereign within the private sphere where the authority of law does not extend. The family and matters related with it, sexuality and other such issues are relegated to the private sphere.

Liberal feminists have argued that it is this exclusion that has prevented the private sphere from being governed by the same emancipatory ideas of justice, rights, equality and freedom that govern the public sphere. Liberal feminists would typically employ the ideas of individual privacy, and rights and autonomy to ask for reproductive rights for women, or for provisions relating to abortion. Thus, abortion or contraception, they argue, should be decisions left to the autonomous individual to decide upon using her rationality in conditions of privacy. The government or any other institution should not have the authority to intervene in these matters. Suitable legal reforms would be needed to enable women to experience autonomy and privacy within the private sphere as well. The underlying assumptions in these arguments are that since women were relegated to the private sphere, they were denied the status of the individual with autonomy and privacy. Within this approach, feminist efforts have sought an extension of these values to the private sphere. Thus, ensuring through legal reforms a private sphere based on the principle of autonomy and privacy for both men and women would be the goal for feminists within this approach. Liberal feminists would frown upon any special provisions in keeping with their commitment to the idea of equality. Although the Marxist and the liberal approaches are very different, there is a basic similarity in the two approaches stemming out of a tendency to present a male point of view as the universal point of view. Feminism has questioned the universal claims of both these approaches.

Cultural feminism holds that women value—and have a special competence for—intimacy, nurturing and relational thinking, unlike men who value autonomy. The focus of cultural feminists is on the distinctiveness of women and they, hence, would not desire equal treatment of men and women by law. Treating them equally would force women to adopt 'male' values like fierce individualism and competitiveness. Instead, laws should recognise the different ways in which women relate to the world.

Radical feminists, on the other hand, argue that it is women's connection to others that is the source of their miseries and subordination. In fact, they argue that focusing on women's distinctiveness leads to further reinforcement of women's subservient role in society. They hold that the history of women's subjugation is more or less an account of the 'special' characteristics, on the basis of which their subordination has been justified. Since women suffer subordination, laws have to focus on this aspect and redress these special disadvantages through special provisions. They hold that invasion and intrusion, a consequence of women's connection with others, is the story of women's lives and not intimacy and nurturance as cultural feminists would have it. Radical feminists seek individuation but not the kind of autonomous individuation that liberalism bases itself upon. Rather, Robin West describes it as the right to be the sort of creature who might have, and then pursue one's own needs. Conventional liberal understanding of individual autonomy implies that human beings possess rationality and it is through their ability to make autonomous choices that their rationality is realised and their individuality reaffirmed. It is based on the understanding that each individual is distinct, separate and exclusive, and hence, must have the autonomy to make free choices to affirm her/his individuality. The ability to posit goals and to work towards it is crucial for affirming individuality within the liberal framework. On the other hand, the lives of women, radical feminists suggest, are so taken over by intrusion and invasion (the nature of sexual intercourse and pregnancy being prime examples) that their primary fear is of being taken over and being occupied from within. This occupation denies women the ability to determine their ends; their ends get 'displaced' even before they are formulated. Women become incapable of articulating their own interests in an autonomous sort of way. Their lives become so connected with that of others that it is impossible for them to posit their own ends or think of themselves as 'I'. Radical feminists, therefore, are seeking for women an individuation that enables women to become an ends-making creature. West suggests that the notion of 'human beings' assumed by conventional legal theory is vastly different from the articulations made by feminists. According to conventional legal theory, human beings value autonomy and fear annihilation, while at the same time dreading the alienation that would be the inevitable result of such autonomy. Women, according to feminist legal theory, value intimacy, and fear separation, and at the same time long for individuation.

Existing jurisprudence, West argues, is masculine because the existing laws are 'masculine' in terms of their intended beneficiary and authorship. West goes on to suggest that women's absence in this jurisprudence stems from the absence of women as human beings in law's protection. Traditional jurisprudence has thought of only men while talking about human beings. Women are perceived as either their belonging or their wards, lacking in autonomy, and an individual and distinct identity. Hence, she concludes that a truly ungendered jurisprudence is possible only when the law begins to take women's lives as seriously as it does men's.

THE INDIAN CONTEXT

Insights from North America on feminist engagement with law were initially based on the common experience of women's oppression based on gender. Such an approach, while valued for its fresh insights, obscured the differences that exist among women. In the North American context, the most obvious difference was that of race. Voices of women located differently added a new dimension to feminist legal studies. Thus, the tendency to curb a totalising theory based on gender alone was avoided. In our context, this is of obvious significance, given the differences of caste, religion, ethnicity, and so on. Ratna Kapur, in the introductory chapter of her book, *Feminist Terrains in Legal Domains*, has talked about the considerable scope for expansion of feminist legal studies in India. She contends that by recognising the multiplicity of women's experiences based on race, caste, religion, marital status and their mediation of gender, the hegemonic nature of law can be exposed and deconstructed.

Feminists in India have engaged with law and have been rather successful, especially in the context of laws related with violence against women. Through the 1980s, feminist groups in India demanded legislations of various kinds, in the hope that this would prevent violence against women.

Their efforts were successful to the extent that they were able to bring about changes in the existing legislations, and wherever needed bring-in new legislations. Legislations related to dowry, *Sati* and indecent representation of women were some of the most significant ones. Despite the legislations, problems remained with its implementation which, at best, remained partial and conservative.

This became the context within the feminist movement in India for the evaluation of a legal campaign as an effective strategy for change. Nivedita Menon identifies the major positions on this debate within the women's movement. The first position seems to realise that laws alone are not enough but are surely important. Legal campaigns are seen as part of a broad strategy to create legitimacy and generate public awareness. Laws are also expected to provide short-term redressal.

Madhu Kishwar, Flavia Agnes and others represent the second line of thinking on this issue. This position is rather sceptical of the efforts being made for legislations. They are of the opinion that every successful attempt involves an increase in the state's powers, because it is, after all, the state that would monitor the implementation of the laws. The result is an increase in state control without a strong commitment to implementation.

Menon identifies Gail Omvedt's rather unenthusiastic response to legal campaigns as the third position. Omvedt believes that in the absence of mass-based militant politics, legal campaigns are rather futile. The way out, perhaps, is to be found in Nandita Haksar's suggestion that legal campaigns are useful only when the movement has strengthened itself enough to be able to carry the legal reforms forward.

While the struggle against women's subordination has most certainly looked beyond legal reforms, Menon expresses her doubts regarding legal campaigns on two definite grounds. First is the realisation that legal reforms often work against feminist interests. Second is a reason more specific to postcolonial societies like ours. Menon argues that in societies such as ours, a modern legal framework was introduced as part of the requirements of colonial administration. In Europe, the context for a modern legal framework was the collapse of feudalism and the emergence of capitalism with its basis in individual rights and freedoms. On the contrary, it was colonialism that initiated us in the practices of modernity. The core of this initiation was not individual freedom or rights, but a violent and disruptive system—colonialism. Hence, Menon argues that laws in our context do not necessarily possess the same emancipatory potential that its European counterparts possessed. (Of course, the potential even there has been limited.)

Feminists in India do realise that the state and its structures are patriarchal, but despite that, they are optimistic about changes that laws influenced by feminist intervention can bring about. This makes them ask for legislations in areas of 'judicial void' of family and sexuality, traditionally considered to be in the private sphere. Perhaps, as Nandita Gandhi and Nandita Shah have suggested, this is because it is easier to campaign for legal intervention by the state than it is to challenge customs and traditions within the family.

Clearly, the time has come to review the relationship between laws and the public–private dichotomy. Menon is of the opinion that the 'private' is not private because laws refuse to intervene in this sphere; rather, it is private because the laws have so framed it by its refusal to intervene in this sphere. She cites the example of a judgement made by the Delhi High Court that expressed the inability of Constitutional law to intervene in the domestic relationship between husband and wife, since in the opinion of the court, Constitutional provisions have no relevance within the privacy of the home. Menon is, therefore, establishing the fact that it is law that actually determines the public–private dichotomy and upholds it by either intervening or refusing to do so. In other words, there is no natural demarcation between the public and the private that exists prior to law. It is law and societal norms, and such others, that together carve out this dichotomy between the public and the private.

A more fundamental problem set out by Menon is the relationship between the language of rights and laws. Legal discourse by nature requires universal categories. Social movements while asking for change invoke the issue of *their* rights and present *their* claims as though they are universal. Rights are by nature specific to a particular perspective and make sense only within a particular discourse, while legal reforms that these movements might ask for are based on the principle of universality. Thus, Menon identifies a contradiction between the universality required by legal discourse and the multilayeredness of the discourse of rights.

THE INDIAN CONSTITUTION: WOMEN AND FAMILY

The Indian Constitution grants men and women equality before law and equal treatment by law. Ratna Kapur and Brenda Cossman in their article titled 'Familial Ideology and the Constitution' have suggested that the language of equality has played a central role in the struggle of women's movement to bring about social change. But in its guise as formal equality, it is often used to stall moves formulated specifically to improve the conditions of women. Formal equality is understood as equal treatment to all those who are same. The substantive approach is more concerned with the impact of law. The substantive approach is keen to remove the disadvantages and discrimination faced by marginalised groups. Thus, the former approach is concerned with sameness while the latter is focused on disadvantages. This debate is almost endless in political theory and is linked with different concepts of liberty. The roots of this idea are clearly traceable to the eternal debate in political theory on the relationship between liberty and equality. One position sees the concept of formal equality before law as the only guarantee of individual liberty, as a narrow construction of equality. The other position sees this as a farcical defence of both equality and liberty arguing for a wider understanding of both equality as (substantive equality) and liberty. If liberty were seen as nothing more than being left alone, then the choice of formal equality would follow. This position assumes that any interference in the name of equality would amount to violation of liberty. People on the basis of their rationality make different use of the liberty that they enjoy; the different results (for example, some might become rich, and others destitute and poor) have no bearing on the extent of the liberty they enjoy. Any attempt to bring about equality is completely misplaced according to this view, because equality lies in being treated equally by law and having the same kind of liberty. The second position argues that equality has meaning only when all individuals are able to use the liberty they have in a way that helps them to realise their potential.

Kapur and Cossman have identified three different approaches in law to the issue of gender. A protectionist approach believes that women are different from men and are weaker, and therefore, in need of protection. This approach in their opinion essentialises the differences and takes gender differences as natural and inevitable. There is no attempt in this approach to examine the reasons for the differences and the impact of the differential treatment on women. Thus, often in the name of protecting women, this approach reinforces the subordinate status of women. An example of this would be laws that deny women basic civil and political rights on the grounds that women, being different, need protection.

The second approach mentioned by Kapur and Cossman is based on the idea of sameness. For the purposes of law, men and women are treated as being same. Within this approach, no law that seeks to provide women with special protection would be acceptable, because it would be seen as a violation of the principle of equality. In the third approach, women are understood as a historically disadvantaged group, who, therefore, require remedial action. Working within this approach would mean taking steps for recognising gender differences as being significant from the legal point of view.

Feminist legal scholars have demonstrated that the so-called neutral approach that guides the formal equality framework is not neutral at all; rather it is based on male standards and values. In this framework, women would qualify for equal treatment by law to the extent that they are able to internalise male standards and norms.

Kapur and Cossman contend that the dominant judicial discourse is guided by the formal equality approach, and at times, the protectionist approach. The perspective that guides the dominant judicial discourse is embedded in what Kapur and Cossman describe as familial ideology. This ideology allots a specific role to women within the family, and accepts sexual division of labour as an inevitable, natural and universal fact. This is despite the obvious fact that there is no universal family in India. But it is still possible to talk in terms of a dominant ideology of the family within law. This guides law's understanding of what the family is and what it should do. It is seen as the basic building block of society and as being natural, and hence, prior to social relations.

This ideology also accepts certain roles and functions for women and men strictly on the basis of gender. Women are allotted the roles of wives and mothers, and it is their responsibility to manage the home and care for the children. Men are expected to earn and support the family financially. This ideology is naturalised through a variety of cultural and religious symbols. Thus, if the law does treat women differently, it is not discriminatory but is simply protecting the natural roles that women play. What is being missed here is the fact that differences do not exist in a vacuum but acquire meaning and significance within a complex social web of relationships. Men and women are different but men are treated as the point of reference, and the yardstick for measuring the differences is man. If differences were to be recognised as a consequence of social relationships, then they would cease to appear as natural and inevitable, and can thus be changed through legal provisions. On the contrary, if they are seen as natural then the law can only uphold the differences.

Kapur and Cossman have examined the Indian judiciary's approach in this context. They find that the judiciary accepts the specific social consequences of biological differences as natural and inevitable, and thus bases its judgments in cases related with issues of divorce, restitution of conjugal rights, adultery, custody of children, and so on, from this perspective. In a letter titled 'Ants in the Pants' to the journal *Manushi*, Mary Roy who fought and won against Christian patriarchy in Kerala on the issue of inheritance would be very interesting. In her own inimitable style, she observes how the Supreme Court struck down the Travancore Christian Succession Act in 1986. The Indian Succession Act replaced the Act. The former act stated that daughters would inherit only one fourth of the share of a son or a sum of Rs. 5000.00 whichever is less. The latter divides the intestate property equally among sons and daughters, and the widow inherits one-third share. Time and again after the judgement, the male-dominated church and the legislature have heard powerful sections of the community voice their concern about the inconvenience caused to Christian men by the new act. In fact, repeated attempts are made by powerful Christian legislators to reintroduce the old act. On the basis of an examination of various cases and the judgment announced by the courts in India, Kapur and Cossman conclude that law is based on familial ideology, according to which only husbands, fathers and sons are entitled to own and inherit property, and hence, men's right to ensure that only their biological offspring inherits their property is recognised by law.

The Hindu Succession (Amendment) Bill 2004 sought to amend the Hindu Succession Act, 1956. The Rajya Sabha passed it on 16 August 2004. Although all the parties supported the bill, the BJP benches were deserted while the bill was being passed. This Bill has moved the Hindu women closer towards enjoying the same rights as men in inheriting their ancestral property. The 174th report of the National Law Commission had observed that denying women an equal share in their ancestral property amounted to violation of the Article 14 and 15 of the Constitution. They argue that familial ideology which constitutes men and women as different immunises the legal provisions from judicial scrutiny. The gendered construction of men and women as being different, influences the way in which law criminalises adultery, for example, and the different significance of the adulterous conduct of men and women that are accepted by the legal framework. After all, adultery committed by the wife, could lead to the husband's rights to pass on his property to his own biological offspring being violated.

Law continues to hold the family as private and, hence, beyond its purview. Women are seen as belonging to the private sphere and this public–private dichotomy is used to justify the insulation of women's subordination within the family from the law. Discriminatory treatment, ranging from dowry and unequal inheritance to sexual assault, are justified on the grounds that they happen within the private sphere of the family, and hence, the law can only be of limited relevance. The legal framework has not thought it necessary to examine the nature of marriage and women's role within it. Laws have been amended but are yet not comprehensive enough to include wife battering. The law leaves many loopholes; for instance, it makes both the taker and giver of dowry guilty. Nandita Shah and Nandita Gandhi point out that under prevailing conditions, the givers can hardly be expected to give evidence. The law also does not seem to recognise the peculiarly vulnerable nature of the bride's family.

Thus, feminists realise that there is a sharp difference between the dominant legal discourse based on familial ideology and the feminist vision. But this need not lead them to abandon their engagement with law. Kapur and Cossman describe law as a site of complexity and contradiction, and feminist engagement with law should recognise this.

SOME IMPORTANT LEGAL CAMPAIGNS

The Indian women's movement has a long tradition of engagement with laws. However, doubts about the impact of legal reforms on the lives of ordinary women still remain. In the light of this, a look at some of the important milestones would be instructive. After a series of custodial rapes, changes were brought about in laws relating to rape. The changes widened the definition of rape and recognised the scourge of custodial rape. The new law (Criminal Law Amendment Act 1983) recognised that people in official position could commit rape, and it shifted the onus of proving innocence on to the man in the case of public servants. Of course, at that juncture, there was no recognition of marital rape, although the situation has changed today. Women's organisations do recognise that within the existing context, these laws would be of limited efficiency.

Women's groups have conducted another big and emotional campaign on the issue of dowry. The nerve-centre of this campaign was Delhi that had the dubious distinction of reporting a very large number of dowry related murders and suicides. Women's groups used public rallies, demonstrations and street plays to raise awareness about the issue and create public support for their campaign.

The public outrage against the *sati* in Deorala in 1987 led the legislatures, both at the central and the state level, to rush through new legislations. Gandhi and Shah point out that these legislations held the woman also an offender. Clearly, the lawmakers persisted in seeing the woman as an autonomous person with the ability to make free choices, completely ignoring the exploited and vulnerable status of the woman.

In 1987, Roop Kanwar, a young woman, committed *sati* in a relatively well-developed village of Deorala in Rajasthan. Married to a headmaster's son, the family was definitely not poor. Her husband suffered from some mental illness and they spent only six months together as a couple. After her husband's death, his family announced that Roop Kanwar was to 'become' *sati*; her natal family was not informed. Reports suggest that she tried to run and hide but was dragged and drugged, dressed in her bridal clothes and was set afire by her brother-in-law who was a minor. Subsequent to this, the site became a popular pilgrim spot. Feminist groups all over India mounted a huge campaign (the details of which are in the next chapter).

Women's groups have focused on representation of women in the media. They have campaigned against the exploitative use of women's bodies for advertising and other commercial purposes. In response to these concerns, the Parliament passed the Indecent Representation of Women Bill in 1986. Shah and Gandhi have drawn attention to the drawbacks in this law.

It has a very vague definition of what is indecent and confuses indecency with obscenity, besides giving tremendous powers to gazetted officers to seize material and conduct raids.

The other controversial aspect has been that of family law. Whenever women have sought the help of law in matters relating to family, the response has been that this would endanger religion or that excessive modernisation would lead to break-up of the family. In the 1980s, this issue became very controversial in the light of the Shah Bano case.

On 23 April 1985, the Supreme Court, in response to a petition filed by the 75-year-old Shah Bano, ruled that she was entitled to maintenance by her husband. The bench invoked the provisions of Section 125 of the Criminal Procedure Code. The application of the criminal procedure code and the sidelining of the Muslim Personal Law, as well as the suggestion for a Common Civil Code made the judgement unpopular. The conservative sections within the Muslim community immediately responded by raising the issue of minority rights. Shah Bano's appeal for maintenance was upheld by the court. This was immediately seen by a certain section of the Muslim community as a threat to their community's identity, for, in their opinion, Islamic law had provisions for protection of the rights of a divorced woman and any interference by the law courts would tantamount to interference in their personal laws. Earlier, in the 1950s, Hindu men had expressed similar reservation regarding the Hindu Code Bill that was intended to empower women within the Hindu community.

Shah and Gandhi have argued that the judgement itself in the Shah Bano case pronounced by the Supreme Court was not problematic but it was the manner in which it was worded that stirred a controversy, finally leading to the passage of the Muslim Women's (Protection of Rights on Divorce) Act 1986. This act supposedly protected Islam, and as Shah and Gandhi have said, gave to the Muslim man more control over his wife. Thus, in the guise of religious freedom, women of the Muslim community were denied basic Constitutional rights.

It was in this context that the debate on uniform civil code became central to the politics of the 1980s and the 1990s. The code has a long and controversial history. Even while the Constitution was being framed, this issue was raised; but given the heterogeneous nature of the Indian society, it became difficult to reach a consensus. The debate on this issue continues. The uniform civil code is advocated by sections of both the liberal and the majoritarian Hindu right. The latter maintains that separate civil codes for different religious communities go against the principles of secularism. Feminists, who earlier supported this idea, have modified their stance now. They voice their concerns over the possibility of a homogenised code, based largely on the practices and assumptions of the upper-caste North Indian Hindus, compromising the essence of diversity and secularism inherent in the Constitution. Feminist groups, in this new context, have adopted a nuanced position on the issue. In their opinion, equality and dignity, and not necessarily uniformity, should be the guiding principles of a uniform civil code.

CONCLUSION

It is a fact that despite the existence of progressive laws, women seldom do take advantage of it. Very often they do not know their rights or else issues like family honour and traditions prevent them from doing so. What has generally been observed is that it is easier for women to fight the state than it is to question the injustices within the family. Women who have done so have found themselves isolated from their families and communities. Nandita Shah and Nandita Gandhi accept the rather unfortunate fact that in the absence of support that the state should provide to women in distress; the family is more often than not the only alternative. Women's organisations find it difficult to extend support over a long period of time, and thus, being alienated from one's own family or community context is a rather frightening prospect for most Indian women. And it is, perhaps, this fear that prevents many of them from appealing to law in the context of injustices heaped upon them by their families and communities.

Of course, in asking for legislation, there is always the risk of increasing state control and supervision. The other rather unfortunate fallout is the uniformity and homogenisation that law-making necessitates. We go back to the question that Nivedita Menon has asked: does law have the capacity to pursue justice? Menon argues that justice cannot be conceived of in a uniform sense. The discourse of law, she argues, is dependent upon a set of self-evident and universal set of values. What exist are multiple definitions of justice; what law seeks to do, however, is to homogenise these differences. Hence, there is a fundamental discord in her opinion between the discourse of law and the pursuit of justice. Does that mean that feminists need to give up fighting for legal reforms? The answer is no, because by doing so, laws will not go away. Laws exist, and therefore, it is important for feminists to engage with laws in order to negotiate some spaces that are, as Menon puts it, 'outside and around it'.

POINT FOR DISCUSSION

- There has been a proposal to fix the death sentence as punishment for rapists. While this has found many supporters, there are others who are against it. Some oppose the death sentence under any circumstances, and others, while opposing death sentence, are also worried that this might actually make convictions for rapists fewer, apart from reinforcing the conventional notion that 'rape is worse than death'. Discuss.

REFERENCES

Bartlett, Katharine T. and Rosanne Kennedy (eds) (1991). *Feminist Legal Theory: Readings in Law and Gender*. Boulder, CO: Westview Press.

Basu, Srimati (2005). *Dowry and Inheritance*. New Delhi: Kali for Women.

Kapur, Ratna (ed.) (1996). *Feminist Terrains in Legal Domains.* New Delhi: Kali for Women.

Menon, Nivedita (2004). *Recovering Subversion*. New Delhi: Permanent Black.

Shah, Nandita and Nandita Gandhi (1992). *The Issues at Stake*. New Delhi: Kali for Women.

11

Women's Movement in India

THE PRE-INDEPENDENCE PERIOD

The account of the women's movement in India is long and inspiring. It can be divided into the pre-independence and post-independence phases. Before narrating the history of the Indian women's movement, it is pertinent to point out that the term 'Indian women's movement' is, today, highly contested. The discomfort stems from the belief that the term 'Indian' obscures all other politically relevant divisions such as caste, class or religion. Given the differences in caste, religion and class, it is indeed very difficult to talk in terms of a homogenised category of 'Indian' woman, for this would not adequately address the differences that exist among Indian women. After all, a Muslim woman in Gujarat would have a very different understanding of what it means to be an Indian from that of the understanding of an upper-caste, upper-class Hindu woman from Delhi.

Radha Kumar (1998) in her book *The History of Doing* suggests that while colonialism and the struggle against it was the most important influence on the feminist movement in the pre-independence period, in the post-independence period, democratic politics and institutional structures have been the most important influences. This, obviously, does not mean that the two phases are unrelated.

It was in the nineteenth century that women's issues became important. The Social Reform Movement had the 'woman question' as its central concern. There seemed to be a belief that the status of women determined the claims of modernity and, indeed, of nationhood itself. In the context of the anti-colonial struggle, therefore, this issue gained momentum and added relevance. The emerging new Indian elite educated in Western ways sought to remedy the worst aspects of the existing patriarchal structures. In this enterprise, they sometimes sought the help of the British government. These efforts were also guided by the desire on the part of the Westernised Indian elite to create a new Indian woman, who would be able to share her sensibilities and approach to life. It is, perhaps, because of this desire that education for women became such an important issue within the reform movement. The other big issue was, of course, the campaign against *sati*.

There were two kinds of opinion within this newly emergent Indian elite: one that sought the intervention of the government and the other that resisted it. Lata Mani argues interestingly that both sides were, of course, not prepared to grant agency to women. They merely used the 'woman question' as the site on which they could carry on their discourse and definition of Indian identity and tradition.

A small group of elite women benefited from the efforts of the male social reformers and the changes brought about by the British government. Most of these efforts were, however, located within the language and understanding of upper-caste men. This not only glossed over the experiences of women belonging to marginalised groups and castes, but, indeed, took away from them their traditional freedoms and rights. The most well-known example would be that of matrilineal communities like the Nairs in Kerala, who in the context of colonialism rethought their family life along the lines of modernity and felt contemptuous of their traditional family structures. The only respectable family structure seemed the nuclear family, as it had emerged in the West. The various legal campaigns led by the English educated Nair men for the transformation of matriliny resulted in Nair women losing out on many aspects of their hitherto secure and free life.

A stocktaking of the results of the social reform movement would show that the changes brought about as a result of these efforts converged with the interests of the colonial state, capitalist employers and indigenous elite men. Thus, a new kind of patriarchy was being created to replace the existing one. By the end of the nineteenth century, the social reform movement began to bear fruit. Women's education came to be accepted, and many women made independent evaluation and took initiative to ameliorate the status of women. Women in Bengal pioneered most of these efforts, although similar efforts were being made elsewhere also. Women's role as mothers came to be glorified. An educated mother's ability to train and nurture her sons and support her husband in the task of nation-building came to be emphasised. Indian women, it was hoped, would be mothers of the Indian nation and not mothers of the British Indian Empire.

The early twentieth century witnessed acceleration in the pace of women's participation in nationalist politics. One of the most well-known organisations set up for this purpose was the All India Women's Conference established in 1927. This and many similar organisations were concerned with eradication of social problems affecting women and made many attempts towards popularising women's education. Although they began with a commitment towards these issues, it was not before long that nationalist politics engulfed them.

From the 1920s, nationalist politics began to make a conscious effort to address women. This was also the time when Mahatma Gandhi became a part of the national movement. By the 1920s, Radha Kumar identifies two distinctive rationales for women's rights. The first was based on women's socially useful role as mothers. The second position based itself on the belief that men and women had same desires and needs, and hence, need the same kind of rights.

The Salt Satyagraha in 1930 marked a new high in the number of women who participated in the national movement. Very soon separate organisations were set up to mobilise greater participation of women. Participation in this movement helped most of the upper-class women activists to come out of their elitist moorings and, this in turn, had an impact on the working of women's organisations.

Gandhi's influence is acknowledged as one of the most important reasons for increasing women's participation in the national movement. From his experience in South Africa, Gandhi concluded that women have an extraordinary capacity for self-sacrifice. His appeal to Indian women was based on this conclusion. He argued that women have a great ability to tolerate suffering and, hence, were ideally suited to carry out the politics of non-violence. This idea was derived from his understanding of women's role as mothers. Because of this mothering capability, Gandhi argued that women are preceptors for men. He subscribed to the position that men and women are biologically different and, hence, have different roles to play.

There is no doubt that Gandhi legitimised women's participation in public activities and politics. But the basis of his understanding was firmly located within traditional upper-caste Hindu patriarchy. He hesitated to acknowledge the need for expanding the role women played in politics. He argued that the home is an important arena with far-reaching impact on the world outside. It was the woman's job to bring about change in that domain. However, he remained unconvinced about expanding their role in the world outside. The compulsions of politics made him change his stand in later years. Gandhi's support of the women's cause led the already liberal sections of the Congress to commit themselves to the cause of women's equality.

It is this commitment that led the Congress party to draft the Fundamental Rights Resolution at the Karachi Session of the Congress party in 1931. The basic principle of equality between sexes was accepted. After independence, therefore, the Constitution makers unhesitatingly accepted this idea.

Women in pre-independence India became active participants in the communist as well as the other revolutionary organisations. They were actively involved in working class struggles, peasant movements and adivasi uprisings. Of course, the domination of the Congress ideology meant that most of these efforts were overlooked.

THE CONTEMPORARY WOMEN'S MOVEMENT IN INDIA

Independence came in 1947 with the promise of a new beginning. The hope was that within the democratic framework guaranteed by the new Constitution, Indian women would find greater autonomy and freedom. The economic and social changes, it was hoped, would ameliorate the conditions of the poor and marginalised sections of the society, and empower women. The immediate years following independence were, thus, marked by hope.

By the mid-1960s, however, the consensus put together under Jawaharlal Nehru's leadership was beginning to crack. India's defeat in the war with China, an adverse economic scenario, and finally, Nehru's death led the Congress that had been the undisputed party of power to experience dissent, and finally, electoral defeat, albeit in state assembly elections. There was a growing realisation of the fact that the Congress party was unable to fulfil all the promises that it had made during the national struggle. Economic development was taking place but there was no place in this for the vast majority. This discontent was channelled through various political forces and groups, and women became a prominent part of these movements. Ilina Sen in her essay Women's Politics in India has brought out the essential difference between the mobilisation of women in politics in this phase and the mobilisation that happened earlier. She contends that in this phase, the accent was not solely on mobilising women but on introspection of how and why women continued to be subordinated. Thus, the women's movement was being revived after a lull in the 1950s and the 1960s. Interestingly, the movement this time round was unfolding in the context of contemporaneous radical movements.

The Left parties that had been the beacon of radical politics were now getting fragmented. Many adherents of Left politics left the formal political party organisation and became part of other radical movements that were asking fundamental questions. The women's movement benefited from this general mood of investigation and became a part of this new political ethos. Women became a big and important part of landmark campaigns like the Shahada, Dhulia, Self-Employed Women's Association (SEWA) and Nav Nirman, among many others.

The Shahada movement emerged in the adivasi areas of Maharashtra. Harassment by the local landlords, and conditions of famine and drought led the adivasi people to organise themselves into the Shramik Sangathana in 1972. They directed their efforts in the direction of famine relief and reclaimed land for cultivation. The movement, thus, became very popular among the labourers, especially the women. It was women who mobilised men to join the movement and remained steadfast in their negotiations with the landlords. As women's militancy and participation grew within the movement, gender concerns and issues came to be raised. These women were far removed from the stereotype of feminists in India, that is, Westernised, university-educated and urban.

Radha Kumar discerns a pattern in the development of the Shahada movement that went from being a social reform movement to a Sarvodaya movement, and finally, a far Left one. Thus, with the development of militancy in the movement, the scope for raising questions related to gender concerns became possible. She points out that whenever a community becomes conscious of its own oppression, and is actually able to express it through a large scale movement with active involvement of women, there is bound to be an examination of the subordination of women, by women themselves. In the Shahada movement, this examination centred on the issue of wife-beating and alcoholism. Women organised themselves into groups that would raid liquor dens and come to the assistance of any woman who was beaten by her husband. In this, the activists were guided by a clear feminist understanding that alcohol was only a subsidiary problem; the main issue was wife-beating which was unacceptable. Thus, a clear anti-patriarchal sentiment imbued the Shahada movement.

Ela Bhatt pioneered the Self-Employed Women's Association or SEWA. Formed in 1972 in Ahmedabad, Gujarat, this was an effort guided largely by Gandhian principles. SEWA focused upon the exploitation and low wages paid to women in the informal sector. These women faced harassment by the civic authorities and their work was not recognised as socially useful. After a long struggle, SEWA was able to get recognition as a trade union. This was, indeed, a tremendous achievement since its members did not work either in a factory or for a particular employer.

SEWA remained within the Gandhian framework and focused upon reformist efforts. The Shahada movement was, thus, closer to the feminist political sensibilities than SEWA, which, too, kept its distance from the feminist movement.

The anti–price rise agitation that spread throughout Gujarat and Maharashtra in the 1970s is noteworthy from the point of view of the number of women participants it was able to attract. A United Women's Anti–Price Rise Front was formed to mobilise women against inflation.

Women from the communist and socialist parties were involved in its organisation. From Mumbai, the movement spread to Gujarat and became the foundation of the Nav Nirman movement that started in 1974. This movement against price rise soon became a movement that questioned the very basis of the Indian state. Their critique of the Indian state and parliamentary democracy was inspired by Jai Prakash Narayan's concept of 'total revolution' that was beginning to gain popularity in Bihar.

Both the anti–price rise and the Nav Nirman movement involved many women, but did not necessarily raise questions related to women's subordination. For instance, the most obvious question would have been to examine why was it that only women were concerned about the rise in domestic expenditure? In fact, the movement through many of its actions seemed to reinforce traditional norms of contempt for women, as when they offered bangles to those in power suggesting that they were not manly enough to be in power.

The call for 'total revolution', on the other hand, raised far more difficult questions. The movement, involving many women and students, questioned the existing power structures in the state and society. They challenged the institution of the family and the role of women within this structure. Apart from unequal property rights for men and women, the movement even re-examined the whole nature of male–female relationships, and even the issue of female sexuality. The main proponents of this feminist critique of patriarchy were the young men and women, who were part of the Chaatra Yuva Sangharsh Vahini, the vanguard of JP's movement.

One of the most important struggles that the Chaatra Yuva Sangharsh Vahini was involved with was the Bodhgaya Math struggle. The Math controlled the lives and lands of the poor peasants of this area. Interestingly, when the poor began to ask for land rights, there was a clear recognition of women's rights to ownership of property. While most of these landmark political developments were unfolding in rural India, urban India, too, witnessed the strengthening of feminist activism and politics.

It was in this context that the autonomous women's movement emerged in India. One of the first groups to be formed was the Progressive Organisation of Women (POW) in 1974, in Hyderabad. Most of the women who were part of POW were drawn from the Maoist groups that were very popular in Andhra Pradesh. The POW identified the sexual division of labour and the cultural justification of this division on which women's subordination is based as its main adversaries. They saw the need to challenge the existing economic system based on capitalism, and sought its replacement by socialism which they argued would bring in a culture of equality.

In 1975, many new organisations and efforts that were beginning to ask fundamental questions about women's subordination began to emerge, especially in Maharashtra. This was a significant year because internationally the UN had declared it as Women's Year. For the first time, International Women's Day was celebrated in India on 8 March. Most of these efforts came from women within Maoist groups. Radha Kumar finds the gradual realisation of the connection between patriarchy and caste; especially the coming closer of the anti-caste Dalit movements with feminist groups, a very significant development in this period.

These groups were different from the ones in the earlier phase in that they stressed on the sexual oppression of all women and not just of certain categories of women like prostitutes. Of course, within them there were different explanations for women's subordination. Some groups attributed women's sexual oppression to their economic dependence on men, while others argued that women's enslavement was a consequence of their reproductive functions. Thus, it was a clear divide between those who held biological differences to be the root cause of women's oppression and others who did not wish to predicate women's oppression upon these biological differences. The latter group argued that women's subordination was not a consequence of their biological differences but was based on an unequal sexual division of labour that was centuries old.

The year 1975 was also the year, when the then Prime Minister Mrs Indira Gandhi declared Emergency. The two-year period till 1977 saw most political activists either behind bars or engaging in underground political activities. This became the context for a serious and complete re-examination of the foundations of Indian democracy and the nature of the Indian state. The new women's groups that were coming together at this time were engaged in a re-examination of one of the fundamental assumptions of the Indian society—the sexual division of labour and the subordination of women. Hence, they declared themselves to be feminist, although many of these women belonged to the traditional Left groups. Left parties have, by and large, been sceptical of feminist ideology and politics seeing it as divisive and more seriously as bourgeois. Perhaps, it is because of this that these groups decided to be autonomous and not affiliated to any big political party. Soon these groups formed all over the country began to come together, share their ideas and strategies, and form networks. It is, thus, that the current phase of the women's movement began in India.

This is not to suggest that there was complete uniformity in the understanding, politics or strategies of these diverse groups despite the fact that most of them belonged to far Left groups. In the 1970s, the most important questions for these groups were of self-definition and of representation. Radha Kumar explains the dilemma these groups faced vis-à-vis the question of organisation and representation. Not all groups felt confident of being effective organisers or representatives. Most of the activists in these groups were drawn from urban, educated, middle-class backgrounds. This, they believed, created a wide gap between them and the peasant and working class women they were seeking to organise and hoping to represent. Still others believed that while the issue of women's subordination was very important, it, however, had to be linked with other mass movements. They sought space within existing mass organisations like trade unions and peasant bodies for raising feminist issues. Still others hoped that with the gradual spread of their ideals, organisations would spontaneously be formed. This last group, obviously, was not very hopeful of arousing feminist sensibilities within the existing organisations. These differences often led to sharp disagreements.

Most groups, however, agreed upon the desirability of autonomy. Existing political parties were seen as hierarchical and entrenched within the power structures of the society. Some groups believed that it was possible to transform them, while others believed that the institution of the political party would never lend itself to the radical and democratic political vision that feminism espouses.

It was in 1977 with the end of the Emergency that a group of women in Delhi came together and set up a journal called *Manushi* that was to be both in Hindi and English. Many such efforts were begun elsewhere, apart from documentation centres.

Two issues, towards the end of the 1970s and through the 1980s, galvanised women's groups further. The forceful campaign against rape, and the highly charged and emotional campaign against dowry brought in new energy into the movement. As early as 1975, the POW in Hyderabad launched a campaign against dowry. But the overall political climate, thanks to the Emergency, was not conducive to the campaign taking off in a big way. Soon after the lifting of Emergency, Delhi became the centre of a forceful campaign against dowry. In the democratic upsurge following the defeat of Indira Gandhi's government, the movement found many supporters. Delhi spearheaded the campaign also because it had the dubious distinction of a very high number of deaths of young brides that everyone suspected was related to unfulfilled dowry demands, but were reported as either accidental deaths or suicides. These deaths were seen as private affairs and not open to the state for investigation. Feminists insisted that the disproportionately large numbers of women who died in fire accidents was definitely related to harassment related to unfulfilled dowry demands and were, thus, murders. The movement gained popularity. Public campaigns, protest marches, and street plays and posters were all employed to arouse consciousness against dowry. They systematically recorded the last statement of a dying woman, assisted the woman's family in reporting the death to the police (this was not being done till now) and collected evidence from friends and family. Under pressure from the massive success of the anti-dowry campaign, the government in 1980 passed a law against dowry-related crimes. Like all legislations, this one also has its limitations and loopholes. D. N. Sandanshiv and Jolly Mathew in the book *Dowry and Inheritance* by Srimati Basu evaluate the efficacy of the legal reforms. Laws relating to dowry come under criminal laws and, therefore, like all other criminal laws are bound to be limited in its effectiveness. They argue that ultimately these laws would be effective only when backed by community action, public legal education and sensitising all levels of implementation agencies. Of course, education and economic opportunities for women are very important. Often the offenders in dowry-related cases do not see themselves as guilty nor do the courts sometimes treat these cases with any degree of urgency. Another stumbling block that they identify is the role of bail. Despite the Supreme Court's cautionary advice, sessions and high courts frequently grant bail in cases related to domestic violence and dowry.

The next big issue that feminists took up in the 1980s was the issue of rape. Women's groups had been consistently protesting against rape by landlords and employers in various parts of the country, but two incidents of custodial rape by the police sparked off an agitation that marked a new phase in the feminist movement in India. Rape has been an important issue in the feminist discourse internationally. The issue of rape and how it is discussed tells us a great deal about how societies and communities perceive a woman's body. It is common to use rape to establish power and authority over an individual, as in the case of landlord raping women workers employed by him, or the wives of the workers employed by him. It is almost seen as a right that the landlord has over his workers. Rape is also used to establish the superiority of caste groups, or to prove the vulnerability of the minority community. It is also used to 'humiliate' the vanquished in war. A young 17-year-old woman called Mathura was raped by policemen. The courts acquitted the policemen on the grounds that since she had a boyfriend, she was of dubious moral character and, hence, cannot allege rape. This and later in 1980, the rape of a woman called Maya Tyagi, once again by policemen in Haryana, made the issue of custodial rape central to feminist concerns. The Forum Against Rape was established in Mumbai in 1981 that later came to be known as the Forum Against Oppression of Women. Their forceful campaign resulted in the government responding with an extremely radical piece of legislation that shifted the onus of proof onto the accused among many other provisions like 10 years imprisonment and *in camera* trial.

Subsequent judgements in many rape cases disappointed the feminists who discovered that the quick response from the government was little more than political opportunism. The attitude towards rape, and the problem of marshalling medical evidence, especially in rural and small town India—all made the legislation rather redundant. The courts continued to look at past conduct of the woman to condone rape. Feminists continued to protest against this, and the National Front government in power in the early 1990s promised changes. The painful realisation, however, was that despite the enactment of radical legislations, it was the terrain of implementation and interpretation of the law that was difficult to negotiate. Feminists also drew attention to the fact that the technical definition of rape itself was problematic because it did not recognise the basically violent nature of rape, since it recognised only the forceful penetration by the penis of the vagina as rape. By the end of the 1980s, the number of rape cases that were registered by the police had more than doubled as a consequence of the changing social attitudes that emboldened more women to report rape.

With the experience of two successful mass campaigns behind them, feminist groups began to diversify their activities to include running of legal aid centres, media monitoring groups, and so on. They began setting up counselling centres and health care facilities. These new efforts differed from the somewhat similar efforts in the past. The guiding principle now was the interrelated nature of the problems that beset women, and their origins in women's subordinate position in society. Thus, a feminist and not a social welfare approach began to guide these efforts. In doing this, there was a conscious effort to translate into reality the feminist ideal of sisterhood. It was hoped that the existence of organisations run by women for other women would create this sentiment and create avenues for women to come together outside of the approved familial context.

The *sati* that took place in Rajasthan in 1987 was yet another issue that became the focus of the feminist campaign in the 1980s. At the heart of the campaign was not only the act itself but also the subsequent glorification of *sati* and the half-hearted attempts by the state to control this. More worrying was the sight of women who enthusiastically marched through the streets of Jaipur and other cities to demonstrate their support for the practice. A section of the intellectuals argued that being alienated from their traditions and culture, feminists and others who opposed *sati* were unable to understand the discourse and the logic of *sati* as an example of self-sacrifice.

The support for *sati* that came from within the Rajput community spoke of *sati* as being one of the distinguishing features of their community's identity. This practice, they argued, was part of the personal laws of Hindus and should be kept beyond the purview of the state. In the context of the Muslim Women's Protection Bill, they demanded that the state should show the same discretion with respect to the family laws of Hindus. The issue of *sati* became the site on which the secular credentials of the Indian state were to be evaluated. The Indian state was repeatedly being accused of accommodating interests of the minority community, while interfering with matters of personal law of the majority community. This, they argued, made the secular claims of the Indian state rather suspect.

The pro-*sati* campaign posited the traditional Hindu woman against the alienated, Westernised, feminist woman who could not share the sentiments and understanding of her sisters. Of course, closer examination did reveal that most women, perhaps, wholeheartedly supported the worship of *sati* while being unsure of the desirability of its practice. However, facing women who were pro-*sati* forced the feminist movement in India to take up issues of culture and tradition as well as communities and representation. The legislation (Commission of Sati Prevention Bill) that followed the feminist campaign against *sati* did not bring much consolation because it had far too many loopholes, and considered the woman who commits *sati* also an offender. This would let the family members of the woman to go scot free, despite the fact that they aid and abet the act.

Culture became the new focus of research and analysis. The attempt was to take a close look at traditions, and identify possible allies within the tradition. For this, it became necessary to reinterpret traditions and redefine it wherever necessary. One of the favourite figures that lend itself to such attempts was that of the Mother Goddess and Kali. The attempt was to present Kali as a symbol of power and energy, a feminist icon, far removed from the docile, domesticated goddesses of the traditional Hindu pantheon.

There were other efforts made to identify the spaces that were already available to ordinary women in the traditional context. The example Radha Kumar cites is of pregnancy. Women in traditional contexts often use this condition to extract concessions for themselves.

Much research was focused on trying to find precursors of the contemporary feminist movement. History, therefore, became a very important arena of research. It is in this context that the Chipko movement of the early 1970s, that was hitherto seen as an environmental movement to save the trees and forests of Uttaranchal, suddenly made an appearance as an illustration of women's special bond with environment. This eco-feminist reconstruction has not been without its critics. The obvious criticism emerges out of a discomfort with the essentialist nature of the eco-feminist assumptions that defines women's nature in an eternal and unchanging sort of way.

The most well-known position on eco-feminism is that of Vandana Shiva. She argues that colonialism commercialised India's forest and disrupted the traditional nurturing relationship that women had with nature and forest wealth. She alleges that commercial forestry in collaboration with patriarchy violates the natural life of the forest and its resources, thus, adversely affecting the economic and social lives of the communities that depended on these forests for their livelihood. Women, she says, have always understood the life of the forests and have respected its resources. In making this argument, she invokes many elements of upper-caste Hindu philosophy, especially the whole discourse of the Mother Goddess and the principle of *Prakriti* that she describes as the 'feminine principle'. The Chipko movement, in which hundreds of women participated, had as its public face a few well-known men. Although men were also part of the Chipko movement, they were driven more by the need to secure local interests in commercial forestry, whereas, she suggests, the women were driven by the need to sustain and protect the forest, and its resources. Many feminist scholars have challenged this presentation; some like Gabriel Dietrich have expressed their discomfort with Shiva's unproblematic use of Hindu upper-caste idea and concepts that would not only exclude a whole range of women but are of suspect feminist lineage. Besides, in the context of Hindu right wing politics, such attempts are politically rather problematic. To suggest that pro-colonial ecological systems were sustainable is only describing a part of the picture. Ecologically sustainable systems, as we have seen in India, could also be hierarchical as well as patriarchal at the same time. Caste division of society and caste based division of labour were, after all, the foundation of pre-colonial ecosystems. Bina Aggarwal has questioned Shiva's unduly romanticised picture of pre-colonial Indian society, for, she argues, pre-colonial India had its own systems of power, domination, control and hierarchy. Aggarwal has also expressed discomfort with Shiva's attempt at essentialising women's nature as being universally nurturing towards nature. This position seems to ignore the fact that men and women do not have an essential way of relating to nature; rather it is mediated by their relationship with the material world.

Meanwhile, academia and research institutes in the 1980s incorporated women's studies as the focus of their research and eventually teaching. Feminist issues and movements began to show a clear impact on media as well as medicine. Health care and related issues became very important points of reference. Malnutrition has been recognised as a major health hazard for women. But it is common to justify women's intake of nutritionally less healthy food on the basis of the supposedly less amount of work that women do. Shah and Gandhi point out that it is not a specific kind of work but the overwork that women engage in that becomes a health hazard. The double burden of work, both in the public and the private sphere, is the problem. Time spent in collecting fuel, food or water is not recognised as work. Breathing the smoke in the kitchens that use traditional fuel like cattle dung, agricultural waste, and the like, is very harmful because of its carcinogenic character. Feminist health campaigns have pointed out that health policies of the state must have a more holistic and non-sexist attitude towards women's health. The guiding principle should not be to see women as potential child bearers and mothers, but as people who have a quintessential right to health care. It is in this context that one of the biggest feminist campaigns of the 1980s unfolded on the issue of contraceptives. After a storm of protest against injectible contraceptives in the West, it was tried out in India in the 1980s. Apex medical bodies began to try these drugs on women who had no information about the negative side-effects of using these injectible contraceptives. Activists stormed meetings that were being held to study the feasibility of this injectible contraceptive called Net-N, and soon realised that a ban on this alone would not be of much consequence.

The next big campaign was against High Dose Estrogen Progesterone formulations, popularly referred to as EP drugs. This drug came to be used for a variety of gynaecological conditions, but the fact that it could create congenital heart conditions in the foetus was not revealed. A high voltage campaign by women activists in the field of health and sustained discussions with government health authorities resulted in the banning of this drug in the tablet form.

A medical diagnostic test called amniocentesis has been the other issue that feminists interested in health issues have taken up. This test that analyses the amniotic fluid surrounding the foetus is meant to detect over 70 genetic diseases. It is also capable of revealing the sex of the unborn child. Health activists have campaigned against this test because in our country this test is used primarily for the latter purpose, and if the foetus is found to be female, an abortion follows. This abortion itself being carried out in the second trimester of the pregnancy has chances of turning fatal, besides resulting in physical dislocations in the foetus. It was a difficult campaign to take-off, given the son loving cultural context, but in response to the campaign, legislations not banning but 'regulating' the tests have been passed. Maharashtra passed the first law in this regard in 1986, but among the many other dissatisfactory provisions, it held the woman undergoing the test, also, guilty.

The Pre-Conception and Pre-Natal Diagnostic Techniques (Prohibition of Sex Selection) Act and Rules 1994 (as amended up to 2002) (the PCPNDT Act) mandates that sex selection by any person, by any means, before or after conception, is prohibited. Then, there is the legally binding Code of Medical Ethics, constituted by the Indian Parliament in the Medical Council Act 1956, that many doctors conveniently ignore. The consistent practice of sex selection tests is bound to get reflected in the national census. The 2001 census registered a decline in the child sex ratio in 80 per cent of the districts in India. The juvenile sex ratio, which stood at 976 in 1961, fell to 927 in 2001, for the country as a whole. The PCPNDT Act mandates that any person conducting ultrasonography or any other pre-natal diagnostic technique must maintain proper records. The Act requires the filling-up of a written form, duly signed by the expectant mother, as to why she has sought diagnosis. Violations are punishable by imprisonment and a fine. The child sex ratio for the country stands at 927 in 2001, down from 945 in1991. But, in India, all statistics hide more than they reveal—if we disaggregate data, we find great inequalities both between states and within states. The more prosperous states like Haryana, Punjab, Delhi and Gujarat show ratios, which have declined to less than 900 girls for 1000 boys. Further disaggregation of data shows that 70 districts in 16 states and Union territories of the country have recorded a decline of more than 50 points in the sex ratio in the last decade.

Take a look at some statistics regarding the sex ratio in various parts of our country (Table 11.1). What we see is the number of women listed in the table to every thousand men in our population. By and large, the world over, the trend is of more women in the human population to every thousand men, but in India the picture appears to be rather different. However, within India itself there is a great deal of difference. A very prosperous union territory like Chandigarh had only 773 women to every thousand men. If we turn our attention to the capital of the country, the figures are even more dismal. However, the state of Himachal Pradesh does have a couple of districts at least that report figures closer to the international norms. If we turn towards Kerala, we see a completely different scenario with eleven out of the twelve districts reporting more than thousand women to every thousand men in the population. A lot of interesting analyses of the issues that result from these findings are available, but clearly the number of women in the population has something to do with the overall status of women in a particular society, which, in turn, is linked to the property norms, family, marriage and kinship patterns, education and a whole host of other factors.

In 1999, The Pre-Natal Diagnostic Techniques (Regulations and Prevention of Misuses) Act was passed. The Act permits the test only under certain specific conditions and only for the detection of a limited number of abnormalities in the foetus. Revealing the sex of the foetus is, however, prohibited. Several loopholes in the proposed law were identified only to be ignored. For instance, the information regarding the sex of the foetus is not to be revealed to the woman or her relatives but does not prevent such information being shared with a non-relative. It also treats the woman as

TABLE 11.1 Sex ratio and population density in 1991 and 2001

(a)

Code no.	*State/Union territory/District*	*Sex ratio*	
		1991	*2001*
4	**Chandigarh**	**790**	**773**
1	Chandigarh	790	773

(b)

Code no.	*State/Union territory/District*	*Sex ratio*	
		1991	*2001*
7	**Delhi**	**827**	**821**
1	North West	822	820
2	North	819	826
3	North East	837	851
4	East	846	845
5	New Delhi	793	791
6	Central	872	843
7	West	848	830
8	South West	795	783
9	South	807	797

(c)

Code no.	*State/Union territory/District*	*Sex ratio*	
		1991	*2001*
32	**Kerala**	**1036**	**1058**
1	Kasaragod	1026	1047
2	Kannur	1049	1090
3	Wayanad	966	1000
4	Kozhikode	1027	1058
5	Malappuram	1053	1063
6	Palakkad	1061	1068
7	Thrissur	1085	1092
8	Ernakulam	1000	1017
9	Idukki	975	993
10	Kottayam	1003	1025
11	Alappuzha	1051	1079

Contd.

Contd.

(d)

Code no.	*State/Union territory/District*	*Sex ratio*	
		1991	*2001*
2	**Himachal Pradesh**	**976**	**970**
1	Chamba	949	961
2	Kangra	1024	1027
3	Lahul & Spiti	817	804
4	Kullu	920	928
5	Mandi	1013	1014
6	Hamirpur	1105	1102
7	Una	1017	997
8	Bilaspur	1002	992
9	Solan	909	853
10	Sirmaur	897	901
11	Shimla	894	898
12	Kinnaur	856	851

an offender unless she can prove that she has been coerced. It is, indeed, strange that in a cultural context where women seldom make autonomous decisions, they should be thought of as being capable of taking decisions on this issue. The fact is that the law obviously has not had much effect. The 2001 census figures show a further decline in sex ratio, especially in the 0–6 years age group, suggesting a large-scale femicide of female foetuses and female children.

Nivedita Menon has raised the issue of femicide of female foetuses as being distinct from the issue of abortion. Steering clear of the use of the word foeticide, she implies that the use of this word does not leave much room for feminists to defend abortion, on one hand and on the other hand, ask for a ban on selective abortions based on the sex of the foetuses. The point that she makes is that people have rights not in an abstract, ahistorical sense but within a particular context. Given the son loving and misogynist context of our country, and given the fact of alarmingly disproportionate sex ratios, it is perfectly possible for feminists to argue both for the woman's right to abortions as well as a ban on femicide of female foetuses. Patriarchy creates specific kinds of constraints because of which abortion must be made accessible to women. It is these constraints that produce a society that seeks femicide. As a consequence, the numbers of women would shrink even further and, the world over, it has been seen that societies with fewer women than men are invariably more sexist.

Hence, selective abortion of female foetuses should be prevented. This insightful line of argument frees feminists from the seemingly contradictory stand they took on the issue of abortion, on one hand, and femicide, on the other. This understanding would free feminists, as Nivedita Menon has argued, from being forced to choose between the rights of future women to be born versus the rights of existing women over their bodies.

CHALLENGES TO THE WOMEN'S MOVEMENT

Towards the end of the 1980s, feminists began to understand that the category of woman is far too universal and undifferentiated. In the context of caste, community and class among many other differences, it was no longer possible to talk in terms of women. This made essential a shift away from the unmarked nature of the definition of citizenship. But it was this unmarked nature of the definition of citizenship that made it possible to talk in terms of equality and justice in an unproblematic sort of way. If differences were to be acknowledged, then the traditional terms of discourse seemed to be faltering.

The closing years of the 1980s and the 1990s have seen a new kind of political contest gaining in importance. Politics of backward caste, Dalit and minorities seeking their share of power in the Indian state has been offset by the attempts by the Hindu right to define the nation itself. The latter have tried repeatedly to present a monolithic picture of the Hindu society that is united by its hoary past. This vision glosses over all kinds of internal differences, especially the ones based on caste, and in its own unique way, on gender. This political group does perceive caste, and to a certain extent gender politics, to be potentially divisive forces. The spectre of minorities and backward castes cornering all the benefits that the state has to offer, has driven many sections of upper-caste India into the arms of Hindu right wing politics. It is in this context that the entire campaign for the construction of the temple at the controversial site of the Babri Masjid in Ayodhya should be located.

Feminists, to their dismay, discovered that women were enthusiastic participants not only in the anti-Mandal agitation (discussed in Chapter 7) but also in this new more militant Hindutva campaign. As Tanika Sarkar (1995) has shown, a new kind of woman activist was thus being created who consciously wished to distance herself from the feminist activist. Their activism often had the blessings of the family and was seen as an extension of their nurturing role in the family. The new breed of women activists have been described as being not home breakers but as torchbearers of the Hindu tradition. Their activism in most cases has not involved or permitted any challenges to traditional family structures and practices. Women's roles are accepted as given and immutable. These women activists of the Hindu Right clearly show that women could come together and even be engaged in politics without necessarily challenging patriarchy. On the contrary, the way they come together and their manner of working wins approval from patriarchal structures.

Community politics, especially majoritarian politics, in the Indian context has posed one of the biggest challenges to the women's movement. The enthusiastic participation by women in large numbers in the Ram Janma Bhoomi campaign made feminists in India rethink the whole issue of community and politics. This process, undoubtedly, began in the context of the Shah Bano case. The conservatives within the Muslim community alleged that the Supreme Court judgement endangered Islam and took away the rights of the Muslim community to their unique identity, which was, in part, derived from their special family laws. The Hindu communalist used this opposition as a vindication of their long standing argument about the barbaric nature of Muslims.

Thus, essentially an issue about the rights of women became the peg on which to conduct the entire debate on secularism in India. The 1980s had witnessed increasing communal assertions by the majority community. The anti-Sikh riots following Indira Gandhi's assassination in 1984, and the general mood of distrust and animosity towards the minority communities characterised the 1980s. The aggressive campaign for the temple in Ayodhya that followed soon after, seemed to have the tacit approval of the state.

The middle-class, upper-caste Hindu male had convinced himself of being besieged by the frightening forces of minority politics, Dalit and backward caste movements, and feminist women. The fear stemmed from the belief that old and familiar structures of authority and power would be pulled down. This fear is the basis to a great extent of Hindu right wing politics that grew in strength in the 1980s.

Sections of the minority communities were, in the meanwhile, swamped by the fear of the state's attempts to homogenise their distinctive identities. The agitation for the temple and the judgement that supposedly challenged Islam, came to be linked and seen as an onslaught on the minorities, especially the Muslims. Feminists learnt many lessons through the course of these years. One important lesson was that the 'community in danger' argument is very appealing; and as part of protecting the community, one of the demands is regulation and control over the woman of 'our community'. They also learnt that the state very easily succumbs to such demands, even at the cost of withdrawing basic Constitutional rights of women (in this case of the Muslim community). These lessons, among many others, forced the feminist movement to rethink the whole issue of an undifferentiated, uniform civil code not based on specific religious laws that they had been campaigning for. The campaign stemmed from the conviction that all existing family laws based on specific religious codes and practices were discriminatory to women. However, in the highly charged and communal milieu of the 1980s and the 1990s, any demand for such a code has become politically suspect. Flavia Agnes has been quoted as saying that with the rise of majority communalism, it is not possible to discuss the Uniform Civil Code as a non-sexist code any longer. Equal citizenship in the context of attempts by politicised religious groups to gain hegemony over the state can hardly be discussed.

Is the choice for women, then, between state control and regulation, on one hand and community control, on the other? Kumkum Sangari has argued that posing the choice, thus, obscures the possibility of feminist agency. In her opinion, women should not be in a position where they need to choose between patriarchy regulated by the state or by the community. Rather their struggle should be for the recognition of gender justice as a principle and a social horizon. Every action in society needs to be evaluated at all times on the basis of the principle of gender justice. In other words, gender justice should be a principle that is always being strived for. It should be impossible to announce the achievement of gender justice.

The Hyderabad-based women's group Anveshi has words of caution that deserve to be mentioned here. While the discourse of citizenship based on universal ideal of equality and justice has an emancipatory potential, it also tends to homogenise and marginalise other understandings of justice. Women are perceived as a universal category, based on biological differences from men. What about different understandings of rights and justice that are emerging out of movements based on caste, class or religion, they ask. Hence, they suggest that any demand for a singular conception of gender justice is problematic. Does that, however, mean surrender to relativism? Their answer is no. What they suggest is a re-examination of dominant meanings of terms such as justice, equality and rights.

In this complex context, hence, there is no consensus possible within the feminist movement on the issue of Uniform Civil Code (UCC). The fear of the Hindu right wing inscribing its agenda over the UCC has unnerved those who were at the forefront of the demand.

Caste is an issue that women's movement had not paid much attention to in the past. By the end of the 1980s, it became clear that it was no longer possible to talk of the Indian woman as a universal and undifferentiated category. The autonomous women's movement in Sharmila Rege's opinion left Brahminism unchallenged. She recognises the fact that while the autonomous women's movement did raise issues concerning Dalit and adivasi women, it did not allow for the emergence of a feminist politics centred on the experiences and problems of women from the most marginalised sections of our society. While the movement did raise issues of sexuality, in her opinion, they remained within the framework of lifestyle choices, missing the essential linkage between caste and sexuality. In post-Mandal India, it is no longer possible to pretend that universal categories exist. Upper-caste women suddenly discovered their commitment to the ideals of merit and efficiency, and joined their men in the virulent campaign against reservations. It is, therefore, clear that the Indian women's movement has to address the issue of caste from a gendered perspective.

CONCLUSION

This has been a very brief survey of the contemporary women's movement in India. There are many more issues and campaigns beyond what has been presented here. But even this brief examination reveals the complex and interrelated nature of most of the issues and campaigns raised by the women's movement in India. It has addressed issues of work, wages, education, health, family laws, culture and aesthetics, history, law, participation in contemporary politics, environment and sexuality. The sheer diversity of issues raised by the women's movement makes it vibrant and dynamic and somewhat difficult to define. A vast number of organisations and groups would like to be included in this collective called the Indian women's movement. Party affiliated groups as well as autonomous groups are both present.

One of the biggest challenges to the women's movement in India undoubtedly comes from the Hindu right wing efforts to mobilise and organise women politically. Other kinds of criticisms also need to be taken stock of. Conventional Left groups, for a long time, were suspicious of the women's movement, dismissing it as essentially a bourgeois movement that talks of waging war on men, thus weakening chances of worker's unity. Today, however, most political parties have appropriated the issues and demands of the Indian women's movement with not very happy consequences. A major dilemma facing many of the groups is the question of funding which either comes from international donors or from the government. This does place certain constraints upon their working. The problems facing Indian women are complex and diverse, and hence, the response also has been diverse. Women are located in different cultural contexts and no uniform answers would be satisfactory. The search, however, should be able to strike a balance between respecting diversity while creating a just and egalitarian society.

POINTS FOR DISCUSSION

- Discuss the coverage given to the contemporary women's movement in India by the press. Is it possible to discern any patterns?
- The International Women's Day was celebrated in India for the first time in 1975. Try and look at the newspaper coverage of the event back then, and how different is it today?

SELECT BIBLIOGRAPHY

Chaudhuri, Maitrayee (2004). *Feminism In India*. New Delhi: Kali for Women.

Kapadia, Karin (ed.) (2002). *The Violence of Development*. New Delhi: Kali for Women.

Kumar, Radha (1998). *The History of Doing*. New Delhi: Kali for Women.

Sarkar, Tanika and Urvashi Butalia (eds) (1995). *Women and the Hindu Right: A Collection of Essays*. New Delhi: Kali for Women.

Section III Environment

12

Environment and Sustainable Development

> The first UN Conference on Women was held in Mexico in 1975. In preparation, I researched the needs of Kenyan women and learnt that what they wanted most was clean water to drink, cooking fuel—mostly from wood—and food from land. These issues, I realised, were all intimately connected to land. It became clear to me that many of the problems communities were facing were the result of environmental degradation ... The Norwegian Nobel Committee has challenged the world to broaden the understanding of peace: there can be no peace without equitable development; and there can be no development without sustainable management of the environment in a democratic and peaceful space. This shift is an idea whose time has come.
>
> —Prof. Wangari Maathai, Winner of the Nobel Peace Prize 2004

This section of the book seeks to explain that it is the issues of environment that highlight the fact that there is something wrong in the modern model of development. Further, they show what kind of fundamental changes are required in it, if the human race is to survive and survive well, over a long period of time, and how these are to be achieved. Thus, this link between the two is not quite obvious, because each of the terms is very heavily loaded with associations built up over the years. So, these two terms need to be explained before anything else would make sense. For this reason then, we will take them one by one—the concept of development itself, the environmental critique of development and, finally, how the concept of sustainable development emerges from these critiques. You will find that the second and third sections themselves have a number of smaller sections, so arranged as to distinguish clearly for you the separate modes of thought, while trying to convey their linkages.

THE CONCEPT OF DEVELOPMENT

Development is a concept that denotes the significant rise of the production of an increasing range of goods and services that substantially improved the quality of human life. These were labour-saving machinery, faster modes of travel and communication, more fluid and mobile forms of money, medicines with greater ability to fight killer diseases and healthcare systems that enabled increasing life expectancy. These were all possible because a number of significant changes combined in society—the change in the ownership and use of capital, the consequent changes in the structures of societies, and the changes in the pattern, extent and direction of the use of natural resources for the use of human beings. Further, these changes first occurred in certain societies, and at certain periods of time, these being in Western Europe and the United States from roughly the sixteenth century onwards. The imperialism and colonialism of the eighteenth century were important factors for pushing these forces of development forward by providing additional resources of every kind from the colonies. The progress of the imperialist countries, a source of fascination for the colonised, also served to undermine the latter's achievements historically, while making their present and future worse by continued subjugation. Thus began the process by which the historical trajectory of Europe, its specific economic, social and political developments became the reference point for the direction in which all other countries of the world must move. This is what makes the concept of development 'Eurocentric' and also capitalist. Thus, Adams (2001: 6) refers to Goulet's (1995) analysis arguing that the word 'development' is used both descriptively (to describe what happens in the world as societies, environments and economies change) and normatively (to set out what *should* happen) [emphasis original].

The process was consolidated by the end of the Second World War, by which time, imperialism of the nineteenth century kind was over, but a new world order was taking shape. (This has been discussed in detail in the chapter on UNEP.) Development, denoting what we have discussed above, became the dominant wisdom and the focus of policy and politics for governments in most countries, especially the newly independent ones, seen as backward and required to 'catch up' with the West. Economic growth, of the kind developed and practised by the West, would be a means by which widespread hunger, poverty and disease would be eradicated in these countries. D'Monte (1985: 3) points out, 'Most planners in Third World countries have their schooling in welfare economics which, ... "furnished the paradigm within which conventional development economics operates".' He (ibid.: 3) also quotes Farvar and Milton who argue that while goals of development may be 'conceptualised by sociologists and politicians in a developing country, but the means are prescribed primarily by economists.' Thus, Adams (2001: 7) argues that the word 'development' then came to mean the projects and policies, the infrastructure, flows of capital and transfers of technology, which were supposed to make that imitation possible. Development thus involved the imposition of the established world order on the newly independent periphery. However, it is well known that even today, more than 50 years after this exercise was begun, development continues to be elusive for a significant proportion of that periphery. This is what prompts the question—what is wrong with development as we know it?

Two sets of ideas in opposition to the concept of development can help us answer this question. There were principally two critiques of development, one focused on the capitalist system, the principal base for development, and the other on the concept of development itself. Socialist ideas of the nineteenth century opposed capitalism, in as much that its admirable achievements—economic prosperity and democracy—did not reach the majority. This majority were in fact the workers, essential to run modern machinery, the hallmark of capitalist enterprise that worked in unhealthy and difficult work conditions, and were paid wages that were never a fair share of the profits from enterprise. This happened because the process of manufacture for development was enabled by the ownership of capital by a few, and they made the decisions on sharing the benefits of prosperity. Thus, development that was meant to liberate from forms of human bondage—like slavery and feudalism—fulfilled this promise only to a limited extent. Further, they have argued that with each new stage of 'development', this aspect is becoming even less significant. Therefore, these issues need to be resolved if development is to be truly successful.

The second critique of development came up in terms of the methods of development itself—particularly the manner in which it uses nature. D'Monte (1985: 5) points out, 'Traditional neo-classical economics treated the environment in two ways. One was to view it as an "externality" with either positive or negative impact on the cost of operation of an individual firm; the other was to treat it like a commodity for which, like any other, the consumer was expected to pay a price.' Industrialisation even today relies to a great extent on Nature's bounty of resources for its main focus—to produce newer goods for human use. These resources include not only those regenerable in principle, like plants and animal life, but also non-renewable resources like fossil fuels. The issue posed is, knowing that these are finite, do we not have to consider alternatives: products that do not rely on these resources or perhaps even reduce our reliance on these products? Another negative effect of industrialisation is that it has continually polluted and created an imbalance in the resources of nature, like discharging chemical effluents into rivers and soils, and building large dams across rivers to generate electricity. This critique focused on the environment as a crucial factor in development, forcing a rethink on the concept of development itself, eventually making way for the concept of sustainable development. We will discuss these in the next two sections. Before we take them up for discussion, however, it is important to make one qualification. The environmental critique is sourced from both, movements and academic/policy writing. Both of these, in their life of 30 years or so, have moved from being focused on issues and regions to concepts and theories. There is heterogeneity within broad positions of agreement, while surprising overlaps are visible in otherwise polar opposite positions. Besides, it is a vast body of literature by now and any attempt to summarise it would be futile. Hence, the following sections can serve only as pointers and carry references for those whose curiosity is aroused.

However, before going into these, it is important to remember that industrialism and its hazards—physical, social and moral—had its early modern critics, especially form an ethical viewpoint, which brings to mind Tolstoy, Ruskin and Gandhi. While Gandhi's critique of modern civilisation and its problems may be familiar to us, writers Leo Tolstoy and William Ruskin were also stringent critics of the way of life that modern industrial society stood for—away from nature and so, away form their inner selves. Both of them also carried out experiments in alternative ways of living, in fact, one of which, Tolstoy Farm is what inspired Gandhi to a great extent. There were critics from early foresters and engineers as well, who believed that modern industrialism could simply not be efficient in the long run—that the proportion of resource-use to resource-waste would make them into unproductive technologies in the long run, however efficient they might look in the late nineteenth century. And as will become evident in the chapter on Industrial Pollution later in this section, how right they were!

But, perhaps one of the most powerful post–Second World War critiques, that Guha (2000: 69) believes 'began modern environmentalism', is the publication of a book by Rachel Carson, called *Silent Spring*. This book identified 'the central problem of our age', to be the 'contamination of man's total environment with substances of incredible potential for harm', that is, the new chemicals like DDT patented during and after the Second World War, and enthusiastically adopted by farmers as pesticides, and welcomed by scientists.

Guha (ibid.: 72) argues that while

> environmentalists had been for some time been concerned with the protection of endangered species or beautiful habitats; it was *Silent Spring* that helped them move further, to an appreciation that…nature was, in sum, 'an

> intricate web of life whose interwoven strands lead from microbes to man'. The interconnectedness of all life called for a modest, gentle and cautious attitude toward nature, rather than the arrogant, aggressive and intrepid route taken by synthetic chemistry and its products. Otherwise the web of life could very easily become the web of death.

This recognition is the beginning towards recognising that there are several aspects to this interconnectedness that need to be further understood and explained. That is, all human beings were not connected to nature in the same way. There was a web of inequality that gave it a particular character and it is through this that we will seek to understand the environmental critique as it developed in the 1970s.

THE ENVIRONMENTAL CRITIQUE OF DEVELOPMENT

To begin with, if we were to relate the two critiques of development discussed above, social inequality, that is, inequality *between human beings* that resulted from development, was seen separately from the inequality *between human beings and nature* also resulting from it. That is, as a result of the policies of development being planned with just a few in mind and ignoring the rest, and the fruits of development, therefore, being unequally distributed, inequality amongst human beings increased. Second, because policies of development did not take into account how nature could be used without being abused or destroyed, development created inequalities between human beings and nature. Over time, much of the lessons learnt from the environmental critique have been as to how closely the two inequalities are actually related. And further, that the sooner this closeness is recognised and policy/politics targeted towards it, the more likely their success.

The early critiques in most parts of the world were invariably on single, disparate issues that highlighted the visible or possible ill effects of development processes on aspects of nature. In India, the Silent Valley campaign was a good example of this. So, concern for the environment would be protecting it from the development process, if necessary. While the response of policy makers to this issue was positive, most times, they tended to ignore its significance in a larger rubric of policy. D'Monte (1985: 5) says of the responses of policymakers in India, 'Environment was seen as a "bottomless pit" with unlimited capacity to withstand stresses: its impact was believed to be temporary and marginal, it could be isolated into small segments of which specific policy decisions could be made.' Thus, this perspective had little to offer by way of an understanding of any kind of inequality.

This was true to an extent of the critique of development offered by Marxist political economy in the mid-twentieth century. The development of underdevelopment and uneven development arguments demonstrated the unevenness and implicit unfairness of the development processes between territories and people. Simply put, they argued that the way in which the international economic system is structured, 'development' can never be even throughout the world and that the development of the North would always be at the expense of the South. Further, that the South's particular economic linkages with the North would never make it possible for the former to develop independently. Thus, they provided insights into the inequalities that govern international economic relations, that is, of the Bretton Woods system that had dominated until then since the 1940s. However, as Redclift (1984: 1) demonstrated, 'The environment has not, in fact, been interpreted within the framework of global economic relations. It has not been part of the political dialogue about development and the analysis of underdevelopment.' He (ibid: 2) argued further that this occurred precisely because Marxists were concerned over the distributive aspects of development, whereas

> the environment was rarely looked upon as a distributive issue... It was a 'given' in the development situation of most countries, over which they had little control. Rather like the climate, natural resources were distributed according to rules that man did not invent, thus disputes between men about them were not inherently environmental. These disputes had their origin in the international economy and the class structure of individual countries.

What Redclift meant was that the crux of these arguments actually rested on the unequal relationships between the global North (the industrialised countries) and the global South (the developing world), on one hand, and the unequal relationships between classes and people within the South, on the other. This was because the former had both high levels of production and consumption that continued to increase relentlessly for more than 200 years, thus negatively impacting their own environment. At the same time, the latter had been exploited by the North for both the above processes for a long time, resulting in their economies becoming subservient to them. As a result, the environmental degradation of the South was clearly linked to its external unequal position, as, also, the inequalities within it. But this crucial link between the two inequalities was missing in this critique, not by oversight, but a refusal to recognise its importance. These were accepted with only the greatest difficulty in the critique of the environment and continue to be important obstacles in policy-making at both international and national levels.

At this point, it may be opportune to point out that theoretical Marxist political economy did not in any way indicate the environmental situation in the socialist states of the same time. The critique of capitalism (offered by Marxism) that was at the heart of these political systems *did not include* a critique of capitalist technology that was responsible for environmental degradation. It was focused on the critique of unequal distribution of the profits generated by that technology. Further, because in all these states, the policy was to take all decisions centrally, without adequate attention to, and the involvement of, local people, disastrous decisions were taken. For example, around the Aral Sea, which practically destroyed it and the effects of which have been very hard to resolve in the long run. Thus, some of the worst industrial disasters of the world, comparable to Bhopal, occurred at Chernobyl and the Soviet State was just as careless about its people as the Indian state was about the victims in Bhopal. Being a superpower at the time of the accident, it was narrowly concerned about protecting its image in the Western world, and so hid the facts as well as it could.

What it did imply, though, is that the environmental critiques developed in national and international contexts almost simultaneously. Environmentalism of the 1960s and the 1970s was spread out in different parts of the globe, with people taking up issues of local significance, while trying to relate to the trends outside. Two developments proved crucial—one was the failure of development to alleviate poverty in most parts of the globe and the reactions that the failure evoked. The other was the initiative taken up by the UN system to respond to issues of environment and the impact it had on the developing world in particular. The failure to alleviate poverty implied the persistence of economic and social inequalities and it was clear that the trickle-down effect of developmentalist works of the state were not actually taking place. When the question 'why does this not happen', was posed, one of the answers that came up was that while the poor actually subsist on nature, development is systematically destroying nature, and thereby, taking it further out of their reach. So, the need was perhaps, as Agarwal and Narain (1985: 362) put it, to 'modify the development process itself in a manner that will bring it into greater harmony with the needs of the people and with the need to maintain ecological balance, while increasing the productivity of our land, water and forest resources.

Thus, the link between environment and development through poverty, or the inequality of income between human beings that causes some to live in conditions of extreme frugality, has become the most important. Adams (2001: 15) argues,

> It is recognised that tight and complex links exist between development, environment and poverty...The poor often endure degraded environments,

> and in some instances contribute to their further degradation. Urban air and water pollution are both rising rapidly, even in those countries in which economic growth is taking place, and the degradation of agricultural, forest and wetland resources is extending the depth and breadth of deprivation in many rural areas.

This understanding is more finely tuned than the earlier argument that sought to lay the blame of environmental degradation only at the door of the rich, whether in the North or the South. While that blame must continue to be accorded, the additional crisis caused by the sheer helplessness of their situation that makes the poor degrade their natural environment, needs to be highlighted to show the urgency of the situation. A very pertinent example of this is what has happened to grazing lands in India. The colonial policy of bringing more and more land under cultivation in order to earn more revenue was continued by the postcolonial state, in order to increase food production and land for agro-industry crops, which meant that village grazing lands were treated as revenue wastelands converts into no man's lands subject to overuse (Gadgil and Guha 2000: 24). Because this was accompanied by agricultural practices that did not leave crop residue as fodder for cattle, as was the practice earlier, it meant that livestock owners had to perforce take their cattle to feed in lands that should not have been used, leading to their degradation. At the same time, the increasing demands of the domestic dairy and meat requirements as well as the international leather market, has meant that there is further degradation of grazing lands. So, as Gadgil and Guha (2000: 25) point out,

> state interventions to organise dairies, to provide cattle and goat purchase loans, or to promote leather exports have primarily helped to enhance the availability of dairy products and meat for city dwellers, to generate income for farmers with irrigated lands and to bring in foreign exchange, all at the cost of the degradation of India's forests, grasslands and water bodies.

This is examined in detail in the section on sustainable development.

The Gandhians in India and several scholars in Europe have been amongst the most severe critics of 'development'; among them Sachs (1993, 1999) is perhaps the best known. Gandhi had offered a critique of modern civilisation in *Hind Swaraj* (1909), which became the basis of his critique of British rule in India. He argued that the basic characteristics of modernity destroy the relationship between human beings and nature, making unnecessary reliance upon new technologies (even when they are not 'needed' as in an economy where labour is in abundance, as in ours) and increased consumption, a cornerstone for progress. This creates violence and conflict antithetical to true progress. Hence, he was in favour of retaining (and not returning to) the structure of work and consumption of the village community in India that he understood to uphold values of harmony between human beings and nature, and thereby, between human beings as showing the way forward. He felt that too much of this fabric had been destroyed by modernisation and colonisation, and believed that fighting British rule meant fighting this aspect, and that real Swaraj would mean exploring a future based on these ideals and not, 'British rule without the Englishman'. His ideals were exemplified in the structure of his ashrams, where commitment to vegetarianism, natural products like khadi, and equal responsibilities of work, were meant to bring-in harmony between humans and nature, and amongst human beings. After Gandhi, these became the basis for the Gandhian understanding of environment. The most well known Gandhians in this respect are JC Kumarappa, Mira Behn, Baba Amte, Anna Hazare, Chandi Prasad Bhatt and Sunderlal Bahuguna, to name but a few. Meera Behn in the 1950s wrote eloquently for an oak oriented forestry that would help peasant livelihoods in the Himalayas (as opposed to conifer centred monoculture that were market and industry driven); Elwin was an early upholder of adivasi rights to hunt, and do slash and burn, both as a scholar and a policymaker; Kumarappa was an early visionary and practical worker on decentred energy systems in the 1940s! While Baba Amte and Anna Hazare have taken Gandhian initiatives and built Gandhian institutions, whilst moving into struggles against the system later in their lives, the latter two started by leading people's movements and struggles based on Gandhi's methods of resistance, and then cementing those efforts on the ground with institutional interventions. While they are widely admired, the dominant discourse of development overwhelms the public imagination and does not accord them plausibility at a wider level.

Sachs' (1999: 17) critique of development, exemplified in his book *Planet Dialectics: Explorations in Environment and Development* (1999) is searing in its denouncement of the very idea of development:

> that the essential reality of a society consists in nothing else than its functional achievements; the rest is just folklore or private affairs. From this viewpoint, the economy overshadows every other reality; the laws of economy dominate society and not the rules of society the economy. This is why, whenever development strategists set their sights on a country, they see not a society that has an economy, but a society that *is* an economy.

Sachs (ibid.: 19) bemoans how it has affected the Third World, when he states,

> In the last decades, similar radical changes have taken place in large parts of the Third World as the economic ideology has tightened its grip. Traditions

> of sufficiency have been pushed aside, local exchange relations dissolved, collective forms of ownership broken up, and subsistence economies wiped out.

Thus he (ibid.: 22) believes,

> In these circumstances, the 'development' concept loses its reassuring connotations for the future: slowly it is being substituted by the concept of 'security' ...There are already many development projects that have little to do with taking a country along the road to progress and simply content themselves with trying to prevent the worst on a once-only basis.

Apart from these broad critiques, those that focus on specific inequalities are equally important. In recent years, there has been an increasing focus on linkages between gender and the environment in development research, policy and practice. Gender–environment relations are seen as integral to the social and economic organisation which mediates peoples' relationships with their particular environment. Gender is also viewed as a key dimension of social difference affecting peoples' experiences, concerns and capabilities in natural resource management (Leach et al. 1995). Masika and Joekes (1997) point out that there are significant differences between women's and men's experiences of poverty and environmental change because of gender inequalities in the ability to have command over environmental resource entitlements (for eaxmple, land, trees, and so on), labour and income. These inequalities leave women with limited flexibility to respond to environmental changes in ways which maintain environmental resources. Thus, they (Leach et al. 1997: 6) identify three factors, which, if ignored, can further deplete the environmental capital:

1. experiences of poverty and environmental change are gender-differentiated;
2. environmental security is mediated by gender relations;
3. women and men have both conflicting and complementary interests and roles in environmental management.

Thus, these analyses as well as many hundreds done across the globe by now, demonstrate how gender relations have a powerful influence on how environments are used and managed over time, and the effects of this on patterns of ecological change.

A major critique has emerged from the studies on the widespread loss of biodiversity resulting from denuding of forests for expansion of agriculture and feeding the timber industry, mining of hillsides and other fragile ecosystems for industrially profitable minerals and metals like iron ore and asbestos, stone quarrying for purposes of both construction and precious stones, and deep-sea fishing and trawling for global fishing industries. A fine precis of this is in James Gustave Speth's new book on *Global Environmental Challenges* published in an Indian edition by Orient Longman (Delhi, 2005). Much of this loss is irreversible and has been compared in its impact and scale to past waves of extinctions such as those that wiped out the dinosaurs.

From all of these analyses, it can be discerned that environmentalism, as a critique of developmentalism, as also a focus of critical reflection and political mobilisation, has many points of entry and arguments. Many typologies and critical analyses of these, trying to classify them into categories of thought and action have been attempted, but we cite a few examples. Krishna (1996: 36) identifies three: popular, managerial and progressive. She defines them as those derived from Gandhi, from a 'scientific' understanding of environmental problems and those from radical politics slowly articulating the centrality of the question of environment and natural resources, respectively, while recognising that these cannot be watertight compartments. She identifies the elements of one in the other and demonstrates how they are bound to influence each other in the common cause. Gadgil and Guha (2000: 98) identify seven strands of the environmental movement in India, which are possibly more exhaustive in their description of the differences between them, while emphasising the relationship between ecology and equity focused on by them. Similarly, Blaikie emphasises the political dimensions of rights over resources, stressing the need for those seeking to understand environment–development related problems to explore the links between environment, economy and society, that he calls 'political ecology'(Adams 2001: 15).

Movements in India that indicate many of these characteristics are discussed in the last chapter.

SUSTAINABLE DEVELOPMENT

In the spectrum of the environmental critiques of development referred to above, the one that lies in between the extreme positions has been that of sustainable development. In fact, it borrows from and is able to host different kinds of ideas, which might even look as if they are going off in opposite directions. This is why it is very difficult to define exactly, but also possibly why it has become dominant in the discourse of environment in recent times. As with most ideas discussed here, this, too, has grown out of the two levels at which arguments are made: that of the civil society and the state.

In the classic sense, civil society is the realm of a large number of non-state actors, which nevertheless play very important political roles—like that of organisations/associations of ordinary people, of the circle of competitive entrepreneurs that comprise economic activity, of social movements focused on specific issue/s and any other sporadic campaigns and activities that may take place from time to time. This space is characterised by competition amongst these elements for power to dominate the priorities and focus of its concern, by continuously intervening and articulating this position in it. Since their power is uneven, their capacity to intervene and articulate will, naturally, be uneven as well.

On the other hand, the state comprises the formal institutions of government and the non-formal sources of power as in different political groups, and so, is also an arena of competition. The competition is between the different elements that make up the government and those powers from the civil society that seek to continuously influence it to make policy and take decisions that would be in their favour. These would include international policy and political institutions as well. From both of these sources, two trends can be identified: (1) certain patterns of conceptualisation, and (2) certain instruments of policy and action. While the instruments of policy and action have been discussed in a separate chapter, the former will be discussed here.

The messy concept of sustainable development is best understood in terms of *three major strands of thought and action*—the reformist and the radical strands at two ends, and one in the mean position (in the statistical sense of the term). Adams identifies the reformist view to include theoretical dimensions of market environmentalism, ecological modernisation and environmental populism. This constitutes the mainstream of the sustainable development discourse. The radical strand that he identifies include ecosocialism, ecoanarchism, deep ecology and ecofeminism (Adams 2001: 18), and these he finds clearly located on the periphery, that is, on the margins of the discourse. The one in the mean position is a critique that genuinely lies between these two and could be called the ecology–equity critique. They will each be explained briefly.

The Reformist Strand

Market environmentalism, expectedly, presents the market as the most important mechanism for mediating between people and regulating their interaction with the environment. It follows the conventional logic that market prices rise as resources become scarce, automatically leading people to innovate to finding cheaper sources or ways of using resources more efficiently (ibid.: 104). At the same time, it believes that open-access resources are liable to over-exploitation, while private resources are more efficiently used, thereby, justifying the privatisation of resources. Thus, they argue that further the market exchange penetrates into the environment, the greater the efficiency of environmental management. However, it does not advocate an unregulated dependence on the market. This calls for accommodating some state control, and making way for another concept.

Ecological modernisation is a manifestation of the Brundtland report (discussed in the next chapter), which is about economic growth in a capitalist economy, working within the constraints of ecological sustainability. It involves working towards improved and more 'rational' planning, management, regulation and utilisation of human use of the environment. This could be achieved by applying better science to solve human problems because 'the environmental degradation associated with industrialisation is a "design fault", a failure of rational environmental management.'[1] Thus, institutions can change and actors within them can learn. Thus, the very same participants in the path of modernisation can now restructure their relationships to make the above possible—that is, states and citizens can plan and work together, the public and private enterprise can collaborate, and while the state reduces its burden on the front of regulation, industry can focus on self-regulation. The last has led to the very important new idea of corporate social responsibility, which is being picked up by corporates in both the developed and the developing world. At the same time, responsible citizenry can help create the 'green consumer', who by refusing to buy products that destroy the environment irrationally (like paper made from recycled materials rather than from wood), can make them unprofitable to produce. This would eventually operate as a regulatory force in the market.

Environmental populism is the political facet of the mainstream thinking on sustainable development. It is so in the sense that it seems to pick up certain ideas that directly affect dimensions of power structures in society and link them with the environment. Additionally, it posits ideas that seem to be rather challenging of the development discourse and link them with the earlier linkages as well. It is founded on the idea of 'ecodevelopment', which Sachs explained as 'an approach to development aimed at harmonising social and economic objectives with ecologically sound management, in a spirit of solidarity with future generations' (cited in Adams 2001: 114). Thus, it directly adopted the idea of 'basic needs' that were the hallmark of the debates on development in the Second Development Decade of the 1970s, emphasising on the morality of development outcomes. It also called for 'participation'—by people from the grassroots and making them active in decision making for development. This last would enable the poor to also focus on what they considered to be their needs, rather than those that did not understand their context, but sat in positions of power to do it for them. And most interestingly, it adopted the idea of 'appropriate and intermediate technology', accepting thereby that the approach of the big industry, based on capital intensive technology was not the ideal solution for many poor parts of the world.

Each of these ideas would appeal to the popular imagination, giving the impression that governments or powers that can see reality from the point of view of the poor at last. However, if we look closer, we find something else. Actually, focusing on basic needs means: *make some adjustments and make the poor feel better*. However, it does not make any changes that disturb the basic power structure. So, this serves to shift the focus of policy away from any fundamental redistribution of wealth or decentralisation of power. Genuine 'participation' requires the dismantling of deep social and cultural strangleholds that are in place, but these are precisely those that the current powers-that-be benefit from. Thus, unless politics, even more so than policy, targets it, the strangleholds would continue. Finally, appropriate technology for all its great value and contribution, makes for the belief that 'alternative technologies' are not a possibility. That is, means of better production can only be based on modern scientific knowledge structures and no other knowledge has produced anything like it in the past, nor can it legitimately produce any such thing in the future[2]. Together, Adams views these as a neo-populist vision of the world being allied with a call for more technically sophisticated environmental management.

The Radical Strand

Ecosocialism draws upon the critiques and debates of socialism referred to in the preceding paragraphs. Some analysts seem to see an incompatibility between socialist and environmental movements (between red and green alternatives), on grounds of their social vision, who they identify as enemy, method of analysis, organisation and ideology, among other things (Friberg and Hettne 1985). And others, like Pepper, argue that ecocentric thought is inherently anti-capitalist (quoted in Adams 2001: 155). Adams points out, very well though, the several points at which environmentalism and socialism come very close to each other and indeed sometimes converge in their concerns. He indicates how they both refer to the innate tendency of capitalism to destroy itself, by its greed for natural resources and that of over-production. The Marxist focus on the alienation of people from land runs parallel to the environmentalist focus on the alienation of people from nature; the commoditisation of human labour is parallel to the commoditisation of nature. From this, then, Adams (2001: 159) concludes, 'there is more to Marx in environmentalist thought than might first appear' and 'Ecosocialism remains an important influence on debates about sustainable development.'

Ecoanarchism refers to the body of critical thinking on the environment that is influenced by anarchist thought. Anarchism is the name given to a principle or theory of life and conduct under which society is conceived without government. Harmony in such a society is obtained not by submission to law or by obedience to any authority, but by free agreements concluded between the various groups, territorial and professional, freely constituted for the sake of production and consumption, as also for the satisfaction of the infinite variety of needs and aspirations of a civilised being. In a society developed on these lines, the voluntary associations which already now begin to cover all the fields of human activity would take a still greater extension so as to substitute themselves for the state in all its functions.[3] Acquiring the status of a political ideology that can be traced back to Proudhon who first used this word in 1840, it implied, for post-revolutionary France, that the Revolution would be complete only when they could run society without a government and people could return to village communities, their common lands and abolish feudal rights, along with many other economic measures. By bringing these ideas closer to environmentalist ones, Bookchin (cited in Adams 2001:162), one of the well-known ecoanarchists argues, 'in the final analysis, it is impossible to achieve harmonisation of people and nature without creating a human community that lives in a lasting balance with its natural environment.' Further, he states (cited in ibid. 2001: 163):

> The anarchist concepts of a balanced community, a face-to-face democracy, a humanistic technology and a decentralised society—these rich libertarian concepts—are not only desirable, they are also necessary. They belong not only to the great visions of a human future, they now constitute the preconditions for human survival.

Deep Ecology is a perspective that contrasts with all the above described perspectives, in as much that it seeks to place a value on nature for its own sake, over and above its value for human beings. Thus, deep ecology ideas would be described as 'biocentric', while the latter, 'anthropocentric' (centred on the human). The concept is drawn from the writings of the Norwegian philosopher Arne Naess, who in turn derived his ideas from Spinoza and Gandhi. He argued that protecting the environment for the interests, long or short term, of humans meant an innate separation of human beings from environment. Further, if this approach were to be followed, it would actually never place human beings and all other parts of nature at par, as also leading to making differences, between which human beings should be better protected or taken care of in the present or the future. If we were to correlate this simple explanation with the basic focus of this book, then we find that deep ecology *relates to the basic issues of inequality* we have posed—*of that between human beings and nature and between different communities of human beings* in the most definitive way. However, what remains to be analysed is the extent to which this idea is translatable into policy instruments and political action, a discussion that is beyond the scope of this book.

Ecofeminism seeks to take the gender critique of environmentalism (summarised above) several steps forward by combining it with deep ecological perspectives. Two strands may be identified within this perspective. One is what is described as 'essentialist ecofeminism' and the other as 'social ecofeminism' (Martinez-Alier 1998: 318) . The two most famous proponents of each are Vandana Shiva and Bina Agarwal,[4] respectively. Shiva argues in her work *Staying Alive* (1988) that women and nature were similarly exploited by the patriarchal order of society by Western Science, that believes in similarly subjugating and destroying women and nature. Beginning from the position that women were carriers of the values and characteristics of nature, that is, nurturing, caring and recreating, she believes that the only lasting way of protecting the environment is to combine the principles of feminism and (deep) ecology. The specific image of women that Shiva believes in is one that embodies the 'feminine' principle of nature, unconfined to context of Culture or Time. It has been widely criticised on mainly two grounds: first, that it bases itself within gender analysis, but clearly outside the frame of feminism; and second, that it bases itself on a universalistic understanding of both women and environment.

Bina Agarwal's analysis (cited in Sandilands 1999: 60)

> centred on the ways in which material conditions (especially immediate ecological degradation) adversely affect, and thus politicise, poor peasant women in India. ...Thus, women's grassroots activism is not so much about preserving their subsistence activities, as it is about questioning the relations of structural inequality in which specific women experience environmental degradation on a daily basis.

In a path breaking book, Agarwal (1994) demonstrated how the single most important economic factor affecting women's situation in the gender gap is their lack of command over property. Agarwal has been criticised, too, from an even more complex position of how her argument can be read as a critique of not only what happens in South Asia, but also, how her approach helps to understand and critique the North American ecofeminist approach (which we have not discussed here). We will not go into those arguments here. What is important to understand and appreciate, at this point, is that a range of ideas have come up in the last 30 years or so, and when we discuss these issues currently and in the future, the complexities they throw up should become the commonsense basis for them.

The Ecology–Equity Critique

Presented in the body of the work of two people, an eminent scientist trained in ecology, Madhav Gadgil and an eminent sociologist,

Ramchandra Guha, both with a common interest in history, this critique is offered in the context of India. It is in two parts, the first of which is an original theoretical framework of making sense of what actually the issues are, from an ecological point of view. This means evaluating the exact impact of developmental policies that include the social, economic and political—on different kinds of ecosystems and the people that live in it. The most important aspect of that framework is a new set of categories to locate and analyse the relationship of different social groups, to specifically reflect the relationship between people and nature. These categories are those of ecosystem, people, ecological refugees and omnivores, discussed in detail in the 'Introduction' (Understanding Social Inequality) to this book. The second moves 'from analysis to construction, arguing for a new environment-friendly agenda for development'(Gadgil and Guha 2000: 5). The analysis leads them to

> firmly believe that prudent, sustainable use of India's environmental resources is in the interests of a vast majority of India's population. It is, therefore, entirely possible to construct a development agenda that is at once in the interests of a majority of people and the country's environment.(ibid.: 6).

What makes this argument more credible than others of its ilk is its recognition of both the limitations posed by contemporary dispensations of power and the belief in the enormous potential of the Indian society being able to work out their sketch of an alternative. They also state with conviction that the liberal economists' clamour for efficiency, which has dominated the development discourse, (as we have seen in this chapter), has to now reckon with two other compelling parameters, identified by protest movements and the reality of ecological degradation—those of equity and ecology. This is a very carefully worked out response to a range of positions—on one hand, to the stubborn policy makers who cannot see the significance and the possibility of balancing efficiency with ecology and equity. And on the other hand, they address themselves to the movements that have raised the issues of ecology and equity, urging them to consider alternatives carefully, work out a middle ground of ideas, such that some space for negotiating interests on all sides is possible. We shall take this up for discussion in detail in Chapter 16, when we discuss environmental movements in India.

Political Ecology

A perspective that brings political economy and environmentalism together, it has many proponents worldwide. But instead of trying to summarise their positions here, a quote from an article reflecting on the potential of this approach, as different from all of those discussed above, might be thought provoking. Dunu Roy (2002), one of the most reflective thinkers and participants in the environmental movement in India, wrote of the lessons we have learnt from our experiences over the years,

> that the nature of knowledge, of learning, is determined by class interests and the conflicts between them. Thus, our university is as much prey to the political economy of production for greed (while millions teeter on the brink of survival) as is any other institution in civil society. We have to see our university as part of the world and, hence, the environment is everything, and we have to grasp the linkages between all phenomena. In particular, we have to comprehend the linkage between environment and work, between the food-gatherer and the tool-producer.
>
> The challenge that such an exploration throws up is not merely a change in lifestyles, but a revolution in state and society; not just the right to be human, but in defending and enlarging human rights. This is the heart and the brain and the muscle of political ecology—that we hauntingly wage war against all oppression and exploitation, against all injustice and violence, against war itself.

This is true of all of the main currents of thought on environment and development discussed here. This description is by no means exhaustive and the list can include many more strands and can be differently classified as well. What is important to note at the end of the day, however, is that all these strands of thought offer a series of sources of reflection, helping us to understand one of the most important concerns of our time.

We conclude this chapter with a reference to a very strong critique of the concept of sustainable development. Sachs argues that sustainability provides a way out of criticising the fundamentals of development, by offering a better mode of development. But the ideology of developmentalism that underlies it, he believes, is irreconcilable with the needs of a balanced environment and the future of the planet. To quote Sachs (1999: 27–28),

> Reaffirming the centrality of 'development' in the international discussion on the environment surely helps to secure the collaboration of the dominating actors in government, economy and science, but it prevents the rupture required to head-off the multifaceted dangers to the future of humankind. It locks the perception of the ecological predicament that stimulates the pernicious dynamics, and hands the action over to those social forces—governments, agencies and corporations—that have largely been responsible for the present state of affairs. This may turn out to be self-defeating. After all, the development discourse is deeply imbued with certainties like progress, growth, market integration, consumption and universal needs, all notions that are part of the problem, not of the solution. They cannot but distract

attention from the urgency of public debate on our relationship with nature, for they preclude the search for societies that live graciously within their means, and for social changes that take their ideas from indigenous ideas of the good and proper life.

NOTES

1. This is a widely shared belief particularly amongst scientists that dominate development planning models and so, even in few universities, when work on the environment is being carried out, it is usually by science departments.
2. There is a considerable body of literature on appropriate and alternative technology that cannot be cited here.
3. http://flag.blackened.net/daver/anarchism/kropotkin/defanarchy.html
4. These thinkers are also discussed in detail in the section on gender in this book.

REFERENCES

Agarwal, A. and S. Narain (1985). *The State of India's Environment: The Second Citizens' Report*. New Delhi: Centre for Science and Environment.

Agarwal, B. (1994). *A Field of One's Own: Gender and Land Rights in South Asia*. Cambridge: Cambridge University Press.

Adams, W. M. (2001). *Green Development: Environment and Sustainability in the Third World*. New York: Routledge.

Centre for Science and Development (1985) *The State of India's Environment 1984-85: The Second Citizen's Report*.

D'Monte, D. (1985). *Temples or Tombs? Industry versus Environment: Three Controversies*. New Delhi: Centre for Science and Environment.

Friberg, M. and B. Hettne (1985). 'The Greening of the World: Towards a Non-Deterministic Model of Global Process' in H. Addo et al. (eds) *Development as Social Transformation: Reflections on the Global Problematique*. Sevenoaks: Hodder and Stoughton.

Gadgil, M. and R. Guha (2000). *Ecology and Equity: The Use and Abuse of Nature in Contemporary India*. London: Routledge.

Gandhi, M. K. (1909). *Hind Swaraj*. Ahmedabad: Navjivan Press.

Goulet, D. (1995). *Development Ethics: A Guide to Theory and Action*. Zed Books: London.

Guha, R. (2000). *The Unquiet Woods: Ecological Change and Peasant Resistance in the Himalayas*. New Delhi: Oxford University Press.

Krishna S. (1996). *Environmental Politics: People's Lives and Development Choices*. New Delhi: Sage Publication.

Leach et al. (1995). 'Gender Relations and Environmental Change'. *IDS Bulletin*. Sussex: Institute of Development Studies.

Masika, R. and S. Joekes (1997). 'Environmentally Sustainable Development and Poverty: A Gender Analysis'. *Bridge Bulletin* Report No 52. pp. 1–16.

Martinez-Alier, J. (1998). 'Environmental Justice' (Local and Global) in F. Jameson and M. Mayoshi (eds) *The Cultures of Globalisation*. Durham, NC: Duke University Press.

Redclift, M. (1984). *Development and Environmental Crisis: Red or Green Alternatives?* London: Methuen.

Roy, Dunu (2002). 'Environmentalism and Political Economy'. *Seminar*. August.

Sachs, W. (ed.) (1993). *Global Ecology: A New Area of Political Conflict*. London and New Jersey: Zed Books.

Sachs, W. (1999). *Planet Dialectics: Exploration in Environment and Development*. London and New York: Zed Books.

Sandilands, C. (1999). *The Good-Natured Feminist: Ecofeminism and the Quest for Democracy*. Minneapolis, MN: University of Minnesota Press.

Shiva, V. (1988). *Staying Alive: Women, Ecology and Survival*. London: Zed Books.

Swedish International Development Cooperation Agency (SIDA). *A Gender Analysis Report*, prepared for the Gender Equality Unit.

WEB SITES

1. http://www.un.org/millennium/index.html
2. http://www.un.org/millenniumgoals/index.html
3. http://www.un.org/millennium/declaration/ares552e.pdf

13

United Nations Environment Programme: Rio, Johannesburg and After

THE BACKGROUND

In order to understand the role of the United Nations (UN) in the international arena of environmental negotiations, indeed, the character of negotiations in general, it is important to recall the founding of the UN system and the relationship between its different components. The name 'United Nations', coined by the United States President Franklin D. Roosevelt, was first used in the 'Declaration by United Nations' of 1 January 1942, during the Second World War, when representatives of 26 nations pledged their governments to continue fighting together against the Axis Powers.

In 1945, representatives of 50 countries met in San Francisco at the United Nations Conference on International Organization to draw up the United Nations Charter. They finally signed the UN Charter on 26 June 1945. The United Nations officially came into existence on 24 October 1945, when the Charter had been ratified by China, France, the Soviet Union, the United Kingdom and the United States, and by a majority of other signatories (United Nations 2000).

What is important for the purposes that we have outlined earlier is a deeper understanding of this organisation. Two aspects of this impact, that is, the issue of environmental understanding and negotiations at the international level, are particularly important. First, the unevenness of relationships between the member countries—some are more powerful than others—and the reasons for this need to be understood. Second, there is unevenness between the organisations of the UN—again, some are more powerful than others, despite ostensibly being equal parts of the same rubric. We will attempt to explain the nature of these relations and what impact they have on the policy and practice on the environment by the UN.

One of the most important developments of the creation of the UN system is the Bretton Woods system, which brought a host of financial and monetary institutions under the World Bank Group. The reasons for its development lay in the combination of circumstances that existed in the first half of the twentieth century. The world in 1945 was replete with colonised countries that had been acquired by the Europeans in the eighteenth century. However, the imperial order was in disarray for a number of reasons, principally that the colonisers were losing the great economic control they had created. Hence, many of the colonised countries were well into anti-colonial movements, knowing the weakening grip of the colonisers, yet, not quite in a state to create tenacious institutions of their own. The latter process would take many years, that too in a situation of combating the poverty and decay fostered by colonialism. At the same time, the world was closely networked into a web of relationships—economic and cultural—that would steer the directions of trade and other agreements that these newly independent colonies were going to make in the post-colonial phase. On the other hand, the space created by the decline of Britain's imperial strength and obvious dominance of world politics until then was occupied by the United States. The combination of these two factors made the Bretton Woods movement what it became.

The Bretton Woods system is commonly understood to refer to the international monetary regime that prevailed from the end of the Second World War until the early 1970s. Taking its name from the site of the 1944 conference that created the International Monetary Fund (IMF), the World Bank and the General Agreement on Trade and Tariff, the Bretton Woods system was history's first example of a fully negotiated monetary order intended to govern currency relations among sovereign states. The common view (among the countries of Europe and the US) at the Conference was that the depression of the 1930s and the rise of fascism could be traced to the collapse of international trade and isolationist economic policies.[1] The institutions which were planned at Bretton Woods to oversee this arrangement include the World Bank, launched late in 1945 and officially called the International Bank for Reconstruction and Development (IBRD), intended to provide long-term loans to states for reconstruction after the devastation of the War; the IMF (International Monetary Fund) launched in 1946 and intended to finance short-term imbalances in international payments and help maintain fixed exchange rates, linking all currencies to gold via the Dollar Standard; and in October 1947, the General Agreement on Tariffs and Trade (GATT) to oversee the dismantling of trade barriers.

In principle, the regime was designed to combine binding legal obligations with multilateral decision making conducted through an international organisation, the IMF, endowed with limited supranational authority. In practice, the initial scheme as well as its subsequent development and the ultimate demise were directly dependent on the preferences and policies of its most powerful member, the United States.[2] The conference rejected proposals by the eminent British economist John Maynard Keynes that would have established a world reserve currency administered by a central bank and created a more stable and fair world economy by automatically recycling trade surpluses to finance trade deficits. Keynes' notion did not fit the interests of a US eager to take on the role of the world's economic powerhouse. Instead, the Conference opted for a system based on the free movement of capital and goods with the US dollar as the international currency. The Fund and the Bank were limited to managing problems related to deficits, and to currency and capital shortages.[3]

While this system worked until 1958—that is, well enough to serve hegemonic interests certainly, as also to stabilise battered European currencies—it began to falter thereafter. The balance of trade crisis of the United States on one hand and its continued power of convertibility (of dollar into gold) on the other was causing great strain to the system and a breakdown was imminent. It was at this point, between 1971 and 1973, that the convertibility of the dollar into gold was suspended, freeing the US dollar to find its own level in currency markets and the monies of all the industrial countries were set free to float independently. With these decisions, both the par value system and the gold exchange standard—the two central elements of the post-war monetary regime—were effectively terminated. The Bretton Woods system passed into history. Thus, while the US lacked effective control over the dollar exchange rate under the prevailing rule of the game, it still alone had the power, among governments, to unilaterally change the rules themselves, as the US policymakers deemed fit.

The countries of the South played an active role in challenging the hegemonic power of the US in this system and applied continuous pressure for counter forces throughout. The creation of UNCTAD and the call for a New International Economic Order were means of countering the GATT, whose structures had become very difficult for them. Today, the vast majority of major world currencies move independently of one another and are actively traded for speculative purposes by banks, hedge funds, brokerage houses and individuals.

One of the most important issues that came out of the debates between the countries of the North and the South was that of environment and its relationship with development. The debate that we have referred to in Chapter 12 was raised throughout the 1960s in international meetings on conservation and protection of nature. The criticisms ranged from exhorting the developmentalists to finance and support environment-friendly technologies, to offering alternatives to the model of development itself. At the peak of the Cold War, a fundamental critique of development seemed like a critique of capitalism and, therefore, of the US axis of power, which it partly was. Historically, both capitalism and the power of the US have survived not only by brute force, but also by creating concepts and institutions that accommodate dissent (this is explained by the term hegemony, used a lot by political scientists). It is in this context that the UN initiatives—the Stockholm Conference of 1972, the articulation of the concept of sustainable development and the creation of UNEP—can be understood (Adams 2001). It has taken much longer for it to be understood that the modernist frame of development was actually common to capitalist and socialist systems, particularly in its technological base, though not in its distributive focus.

THE UNEP

The United Nations Environment Programme (UNEP) was the outcome of the first UN Conference on Human Environment held in Stockholm in 1972 and brought the idea of sustainable development on to the international agenda. But its formation was strongly opposed by the existing UN agencies. UNEP is, therefore, not a UN agency like UNESCO or FAO, and these remain responsible for the environmental aspects of their own activities. UNEP seeks to act as a catalyst and thinktank, the 'conscience of the UN system' (Adams 2001: 57). Thus to operationalise this self-image, UNEP works with a wide range of partners, including United Nations entities, international organisations, national Governments, non-governmental organisations, the private sector and civil society. Further, it was the first of the UN bodies to locate its office in Africa (Nairobi, Kenya), that is, outside the First World. A politically astute decision, UNEP seeks to project it as a clear advantage it has in understanding the environmental issues facing the world's developing countries.

UNEP lists its work as follows:

- Assessing global, regional and national environmental conditions and trends.
- Developing international and national environmental instruments.
- Strengthening institutions for wise management of the environment.
- Facilitating the transfer of knowledge and technology for sustainable development.
- Encouraging new partnerships and mindsets within civil society and the private sector.

To ensure its global effectiveness, UNEP supports six regional offices plus a growing network of centres of excellence such as the Global Resource Information Database (GRID) centres and the UNEP World Conservation Monitoring Centre (UNEP-WCMC). UNEP also has major offices in Geneva and Paris, where its Division of Technology, Industry and Economics is situated. UNEP also hosts several environmental convention secretariats including the Ozone Secretariat and the Montreal Protocol's Multilateral Fund, CITES (the Convention on International Trade in Endangered Species of Wild Fauna and Flora), the Convention on Biological Diversity, the Convention on Migratory Species, and a growing family of chemicals-related agreements, including the Basel Convention on the Transboundary Movement of Hazardous Wastes and the recently negotiated Stockholm Convention on Persistent Organic Pollutants (POPs).[4] After the Stockholm Conference of 1972, the next major international meeting of governments on the issue of the environment was held in Rio de Janeiro in 1992.

One of the first important processes that UNEP initiated in the first 20 years of its formation was the production of the document called *World Conservation Strategy* in 1980. It was published under the aegis of 'the Ecosystem Conservation Group', formed by IUCN, UNEP and WWF. Responding to the issues and problems of conservation raised by economic development as such, it marked the first phase in the thinking on these issues. It is important to remember two aspects of this debate at this stage. First, that governments, and policymakers in particular, were just being initiated into the necessity and relevance of conservation. Second, that the inputs into this debate were mostly from scientists and technocrats and, therefore, the focus of conservation was exclusive from the point of view of how the development process was going to carry it out. It argued that *this* needed to be done, that was all. Three objectives were identified:

1. To maintain essential ecological processes and life-support sys tems,
2. To preserve genetic diversity, and
3. To support millions of rural communities as well as major industries.

While it also discussed priorities for national action, it also sought to focus on international actions needed to promote conservation, recognising that many living resources lie partly or wholly outside national boundaries (Adams 2001: 63).

What is important for the purposes of this course, however, is the fact that the WCS fails to recognise the essentially political nature of the development process. On one hand, it suggests that conservation can in some way bypass structures and inequalities in society; on the other hand, it seems to assume that 'people' can exist in some kind of vacuum, outside the influence of inequality, class or the structures of power. The WCS avoids the explicit use of the language and ideas of economics and politics that are fundamental to the development process in terms of social and economic structure, the inevitable political implications of economic change, and the constraints of capital, technical knowledge and manpower. This is why it fails to place ideas, which are essentially environmentalist, into a development matrix (Adams 2001: 69). The subsequent developments in the work of UNEP and international meetings have been an attempt to bridge this gap.

The first of these was the Brundtland Commission Report (1987), entitled *Our Common Future*. It made several significant contributions, beginning by getting the UN General Assembly to address the issue of environment, and that too, together with the issue of development, conveying that the two cannot be separated. Further, it recognised that it was futile to try to tackle environmental problems without considering broader issues of 'the factors underlying world poverty and international inequality'. It identified two concepts: one, of 'basic needs' of the people that ought to primarily guide development action for the poor; and second, the idea of environmental limits, set by technology and social organisation, and not by the physical context of the environment itself. From these, then, it arrived at the now familiar concept of sustainable development. And this is one of the strongest positions argued for in the debate today.

What is important to recognise, though, is that poverty being both the cause and the effect of the problems of environment was addressed as such, to conclude that the focus on growth would continue with an important difference: it would be sustainable, environmentally aware, egalitarian, and integrating economic and social development. These could not have been achieved with a naïve belief or faith in all countries recognising the gravity of the requirements for 'our common future' and coming together in a spirit of 'mutual' self-interest and enlightened multilateralism to do so. Only systematic efforts to 'speed up economic growth while respecting environmental constraints' would have made this possible. These efforts would involve making important changes in international trade rules, giving developing countries a better chance to resist expensive imports and not face protectionism in terms of their exports—two processes that were integral to the Structural Adjustment Programme and had proved to be a major burden on their economies. However, this would challenge the fundamental power relations in the international economy and that could not have been allowed. So, what was actually available for 'the common future' was a world of unequal power structures—between rich and poor nations, and between multilateral agencies. As Agarwal, Narain and Sharma (1999: 311) point out,

> Saving the planet is an expensive mission. The larger part of the world's natural wealth lies in the Southern countries, making them its caretakers. Reeling under the burden of poverty and debt, it amounts to a sacrifice for these nations to save their natural resources for future generations, instead of using them to improve their present standards of living. Their lack of finances also means that they cannot invest in environment friendly technology, and leapfrog out of the destructive development path taken by industrialised countries.

Nowhere was it more evident than in another development of this period, that is, the creation of the Global Environment Facility (GEF). This was a financing mechanism that was set up in 1991 by the World Bank, UNDP and UNEP. The World Bank administers the GEF and acts as the repository of the trust fund. UNEP provides the secretariat for the Scientific and Technical Advisory Panel and supplies environmental expertise on specific projects; UNDP is responsible for technical assistance and project preparation (Adams 2001: 96). One of the most telling assessments of this institution is as follows:

> It was in vague recognition of the fact that the world's ecosystems are suffering due to lack of financial resources—and not the South's call for compensation for damages to the global environment by the North—that the Northern nations set up a fund to save the Earth. This basic fact cast the dice for the fund-to-be—it would come as aid, not as compensation. Ever since the Global Environment Facility (GEF) was set up in 1991, it has been a reminder to the South of the dominance of the financially powerful North in deciding the fate of environmental negotiations. GEF is the only multilateral mechanism providing funds to deal with some of the most urgent global environmental problems facing the world today.
>
> (Agarwal, Narain and Sharma 1999: 311)

The story from here onwards, that is, Rio to Johannesburg and beyond, explains the sharpening of this understanding, but the requirements continue to be on the same lines.

The United Nations Conference on Environment and Development, held in Rio de Janeiro in1992 inaugurated environmentalism as the highest state of developmentalism (Sachs 1999: 27). The incapacity to bid farewell to some of the certainties that had shaped the development era was the major shortcoming of the Rio conference (Sachs 1999: 28).

It had been resolved by the UN that an international conference to assess the situation of the environment and development would be held five years after the publication of the Brundtland Report. This took place at Rio de Janeiro, a major city of Argentina, in South America. By this time, as has been stated earlier, the world was, indeed, a very different place in terms of the range of issues on environment that had been brought up by peoples and movements across the world. At the same time, the economic development situation in many countries that had been advised Structural Adjustment by the financial agencies of the UN had become decidedly worse, making the impact of those policies on environment more sharply visible. Hence, the number of issues deliberated upon at this conference and the kinds of decisions taken reflect the growing concern on these. At the same time, the lack of consensus and what many believe to be the watered-down nature of the resolutions are a testimony to the continuing power of the multilateral institutions, specially the financial ones because most agreements that would expect terms of international trade to be altered in any way were kept at bay. Yet, each of these agreements, dogged by trouble as they were, marked important steps forward for the issues at hand.

In terms of the conference itself, a large number of preparatory meetings called PrepComs and a number of regional meetings were held before, trying to hammer out the issues as they ought to be presented finally. Also, Maurice Strong, the Chairman of the Conference, who had been with the international environmental negotiation process since Stockholm, brought many NGOs to participate in the process. This was a clear recognition of the fact that the responsibility for protecting and preserving the Earth's environment had been undertaken by more than national governments, and so those organisations ought to be part of the deliberative and decision making processes as well. While this was a very important step towards a recognition of ordinary people's role in the grand process, the inequalities between different groups was evident as well. Basically, the difference was between the groups of the North and those of the South. But also, within these groups, those well endowed and connected from the North and their partners from the South, were often in a better position to influence government delegations, even while they were excluded from the official negotiating process.

THE RIO CONFERENCE

Four major outcomes are associated with the Rio conference: Agenda 21, the Biodiversity Convention, the Framework Convention for Climate Change, and the Forest Principles. The better known Rio Declaration is a shorter and considerably watered down version of Agenda 21. Let us summarise them here one by one.

Agenda 21

In one of the PrepCom meetings before Rio, Maurice Strong proposed a document to set out how to make the planet sustainable by the beginning of the twenty-first century. This was called *Agenda 21*. By the time it was completed at Rio, it was a large document of over 600 pages that sought to cover a range of issues in three sections. They are social and economic dimensions, conservation and management of resources for development, and strengthening the role of major groups. Each chapter in these sections covers one issue and seeks to set out the basis for action, the objectives of action, a set of activities and the means used to implement them. In this sense, each part of Agenda 21 is a microcosm of the whole, with a particular emphasis on the means of implementation (Adams 2001: 86). A series of key themes that can be identified here are the revitalisation of growth with sustainability, sustainable living, problems of urbanisation (water supplies, health, wastes and pollution), and efficient resource use. Other themes are concerned with global and regional resources, and the management of chemicals and wastes. The final one is perhaps the most important for the purposes of our understanding—the principle of people's participation and responsibility.

The Biodiversity Convention

The aim of this convention was to conserve biological diversity and promote sustainable use of species and ecosystems, and equitable sharing of the economic benefits of genetic resources. While this had its roots in the 1970s environmentalism at the international level that focused on conservation, prompted by Northern states' concern in terms of rainforest loss, it evolved to include new perspectives that became legitimate over the years. The latter principally included the concern of preserving the South's biodiversity, because it was in the world's South that the maximum diversity was to be found and due to its weak economic position, was more vulnerable to exploitation and lack of conservation. Thus, the G–77 countries demanded inclusion of the issue of bioprospecting and biotechnology, and sharing of the wealth generated by the exploitation of biodiversity in the South by Northern biotech companies. However, the convention's basic perspective was to utilise the revolution taking place in biotechnology to preserve and protect genetic resources. The two objectives would be very hard to balance, given that the resources were with the South and the technology to conserve them was with the North (further details on this are discussed in Chapter 14).

Framework Convention for Climate Change

As mentioned earlier, the issue of global warming had been raised by the scientific community since the late 1950s and a World Climate Conference had already been convened in 1979, following the position taken at Stockholm in 1972 that countries should take responsibility for transnational pollution (Adams 2001: 92). Over the years, this agenda was pursued vigorously at many intergovernmental meetings that highlighted the major differences on this issue, the details of which are discussed in Chapter 14. What needs to be referred to here is that while this convention was signed by over 150 states and the European Union, and came into force by March 1994, it contained no legally binding commitments that mattered. Yet the fact that it was signed was, as Adams (2001: 94) puts it, 'a remarkable testament to the urgency with which global climate change was viewed in the early 1990s.'

Forest Principles

Like the other two issues, threat to forests had for long been on the agenda of the international community. Again, it was one that split it straight down the North–South divide—with the curiously complex position of the South on not wanting to support an agreement that did not allow them to exploit their natural resources for economic gain. Further, they argued that, if indeed, they did so for the sake of protecting the global environment, then the opportunity cost, as it were, ought to be provided globally. As a result of the bitterness of the dispute, no legally binding document was signed on this issue either. Instead, a political document, avoiding specific commitments and repeating the familiar arguments about the social, environmental and economic importance of forests and the need for them to be managed sustainably, was adopted. This was known as the *Forest Principles*.

THE WORLD SUMMIT ON SUSTAINABLE DEVELOPMENT, JOHANNESBURG, SOUTH AFRICA, 2002

The Commission on Sustainable Development (CSD) that was set up to continue policy discussions between summit meetings, convened the final one, a Multi-Stakeholder Dialogue, in Johannesburg in January 2002. The CSD Chairman addressing this meeting condensed the themes arising from his Report on Implementing Agenda 21 into the following five:

1. Making globalisation work for sustainable development.
2. Poverty eradication and sustainable agriculture and livelihoods.

3. Changing unsustainable patterns of consumption and production.
4. Strengthening governance for sustainable development at the national, regional and international levels.
5. Means of implementation—Finance, Technology and Science, Education and Capacity building.

Martin Khor, one of the most powerful intellectual/activist voices of the South, wrote of the WSSD: 'Ten years after the Rio Earth Summit, heads of state concluded the World Summit on Sustainable Development in Johannesburg with an untransparent political declaration and a weak implementation plan.' Although the Rio Summit failed to consider the issue of international environmental governance (IEG), it has since become clear that this is a critical component for the implementation of the concept of sustainable development. The First Global Ministerial Environment Forum (GMEF), in Malmo in May 2000, stressed the importance of 'a greatly strengthened institutional structure' for IEG, and when environment ministers met in Cartagena in March, they continued the discussion with this goal in view of preparation for the Johannesburg Summit.

Against the backdrop of spreading financial instability and mounting debt crisis, the continuing North–South divide on trade, debt and finance resulted in a stalemate on these critical issues at the WSSD. Talks were deadlocked because developed countries, particularly the US-led Juscanz group (Japan, US, Canada, Australia and New Zealand), refused to commit to crucial paragraphs spelling out the relationship between globalisation and sustainable development, and the language firmly committing developed countries to concrete action on debt, financial contributions and fair trade. While the WSSD Plan may not have the binding force of a WTO agreement or a multilateral environmental agreement (MEA), the programme of action endorsed by heads of government and by the UN does represent an expression of political will and commitment on the part of all UN member countries.

At the same time, there were deep concerns that WSSD's emphasis on market-based, private sector financing of the Summit's five priority programme outcomes—water, energy, health, agriculture and biodiversity (WEHAB)—would undermine government commitments. The shift towards private–public partnerships in both the Type I (obligatory on governments) and Type II (voluntary) outcomes of the WSSD represents part of a wider abdication of responsibility on the part of developed countries to fulfil their commitments to facilitate sustainable development in the South. Furthermore, allowing agencies such as the World Bank to initiate the implementation of crucial programmes and totally endorsing the WTO work programme would once again limit the policy choices of developing countries in their attainment of sustainable development (Goh Chien Yen and Celine Tan). Thus they conclude,

> The WSSD text on the international financial system does not meet the much needed reform agenda and many issues of immediate concern to developing countries. Objectives commonly shared by developing countries include: more balanced and symmetrical treatment of debtors and creditors regarding codes and standards, transparency, regulation and crisis management; more stable exchange rates among the major industrial countries, especially with respect to their effects on capital flows, exchange rates and trade flows of developing countries; less intrusive conditionality; and above all, more democratic and participatory multilateral institutions and processes.

The relationship between the rules of WTO and multilateral environmental agreements was another controversial area at WSSD. This has been a sticky issue ever since the Uruguay Round, with the trade and environment regimes often contradicting each other. Several attempts have been made to clarify this relationship in the past, but without success. WSSD was no exception in this regard. At one point in the negotiations, there was a genuine fear that all environment agreements would have to be made 'consistent with WTO rights and obligations', thus giving the trade body more power. After protracted negotiations, however, it was only decided that governments 'enhance the mutual supportiveness of trade, environment and development'—leaving existing controversies unresolved (Sharma, Mahapatra and Polycarp. 30 September 2002).

Unwilling to commit to a concrete sum of money over a concrete period of time to fund sustainable development in the South, the US came up with the idea of partnerships (also called 'Type II agreements' in WSSD jargon) during the preparatory process of WSSD. Several aspects of these partnerships are designed to suit the US foreign policy. They are voluntary; involve no firm multilateral commitments for funds or deadlines on part of the US government; bring corporations firmly into the picture giving them a free hand to promote their interests through such partnerships; and best of all, ensure that responsibilities remain fuzzy. There are no rules to govern partnerships—only a set of flimsy guidelines that were not even discussed in Johannesburg (ibid.). The Indian delegation had loudly opposed such partnerships before the summit, saying they would find them acceptable only if four conditions were met. They wanted the goals of the partnerships to have clear linkages with the final Plan of Implementation to ensure that they did, in fact, work for the goal of sustainable development and not against it for the partnerships to be country driven, not donor driven for each partnership to be no less than US $5 million, and an assurance that the partnerships would involve 'new and additional' funds, and not merely be a repackaging of existing aid. Other governments had similar misgivings.

NOTES

1. http://www.newint.org/issue257/simply.htm
2. http://www.polsci.ucsb.edu/faculty/cohen/inpress/bretton.html
3. http://www.newint.org/issue257/simply.htm
4. http://www.unep.org/Documents.Multilingual/Default.asp?DocumentID=43&ArticleID=3301&l=en

REFERENCES

Adams, W. M. (2001). *Green Development: Environment and Sustainability in the Third World.* New York: Routledge.

Agarwal, Anil, Sunita Narain and Anju Sharma (eds) (1999). *Green Politics: State of Global Environmental Negotiations*. New Delhi: Centre for Science and Environment.

Sharma, Anju, Richard Mahapatra and Clifford Polycarp (2002). 'Dialogue of the Deaf'. *Down to Earth*. Delhi: Centre for Science and Environment. 30 September.

United Nations (2000). *Basic Facts About the United Nations*. New York: United Nations Publications.

14

Issues of Industrial Pollution, Global Warming and Threats to Biodiversity

INTRODUCTION

By now, we have discussed enough the theoretical arguments about environment and a whole set of international organisations in the area for you to understand what goes into the making of these issues. So, issues of the environment, as we know them, do not just happen to be there, but are constituted by politics and mobilisation, and often have to face contestation from the state and other structures of power. Following from our understanding of 'commonsense' in the Introduction, you may remember that any issue always has a commonsense to it. *The real challenge in understanding is to be confident of being able to go beyond the commonsense and analyse any issue of the environment for oneself.* So, this chapter is written with this intent—in two parts. The first, short, part will just spell out the questions that need to be asked in order to better understand and analyse the issues of environment. The second part comprises three sections on each of the three issues meant to be studied for the course, in which you will get the details of the issue that will be presented by following the question guide spelt out in the first.

How Does One Think About and Analyse the Issues of the Environment?

The first question to ask is what exactly *is* the issue? Say, something like the Bhopal Gas Tragedy—was it about the making of the gas, or the leak, did it kill people, and how many died and so on. Next, we need to know how and where did it begin. This may not always be obvious—say, the tsunami disaster. It is important to know the exact context and location of the question. Sometimes, exploring this question reveals the linkages of the problem to the steps that precede it (the backward linkages), which then help to explain it in its *entirety*. For instance, if you were to explore the backward linkages of the Bhopal Tragedy, it is then that you would discover the range of factors and contexts that actually contribute towards an issue, giving depth to the understanding rather than seeing it as some sensational incident.[1]

Along with this, we would need to know *who did it affect* and *how, in what manner*. This would be a difficult one, because if one were to study an issue of *environmental change*, then as McNeill (2001: xxiii) points out, all changes are good for some and bad for others ... It depends on whose interests one rates over others. But if there is clearly a disaster of some kind, it is usually clear who *exactly* it affects negatively and the effort should be to identify them unequivocally.

What Is the Scientific/Ecological Explanation for It?

Most issues related to environment by definition are those that concern the physical and natural world. So, the first source of understanding would be from the physical and natural sciences, regardless of one's disciplinary training. However, this would not be enough. 'Environment' is constituted by not only the physical and natural world, but in *the way in which* human beings construct their relationship with it. Therefore, by this definition, the understanding of *every issue of the environment must have a scientific, a social-scientific and philosophical component to it*. Together, they constitute a comprehensive explanation.

Who Began and Continued the Mobilisation Around It?

In the case of disasters, mobilisation begins almost immediately—by victims, those speaking on their behalf, media, and such others. However, environmental issues that are identified as they occur and acquire significance are a different matter. Often, it is when individuals or communities identify a problem, begin to ask questions and seek answers that an issue is recognised. Studying the mobilisation around any issue invariably reveals a long story of some people doggedly asking uncomfortable questions, challenged or put down by powerful vested interests, struggling to mobilise public opinion and whether they are able to carry the argument through. While there can be no ultimate triumphs and losses in these conflicts, great lessons can be learnt about harsh realities and where larger thinking on these issues is headed.

What Was the Response of the State to That Mobilisation and Was It Repressive?

Given the commitment of states and governance to the idea of 'development', in most cases, there are reports of state repression against mobilisation around issues of environment. The case of Kashipur in Orissa and the tribal movement against bauxite mining in that area is an interesting case in point. However, it must not be seen as if it's only in India or the Third World that the state is repressive. Even in the bastions of democracy, notably the US, there is little tolerance for people's opposition to big projects. The history behind the passing of the US Environment Protection Act (1970) is a grim testimony to this point.

What Has Been the Status of This Issue Internationally? Any International Agreements?

Many issues in the last 30 years have been discussed internationally, especially when multinational corporations were involved. An example of this is the Shell Corporation in Nigeria and the sad story of the repression of activists opposing the pollution of rivers and fields by the activities of Shell. The trial and subsequent execution of Ken Saro Wiwa attracted widespread international criticism and discussion, but it was a case in which the international community was unable to check the repression of the movement by the combined strength of the Nigerian state and big international business interests.

Where Is the Issue Now?

To complete the understanding of any issue always requires that one refers back to what the contemporary status is. As stated earlier, these issues do not reach a resolution easily and it is always revealing to return to them.

We have created this framework to analyse/understand any issue of environment as one that is an application of McNeill's (2001: xx) perspective on understanding ecological history as a whole: 'Modern ecological history of the planet and the socio-economic history of humanity make full sense only if seen together.' Before we go into the analysis of specific issues, let us have an overall picture of the impact that human beings have had on the natural environment.

TABLE 14.1 The impact of human beings on the Earth in the twentieth century

Spheres of the Earth	*Nature of Human Intervention*	*Fallouts*
BIOSPHERE Land, forests	Crop agriculture, plantations, making medicines, large cities	Threats to biodiversity, endangered plant and animal species
ATMOSPHERE	Released gases from industries, regular air traffic	Air pollution, climate change
HYDROSPHERE Rivers, lakes, seas, oceans	Used groundwater, tamed floods, drained wetlands, tinkered with coastlines, incessant fishing, dammed rivers	Lowered water levels, reduced quantities of marine life, drowned habitats for dams
LITHOSPHERE Outer shell of rock, floating on molten rock	Mining for minerals and metals	Polluted soils, air, water and even the food chain
PEDOSPHERE Soil—a membrane between the lithosphere and the atmosphere	Application of chemical fertilizers and pesticides	Soil pollution

I

INDUSTRIAL POLLUTION

Let us recognise the basic *commonsense* on industrial growth—that it has been the most phenomenal achievement of the humankind. McNeill (2001: 6) points out that,'The world's economy in the late twentieth century was about 120 times larger than that of 1500. Most of this growth took place after 1820. The ... whole period since the Second World War saw economic growth at rates entirely unprecedented in human experience.' So, 'on average, we have nine times more per capita income than what our ancestors had in 1500, and four times as much as our forebearers had in 1900' (Ibid.: 7). What dazzles, always blinds as well, and when we open our eyes wide and look at this phenomenon more carefully, we find that there is a heavy social price and a heavy environmental price to pay for these rates of growth. This price is industrial pollution, which we will seek to understand.

As is evident from Table 14.1, industrial pollution affects each and every aspect of the Earth's environment. The effluents and gases affect both the hydrosphere and the atmosphere, while the technologies of production that they have invented and applied, and methods of extraction they have used, whether for minerals or metals or medicinal plants, have had a significant negative impact on the lithosphere and the biosphere. In other words, the impact of industry is felt on the soil, the rock beds, the forests, lands, the water bodies and the air, that too, all the way up to the ozone layer. McNeill (2001: 27) reports:

> One major source of soil pollution was the mining, smelting, refining and use of metals such as lead, cadmium, mercury and zinc…even in small doses these metals are dangerous to human (and other life)… they infiltrated soils, (as well as air and water).. lead and cadmium emissions increased about 20 per cent between 1875 and 1975.

Throughout his fascinating book, *Something New Under the Sun: An Environmental History of the Twentieth Century World*, he acquaints us with many similar realities in terms of industrial pollution affecting different parts of the Earth. Let us turn to look at the history of pollution in a country which is in the 'commonsense' of our consciousness, the epitome of economic growth, based on industrial achievements and one that most of us long to emulate, if not go and live in: the United States of America (USA).

In the US, industry is the greatest source of pollution, accounting for more than half the volume of all water pollution and for the most deadly pollutants. Some 370,000 manufacturing facilities use huge quantities of freshwater to carry away wastes of many kinds. The waste bearing water, or effluent, is discharged into streams, lakes or oceans, which in turn disperse the polluting substances. In its *National Water Quality Inventory*, reported to Congress in 1996, the US Environmental Protection Agency concluded that approximately 40 per cent of the nation's surveyed lakes, rivers and estuaries were too polluted for such basic uses as drinking supply, fishing and swimming. The pollutants include grit, asbestos, phosphates and nitrates, mercury, lead, caustic soda and other sodium compounds, sulfur and sulfuric acid, oils, and petrochemicals.

In addition, numerous manufacturing plants pour off undiluted corrosives, poisons, and other noxious byproducts. The construction industry discharges slurries of gypsum, cement, abrasives, metals and poisonous solvents. Another pervasive group of contaminants entering food chains is the polychlorinated biphenyl (PCB) compounds, components of lubricants, plastic wrappers and adhesives. In yet another instance of pollution, hot water discharged by factories and power plants causes the so-called thermal pollution by increasing water temperatures. Such increases change the level of oxygen dissolved in a body of water, thereby disrupting the water's ecological balance, killing off some plant and animal species while encouraging the overgrowth of others.

POINT FOR DISCUSSION

Taking the above example, make a presentation and have a discussion on these issues amongst yourselves? Resources you can use for this:

- McNeill's book cited above.
- Films: *Erin Brokovich* starring Julia Roberts and *Class Action* starring John Travolta.

Further, it is estimated that 10,000 deaths occur each year in the US due to routine industrial accidents; another 100,000 deaths occur due to occupational diseases; and 30,000 deaths and 20,000,000 serious injuries due to unsafe consumer products. This list does not include an estimated 90 per cent of cancers that may be environmentally induced (that is, from industrial products and byproducts).[2]

The above information implies that the country with such a high level of industrialisation is one that is likely to have a commensurate level of pollution as well. At the same time, we hear that there are now strict controls in place, created by law and that those have made a great difference to the quality of air, water and soil in the US. Also, that citizens are very aware and active in protecting their rights, which keeps industries on their toes. We will take it up in some more detail in the section on biodiversity.

The fact of the matter though is that these chemicals are integral to modern life and we cannot simply do away with them or stop using them. The key issue is that since they do not degrade and instead enter the food chain causing long-term damage to the human system, a change of focus on their disposal is urgently required. For this, a simple mantra, perhaps, would work well—the human mind that could think of the complex science to understand and use these chemicals can surely find a way of disposing them, especially if it means saving the human race itself. A good example of this last thought process is evident in Japan's environment miracle, which we have summarised from McNeill (2001) in Box 14.1.

In other words, unless there is a close focus on the built-in pressures on the industrial process itself, with safeguards against the possible pollution it might inflict on the environment, a clear correlation between higher levels of industrialisation and higher levels of pollution is evident. This was recognised by people affected by industrial pollution and the initiatives taken by them since at least the 1960s—pressurising governments to lay down strict standards for preventing pollution and insisting that industry abide by them and pay if there was any damage or slip-ups. The latter is what laid the foundations of the environmental movements in the US and Europe, and inspired many movements in other parts of the world. *Erin*

BOX 14.1

The Japanese Environmental Miracle 1965–1975

Between 1868 (the Meiji restoration) and 1945, Japan was focused on achieving the standards of industrialisation without any intervention/support from the West. From 1945 to 1965, it focused on a clear recovery from the defeat in the Second World War and achieved tremendous economic and commercial success. But these were done regardless of social and environmental costs. So, for these 100 years, it was 'a polluter's paradise' (Hashimoto 1989, quoted in McNeill 2001: 9). This was contributed to by the mining and smelting industry early on, spreading to many parts of Japan and causing the maximum air pollution. While there were intermittent protests over these throughout, the intense nationalist fervour for development justifying some negative fallouts prevailed. This was further complicated by increased automobile use in cities like Tokyo by the mid-1960s.

In the early 1950s, an unusual coalition of academics, industrialists and local bureaucrats formed, to act upon the health consequences of Ube's (a city in southern Japan) foul air. A leading industrialist saw the difference the city of Pittsburgh had wrought with its initiatives and convinced his peers that this was possible in Ube. The bureaucrats composed new regulations on emissions and this was implemented strictly. Its success ensured that the national law was designed along its lines. Citizen action drove the next stage—in 1967, asthma sufferers in Yokkaichi sued the giant petrochemical complex operating there since 1959. The damages they won, illustrating pollution and health concerns, prompted many other prefectures in Japan to cancel planned industrial complexes of its kind. Pollution control became a major issue in national politics, with people and authorities learning more and more about it and in 1970, when a particularly bad smog episode happened in Tokyo, a new agency to monitor environmental affairs and many antipollution laws came into effect. It was at this point that Japanese industrialists understood the significance of investing in cleaner technologies and by 1975, the skies in Japan got very much cleaner.

Behind this remarkable turnaround was a result of a large number of factors—combined with citizens' awareness and action, very basic material changes also took place—coal use gave way to oil and other energy sources, massive saving of capital by the Japanese allowed for substantial investments, a proportion of which could go to pollution control, and a careful study of and adaptation from laws abroad enabled the creation of effective legislation at home. This was the Japanese environmental miracle.

Brockovich, the highly successful film, made in the US a few years ago, is based on a story of the same theme.

The other result of the work of movements and pressure groups on this issue and the response of the US government to them was the legislation called the Environment Protection Act, passed in 1970. This actually enabled people to have some legally enforceable safeguards with respect to very powerful industry interests, which always fought the claims of ordinary people, on grounds of insufficient or unscientific information.

Over time, the enforcement of this Act and the many activities around it—the prolific literature and active debate and discussion in different forms of the media—has led to another development. There is an attempt, on the part of industry in the West, to recognise that there is possibly a responsibility to understand the issue and respond to it, instead of just being hostile to people's demands. The advocacy of many groups has encouraged it to understand that if the resources on which their profits are based were to be destroyed, their survival itself was at stake. So, the response has been across a spectrum. At one end of this is the attempt by industry to support research on and adopt greener technologies to alter the very production process that causes pollution, at the other end are industries that are not very keen to spend money or energy on this, but not able to resist the pressure of the issue and so making some kind of token concession to the locality or people affected by pollution. In any case, there is clearly now a trend *within industry*—it is not externally driven alone—to respond to the question of the environment. This trend has also a name—it is called Corporate Social Responsibility. We now turn to examining closely two instances of industrial pollution in India, following the parameters set out in the first section of this chapter.

The Case of Small-scale Industrial Units in New Delhi, India

What exactly is the issue? According to estimates that the Delhi government submitted before the court, there are 1,26,218 small-scale industries (SSIs) in Delhi, of which 97,411 are located in the non-conforming areas as per the Master Plan of Delhi (Non-conforming industries are located in unauthorised colonies, *lal dora* villages, resettlement colonies, the walled city and other residential pockets). Of these, 2,224 are stated to be polluting and these have been shut down. Some 20 lakh workers are estimated to be employed in the SSIs and tiny units.

How and where did it begin? The immediate context was that of a directive issued by the Supreme Court in September 2000 to close polluting industries in a bid to clean the city. In November, the Supreme Court set a deadline for shifting out all polluting industrial units from the capital's residential areas.[3] The more long-term context of this issue lies in the history and significance of SSIs in India as a whole, and the attitude of the government to it, as also its history specific to Delhi.

Small-scale industries have been nurtured by successive governments as part of the Industrial Policy Resolutions, with 'uninterrupted focus in all plans and the list of goods reserved was constantly upgraded. By the late 1980s, protection for SSI sector reached its peak' (DTE 15 October 2002). This attention was justified on the grounds that they fulfilled multiple objectives of decentralised industrial development, equitable distribution of income, utilisation of resources and generating employment. And in these, they have had some success—these industries are the largest supplier of mass consumption items, manufacturing close to 7,500 products, account for 90 per cent of export products and employ close to 19.2 million people. The one aspect that was not monitored ever was that of their location. Hence, they came up in all kinds of non-conforming areas and especially in a fast growing city like Delhi. The other neglected aspect was that the requirement for environmental clearance for technologies used by these industries was minimal, with only 17 industries in the red category identified by the union Ministry of Environment and Forests (MEF) requiring it. For others,

> a mere acknowledgement by the state pollution control board serves the purpose of consent and there is no need for the industry to obtain periodic environmental clearance till such time that a unit modifies or changes its processes of manufacturing. The Delhi based National Productivity Council estimates that small scale industries were responsible for 65 per cent of industrial pollution in 2000...(and) contributed to 40 per cent of wastewater generation in 2001.
>
> (DTE, 15 October 2002)

This is when the enormous environmental costs of this policy neglect became visible and led to an extreme order like that issued by the Supreme Court .

Who did it affect and in what manner? As was to be expected, the owners and workers of the SSIs, who faced the prospect of loss of livelihood, took to the streets, creating a crisis of law and order for the government. As the rampaging mob began burning government-owned buses, the police resorted to several rounds of firing. Three persons were killed and several others injured. On 20 November, owners of the industrial units called a Delhi *bandh*, which was supported by all the trade unions.

The unions, meanwhile, launched independent action in various parts of Delhi. In a rare occurrence, workers and owners came together on a common platform. In the discourse on pollution and relocation of industrial units, the case of thousands of workers in the unorganised sector was being overlooked. In the majority of cases, the owners did not even pay them minimum wages, leave alone other benefits.[4]

What is the scientific/ecological explanation for it? According to the Draft Master Plan of Delhi 2001 (hereafter MPD 2001), in 1981 there were about 46,000 industrial units, of which 77 per cent had fewer than 10 workers and 16 per cent had between 10 and 20 workers. It was estimated that by 2001 the number of units would increase to 93,000. It noted that the percentage share of workers in the industrial sector among the total workforce had constantly increased and a considerable change had taken place in the industrial structure in the last three decades, more so after 1975. Two kinds of industries grew rapidly: those involving electrical and electronics goods, and those involving rubber, plastic and petroleum products. MPD 2001 faulted the 1962 Master Plan for not proposing a monitoring system to register the changing socioeconomic profile of the community as well as the physical structure of the city, for certain other reasons. The absence of such a framework had led to unintended growth, in the form of unauthorised colonies, squatter settlements, the informal sector and the non-conforming industry, all of which needed to be monitored. It was forgotten that government agencies, such as the Municipal Corporation of Delhi (MCD), had issued licenses to the majority of these units and many of them were paying sales tax! The anger of the factory owners was, therefore, palpable.

Dunu Roy, director of Hazards Centre, a technical support group for community and mass organisations suggests that the concept of non-conforming *vis-à-vis* conforming is part of a mindset. He says that the formal system of planning in Delhi represented by the Master Plan has never taken into account the informal dynamics, including the fact that Delhi, compared to the rest of the country, has low overhead costs and the highest minimum wage. According to him, this has been one of the major reasons for the large-scale migration and concentration of small business and industry in Delhi in the last three decades. The units relocated following their classification as hazardous have been replaced by new ones although their pollution potential is not known. Industry and residential areas had traditionally coexisted in Delhi and the Master Plan failed to recognise this pattern, he said. Instead, while major violations of the Plan, like that of the Asiad Village complex, took place, no petition took cognizance of this. The focus was on deindustrialising Delhi, an elite interest that took no cognizance of the fate of the 7.31 lakh workers who depend on it.[5]

Who began and continued the mobilisation around it? Janwadi Adhikar Manch, a group that was formed in response to the plight of the workers who had lost their jobs and livelihood and had no one to speak up for them, focused on trying to actually get their compensation from the owners of the factories, as the Supreme Court had directed. They found out that loopholes left in the judgment allowed the owners to terminate the services of the workers a day before the deadline and not paying them the fair compensation. In order to cover their tracks, they then alleged that the workers did not want to come back for work. Also, when asked about occupational hazards of the technologies they were using and the high incidence of tuberculosis, and so on, amongst the workers, in order to get away they simply lied that these did not exist. The Manch then held public hearing on these issues, bringing people of eminence as well as commitment to hear the grievances of the workers. This produced a series of revelations and scathing attack on the combined oppression of the police and the owners on the workers and the bleak future they faced. Most of them were from very poor villages of Bihar and UP, and had moved to Delhi precisely because their own villages did not have any opportunities, either of income or any other facility, given that most development allocations were biased towards larger regional centres.

What was the response of the state to that mobilisation and was it repressive? The government was caught in a situation of its own making, with the responsibility for the units they had protected so far, yet bound to maintain law and order, and even more importantly, abide by the directive of the Supreme Court. Besides, it is very important to remember that the government is not a set of institutions apart and above ordinary people—in fact, it is intended to represent it, which also means that it comes from within it. This would imply that some of these representatives would have clearly wanted to represent the interests of the units, polluting or otherwise. That is why, in situations like this, we find governments struggling to find solutions. From a simple environmental point of view, it might seem simple—that is to close the units down—but it is not as straightforward as that. And it is the government that needs most of all, *to strike a balance between different interests*. (This is a clear application of the quote from McNeill, cited earlier in the chapter.) Thus, the government of Delhi was very harsh sometimes, and conciliatory at other times.

What has been the status of this issue internationally? Any international agreements? With respect to SSIs, these questions themselves can be understood in two different ways. First, are there significant international developments with respect to this sector? Second, regarding these kinds of production systems, are there important international norms that can provide guidelines as to how can the Indian state, and the industrialists and workers respond to this issue. As for the first, the international economic scenario, with its requirements for the removal of quantitative restrictions, except on a few items, has meant that a significant measure of protection has virtually disappeared. So, SSIs now face competition from very cheap imports from countries like China. In the case of certain products where consumer usage is widespread, imported goods could be available at far lower cost than domestic goods (DTE October 2002). Further, many countries, including the US, have been pressing for the inclusion of environmental and social causes as the part of the rules of the World Trade Organisation (WTO). Once this is done, it will mean that environmental costs of production will be taken into account in trade. This would put polluting SSIs in India at a disadvantage in the global market and may have to close shop leading to loss of exports and of trade.

Another area of concern for Indian SSIs is the agreement on Trade Related Intellectual Property Rights (TRIPS). 'For Indian SSIs, which are so much used to reverse innovation (taking a product and breaking it backwards to learn the intricacies of production), this may spell doom since under the strict Intellectual Property Rights (IPR) regime, the burden of proof will lie on the infringer,' says K. P. Nyati, Head, Environment Management Division, Confederation of Indian Industry, New Delhi. As a result of all these pressures, these industries are slowly coming around to the view that it would serve them well to become environment friendly.

Have any alternatives/policy guidelines been offered by any knowledgeable party? An analysis offered by The Energy Resources Institute, New Delhi, offers the following policy guidelines:[6]

- Compulsory registration of all industrial units with industrial department and development of database showing industrial unit location and/or expansion.
- Application for new units or expansion should be accompanied by an environmental clearance certificate.
- Non-polluting sectors like electronics should be promoted.
- No hazardous units should be allowed.
- Special efforts for promoting industrial units and developing supporting structures in adjoining areas of Delhi should be introduced.
- 'One window' approach should be strengthened by adequate training in environmental matters and for registration of new units, building the data base, processing applications for environmental considerations, and so on.
- Household/cottage units should be regularised and permitted within the prescribed norms to take care of the pollution.

Where is the issue now? What can we learn from it? This is a case study that amply illustrates two realities. The first is that the structures of inequality are fundamental to the issues of the environment and development, which we have discussed in great detail in this book so far. Second, a more fundamental issue, and one which we have begun to raise only in this chapter, is that *this is a problem of the design of modern technology itself*, that is, it is meant to focus on the creation of a specific product, but not at all designed to check the toxicity of what it leaves as a residue from that process—whether it is smoke or waste chemicals or solid waste or anything. The entire attention was not only on the quality of the product, but also how fast it could be made and the larger numbers in which it could be made. These were unquestionably guided by the basic motive of industrialisation—profit from the human desire to want more and want better. So, is it at all possible to have all of them at once? This is the question that has been pondered over a great deal, with respect to almost all modern industry. Here, we will look at some specific arguments for this case.

The main issue in creating technologies that are non-polluting is capital, that is, money. Those that have already invested money in technologies for these products do not want to pay for the costs they are inflicting on the environment. These are adopted by both small and large industries, but particularly the former, partly because the law has been lenient with them. On the other hand, the bigger industries have taken advantage of this leniency by outsourcing many of their products to SSIs, thereby escaping the investment to be made in pollution-controlling mechanisms.

The larger issue in all of this is of course the attitude we have towards creating modern technologies. In countries like India, a large number of technologies are mechanically adopted from the industrialised countries. These also become cheaply available when they become obsolete (out of date; replaced by newer technologies) in those countries. Given our fascination for their technology and our low self-esteem in building technologies that serve our purposes, these are the technologies investors look out for. And our higher education institutions of technology have not done much to alter this mindset over the last 60 years or so. Unless we are able to think, as they say, 'out of the box', that is, begin from scratch about all our requirements, seek to balance them and be confident that we can come up with competitive technologies, which local capital would invest in, we are not likely to find solutions to long-term problems like those of technology and environment.

BOX 14.2

The same human mind that created the technologies that turned out to be polluting is the mind that has the capacity to make them less so!

The same people that invested money in creating the first kind of technology should know that in it is in their interest to do the same for the latter!

The Bhopal Gas Tragedy[7]

What exactly is the issue? One of the worst industrial disasters in the history of the world, the tragedy of Bhopal is not so much the event of the disaster itself, but the poor record of public policy, politics, and indeed, public opinion, that has been unable to deliver justice, compensation and hope for the affected people of Bhopal. It is one of those environmental issues of the Third World that caught the attention and imagination of the international community, and is a lesson for anyone who wants to understand the politics of environment issues anywhere.

How and where did it begin? Who did it affect, how, and to what extent? On the night of 2 December 1984, deadly vapours of Methyl Isocyanine (MIC) gas engulfed the sleeping town of Bhopal, killing 3,500 people over the next few days. The gas escaped from Union Carbide, a US based multinational company that produced pesticides. Thousands were woken up close to midnight coughing violently, eyes burning and soon finding it difficult to breathe. People fled the town in thousands but wherever they arrived they had to be hospitalised and provided some antidote. Had it not been for the two lakes of Bhopal which came in the way of the gas cloud and neutralised it, an even bigger tragedy could have taken place.

What is the scientific/ecological explanation for it? Even though the explanation of what happened that night in the factory remains controversial, it is more or less known that the pressure in the MIC storage tanks built up alarmingly because of an extremely violent chemical reaction and the MIC vapour escaped, rupturing the sage disc and popping the safety valve. The safety devices that were meant to minimise any harm in the event of an accident, failed that night. What's more is that no one in the factory had any idea of the chemistry of MIC, thus proving to be fateful for the large number of people that inhaled it and required accurate antidote. The significant issues that can be identified on the basis of this great tragedy are as follows:

- Immediate issues of the operation of the plant, rather the lack of them.
- The larger issues with respect to the agricultural development policies of the Indian state.

The immediate issues were about the errors in maintenance and running of the establishment that led to the leakage. It was endlessly debated as to how a multinational company, which supposedly followed better work practices could be so irresponsible. However, an examination of their records world wide showed that Union Carbide had been particularly lax about health and safety in the Third World, with examples from Puerto Rico, Jakarta and other Third world countries. This clearly demonstrated the company's laxity of awareness and appreciation of the context of poor countries in which they work. Thus, concern for environment was clearly conditional upon the existing wealth of the environment they were functioning in.

The larger issues[8] about the purpose served by such a plant were equally significant. Union Carbide's coming to Bhopal was welcomed by all, because it meant jobs and money for Bhopal, and foreign exchange for the country, with rising demand for pesticides after the Green Revolution. Green revolution techniques of hybrid plant varieties had already come in for criticism because of their continuous dependence on chemical pesticides and fertilizers, not to speak of large supplies of water (CSE 1985: 207). By the time the tragedy struck, there had already been a great deal of questioning as to whether such a capital-intensive form of agriculture (that is, one that required expensive fertilizers, pesticides and water) was the only solution to the hunger problem of the Third World, and whether the jobs and money it generated, on one hand, were not actually taking away long-term livelihood options in agriculture. The breakdown of the Bhopal plant and its acute impact on the thousands of poor people who lived around it only served to highlight the tragedy of this policy. Further, it reiterated the unequal relationships between the countries that own technologies and those that had to buy it, as did the painful law suits that have dragged on for years, denying even the basic dignity of compensation to the survivors.

Who began and continued the mobilisation around it? There were many groups and people genuinely concerned and committed to the cause of the victims of Bhopal. An account of the mobilisation they carried out and where they stand today is one that reflects the great differences of perspectives that are bound to occur in any movement of these kinds. How the victims should be organised, what issues should be prioritised—whether of compensation, medical relief or rehabilitation—directly result from what the politics of the organisers are. And here, politics does not mean the politics of any political party or one under the cover of unscrupulous politicians, but the position that people take on power structures—of governments and companies—and even the relationship of the poor victim with the middle-class volunteer. Since this cannot be discussed in detail here, do refer to an issue of a magazine called *Seminar* (2004) that takes up these issues in detail.

The Bhopal Survivor's Story (Rumah Rasaq 2004), *Bhopal: A Second Tragedy* (Sunanda and Yogesh Walia 1995), *The Bhopal Legacy* (Nadeem Uddin), *Unravelling the Tragedy of Bhopal* (Gittleman Film Associates), *The Heart Becomes Quiet* (David Christensen and Robin Schlaht), *Hunting Warren Anderson* (Amos Coheny), and *Cloud Over Bhopal* (Gondwana Films/Spanish Television) are some of the films that were made on the Bhopal gas tragedy (Ghosh 2004), which served to create awareness and elicit response from people around the world.

What was the response of the state to that mobilisation and was it repressive? In the 25 years that the Bhopal survivors have fought for justice, they have had to face not one, but two states—that of India and of the United Sates of America. While the Indian government's response has veered from protecting the company to providing relief to the victims and back again, the response from the US has been largely that of protecting the company for most of the time. The last response from one of the US courts (in November 2008) has been supportive of one victim's claim for undoing the harm to the water of Bhopal by the company's policy of dumping the wastes in the premises. The Indian government has also been, on occasions, very harsh to protestors and unwilling to take their claims seriously, while also providing compensation to some of the victims. In all of these responses, it is important to note that the state is not simply the government of the time, but the interests of all of the dominant classes that pressurize their actions. Hence, we see that one Supreme Court judge who allowed the company to build a hospital with the confiscated shares of the company became the chairman of the Trust that runs it. There are many such examples of collusion and contact between politics and business interests, both in our country and abroad. These influence the policies of the governments everywhere. One of the things you can read that would explain all the issues very well is a long interview with Satnath Sarangi, a dedicated activist of this crusade at http://www.corporatecrimereporter.com/sarangiinterview.html

What has been the status of this issue internationally? Any international agreements? And where is the issue now? While this book was being written, a very strong protest by the Bhopal survivors was concluded in New Delhi, its voices incidentally drowned over the clamour by the activists of the Narmada Bachao Andolan, fasting unto death over the raising of the proposed height of the Sardar Sarovar Dam. Nearly 22 years after the tragedy, so many of the basic issues, especially of compensation, remain unresolved.

The victims of the Bhopal gas disaster have not disappeared, writes the lawyer–activist Usha Ramanathan, as do lost memories. Maybe, even if they wanted to, they cannot. For they exist, in large numbers, bearing the continuing burden of the chemical industry's callousness in the matter of risk and safety. Suffering impoverishment, certain only of uncertainty, ill health and pain, incapacity imposed on them by the disaster, injustice heaped on them by the Union Carbide Corporation (UCC), the executive agency of the Indian state, and American and Indian courts, they have fought on. They have found support in local and distant geographies which has helped convert their collective complaints into a cause and to keep alive the pursuit of justice.

By Way of Solutions: The Green Rating Project of the Centre for Science and Environment, Delhi

Since the 1980s, the critique of industry being anti-ecosystem had gathered ground provoking angry responses from them. As discussed at the end of the section above, by the early 1990s, in the West, there was awareness and response by industry to the issue of greening technologies. But that has not happened in India and to give it a fillip, a Delhi-based NGO that has done pioneering work on disseminating information and running campaigns on the environment, initiated a Green Rating Project. The project to rate industries was started by CSE in 1999 as an independent tool to leverage change in the environmental balance sheet of companies. As the pulp and paper industry is extremely environmental-intensive, using large amounts of wood and bamboo as raw material and releasing huge amounts of wastewater into rivers, CSE had rated this sector first in 1999. The re-rating was done in 2004 to check if companies were responding to public pressure to reform their environmental performance. The rating shows that the companies have done so. For instance:

- Only one company had an environmental policy in 1999, and now 16 companies have such policies; 25 of the 28 companies rated today have an environment department.
- The average water consumption of a mill during the first rating was 200 tonnes per tonne of paper produced. This has come down to 135 tonnes today.
- While only one company, the winner ITC Bhadrachalam, has totally eliminated the use of toxic chlorine in its process, the others have cut down on their consumption from 65 tonnes of elemental chlorine used for each tonne of bleached pulp to 40 tonnes by 2002.

- In the 1999 rating, CSE had strongly urged companies to move towards sourcing their wood and bamboo from farmers, instead of depending on government forestlands for raw material supplies. It should be recalled that the voracious appetite for wood of this industry has been the single largest cause of deforestation in the country. The 2004 rating reveals that the area brought under farmland for tree cultivation has doubled—from 20,000 hectares to over 40,000 hectares by 2002. Leaders in this area—Harihar Polyfibres, JK Paper Mills and ITC Bhadrachalam—are getting as much as 80–90 per cent of their wood from farmers, who they are encouraging with their technical help and assured markets.

These improvements are reflected in the fact that the 2004 rating awarded Three Leaves to six companies as compared to 1999 when only three mills could make the grade. CSE's data shows that the industry can work to provide jobs and a growth model. It can provide employment to 0.55 million farming families just from tree plantation, and can make India a pulp-surplus country. The credibility of the rating works as a reputational incentive to drive change in the sector.[9]

This is the kind of innovation that is desperately required for Indian industry. Besides, the growing popularity of this exercise and its effects of generating peer pressure on the industry demonstrate that all initiatives do not have to be taken by the state and the only thing that works is not necessarily the stick of law. If non-state actors were to take up the accountability tracking exercise of the big players in the civil society, people, development and the environment all stand to gain.

II

GLOBAL WARMING

What Is Global Warming?

Gases including carbon dioxide, nitrous oxide, methane and water vapour trap heat from the sun within the atmosphere. Acting like the panes of glass in a greenhouse, they ensure that temperatures close to the Earth's surface are much warmer than they would otherwise be. In this way, the greenhouse effect makes life, as we know it, possible. However, this system has recently come under heavy pressure. Since the Industrial Revolution, humankind has been extracting and burning fossil fuels at increasing rates, releasing significant amounts of greenhouse gases into the atmosphere. As concentrations of greenhouse gases have increased, so has the strength of the greenhouse effect. The Intergovernmental Panel on Climate Change (IPCC), in its third and most recent assessment, published in

2001, suggests that 'there is new and stronger evidence that most of the warming observed over the last 50 years is attributable to human activities'.

The human activities that are responsible for this effect on the environment are the historical use of fossil fuels in industrial processes (in Europe and the United States) and deforestation. McNeill (2001: 109) points out that

> For the 1000 years before 1800, carbon dioxide levels in the atmosphere varied around 270 to 290 parts per million (ppm). Around 1800 an accelerating build-up began, reaching about ... 360 ppm in 1995. ... fossil fuel combustion accounted for about three-fourths of the addition, and deforestation (now mainly in the tropics but in 1900 mostly in North America and temperate Asia), ... accounted for all the rest.

Additionally, most developing countries using modern technologies of production learnt from the developed world, are increasingly becoming partners in this activity.

The use of chlorofluorocarbons in various industrial and commercial machineries like air conditioners and refrigerators were initially favoured because their virtue is that they are very stable and react with almost nothing, until they drift into the stratosphere, where direct UV radiation breaks them up, releasing agents that in turn rupture ozone molecules (McNeill 2001: 111). This leads to depletion of the ozone layer, while increasing the volume of other gases, thereby disturbing the balance of gases and leading to increased warming of the Earth. The IPCC report also states that average global temperatures are projected to increase by 1.4 to 5.8 degrees Celsius over the next 100 years because of the enhanced greenhouse effect. Due to this warming, glaciers and the polar icecaps are expected to melt, causing sea levels to rise by anything between 9 and 88 centimetres in the twenty-first century. The IPCC also expects significant changes in patterns of rainfall—including monsoons—and more extreme weather events.[10]

Agricultural systems contribute to methane emissions through several mechanisms (Reicosky et al. 1995; Rasmussen et al. 1998; Robertson et al. 2000; USDA 2000; Pretty and Ball 2001):

1. The cultivation of soils resulting in the loss of soil organic matter;
2. The clearing of forests to create new cropland;
3. The direct use of fossil fuels in farm operations; and
4. The indirect use of embodied energy in inputs that are energy-intensive to manufacture.

Agriculture, though, is also an accumulator of carbon, offsetting losses when organic matter accumulates in the soil, or in above ground woody biomass used in agroforestry systems or for production of biomass for energy sources that substitute for fossil fuels. Soil organic matter, and thus carbon, can be increased to new higher equilibriums with sustainable management practices. The greatest dividend comes from the conversion of annual crops to agro forests as there is a benefit from both increased soil organic carbon and the accumulation of carbon in woody biomass. Grasslands within rotations, zero tillage (or no-till) farming, green manures and cover crops, and high amendments of straw and manures to the soil, also lead to substantial carbon sequestration. Thus, if this is focused upon as a policy and commensurate investment is made on them, then it is possible that developing countries could significantly contribute to reducing the atmospheric carbon burden.[11]

At the end of the day though, it needs to be remembered that the effect of global warming visible today is the result of accumulation of green house gases over the period of time that the industrialised world has contributed to it and so, needs to take responsibility for it.

> Carbon dioxide is not rinsed out of the air like soot; rather it is very slowly absorbed by the oceans and by living things, at rates that cannot be significantly accelerated. Its impacts, great or small, cannot be reversed quickly. So, the combustion history of the twentieth century has already partly determined conditions in the next several centuries to come.
>
> (MCNeill 2001: 115).

They ought to invest in green technologies using alternate forms of energy, which they have done, but because they are not sure of the returns from those and the present dispensation provides an assured rate of profit, they have not shown much enterprise on this account. It does, additionally, provide a warning to the developing countries that they too need to modify or research into alternate technologies that do no use fossil fuels, so that they do not worsen the problem in the future. The ownership of liability on these emissions is the source of the controversy over the Kyoto Protocol.

III

BIODIVERSITY

Biodiversity[12] is the shortened form of the phrase biological diversity. It stands for the great number of species of flora and fauna, and the ecosystems in which they exist and flourish on the Earth. *Scientists have identified three levels of biodiversity: genes, species and ecosystems*. Genes are the basic unit in hereditary information and their diversity is expressed through terms like subspecies, breeds, races, varieties and forms. Species are the most commonly discussed level of biodiversity, that is, the population diversity of organism that is reproductively isolated from other such population (different crops like rice, wheat and tomato). An ecosystem comprises a biotic community along with its abiotic habitat (soil, stones, air), with some identifiable boundary, making it an ecological complex (ibid: 7). Each of these species has a special role to play in the ecosystem and something to contribute to the growth and movement of the ecosystem as a whole, including the human species. However, as McNeill (2001: 193) puts it,

> by the twentieth century, our numbers, our high energy technologies, and our refined division of labour with its exchange economy made us capable of total transformation of any and all ecosystems. Some remained little affected, such as seafloor vents. But in most of the biosphere, co-evolution gave way to a process of 'unnatural' selection whereby chances for survival and reproduction were apportioned largely according to compatibility with human action.

Thus the developments of the twentieth century transformed biodiversity into an issue of the environment, from being simply an aspect of it.

An understanding of biodiversity would be complete only if the relationship between biological and cultural diversity is recognised. Different human communities have devised a remarkable range of practices, rituals, technologies and social relations in response to the challenges and opportunities presented by their natural surroundings (ibid: 9). The complex juxtaposition of biological and cultural diversity takes place because human beings adapt to nature and nature, in turn, nurtures culture. An understanding of the relationship of societies with their natural surroundings is critical to the development of long-term environmental policies and programmers, as will be evident in the following discussion on threats to biodiversity and responses to them.

Historically, however, the way in which conservation of nature has been discussed, an abiding impression is that concern for preserving nature is that of an aesthetic variety, affordable by only the rich and those who are free from livelihood concerns; that those countries or societies that are already developed in terms of incomes and lifestyles can afford to pay attention to preserving nature in its pristine form. What needs to be understood, however, is not only that biodiversity is not a matter of aesthetics but, also, that in fact it is a matter of livelihood concern for a large number of people. In fact, Ashish Kothari argues persuasively that 'biodiversity already plays a very critical role in our day-to-day existence and is likely to play an even more critical role in the future'. He further argues that there can be no true and long-lasting development if we continue to erode habitat and species diversity. The five grounds on which he substantiates this argument are that

> the components of biodiversity sustain and recreate the quality of air, water and soil that we use; wild plants and animals still constitute the substantial part of the diet of the majority of the world's rural people; the medicinal needs of three-fourths of the population are still directly fulfilled by biodiversity; agriculture still benefits in many ways from it and fisheries, that is a bulk of aquatic biodiversity, contributes about hundred million tonnes of food worldwide, greater than the contribution made by livestock or poultry.
>
> (Kothari 1997: 3–4)

As per our own schema spelt out at the beginning of the chapter, let us begin by understanding how exactly this happened, after which we can explore what has been, and is being, done about it and what can be done in the future.

Whatever Did We Do to Biodiversity

1. Agriculture was mechanised: Prompted by the labour shortages during the Civil War (1861–65), farm mechanisation driven by gasoline first began to appear in the 1920s, setting off a chain of implications—farms began to be made by merging fields, so that tractors could be used profitably, then those crops that lent themselves to machine harvesting were chosen above the others. So, the investment in the machines for that crop eliminated others, leading to monoculture, away from the earlier pattern of the patchwork of crops, requiring new means of controlling pests and insects with chemicals. Monocultures depleted nutrients faster, though the crop yields increased because of more thorough and timely preparation of the fields. *Thus farm mechanisation, by boosting production and prosperity, helped select the winners—among crops, pests and nations—in the twentieth century* (McNeill 2001: 219, emphasis mine).
2. We had the Green Revolution: Since the early twentieth century, people have relied increasingly on a select few plants for food, with about half of the world's calorie intake coming from just three crops—rice, wheat and maize. According to the International Plant Genetic Resources Institute (IPGRI) based in Rome, Italy, at least 7,000 plant species could be cultivated for food, but only 150 crops are grown commercially.[13] This is not simply in order to preserve biodiversity for its own sake, but also that the neglected crops are a

source of micronutrients that are not available in rice, wheat and maize. Thus, the research on the increased production enabled people to have more food, but whether they were being nourished was another matter. So, a problem of 'hidden hunger' was being developed over time, especially amongst the poor.

3. We are now promoting a genetic revolution.
4. We cleared forests for timber, more agriculture, and plantations for tea, coffee and rubber.
5. We fished in the rivers, lakes and most importantly, the seas—the deep seas in search of better and better fish species.
6. We tinkered with coastlines: clearing mangrove forests to 'cultivate' fish varieties, leaving them to face the perils of tidal waves and tsunamis; harvesting corals from the sea to decorate our homes.
7. We have not been able to control our numbers, in proportion to the biodiversity we depend on.
8. We have created expanses of mega cities, in which we have little or no space for other species.

What Are the Threats to Biodiversity on the Basis of Human Intervention?

Speth (2005: 30–32) identifies at least nine separate but often interacting drivers of biotic impoverishment—nine principal threats to biodiversity and to healthy ecosystems. These can be easily correlated with Neill's summary of what we did to biodiversity.

Land use conversion Land use conversion from tropical forests to agricultural uses and tree plantations, draining of wetlands, urbanisation—has meant that more than a third of the world's land surface has been converted for human use, and an additional third could be converted by the end of this century.

Land degradation Land degradation reducing productivity of crop and grazing land, salinisation and water-logging of irrigated lands are leading to desertification on one hand and deforestation on the other.

Freshwater shortages Freshwater shortages caused by heavy and continuous withdrawals for two principal purposes, irrigation and urban sanitary use, lead to serious shortages that could get worse.

Watercourse modifications This occurred due to the channelisation, damming and diversion of all kinds of wetlands.

Invasive species Such species introduced in numbers greater than the local species are a threat.

Overharvesting Overharvesting by marine fisheries, logging, the market for animal parts and birds means that each of them are threatened for survival.

Climate change Climate change can become an important factor in the coming decades in the loss of biodiversity.

Ozone depletion Ozone depletion, that is, the weakening of the Earth's stratospheric ozone shield caused by CFCs and other chemicals affects biodiversity through the influence of the increased ultraviolet radiation reaching the Earth's surface. It can affect plant growth, form and biomass allocation; can change the competition balance in the ecosystems; and can reduce the production of marine phytoplankton.

Pollution As discussed in detail earlier, it can threaten biodiversity through a number of ways.

Who Began and Continued the Mobilisation Around it?

One of the earliest and most decisive legislative and political initiatives to protect biodiversity was undertaken in the United States, when the Clean Water Act was passed in 1972, followed by another exceptional law—the Endangered Species Act. The latter made it unlawful for anyone to collect, kill or otherwise harm any animal that was in danger of extinction, even in his or her own property. This rested on a powerful idea introduced by Aldo Leopold, that of the 'land ethic', which changed the role of homo sapiens form conquerors of the land community to plain member and citizen of it. It implies respect for its fellow members, and also respect for the community as such. He extended it to imply that we have 'obligations to land over and above those dictated by self-interest', and that these obligations stemmed from an appreciation that humans and nature are ecological equals. If we have rights, nature also must have rights. The life that evolved here with us should be allowed to live 'as a matter of biotic right' (quoted in Speth 2005: 24).

The issue of saving biodiversity by no means rested with the passing of legislation, however. Gustave Speth (2004: 24), who went on to found one of the foremost environmental thinktanks in the world, the World Resources Institute in Washington, USA, writes no less than of

> a series of fierce struggles—a struggle to get the act properly implemented, with real estate developers around the country against it; a struggle to get the act reauthorised every few years, since Congress always has kept it on short string; a struggle to find a lasting rationale for species protection that the American public would buy; and, above all, a struggle to save the country's biological wealth in the face of the mounting pressures.

It was around the same time, interestingly, that initiatives for legislation were being taken in India. The context and content were somewhat different, but they are discussed in detail in Chapter 15; so, we will not discuss it here. Other countries, too, saw the development of environmental movements around this time. This was not a coincidence. Despite increasing evidence of destruction of the environment emerging in powerful writings like those of Rachel Carson (*Silent Spring* in 1962), most governments were still dominated by powerful pro-industry interests that could not see beyond their blinkered vision of profits. Yet ordinary people, benefited as they were from the great strides of 'development' in the industrialised and developed world, could see that they needed to take these critics seriously. In the developing world, ordinary people saw the inequality in the benefits of development accruing to only the elite that plundered it, while they themselves were being pushed away from their land, with which they actually had a close relationship of dependence as well as the knowledge to regenerate. Thus, while the impulses were different in different countries, they resulted in a number of mobilisations of people around environmental issues across the globe in the late 1970s and the 1980s. These became manifest in the international agreements that were concretised later.

What International Agreements Were Made on These Issues?

One of the most important initiatives taken to bring governments to discuss the issues of the environment was the Earth Summit in Rio de Janeiro in 1992 (discussed in detail in the chapter on the UN). The Convention on Biological Diversity signed at this summit is one of the most important international agreements on the issue of biodiversity. Many other conventions were signed that address singular wildlife and habitat protection issues.

Where Is the Issue Now?

Speth argues, 'Those conventions have raised awareness amongst governments, provided frameworks for action, stimulated some national planning exercises, and generally had some modestly beneficial effects.' What is more, he believes that 'the process of negotiating these agreements has both advanced the basic principles of international environmental law and instilled in governments an appreciation of such key values such as sustainability, reciprocity and commonality.' Yet, some element of despair and cynicism does appear, when he laments, 'But the bottom line is that these treaties, and their associated agreements and protocols do not drive the changes that are needed' (ibid. 96).

This provides a basic reference point to understand all mobilisation on issues of not only the environment, but against any inequality; that a number of different modes of organisation and their continuity is what makes for some kind of change. People, whether victims or concerned citizens, must raise their voices in systematic and consistent ways that register their protest, which must be followed by some success in enacting legislation and creating policies in favour of those issues and then, the responsibility for actually working in practice, rests not with the administrative aspect of government, but actually, back with the citizens themselves.

Finally, two specific issues of biodiversity are discussed in detail:

1. Genetic modification and weighing its costs and benefits with respect to agricultural produce and the protection of biodiversity.
2. The appropriation of natural resources for human benefit, specially medicines.

Agriculture and biodiversity Genes have become very important in the last 30 years or so, precisely in the light of diminishing biological diversity. Two human necessities are still directly derived from nature—food and medicines. With increasing numbers to feed and maintain health for, it has been argued that scientific intervention to help nature produce more or substitute our dependence on nature with synthetics would be a way out. This is what guided the research and widespread adoption in the 1950s and the 1960s of hybrid varieties of seeds that promised higher yields in wheat, rice and corn production; indeed, in many other food varieties as well. The next breakthrough science has had is at the level of the genes of these varieties. By creating new genes that have a variety of qualities, whether it is resistance to typical pest varieties or vagaries of the weather, or increasing yields, these promise even higher yields and the solution to the problem of supply to increasing numbers. Similar promise is held out if gene pools of medicinal plants can be created and manipulated with in order to replicate, or even better the properties contained in the original plants. This breakthrough has now led to the consolidation of the biggest industries in the world, that is, of biotechnology-based companies manufacturing seeds and plant substances of different kinds and pharmaceutical companies. The former are by now suppliers to millions of farmers worldwide, with a very important proviso for their seeds—they cannot be regenerated by the farmer as was the practice earlier, but have to be bought from the company regularly, thereby ensuring the dependence of the farmer on them.

The governments of many developing countries have been very impressed with giant seed companies and also genetically modified seeds with the temptation of higher yields. This has caused storms of controversies, and India and Zambia offer contrasting pictures on this question. In the former, the government is actively encouraging farmers to adopt genetically modified seeds of cotton, while many groups like Gene Campaign have argued against its use. Their position has been vindicated, sadly, by the crop failures resulting in their inability to withstand precisely the conditions of drought and pests as promised, and farmers, unable to bear the burden of huge losses in their investments have committed suicide in large numbers in the last few years. This is true despite contrasting evidence found in some parts of the country in which the genetic variety was bolstered by irrigation and other very costly inputs which poor farmers elsewhere could not afford. This remains to be resolved. On the other hand, Zambia, a poor sub-Saharan African country is facing a famine condition with people dying for want of food, but has refused genetically modified corn in the form of aid because they are convinced that they do not want it to enter the food chain. A spirited campaign against it in their public sphere has enabled their government to take this stand, inspite of tremendous international pressure for accepting this. It is interesting and important to note that the European Union has refused the same corn, but it is seen by the international community (read *the powerful countries whose companies produce this corn*) as a luxury unaffordable by developing *countries*. This shows up the fickle nature and the double standards of the environment/development debate that we have discussed continuously.

The debate on this issue is very complex, however. Both sides of the issue have very powerful arguments in their favour, usually backed by intimidating scientific evidence. What is important is that these issues are always seen not for their intrinsic scientific value alone, for the simple reason that their use is always within a web of factors—economic, ecological and social—that influence the extent to which the scientific value will find fruition. If any of these factors do not fit the science, the user will not get the benefit of science. This will then raise two further issues—does the user need that particular science alone? Or is it that there can be other options from within the range of knowledge that may already be available from within the ecological and economic system of which the user is already a part? One of the best examples for these questions can be provided by the issue of Bt cotton in India.

Medicines and biodiversity It is well known that even though there are many synthetic compounds that are now the base of biomedical pharmaceuticals, the significance of plant extracts in experimentation for new compounds continues. Further, there has been almost an explosion in the international market for herbal medicines, which these companies are now trying to enter and gain from. In this effort, they are trying to take advantage of two things: the potential of the genetic pool of herbs known for specific medicinal properties and the traditional knowledge of communities that have been using this continuously in their living history. For some products, like antiseptic creams derived from turmeric, there is no need to carry gene pools, because turmeric is freely available and can also be grown under different conditions. But for species that are not easily grown or are only available under difficult conditions or are vanishing, gene pools are the surest ways of retaining access. This way, one can continue to avail biodiversity's benefits without any responsibility towards it in nature outside, but keep it under completely controlled conditions in the laboratory. The implications of this kind of control sought by big international commercial interests has direct implications for the poor of the Third World—farmers, collectors and suppliers of raw medicinal plants, and those that make medicines from them. Of course, many of these groups are not poor, but are nevertheless disadvantaged in this issue because they cannot compete with the bargaining power of the transnational companies that dominate these sectors. They take recourse to the patenting regime of their countries and have attempted to rob the Third World groups of their rights and control over both resources and knowledge in these respects.

With respect to traditional knowledge around genes and plant species, the story is different, at least with respect to India. When it was first learnt that an American company had applied for a patent on a strain of basmati rice and then for an antiseptic preparation based on turmeric, the scientific establishment in India mounted a spirited defence of these as traditional knowledge, garnering every available kind of knowledge source to argue their case. After the turmeric case was won, it was widely recognised that this danger can raise its head again and so a definitive response was required. For once in the history of postcolonial India's policymaking frame, a very good decision was taken and implemented: to put together a Traditional Knowledge Digital Library, accessible to anyone who wanted to take a patent for commercial use. This is a good example of how developing countries that might lack in economic wealth can access a wealth of knowledge, both traditional and modern, and demonstrate a hitherto unknown fighting and staying power on these issues.

The next level in biodiversity, that is, species, are better known in the public realm because of the extensive media coverage that this issue has received from time to time. Across flora and fauna, that is, plants, birds and animals, there has been widespread concern that several overexploited or mindlessly used species are depleting at a rapid rate and slowly becoming extinct. We need to remind ourselves that this issue has to be understood in terms of different species occupying an ecological niche, and their depletion proving to be a destruction of the ecological balance at that point. Hence, these should be a matter of common concern. As discussed in the chapter on UNEP, the earliest environmental negotiation at the international level was for the conservation of many dying species, and it was precisely because this point was not understood that the international discourse on the environment took so much time to garner support. However, today there is a great deal of knowledge about the status of thousands of species and the threats human consumption poses to them. Since it will not be possible to discuss them all here, we will pick up one discussion of great contemporary relevance.

Medicinal plants, as argued above, are a very important and now increasingly more important biodiversity resource internationally. The market for them is growing very fast because of the increasing demand for herbal products worldwide. Most of these plants are still those that grow in the wild and very few are cultivated. Only those communities that have lived beside the ecosystems that support these plants, that is, forests, river valleys and mountains, know the plant varieties and how to harvest them. Often this is their only source of livelihood and in developing countries, regions that are remote from urban centres do not get the benefits of development. In such a situation, the harvesting communities see an opportunity in this growing demand which they may not have again. Also, the growing market has thrown up a complex network of buyers and middlemen, that know the regional, national and international market, and put a great deal of strain on increasing amounts accessed. A combination of these is resulting in overharvesting of the plants, without allowing for enough time for regeneration. So, not only has the scale and extent of harvesting increased, the pressure of the market has also played havoc with norms of collection that would have allowed for regeneration in generations before. Thus, the International Union for Consumer Networks created the Red List of Endangered Species in 1980 and, sadly, that list is growing every year. And so much fieldwork that is reported both in newspaper/magazine reports and academic journals is testimony to the fact that this list is flouted with impunity in the medicinal plants market.

This issue has a direct relationship with the threats to ecosystems. For example, two kinds of perception are common about forests. The first is that they are pristine areas of rich biodiversity which have been plundered for human greed for the last couple of centuries. The other that they are entities where human beings live in an organic relationship with nature. But the reality of their destruction has evinced only one model of protecting/conserving them, that is, by altogether excluding human beings from them. There are others that argue that linking the conservation of biodiversity with development goals and practices, such that both ends are met, is a better way of conserving in the long run. In India, an extensive network of such areas called Protected Areas was created and by 1995, 12 years ago, there were 521 national parks and sanctuaries, covering some 4.3 per cent of the territory (Kothari 1997: 24).

In many areas, the government made rules of limited and conditional use of the forest by the local communities and tribal groups that were historically and culturally dependent on the forest. The idea was to protect the forest from commercial use, while not excluding people who had used it in a sustainable manner for so many generations and could be trusted with it even today. But the experience of the communities with the limitations of the use of forest produce on one hand, and on the other hand, the impunity with which the forest department flouted the rules of felling of trees and setting up factories, has completely altered the terms of discussion on this issue. They no longer feel that they are the real trustees of the forest and instead have to come to believe that if the forest were indeed to be exploited for some material benefit, albeit in the short tune, they might as well be the beneficiaries. Not every community or tribe feels this way, of course, but it is not possible to delve into the details of this here. The debate is very neatly summarised in Kothari's book, *Understanding Biodiversity*. For the purposes of this book, we would state that this conflict over resources, once again brings to light how real structures of inequality ultimately govern the lives of people.

This chapter has dealt with three issues in great detail. At the beginning, we outlined the steps necessary to analyse and understand any issue, and there is also a box that summarises one, briefly along those lines. All these put together should ideally serve the purpose of not only providing some details on some issues but also providing a perspective on understanding the issues of the environment. That would be clear only if the reader were to pick up any issue anywhere in the world and apply the basic questions to it, to discover whether that truly makes for a comprehensive explanation.

NOTES

1. Sadly, many environmental issues are reported in the media only in their sensationalist aspect, not giving enough attention to the deeper contributory factors. This is why even very serious problems remain in the public imagination for a very brief while, returning only on their anniversaries. It must be remembered, however, that some reports can be done differently, and increasingly, there is a small section in the media that is committed to serious and consistent reporting on these issues.
2. George Draffan. http://www.endgame.org/industrial-disasters.html
3. http://www.teriin.org/energy/pollut.htm
4. http://www.frontlineonnet.com/fl1725/17250080.htm
5. http://www.frontlineonnet.com/fl1725/17250080.htm
6. http://www.teriin.org/energy/pollut.htm
7. A wonderful book that was published on this was Hazarika, S. 1986. *Bhopal: The Lessons of a Tragedy*. New Delhi: Penguin.
8. A detailed discussion on these, including a fair amount that was part of the public debate at the time, can be found in *Bhopal Gas Tragedy: Accident or Experiment* by B.N. Banerjee (1987).
9. http://www.cseindia.org/ misc/ 2004paper.html
10. http://www.scidev.net/dossiers/index.cfm?fuseaction=dossierfulltext&Dossier=4
11. http://www2.essex.ac.uk/ces/ResearchProgrammes/CESOccasionalPapers/OccPaper2001-4.pdf
12. Check scidev.net dossier on biodiversity
13. http://www.scidev.net/dossiers/index.cfm

BIBLIOGRAPHY

Agarwal, A., S. Narain and A. Sharma (eds) (1999). *Green Politics*. New Delhi: CSE. Ch.1: 16-122.

Bhatt, S. (1997). *Biodiversity: A Manual for College Teachers*. Ahmedabad: Centre for Environment Education.

Gadgil, M. (1998). 'Let the People Speak'. *Hindu Survey*. 101–137.

Hurst, P. (1990). *Rainforest Politics: Ecological Destruction of South-East Asia*. London: Zed Books.

Kirkby, John, Phil O'Keefe and Lloyd Timberlake (eds) (1995). 'Biodiversity' (Chapter 1), 'Climate Change and Energy' (Chapter 2) and 'Global Warming' (Chapter 10). *The Earthscan Reader in Sustainable Development*. London: Earthscan Publishing Ltd.

Kothari, A. (1997). *Understanding Biodiversity: Life Sustainability and Equity*. 116–130

McNeill, J. R. (2001). *Something New Under the Sun: An Environmental History of the Twentieth-Century World*. New York: Norton.

Meyer, M. and K. Abich, (1993). 'Winners and Losers in Climate Change' in: W. Sachs (ed) *Global Ecology: A New Arena of Political Conflict*. London-New Jersey: Zed Books.

Pretty, J. and A. Ball (2001). *Agricultural Influences on Carbon Emissions and Sequestration: A Review of Evidence and the Emerging Trading Options*. Centre for Environment and Society. Occasional Paper 2001-03, University of Essex.

Ramanathan, U. (2004). Review of *Clouds of Injustice: Bhopal Disaster 20 Years On*. London: Amnesty International.

Rasmussen, P. E., K. W. T. Goulding, J. R. Brown, P. R. Grace, H. H. Janzen and M. Körschens (1998). 'Long-term Agro Ecosystem Experiments: Assessing Agricultural Sustainability and Global Change'. *Science*. 282: 893–896.

Reicosky, D. C., W. D. Kemper, G. W. Langdale, C. L. Douglas and P. E. Rasmussen (1995). 'Soil Organic Matter Changes Resulting from Tillage and Biomass Production'. *J. Soil and Water Conservation* 50 (3): 253–261.

Robertson G. P., E. A. Paul and R. R. Harwood (2000). 'Greenhouse Gases Intensive Agriculture: Contributions of Individual Gases to Radioactive Warming of the Atmosphere'. *Science*. 289: 1922.

Seminar (2004) 'Elusive Justice: A Symposium on the Bhopal Disaster after Twenty Years'. December.

Shiva, V. et al. (eds) (1991). *Biodiversity: Social and Ecological Perspectives*. London: Zed Books.

Shiva, V. (1990). 'Global Warming Caused by Rich Countries'. *Third World Resurgence*, No.1. September. 6–7.

Smith, D. (2003). The Penguin State of the World Atlas (pages 34-37: info on climate change/biodiversity).

Speth, James Gustave (2004). *Global Environmental Challenges: Transitions to a Sustainable World*. New Delhi: Orient Longman.

USDA (2000). *Growing Carbon: A New Crop that Helps Agricultural Producers and the Climate too*. Natural Resources Conservation Service. Washington DC.

Weizsacker, Christine von (1993) 'Competing Notions of Biodiversity' in W. Sachs (ed.) *Global Ecology: A New Arena of Political Conflict*. London, New Jersey: Zed Books.

15

Environment Policy in India

ABOUT THE MAKING OF POLICY

A commonsensical expectation would be that public policy in democratic countries be made on the basis of what people need and want. Further, that both structure and components of policy enable the removal of social inequalities, particularly those that have persisted over a long period of time. However, a close look at the policymaking process tells a different story. The government of a democratic country, in fact, comprises a number of competing interests that vie to appropriate the maximum share of resources available. Since the powerful are, by definition, in a position to do this, they are always able to influence to better their interests and the poor often lose out in the competition. This could be avoided if the representatives of the people take their work of putting the interests of the common person at the heart of a policy seriously and help direct it in that direction. Alternatively, there are those that consider themselves the voice of the people, even without a political mandate like the vote to support it. These are groups and organisations that have mobilised opinion and action on issues that need urgent attention, a different perspective from that being promoted by the government of the day or simply to oppose powerful interests that may actually be pushing through policy that would eventually harm the common person. Thus, policymaking is a complex process that could involve many levels and kinds of people in any polity.

In the past 20 years or so, there has been a great deal of criticism against governments that undertake policymaking without involving the people who this policy will affect. So, models of participation that are viable, easy to manage and provide crucial inputs to policy have been tried out in many parts of the world. Some of the most significant efforts in this direction have been about managing environment, because this is one aspect that directly impinges upon the life of the people. In this respect, the exercise of creating the National Biodiversity Strategy and Action Plan in India was closest to the idea of participatory planning and policymaking. This will be discussed in detail later. But before that, we need to be clear on what exactly public policy is, how it is different from, for instance, legislation on the same issue? Are policies made by the central government applicable to the states in India and such issues. We discuss these next.

ABOUT PUBLIC POLICY

Public policy is an instrument by which governments lay down their intent and direction of work on any matter. It does not have the force of law, but that of political will on any issue and if the government of the day so decides, it can work within the available laws to implement its policies or create a new one in order to do so. Thus, its significance lies precisely in the fact that the government of the day at any time is committed to carrying out what it declares to be its policy, within the purview of its powers and institutions.

It is important to understand, though, that legislation is different. When legislation on a certain issue is passed, it reflects certain political will on that issue. But it is usually confined to a specific issue or specific sets of issues. Further, it usually performs the function of protecting certain interests or subjects of interest, were there to be some violation of that subject. When a law is passed, it means a number of different things, but it does not mean that the government that passes it is declaring any intent on working on that issue immediately. It, however, is very clearly reflective of the larger political, economic and social contexts that would have worked to state the necessity, the provisions and the limitations of the law. Let's take a simple example. A very important issue of the environment is that of forests. Now, India has had laws on forests that protect them, allow collection of wood and non-wood forest products, and so on. Together, these may indicate the broad intent of political thinking on forests, but it is only when a clear set of actions that any government is willing to implement are announced by it, that it can be said that there is a policy on forests in India. Thus, both law and policy are very important for any government to act, but they are different kinds of tools and need to be understood that way.

In India, all laws can be categorised under the three lists provided in the Constitution, defining the jurisdiction of the laws. They are the Union, State and Concurrent Lists, which provide the list of subjects on which the central government or the state governments can make laws, or those on which both may make laws. There are general references to the duty of the Indian state 'to protect and improve the environment and to safeguard the forests and wildlife of the country', as also that of the citizen 'to protect and improve the natural environment including forests, lakes, rivers and wildlife'. Both the Directive Principles and the Fundamental Rights sections refer to environment. At the same time, there is no clear reference, in general, to it in either of the Lists, specifically to forests and wildlife in the Concurrent List. Overall, there are three kinds of legal provisions with respect to environment in India—acts (and amendments to them), rules and notifications.

Policy Inheritance from the Colonial State

A rich array of studies in the field of environmental history of colonial India enables us to understand what exactly the British policy was with respect to India's natural resources and already existing systems of their management. The maximum impact was on the forests of India (Gadgil and Guha 1992), along with water management and irrigation systems (Whitcombe 1993; Sengupta 1985), common property resources (Chakravarty and Kaul 1995) and wildlife (Rangarajan 2001). All of these studies demonstrate that the interest of the British in these resources was linked to the basic purposes they wanted their colony to serve at different points in time and space. These were revenue generation from agricultural land, the supply of sleeper material for the construction and maintenance of railways, the pressure to meet the growing demands to replace the resources of vanishing oak forests in Britain and providing game-hunting opportunities for the colonial and princely state masters. In order to increase revenue from agricultural land, which was the principal source of revenue for the colonial state, it initially encouraged large-scale clearing of forests and increasing land use under cultivation. At this time, its policy had been to recognise forests and waste land, as well as local water management systems (already established and running for a long time), as the property of the village communities within the boundaries that these fell (Stebbing, as quoted in Gadgil and Guha 1992: 123). The intention was to allow the efficiency of the village management systems to operate and provide the revenue, which is all that it was interested in. However, with the expansion of railways and the recognition of the strategic importance of this resource, 'The first attempt at asserting state monopoly was through the Indian Forest Act of 1865. ... it was passed to facilitate the acquisition of those forest areas that were earmarked for railway supplies' (Gadgil and Guha 1992: 123). But this was just the first step to consolidate the control of the colonial state over forests, and a much more comprehensive and stringent law was passed in 1878.[1] Enabling the 'scientific' management of forests towards monoculture of species for commercial purposes, this served a very useful purpose later in the two World Wars as well (ibid.: 135). The development of tea, coffee and rubber plantations, all cash crops, were undertaken by Europeans who were sold these lands cheaply and, eventually, minor forest produce too, which was found to have a variety of industrial uses, was also taken up by the twentieth century (Gadgil and Guha 1992: 137).

One of the most important implications of this policy was the decline in traditional conservation and management systems around the forest. In the precolonial period, these systems were managed by village communities with clear systems of mutual responsibility and punishment for violation of strictures over forest and grazing land use. These were the ways in which many traditional communities kept the use of environment under some kind of control and did not allow its abuse. While great internal hierarchies and inequalities along the lines of caste and gender were most certainly a part of village communities, it is, nevertheless, undeniable from the rigorous and careful work of different historians that some mechanism of mutuality of interests had been worked out whereby all castes and groups had to abide by some basic principles of natural resource management. In today's language then, a decentralised structure of control and management was already in place before the colonial era and it was replaced by the power of the state. This was so not only in the case of forests, but also in that of all the other systems mentioned above. So, the hostile relationship was established between the colonial state and village communities by positing their interests in conflict. This spirit, attitude and relationship are what were carried over to the postcolonial period, when the state simply decided to broadly follow the policies of the colonial sate. This had long-term implications, from the Indian Forest Act of 1952 to the National Biodiversity Action Plan of 2004, as we shall see in the next few sections.

THE POLITICS OF ENVIRONMENTAL POLICY IN INDIA IN THE POSTCOLONIAL PERIOD

It is in analysing the postcolonial policies on environment that some of the approaches stated in the first two sections of this chapter will become clear. The fact that a policy is an outcome of a conflict and negotiation of interests is no better exemplified than in the decisions made by the postcolonial state. The postcolonial state, pursuing a policy of using natural resources simply for economic purposes, encouraging monoculture, and systematically alienating those that subsisted on forest produce and not even bothering to trace how they managed a livelihood, was not very different in its outcomes from the colonial state. The reason for this lay in both, the state's ideology of development and its dominant social base, which we shall discuss next.

The focus of the postcolonial state in India was 'development', that we have seen to be a concept projected and propagated in a specific way by the United States in the aftermath of the Second World War. If the trajectory of the West was to be followed, then the path of development was heavy industrialisation, urbanisation and creation of big networks of power, roadworks and water. In India, unlike many developing countries, there were actually two contending perspectives on the concept of development that would be most suitable for postcolonial India—those of Gandhi and Nehru. While Gandhi had a clearly articulated opposition to the typical 'modernisation' of the West (exemplified in the *Hind Swaraj* written as early as 1909), Nehru was charmed by it and convinced that India needed to and could very easily replicate the Western model, and be counted in the international community as she richly deserved. Given that after independence Gandhi's influence was on the wane and that of Nehru on the rise, postcolonial policy on development reflected this new power equation.

Further, postcolonial policy was a continuation and expansion of the colonial policy, with the difference that the profits of these would accrue to the benefit of the Indian, rather than the British economy. But the great differentiation in the category of the Indian that we have pursued throughout this book was evident in terms of the nature of the social base of the state. The study of political science has shown for a long time now that even in democracies, the state is not some neutral instrument of government, away and outside of the conflicts and struggles of the society. In fact, those that dominate the society are the ones that are most likely to dominate the power of the state (though the curiosity of democracy is that even this is never permanent, and can be overthrown by the power of the people, depending upon how they mobilise support for themselves). So, the ideology that came to dominate thinking in the postcolonial state justified all effects of 'development', especially the negative ones, in the name of 'national interest', because it would help make the nation as great as all the other greats in the world. In the first flush of independence, strengthened by the competitive spirit wrought by partition, this was an irrefutable ideology and the worst consequences of this were, sadly, for the environment.[2]

The first two Five-Year Plans, for instance, focused on agriculture and industry, respectively. This focus was clearly to bring mechanisation and capital-intensive technology to both sectors, aimed at increasing productivity and returns. It must be recognised that this was done in the belief that these returns would then be distributed by systems of the government to reach all sections of society and the implications of this system of development on the environment were not well known at the time. What was apparent and could not be missed were impacts on lives of people that were displaced by development projects like big dams, roads and railways. They lost their homes and villages, indeed, the very physical and natural context by which they had defined themselves for generations. In each case, some kind of compensation was worked out by committees appointed by the government and the losses they incurred were considered necessary for the national interest.

While this line of argument was hard at first to counter, what began to turn the tide was when the livelihoods of people who were dependent on natural resources began to be destroyed. Then, in a direct equation, it became a case of development for some people as opposed to loss for others. A case in point is that of the Chipko movement, which sought to save the trees and forests that provided firewood and other sources of sustenance, from being destroyed by powerful timber interests. Combined with growing international trends of environmental protection exemplified by the Stockholm Conference of 1972, the policy of the Indian government began to undergo a change. It is important to remember, however, that its position at the 1972 conference was very opposed to the focus on environment as a priority, when poverty continued to be such a major issue to be resolved. One of the most memorable quotes of that conference is that from Indira Gandhi, the then Prime Minister, 'Poverty is the biggest polluter'. A close echo was the Brazilian one, 'Smoke is a sign of progress'. As Agarwal and Narain (1985: 363) explain,

> In all those who came from the Third World, there was a sneaking suspicion that the western countries were up to some trick. The West may simply be pushing the environmental concern on to an unsuspecting Third World to retard its technological modernisation and industrial development. It was even argued that having got their riches and affluent lifestyles, Westerners were now simply asking for more affluence: clean air, clean water, and large tracts of nature for enjoyment and recreation, many of which were going to be preserved in the tropical forests and savannas of Asia, Africa and South America.

So, while prior to 1972, environmental issues such as sewage disposal, sanitation and public health were dealt with independently by different ministries without any coordination or realisation of the interdependence of the issues, the systems were altered thereafter. In February 1972, a National Committee on Environmental Planning and Coordination (NCEPC) was set up in the Department of Science and Technology, which was established as National Committee on Environmental Planning (NCEP) in April 1981.

The NCEPC functioned as an apex advisory body in all matters relating to environmental protection and improvement. However, due to the bureaucratic problems that the NCEPC faced in coordination with the Department of Science and Technology, it was replaced by a National Committee on Environmental Planning (NCEP) with almost the same functions. But with the setting up of a separate Department of Environment in 1980, there emerged differences between them as well. The Department of Environment could not, for instance, order inquiry by independent experts as NCEPC could do.

It is in the context of this that the policy to protect endangered species also may be understood. Projects to protect the tiger, the national animal, or a number of other vanishing bird and animal species were undertaken from the 1970s, and have a dedicated following till today. Mahesh Rangarajan details how, from a meeting of the International Union for the Conservation of nature held in 1969, in which 'Experts from across the globe elected to put the Indian Tiger on the "endangered list"… together with a crucial role played by the then Prime Minister of the country, Indira Gandhi, in having the Wildlife Protection Act (1972) drafted and passed, aided by the "new international climate of concern" was able to launch Project Tiger, "a forty-million-rupee scheme, in April 1973"'. What is significant about it is that it not only helped foster an approach that supported protection of a host of other species eventually, but also that it 'played a key role in broadening ecological perspectives … Total preservation was soon extended to lands beyond those of the tiger.' Its expansion, however, brought to light what eventually has become one of the most urgent issues confronting the conflict over natural resources today, which is, preservation/conservation at the cost of people that shared the ecosystem with the endangered animals. Animals were clearly endangered because people killed them relentlessly, but it was not always the people who shared the same space. In fact, most often, the ones that posed a danger to the animals were those that came from outside for commercial interest in the skin, bones and other parts. But for the sake of conservation, those evicted from the Protected Areas were people who were directly dependent on the same natural habitat for food, grazing and other economic activities. And, as Rangarajan (2001: 94–107) points out, the older system 'was neither designed to undertake nor did it seriously even attempt to find serious alternatives for those denied access in terms of fodder resources, firewood or income-generating activities.' And so, 'Once unrest over denial of access began to spread to tribal areas typical of Indian parks, the consequences would be far-reaching, the conflicts more intense' (ibid.).

In the 1980s, the Tiwari Committee which was set up for recommending legislative measures and administrative machinery to strengthen the existing arrangements towards environmental protection, recommended establishing the Department of Environment (DOE) for dealing with various aspects of environment and ecology.[3] So, the Department of Environment was created in 1980 with special interest taken in it by the then Prime Minister Indira Gandhi (D'Monte 1985: 20). The DOE performed an oversight role for the central government. It did environmental appraisals of development projects, monitored air and water quality, established an environmental information system, promoted research and coordinated activities between federal, state and local governments. However, the DOE was criticised by environmental groups who recognised that with its small political and financial base, the agency was weak and symbolic in nature. Environmentalists also recognised that DOE would essentially serve as an advisory body with few enforcement powers.[4]

Under the Rajiv Gandhi government, the policy changed further, and in 1985, the Ministry of Environment and Forests (MoEF) was created. MoEF was more comprehensive and institutionalised, and had a Union Minister and Minister of State, that is, two political positions answering directly to the Prime Minister. The agency comprised 18 divisions, and two independent units, the Ganga Project Directorate and the National Mission on Wastelands Development. It continued the same functions that DOE originally had, such as monitoring and enforcement, conducting environmental assessments and surveys, but also did promotional work about the environment.

The MoEF's implementation of a monitoring system was also aggressive. In 1977, India had 18 monitoring stations for water. By 1992, there were 480 water stations, including 51 from the Global Environmental Monitoring System (GEMS). In 1984, the country had 28 air monitoring stations in seven cities, and by 1994, the National Ambient Air Quality Monitoring Program had 290 stations in 99 cities.

The 1980's witnessed the continuing decline in the quality of environment, together with the Bhopal gas tragedy that had killed more than 2500 people. This spurred the central government to adopt stronger environmental policies, to enact fresh legislation and to create, reorganise and expand administrative agencies. In 1981, the Air (Prevention and Control of Pollution) Act was passed, and in 1986, as a fallout of the Bhopal gas tragedy, the Parliament passed the Environment Protection Act. This was an 'umbrella' legislation designed to provide a framework for central government coordination of the activities of various central and state authorities established under previous laws, such as the Water Act and Air Act. It was also an 'enabling' law, which articulated the essential legislative policy on bureaucrats, to frame necessary rules and regulations. The Act served to back a vast body of subordinate environmental legislation in India. During the intervening years, address-specific-issues acts, such as, The Atomic Energy Act and The Wild Life Protection Act, were passed. The Atomic Energy Act governs the regulation of nuclear energy and radioactive substances. Under this Act, the central government is required to prevent radiation hazards, guarantee public safety, safety of workers handling radioactive substances, and ensure the disposal of radioactive wastes. The Wild Life Protection Act Provided a statutory framework for protecting wild animals, plants and their habitats. The Act adopts a two-pronged conservation strategy: protecting specific endangered species regardless of location, and protecting all species in designated areas called sanctuaries and national parks.

In December 1988, the Union Ministry of Environment and Forest constituted a committee to recommend a framework and an action plan for conservation of resources. Based on the recommendations of the committee, the Government of India adopted a National Conservation Strategy and Policy Statement on Environment and Development (NCS). The preamble to the NCS adopts the policy of 'sustainable development' and declares the government's commitment to reorient policies and action 'in unison with the environmental perspective'.[5]

The next important turn in policy is evident in the 1990s, when the overall economic policy underwent a change. Structural adjustment policies, neo-liberalism and the mantra of globalisation had overtaken international economic fora, and the fall of the Soviet Union and the much touted failure of socialism implied that India's 'mixed-economy' model had begun to lose its legitimacy. Thus, a new trend in liberalising the economy, implying inviting foreign capital and investment was put in place. Invitation to capital in this manner would imply that restrictions on them would have to be minimum. In fact, it was most likely to be dictated by parameters of lending by international financial institutions, resorted to for purposes of covering trade deficits. The most likely negative fallout has been apprehended to be that on environment, given the traditional opposition between them. If one looks at the instance of Coca-Cola at Plachimada, one would realise that these fears are not unfounded. It is possible that for the Indian government, its commitment to issues of environment, such as it has been, would be truly put to test in the era of liberalisation and globalisation. It is in this context, then, that the Draft National Environmental Policy, 2004 can be examined.

DRAFT NATIONAL ENVIRONMENTAL POLICY, 2004

Reasons for a National Environmental Policy

The first question that needs to be addressed when discussing this is: As indicated in the introduction to this chapter, the answer to this question lies in a complex web of political, economic and social factors. Broadly, these factors may be divided into those at the domestic/national level and those at the international.

By the end of the 1990s, the commitment of successive governments to opening up the economy to the influence of international competition was established beyond specific party ideologies. This was believed to be the only way to achieve rapid economic growth, and one that would contribute to higher incomes and growth of the economy in general. As a result, a number of sectors hitherto unexplored, like medicinal plants or non-existent sectors—for instance genetically modified organisms—came up with great possibilities for growth and contributions to the economy. In the case of sectors like medicinal plants, there was a wealth of already existing potential. A great deal of interest was shown by big transnational companies in doing business in the latter, given a huge potential in the agri-business sector. Thus, policies and laws on these sectors became urgent requirements.

Second, national policies for environmental management were already contained in the National Forest Policy, 1988, the National Conservation Strategy and Policy Statement on Environment and Development, 1992; and a Policy Statement on Abatement of Pollution, 1992. The government had also formulated some sector policies such as the National Water Policy, 2002. But the existence of these policies almost in mutual exclusion of each other, allowed only for some kind of piecemeal environmental management, and no more. Cross-sectoral interconnectedness would have to be at the heart of a comprehensive set of actions and this could have been achieved only with a comprehensive policy statement. This would enable an infusion of a common approach to the various sectoral and cross-sectoral, including fiscal, approaches to environmental management.

Third, the 1990s was a time when thinking and action on environment became considerably more complex in the international arena, as discussed in the chapter on UNEP. Given that India had taken vocal positions since the 1970s, it did take the lead in expressing the sentiments and requirements of developing nations, that is, to continuously address the need to balance the interests of environment and development, because they needed both so desperately. In this context, the concept of sustainable development was very versatile, allowing as it did, the interpretation and accommodation of both the objectives, in the most suitable way possible by individual nations. We have discussed this in Chapter 12. India has been no exception to this trend and we will argue later in the chapter that in the Draft National Environment Policy, there has been a clear commitment to continuously balance these two in every provision. Balance is a desirable objective of the policy, except that in the case of balancing between environment and development, the balance towards development invariably results in overwhelming the imperatives of environment. As has been pointed out by many critics, this seems to be the character of balance of the policy.

The fourth influence on the making of the new policy was the increasing awareness about the negative impact of development projects on the environment, in deepening of social inequalities and the violation of the rights of people. This resulted in the increasing momentum of many social movements that took up these issues, for example, the Kerala Fish workers Forum and the Narmada Bachao Andolan, preferring to remain outside the party political process, and instead building up political pressure. While they were individually concerned with specific issues, a consistent position emerging out of the engagement with this politics, both for those on the ground and those in government, was that the close interconnections between issues required a comprehensive policy. This was strong and consistent enough for the government to respond with some legislation and eventually a policy on environment. It must be stated, however, that while the political force of the movements has been considerable, by no means can it be concluded that the environment policy amounted to bowing to pressure from them. If anything, examining the factors substantiates the point made at the beginning of this chapter—the market forces were very strong and precipitated the making of the policy, and governments used this opportunity to create some legitimacy amongst severely critical segments of the polity. An analysis of the components of the draft environment policy 2004 serves to substantiate this argument.

The Contents of the Policy

The Draft National Environment Policy 2004 (hereafter NEP) is a 37-page-long document, seeking to be an umbrella policy covering every conceivable arena of the environment. It identifies the key challenges and states the objectives of policy and the principles on which these are to be achieved. It further identifies strategies and actions that would be created, or when already in existence, taken forward towards the realisation of the objectives. Each of these requires careful and critical analysis. The objectives listed are: conservation of critical environmental resources, to protect and conserve critical ecological systems and resources, and invaluable natural and man-made heritage which are essential for life support, livelihoods, economic growth and a broad conception of human well-being, intragenerational equity in terms of livelihood security for the poor, integration of environmental concerns in economic and social development, efficiency in environmental resource use, environmental governance, enhancement of resources for environmental conservation, legal liability, public trust doctrine and decentralisation. This is perhaps the most comprehensive listing possible.

The principles on which these would be fulfilled are: that human beings are at the centre of sustainable development concerns, that there should be the Right to Development, that environmental protection is an integral part of the development process. It also states that the precautionary approach, that is, cost-effective measures to prevent environmental degradation, irrespective of whether there are unequivocal 'scientific' indicators to support it, should be adopted. It argues for economic efficiency in various public actions for environmental conservation to be realised, whereby the services of environmental resources are given economic value, and such value to count equally with the economic values of other goods and services, in analysis of alternative courses of action. Economic efficiency here refers to its standard definition, that is, maximisation of welfare across all members of a society, given its human, natural and manmade resources, its technology and the preferences of its members. Welfare, again by the standard definition in modern economics, is reckoned as the aggregate of net value realised by each member of society, in his or her subjective perceptions, on a common monetary metric. Thus, we find that the next few principles, polluter pays, cost minimisation, equity, and so on all use the jargon of economic analysis, that has very little credibility in the discourse on environment. This is reflected again in the principle of environmental standard setting which, it argues, must 'reflect the economic and social development situation in which they apply'. Standards adopted in one society or context may have unacceptable social and economic costs if applied without discrimination in another society and context. This is where the 'balance' attempted by the government actually betrays the influence of investor/business interest in the industries that would require regulation and clearance by the government because of their likely impact on the government .

But the most important dimension of the policy that needs to be pointed out at the moment is the way in which it has been evolved and the consultation process that it is meant to be committed to before it becomes final.

The Making of the Policy

In an open letter issued by 64 very committed and well-grounded organisations and people's movements in the country, attention was drawn to the Ministry of Environment and Forests' privileged 'official consultations' over the opinions of communities to the draft policy. This was despite the fact that this large collective had very effectively garnered widespread responses and reactions to the policy, which should have found a listening ear at the Ministry (Open Letter to the Prime Minister by the Environment Support Group, Bangalore). The apprehension that many of these groups have is not unfounded. The most recent experience of the Ministry that people's groups have had with respect to the attitude towards genuine people's participation has been with the National Biodiversity Strategy and Action Plan.

The Ministry had handed over, in an unprecedented and progressive initiative in 2000, the grassroots consultation process on this Strategy and Action Plan to a Technical and Policy Core Group, consisting of activists, professionals and representatives from government, and it was coordinated by an NGO, Kalpavriksh.

Thereafter began a process which envisaged the preparation of 74 independent and worthy of implementing, Biodiversity Strategy and Action Plans (BSAPs) at state (33), substate (18), thematic (13) and ecoregional (10) levels. Apart from this, there were 34 sub-thematic reviews commissioned on topics such as the relationship of biodiversity to thermal power, natural dyes, and such others. The preparation of these plans followed a variety of methodologies including public hearings, yatras, festivals, structured meetings and workshops. Committees and/or advisory groups representing various streams of thought were brought together by the coordinating agency or individuals in order to build in a variety and range of perspectives into the plans. Though there was national-level coordination of the process, and guidelines were issued time-to-time, the BSAPs were prepared in a highly decentralised manner.[6] Despite the sterling efforts at participatory planning, the fruits of which were expected to be accepted as the NBSAP to be implemented, the Ministry altered the official standing of this group when its report was actually submitted in May 2003. At that time, when the entire process was already complete they were told

> that the final draft of the National Action Plan could not be considered as an action plan, but only as a technical report. The justification given for this was that the NBSAP should wait till the National Environment Policy is framed (even though that process started after four years after work began on the NBSAP), as also that a national plan could not be finalised until there is a Cabinet approval for it. This, despite the fact that previous action plans of the MoEF such as the National Wildlife Action Plan and the National Forest Action Plan have not gone through Cabinet approval.[7]

The lesson that can be learnt from the processes of planning of both the NBSAP and the NEP is that, on one hand, there is clearly a scope for genuine recognition for views of common people and community in the planning process, yet the forces that work against this perspective are also fairly strong and can overpower participatory planning at anytime. Therefore, the understanding of how environmental policies are made not only in India but anywhere in the world needs to include the parameters of the people and groups involved. It is also important to recognise that in instances when the government acts in an undemocratic and partisan manner, it does not do so only to protect commercial and industrial interests. A very deep-seated mistrust of the non-modern knowledge that is at the heart of critique of modern technological systems and a fairly dominant disrespect of the common person's understanding are at the heart of the non fulfilment of democratic norms.

The Strategies and Actions of the NEP

The NEP offers a range of reforms and fresh initiatives, not only sectorally but also procedurally. That is, it seeks, on one hand, to enhance and conserve practically every kind of environmental resource to be found in such a geographically diverse country like India (these are the sectors of environment). On the other hand, it offers regulatory reforms which include revisiting laws, the investment approval and improvement procedures and substantive initiatives on environmental clearances, living and modified organisms, and such others. Additionally, it promises to introduce and better environmental standards, management systems and certification. It is not possible here to offer a detailed critical analysis of these provisions. So, what we shall attempt is to indicate towards some positions and arguments available.

One of the most controversial provisions is that of investment approval and improvement procedures. The controversy has its roots in the critique offered by the Govindarajan Committee (2003) on the delays in environment and forest clearances being the largest source of delays in development projects. This was offered at a time when in fact state governments had been already rather careless with overlooking existing environmental clearance. Many groups like the collective quoted above believe that this is a legitimising exercise to avoid environmental clearance approvals in the name of better investment opportunities which are always projected as those in the larger public interests and larger national interests. Indeed, many that work hard to bring fresh profit-making investments in India believe that, by virtue of its potential of returns, they ought to be privileged over their ability to pass environmental clearance regulations. A similar situation is evident with respect to living and modified organism. Biotechnology, as a field of advanced science and technology, has provided enormous possibilities for genetically engineering living organism to fulfil many human requirements and solve many human–nature conflicts. But its interventionist nature and tendency to promote monocultural agriculture practices has elicited bitter criticism from those who believe in the versatility of plant varieties, traditional knowledge that seeks to maintain the versatility and their continued relevance. Thus, the NEP's commitment to promoting the cause of biotechnology does not augur well with the critics who usually represent people's groups and communities.

Ecolabelling is another one of the strategies enthusiastically stated in the NEP. It is the system by which industries acquire a certification of fulfilling environmental norms on the basis of which their products are allowed to be marketed. There are different kinds of ecolabelling and the Indian government has identified one set of norms as the basis of ISO 14000. In this sense, the government's committment to this concept, whereby the industrial sector is given both incentive and yardstick to be responsible to environment, is established. There is a rider, though. It is argued that

> ecolabels, etc., clearly have the potential to be employed as trade barriers, at least by competing firms in the export destinations, if not directly by their governments. The obtaining of an ecolabel, especially one granted by an agency located in a developed country, may involve large transactions costs. However, ecolabeled products may command significant price premia, as well as ease of entry to markets. On the other hand, the fact of a large, rapidly growing, environmentally conscious consumer base in India itself, may provide the required leverage to realise significant advantages from mutual recognition of ecolabeling schemes.
>
> (MoEF 2004: 33).

The ambivalence of ecolabeling, then, is clear, reflecting the typical defensiveness of developing countries with respect to international norms of environmental management systems that have been referred to before.

FUTURE OF THE ENVIRONMENT POLICY IN INDIA

If we accept that environmental policies are made and implemented by both ordinary people and those in authority, then we can expect that conflicts and conflict-resolution mechanisms will become sharper over the years. While international trading regimes will enable greater mobility of products and services across borders globally, the increased competition is most likely to affect terms of trade, of which environmental assessment, human rights violations, and perhaps, even equal opportunities (gender justice) could be an integral part. While the industrial sector and competitive businesses in the Third World would want to take advantage of liberalisation of global trade regimes, they would have to follow regulations and norms set by their respective governments, or else evolve some of their own that would be accepted internationally. The poor and the underprivileged in these countries who are given to understand that globalisation is bound to bring them benefits at the local level are likely to discover conflicts between profitable economic opportunity and fulfilment of democratic rights. In such an event, the task of the environmental movements, focused as they are on specific sectoral issues, would be to walk the difficult track of reconciling a better standard of life with higher democratic principles. They would have to explain and apply to mobilisation, that the physical reality of the health of environment, ultimately circumscribes both opportunity and democracy, a task difficult at the best of times. That is, unless the physical environment and its rich resources are preserved very carefully while the lives of people are improved economically and politically, there will not be much left to improve at all.

A very important resource that can be mobilised and utilised by those who have the privilege and opportunity to understand the complexity of the issues of environment at an early stage would be that of information. Much of what is debated on policies and proposed economic activities that are likely to have a bearing on environment takes place with an incomplete information base. This includes newspaper reports, company statements, editorial positions, and of course, statements by politicians. At the heart of good policymaking, whether contributed by the government or ordinary people, lies a comprehensive information base. India is one of the few countries where at both governmental and non-governmental levels, a very rich amount of information is generated. All too often, though, this information is not intelligently—and with a sense of fair play to all involved—used in the public realm. In fact, very often those that are underprivileged materially are also worse off because they cannot access information and so they lose out in articulating their position well. This is not to state, though, that if they had the accurate information, they would not encounter other forms of repression by the state or other powerful interest in order to prevent them from pressing their point of view. But in many cases , it has been observed, as in the Plachimada Plant case, that having access to accurate scientific information has helped the cause enormously. So, the future, as we see it, lies in determined and informed political mobilisation on the part of common people, influencing public policy towards concerns of environment such that it be understood that those concerns are truly and completely in the national interest. This then takes us to the next chapter on movements.

NOTES

1. A lot of controversy and debate occurred in the intervening years, which shows that colonial history is complex and needs to be understood as such, but this is not the space for it. Please refer to Gadgil and Guha (1992) for the details.
2. It was only the creation of ideologies of interest, of perspectives of people, that is, other political perspectives, therefore, that could possibly counter it. That will be discussed in the next chapter.
3. http://envis.mse.ac.in/loader.asp?lt=legleft.htm&rt=legis.htm

4. See note 3.
5. http://envis.mse.ac.in/loader.asp?lt=legleft.htm&rt=legis.htm
6. http://indiatogether.org/environment/biodiv.htm
7. See note 6

BIBLIOGRAPHY

Agarwal, A. and S. Narain (1985). *The State of India's Environment: The Second Citizens' Report*. New Delhi: Centre for Science and Environment.

D'Monte, D. (1985). *Temples or Tombs? Industry versus Environment : Three Controversies*, New Delhi: Centre for Science and Environment.

Gadgil, M. and R. Guha (1992). *This Fissured Land: An Ecological History of India*. Delhi: Oxford University Press.

Ministry of Commerce and Industry (2003). 'Govindarajan Committee on Investment Reforms'. New Delhi: Department of Industrial Policy and Promotion, Government of India.

Ministry of Environment and Forests (MoEF) (2004). *Draft National Policy on the Environment*. New Delhi: Government of India.

Rangarajan, M. (2001). *India's Wildlife History: An Introduction*. New Delhi: Permanent Black.

Sengupta, N. (1985). 'Irrigation: Traditional versus Modern', *Economic and Political Weekly*. Special number. August.

Whitcombe, E. (1993). 'The Costs of Irrigation in British India: Waterlogging, Salinity, and Malaria' in D. Arnold and R. Guha (eds) *Nature, Culture and Imperialism: Essays in the Environmental History of South Asia*. Delhi: Oxford University Press.

WEB SITES

http://envis.mse.ac.in/default.asp ENVIS Centre (MoEF, Government of India) at the Madras School of Economics

http://indiatogether.org/environment/biodiv.htm

16

Environmental Movement in India

There is no single environment movement in India. A large number of political initiatives, either single-issue-based or attempting to link a number of different issues—together with varying, and at times, competing ideologies—make up its mainstream. This needs to be understood from several different standpoints. One such standpoint would be to contextualise the development and significance of these movements with respect to larger politics. The second would be to classify and analyse the ideological trends in the movements as they have emerged in the last thirty years, to bring our political understanding up to date. Therefore, in this chapter, we will discuss the two standpoints by turns.

As we have discussed earlier and repeatedly referred to it throughout this section, in India, the impact of 'modern development' was already felt in all its negative implications by the late 1960s and early 1970s. While Indian democracy was very proactive and reflected a large number of new concerns, this issue was never adopted by the major political parties. The ideology of development as the saving grace for the nation-state to acquire a new glory—and recover one that was lost—in the international community of nations was too strong a temptation for the Indian elite, especially, given the rich rewards it was able to reap for itself from it. Thus, not only did the educated 'middle class' (do look at 'Understanding Social Inequality' again in case you have forgotten what it means!) not consider it in the planning process, but the political elite did not include it into the mainstream political agenda, too.

But the plight of the people was real and it was bound to have an expression. This was true for not only issues of the environment, but also a large number of other such issues, like those of access to land rights. So, in order to have their views heard, affected people, sometimes with the help of some conscientious educated people or even on their own, began to mobilise their voices and organise protests and have them communicated to the decision-makers and the powerful. These became known as the 'non-party political processes', 'the new social movements'—and a number of different names—basically to set them apart, as being different from the standard kind of politics adopted by the political parties. The environment movement in India needs to be understood as part of this new development.

One other important characteristic of these movements was that they were not guided by any rigid political ideology. The many strands of environmental thought that we discussed in the first chapter in this section, were those that, in the first place, had influenced people leading these movements. But many of them formulated their own understanding and interpretation of what they had read in terms of specific contexts, in which they were applying them and so came up with creative perspectives and explanations. But many of them were overwhelmingly influenced by Gandhian thought and action. That remains the case even today.

There were others that ranged from how development activity had created new and deepened the old structures of inequalities in the Indian society, on one hand, to those offering a critique of the development process itself, on the other. But whichever kind one might identify them with, in their focus and strategies of political action, it can be argued that they reflected the ground realities of the society and inculcated the values of radical and fringe politics, as practised in India for more than a century. As Sethi (2002) puts it, '... hardly surprising that issues of equity and social justice play such a crucial role in our ecological imagination.' These characteristics also accorded these movements a great deal of legitimacy in contemporary politics, making it hard for the powers-that-be to ignore them, despite their dislike of them.

SOME ENVIRONMENTAL MOVEMENTS IN INDIA

Several different kinds of issues have been the focus of these movements in India. Objects of development like dams, hydroelectric power projects, mining and mechanised fishing have been criticised on grounds that they have displaced people from their habitat and taken away livelihoods. Natural resources on which people are directly dependent—forests, land, seeds and water bodies such as rivers, lakes, the sea, groundwater and such others—have been defended by many movements from being over-exploited for fulfilling increasing demands of the market. And finally, many movements have focused on the fallouts of development—pollution (air, water, noise), slum settlements, liquor lobbies—of which, not all are directly related to the environment, but have serious implications for it. We will discuss some of these movements in detail.

Silent Valley Movement

The Silent Valley Movement in Kerala in the 1970s was one of the earliest and fiercest ecological controversies in post-independence India. The protests were against construction of hydel power project on the Kunthi river in the ecologically rich region called Silent Valley. The valley occupies only 8,950 hectares, but is surrounded by the Nilgiri, Nilambur and Attappadi forests that together comprise 40,000 hectares of pristine forest. There is a narrow gorge near the Mannarghat plains, which can be damned to form a reservoir to generate electricity. Technical investigations were carried out only in 1958. Preliminary works started in 1973, but due to shortage of funds, they were discontinued (D'Monte 1985: 31). At this time, no protests were heard. However, three years later, due to the intervention of some conservation-oriented bureaucrats, a task force was appointed by the National Committee on Environmental Planning and Co-ordination to go into the ecological problems of the Western Ghats. The task force submitted a report enlisting the disastrous consequences of such a project, which raised a storm. In January 1978, the Kerala Sastra Sahitya Parishad (a movement aimed at improving scientific temper amongst common people), organised the first mass signature campaign to stop the dam from being built. Nearly 600 academics, students and prominent citizens signed a memorandum addressed to the chief minister. This set off the controversy, beautifully described in Darryl D'Monte's book (1985).

Chipko Movement

The Chipko Movement in Garhwal and Kumaon, in what is now Uttaranchal, also took place in the early 1970s, with people rising against the felling of trees for commercial reasons. The action that had fired the imagination of a whole generation was the hugging of the trees by the women of the villages, to protect them from the contractors' axes, undeterred by threats and eventually triumphant in regaining control over their forests.[1]

These two are perhaps the most well-known of the environmental movements in India. More detailed descriptions of several other movements follow around the different issues listed above. This section is headed by the Narmada Bachao Andolan, also a well-known movement, but one that has lasted for more than two decades, and in its course, has had a far-reaching impact on the focal issues of these movements. This point will be brought out in the ensuing analysis of the movements.

Narmada Bachao Andolan (NBA)

One of the longest running battles against the construction of a dam has been that of the well-known Narmada Bachao Andolan, posited against the system of dams called the Sardar Sarovar Project, to be constructed on the river Narmada. The government's plan is to build 30 large, 135 medium and 3000 small dams to harness the waters of Narmada and its tributaries. The proponents of the dam claim that this plan would provide a large amount of water and electricity, which is desperately required for the purposes of development. Opponents of the dam question the basic assumptions of the Narmada Valley Development Plan and believe that its planning is unjust and iniquitous and the cost–benefit analysis is grossly inflated in favour of building the dams. Over the years, the extensive research conducted on behalf of the Andolan has demonstrated that the plans for the dams rest on untrue and unfounded assumptions of hydrology and seismicity of the area. Further, the construction is causing large-scale abuse of human rights and displacement of many poor and underprivileged communities. The critics also believe that water and energy can be provided to the people of the Narmada Valley, Gujarat and other regions through alternative technologies and planning processes that can be socially just, and economically and environmentally sustainable. Their research also shows how most rehabilitation schemes for people ousted with the building of other big dams have been inadequate. Thus, they have raised a range of issues, first of which is the necessity of such a big dam. They have repeatedly asked for lowering the height of the dam. The second issue is that of the resettlement package, without the proper distribution of which, they have threatened to continue their stay in the villages, where the released water would submerge them, thus resulting in mass suicide. Most importantly, however, they have questioned the model of development itself—arguing, instead, that an alternate model could be truly in the national interest. The NBA has by now become a kind of beacon for the environmental movements in India.

Mithini Village Movement

The village of Sonbhadr is rich in coal reserves. In 1989, the National Thermal Power Project (NTPC) first announced its plans to expand its operation into Mithini. The villagers were given small cash compensation and pressurised to move to a resettlement colony with the assurance that with further expansion, they would be given alternative livelihood options. This promise, however, remained unfulfilled even as displacement seemed imminent. In 1993, a petition was filed in the Allahabad High Court that gained a stay order against further construction until the promise of resettlement was fulfilled. Ignoring the directive, NTPC began to increase pressure on the villagers to leave their lands. In response to this, the movement against displacement took root in Mithini. Even as the villagers moved court to get the 1993 petition implemented, they faced the wrath of NTPC. They were verbally and physically threatened, paramilitary forces were used for intimidation, and the crops of protesting farmers were destroyed. In one instance, the only barrier that lay between the bulldozers and the village huts were the villagers, whole in front of the bulldozers, not allowing them to go further. However, the struggle took its toll. Two-thirds of the families left the village, unable to bear the aggression of NTPC and their own poverty. And only 18 families remained as signatories to the petition. Simultaneously, the struggle gained national and international support. Activists accused the World Bank, a major funding source for NTPC, of violating its own internal guidelines on resettlement of displaced persons and demanded an internal inquiry. In one of the rare success stories in the history of peoples' movements, the panel found that the World Bank rules on resettlement were being violated and under pressure, the NTPC grudgingly gave in. As a result of the struggle, they were able to secure a large compensation package.

Jharkhandi Organisation Against Radiation (JOAR)

The Uranium Corporation of India Limited (UCIL) has three operating mines in Jadugoda, Bhatin and Narwahpur villages of Jharkhand. In the 1960s, land was acquired in Jadugoda for constructing ponds, tailing ponds for dumping nuclear waste, and constructing residential colonies for the miners. Uranium ore is extracted, crushed and processed in Jadugoda and sent to the nuclear processing centre in Hyderabad for further purification into fuel rods. During the purification, depleted uranium mining tailings are discharged as waste, then brought to Jadugoda and dumped in large ponds in the midst of tribal villages, or at times, on roads and even in fields. Radioactive waste from other parts of the country is also dumped in this area. Apart from causing environmental destruction, radiation and radioactive waste have severe health impacts, especially in terms of genetic mutation and slow death. The management of UCIL has stubbornly denied any harmful effects of radiation in Jadugoda and insists that radiation is 'within permissible limits'. The tribals, who work in these mines, are not given any protective devices like respirators, in the absence of which, they inhale dust and radon gas while they work. The initial mobilisation of the tribals was around the issue of their resettlement and rehabilitation. The Jharkhandi Adivasi Visthapit Berozgar Sangh (JAVBS) was formed in 1989. Over the years, the people of Jadugoda have recognised the link between their health problems and radiation exposure. In 1998, the JAVBS was expanded to form Jharkhandi Organisation Against Radiation (JOAR).

The JOAR has been involved in intensive campaigning in schools and colleges on effects of radiation on people and the environment. Soon after Pokhran II, it submitted a memorandum to the Government of India stating that the people of Jadugoda would not let anything that is destructive to humankind be extracted out of their land. In June 2002, the agitation of the people succeeded in preventing the acquisition of 15,000 acres of tribal land for open cast mining. The people of Jadugoda and JOAR are networking with other concerned organisations and peace movements for a nuclear-waste-free Jharkhand.

National Fishworkers Forum

With her 6000-km coastline and innumerable rivers, lagoons, lakes, reservoirs and ponds, India has one of the largest populations of 7 million fisher people in the world. One-third of them depend on marine fishing and the remaining two-third on fishing in a variety of inland water bodies. Despite being generally very poor and relegated to low castes, they have enjoyed a certain autonomy and dignity in the past.

With the introduction of export-oriented mechanised deep-sea fishing and aquaculture in the early 1960s, fishing economy underwent a marked technological polarisation. For the first time, fishing was seen as an industry, in which, anyone with capital could enter. Ignoring the skills and potential of a large number of fishing people, the government promoted technologies like bottom trawling, and so on, for large-scale harvesting of fish, which have depleted the marine resource base over the years. So, the fishing industry became polarised between the modern sector, able to make considerable profits from export, and a traditional sector confined to a domestic market with declining catches and fish stock. The 1970s witnessed violent clashes between the mechanised trawlers and fish workers, since they shared the same fishing grounds. The Majumdar Committee appointed to study the situation proposed the Marine Fishing Regulation Bill. The fish workers, on the other hand, started making new linkages and organising at local and state levels. This resulted in the formation of Trade Unions which came together to form the National Fish Workers Forum in 1979. Thus, it is an all-India organisation that represents the interests of—and unites—these local movements (Kriti Diary 2002).

Beej Bachao Andolan

Up in the hills of Uttaranchal is a place called Jardhargaon, where farmers are working hard to save the great variety of indigenous seeds that abound in different crops. Anticipating the possible imposition of monoculture practice by big transnational companies slowly entering the Indian market with hopes held out for higher yields through modified or laboratory tested seeds, the movement seeks to find ways of systematically saving the seeds of traditional varieties. They argue that these seeds have both quality and quantity yields, and are adapted to local growing conditions to boot, having been mutated naturally. Besides, they produce crops that people of a greater region now have a taste for and, if necessary, can be further mutated in the field for other qualities. Together with this, this andolan works to promote traditional agricultural practices, arrived at over generations of engaging with the terrain of those hills, and adapted to changing rainfall patterns and temperatures. Both of these are protective of certain natural resources and also of existing skills of local communities, recognised even by them as necessary for a comprehensive development process.

ANALYSING THESE MOVEMENTS

Environmental movements can be understood to be a part of what are known as 'new social movements' of the 1960s and the 1970s across the world. These movements came up for reasons specific to the politics of that time. During the Cold War, the two competing ideologies of Liberalism and Marxism had so completely dominated political discussion by their fixed categories of analysis, that some issues could not be included in them. These were issues of peace and disarmament, the models of development and their impact on environment, civil rights, gender, race and ethnicity. The political parties of most democratic countries seemed to be unaware of the importance of including these in their work agendas. As a result, people outside of the political party processes, but concerned about these issues, mobilised others like themselves to raise their voice and call attention of their governments to them. The second wave of environmentalism in India that Guha talks about (we have referred to it earlier in the chapter) has a similar origin.

These movements, therefore, were usually single-issue-based and began as intuitive reactions to what seemed like harsh state action. To begin with, then, most of them had a social base in poor peasants or tribal people, as in Mithini or in Jadugoda. As they progressed, they found support among the urban middle-class intelligentsia of some radical political orientation, but mostly outside of the organised Left. This support was usually in terms of collecting and collating information—about laws, similar issues taken up elsewhere—and reaching out to a larger public by means of all media available. So, whenever any issue gained some kind of momentum, but needed to know whether there were any laws to support its demands, and whether any lawyers or judges would take up cudgels on its behalf, often urban students and professionals would garner support amongst themselves for it. For this, all kinds of information, about similar groups operating elsewhere and studies to support their arguments, would be brought together to be used for different purposes. Chief amongst these, as many movements and their urban supporters realised very quickly, was to interest and inform media professionals about this, enough for them to carry stories/features on these issues in their papers.[2] Each one of these processes took a long time, because they were unfamiliar and unconventional. However, as a result of sustained political action on the ground, combined with inputs of information and support from outside, these movements took mature political positions, not only against the state or models of development, but also in favour of alternatives.

A good example of the growth of the latter is that of Tarun Bharat Sangh, an Alwar (Rajasthan)-based group that, as its primary goal, targeted recovery and conservation of water resources in a drought-prone and semi-arid region. Thereafter, it has espoused the cause of traditional methods of water harvesting for domestic and agricultural use—an idea that increasingly convinces people in other regional and now urban areas, as an innovative and accessible alternative to the water crisis being faced everywhere. Thus, they have been able to project the perspective that development models need not be expensive and capital-intensive options that governments are unable to procure for none except a few. They have shown that it need not be outside the reach of the common person. Further, they have shown how traditional knowledge continues to be sturdy and versatile, and could still be used to advantage. The application of local and traditional knowledge has also conveyed that arguing in their favour does not make for a backward-looking perspective. In fact, that it can be made to work towards solving contemporary problems is a real discovery for the modern world of development. This would enable them to relate to many larger issues of politics, that they would not even have thought of connecting with when they began their struggle.

The unique position of environment movements makes possible such a connection. In all of the movements we have traced, the issue was one of the poor and their livelihood being taken away as a result of development, instead of the other way around. So, these movements bring to light one fundamental insight: *that development's benefits are for some and not always for all*. Hence, it can perpetuate or worsen inequality—social and economic—whereas its mandate and claim is to do the opposite. Yet, precisely on this ground, that of posing workable, road-based alternatives, Gadgil and Guha are of the opinion that, in fact, the environmental movement as a whole is not geared towards alternatives. We will take this up for discussion in the section on criticisms of the environmental movements.

It must be added though that there are a host of movements that are inspired and directed by urban middle-class positions on the environment, though many of them are in the category of non-governmental organisations, rather than movements. Often, they begin as NGOs, but their involvement in the issue/cause makes them take militant positions, making their relations with governments and officials tenuous. Well-known examples of these are Agragamee in the Kashipur region of Orissa, involved in the tribals' protest against bauxite mining in Kashipur, which would lead to environmental disaster—drying up of rivers, deforestation and ecological damage—and the Barh Mukti Andolan of Jamshedpur. Despite their extent of involvement, however, other groups that do not receive external funding for their infrastructure and daily activities, and do not have access to the political power structures, cannot accept them as part of the same political family. A lengthy and complex debate on this persists but there is no space to delve into it here.

For most of the last 30 years, these movements chose to remain outside of the institutionalised structures of politics. Disgusted by the corruption and cynicism of mainstream political actors, they did not participate in the political party/election process. They chose, instead, to challenge it from the outside, giving voice to concerns of people and making political accountability a reality, creating a base of legitimacy as the real representatives of the people. In most of the movements, the commitment of the leadership is to a very simple life, incorruptible in the material terms, which is so blatantly evident and associated with mainstream politicians. Many of these people are not visible in the country's mainstream media, which never makes time and effort to find the genuine leader who still exists. And this is true of most new social movements, even other than those on the environment.

While most of these movements by themselves were strong , it was hard for them to sustain struggles over a long period of time with limited funds and people. At the same time, the state became more and more repressive in pursuing the new agenda of liberalisation and privatisation, implementing policies whether people wanted them or not. This was irrespective of the ideology of the party in power. With increased state repression, it became necessary to demonstrate 'people power', both in numbers and principle, and this required a new orientation. In the mid-1990s then, these movements decided to use their combined strengths to help each other in their struggles. The historic Harsud Convention against

Displacement and Destruction on 28 September 1989 was a landmark event, where over 350 organisations and groups throughout India said 'No' to the present development policies and paradigm and declared their resolve for 'Alternative Development'. After many rounds of discussions with various organisations from 1993 to 1995, a number of organisations and movements, including those involved in the constructive work of developing alternatives in various fields also joined in this endeavour. Gabriele Dietrich, one of the most committed leaders in this group, put it such: 'We are speaking of a second Freedom Struggle. This second Freedom Struggle is about Ecology and Social Justice together.'

From January to April 1996, the main activists of the organisations involved in this process took out a nationwide march from all states, culminating in the National Convention in Gandhiji's *ashram* in Wardha. The National Alliance of People's Movements was thus formally launched. The process of alliance was meant for strengthening diverse movements and coordinating the joint struggle, without giving up their individual identities, on issues common to all organisations (Shanghais).

In the last five years, however, there has been a different focus to the soul-searching of these movements. Relentlessly challenging the state, as they have done from the outside, they now feel the need to storm the bastion from within. So, it is believed by many that the legitimacy and standing that many of the leaders of these movements have, which is much more than elected politicians do, could be utilised more effectively if they are within the state. They could be trusted and would be accountable. Hence, there was a move to create a political front called the Lok Rajniti Manch (People's Political Front). This front did contest for some seats in the General Election of 2004, and expect to move towards a political party, drawing primarily from the constituents of the NAPM. While it is not clear what the outcome of their reflections will be, it can be expected to prove to be a creative intervention in politics.

Achievements

The principal achievements of the environmental movements in India are broadly of two kinds. The first is of introducing new rules and regulations that protected the environment and the interests of marginalised workers/tribals/peasants. An instance of the first kind of achievement is that of the NFWF being able to obtain marine fishing regulations in almost all coastal states of India to protect fish workers, fish resources and maintain 'law and order' in the same. They forced the government to bring out zonal regulations for mechanised boats, night trawling ban, and so on, which enormously benefited the competing capacities of small fish workers.

The second was that of introducing new ideas in the public space that did not exist earlier, making it possible to influence public policy and other interventions in the public space. They have challenged the agendas of dominant politics by exposing their lack of interest in the real issues that affect ordinary people. As Gadgil and Guha (2000: 100) point out,

> Through the process of struggle, the spreading of consciousness and constructive work, action groups in the environmental field have come to develop an incisive critique of the development process itself ... Although perspectives within the movement are themselves quite varied, in its totality this fostering of a public debate on development options constitutes the ideological expression of the environmental movement.

CRITICISMS

There are four kinds of criticisms that have been leveled against the environmental movement in India. By now, familiar as you are with the debates on environment and development, with which we began this section and the manner in which the issues, policies and negotiations have been spelt out in the other chapters, you can probably guess very well what the nature of the criticisms would be.

The first, most standard and powerful is from those who believe that environmentalists focus on the protection of nature *over and above* solving problems of poverty and underdevelopment, which naturally involve costs for some and benefits to others. The environmentalists go against a basic democratic principle that the benefits of the majority should be privileged because they prioritise the whims and wishes of small communities, reducing the significance of big projects to their petty needs. Thus, it is argued that they *do* put petty sectarian interests over the national interest. So, if some people are to be displaced by a dam and some benefit from the redirection of the water for irrigation and electricity, should not the latter be more important?

This debate was played out again in April–May 2005, at the time when the NBA leader Medha Patkar went on an indefinite hunger strike to protest the decision of the government to raise the height of the Sardar Dam (despite the Supreme Court directive to the contrary), pending rehabilitation, which was clearly not complete. During this debate, it became clear once again that the terms of analysis deployed by these critics were very limited—the problem is genuine and the numbers on either side are legion and there are as many thirsting for water as those that will suffer the consequences of the dam being built. The issue has to be of viable alternatives, with least cost to all people and all nature, but that requires a different kind of political will and political power, which can be hoped for in the future.

Second, the critics argue that traditional cost–benefit analysis that used to be conducted by economists to judge the profitability of any enterprise or project could now be amended and improved to be a social cost–benefit analysis, which could accommodate all the issues that the environmentalists raise. Possibly, but as Gadgil and Guha would have us understand, if it is the omnivores that guide the analysis, the record has not been that of making any sacrifices of their own benefits, but always imposing the cost on the others. So, the trust for viable alternatives to mainstream development projects cannot be vested with them. This brings us to the next point of criticism against these movements.

Gadgil and Guha, who are otherwise appreciative of the movements, pose an interesting and significant critique in the lack of ability of the movements to go beyond their standard positions to take on the fundamental positions of their opponents. Thus, in their opposition to modern science and technology, they have not considered that in the long run, focusing on more 'prudent alternatives to prevailing technologies' for production, might be more useful and pragmatic for people. That this is a wise policy is evident from the experience of Korea and Japan. The second issue they raised was that

> the environmental movement focuses too much on the products, and not enough on the processes, of development. Dams ... are not good or bad in themselves ... The problem lies, rather, in the centralised and closed circle of decision-making, ... As things stand, the dam becomes an evil chiefly because the processes of planning and management are distorted by a corrupt, wasteful and unjust machinery of decision-makers.
>
> (Gadgil and Guha 2000: xiii)

While the movements might, by now, be inclined to accept the first criticism—indeed, in the many shades mentioned within the movement, there are many that would actively subscribe to it; the second criticism would be hard for many of them to accept. The reason for this lies, principally, in the extreme suspicion that has been built up in the minds of these movements against the science and technology establishment, and its policies of alienating the poor. So, they believe that yielding to any extent in its suspicion of them would make it vulnerable, and so, there is a tremendous resistance to consideration of these alternatives.

However, this is not a problem of the environmental movement alone. This is the dilemma of all sections in our society that have been critical of exploitative aspects of modernity—they want to continue to be so, but not irrationally. At the same time, they do not want to risk being lumped with those that vehemently support the traditional, in the name of culture and identity, but actually preserve the most discriminatory, unjust and exploitative aspects of tradition. If you look around, you will see this dilemma in those who want to fight for gender justice without advocating the destruction of the institution of marriage and the family; those who want to restore community rights because they are more ecologically sound, but do not want to be trapped in old caste or feudal relations; those who want to propagate the use of traditional medicines, without allowing them to be taken over to unscrupulous god men or manufacturing companies; and many more.

Four, environmentalists have come under criticism from the dominant Left parties, especially in the early years. They accused these groups of narrowing the concerns of politics to the exclusion of the larger issues. So, questioning the environmental impacts of polluting or hazardous technologies was seen as antithetical to the interests of working class politics and the very issues of class, economic models and an overall improvement of the economic life of people. The critique they offered was as much about the issues the movements picked, as the fact that they mobilised political thought and action around single-point agendas. In focusing all political energy on this, the Left parties felt that larger concerns are either buried or postponed in the interest of the issue at hand, thereby deflecting attention away from broader social transformation.

However, these are concerns that these movements have consistently not only countered, but also taken serious cognizance of and used to reflect critically on their strategies and orientation. Consistently focusing on the poor and the disadvantaged, they have demonstrated that they wish the state and other agencies of development to approximate the definition of sustainable development, such that the environment is able to take the burden of development and the poor actually benefit from it. Thus, they have tried to demonstrate how they truly wish to work towards national interest, rather than the other way around. In practical terms, they have tried to substantiate this claim by offering models of and carrying out projects of alternative development that are people, environment and economic benefit-friendly. There are several cases that can be cited. On 28 October 1988, a small dam and ponds for holding rainwater were constructed in the village of Sato in Jharkhand's (then Bihar) Gumla district, which lies about 123 kilometres northwest of Ranchi. The assured supply of water and security against soil erosion and landslips has made the Urao community of Sato now regard 28 October as their real independence day.

In Madhya Pradesh, the inhabitants of Gainda and neighbouring villages, in the district of Jhabua, have used *halma*, a traditional institution for collective labour, to construct numerous civil works that cater to the needs of villagers, with financial support from the government under the Integrated Rural Development Programme (IRDP) scheme (Sharma 2002: 128). Examples like this abound, including better known ones like those of Baba Amte's rehabilitation village for lepers, Somnath and its record rice production and Anna Hazare's Ralegaon Siddhi.

At the end of this discussion, and this book, one can conclude that the complexity of the environmental question demands very careful analysis and understanding. No sweeping political slogans, no dismissive economic models and no superficial reporting can wish away this reality. It can only be hoped that a critical analytical education/exposure to such issues at this early stage will help create a new generation that offers better insights into this question.

NOTES

1. It is very important to know that for every story, there can be another interpretation. For a different analysis of the Chipko movement, please see H. Rangan, *Of Myths and Movements: Rewriting Chipko into Himalayan History.*
2. In the 1970s, environmental journalism was just beginning in India and people like Darryl D'Monte and Anil Agarwal, followed by P. Sainath and Mukul Sharma (to name but a few), did a great deal to create a space to report these movements in the mainstream media that did not otherwise think it in their interest to report it.

BIBLIOGRAPHY

D'Monte, D. (1985). *Temples or Tombs? Industry versus Environment: Three Controversies.* New Delhi: Centre for Science and Environment.

Gadgil, M. and R. Guha (2000). *The Use and Abuse of Nature* (Omnibus edition). New Delhi: Oxford Univeristy Press.

Sethi, H. (2002). 'The Problem'. *Seminar*. 3 August.

Sharma, M. (2001). *Landscapes and Lives: Environmental Dispatches on Rural India*. New Delhi: Oxford University Press.

WEB SITES

http://iref.homestead.com/NFF.html.

http://www.humanscape.org/Humanscape/new/june02/cometogether.htm)

About the Authors

Manisha Priyam, currently a research scholar at the London School of Economics and Political Science (UK), teaches political science at Gargi College, University of Delhi. Her area of research and activity has been the policy and politics of development, especially that of primary education for the rural poor. She has been working with externally assisted programmes for primary education of the Government of India since 1994, providing policy development and implementation support. She has also been a consultant to the World Bank, New Delhi, on various education reform policy research projects. She is an advisor to the Government of Delhi's Mission Convergence, aiming at better service delivery of all social assistance and human development programmes for the vulnerable in Delhi.

Krishna Menon teaches political science at Lady Shri Ram College, University of Delhi. After her postgraduate studies at the Centre for Political Studies, Jawaharlal Nehru University, she obtained a Ph.D. in the subject from the University of Delhi. Her areas of interest include political theory, Indian politics, and feminist theory and politics. Her concern with political theory is to bring it alive in the context of an Indian classroom. She has contributed extensively to the popular series on political theory and Indian politics published by the Indira Gandhi National Open University. She has also been a part of the NCERT's textbook development committee for classes VI to VIII. Her co-authored monograph on issues of gender and migration has been published by the National Labour Institute. Apart from academics, she is interested in classical music and dance. She has worked as a dance critic for nearly three years with the New Delhi edition of *The Indian Express*.

Madhulika Banerjee teaches at the Department of Political Science, University of Delhi. Committed principally to classroom teaching, she has also been actively engaged in curriculum development in political science and allied disciplines like elementary education. She is also interested in fostering an inter-disciplinary orientation in political science, which led her to attempt the section on environment in this book. Her research on the politics of knowledge, medicine and technology is also a reflection of her pursuit of inter-disciplinary connections. Her book *Power, Knowledge, Medicine: Ayurvedic Pharmaceuticals at Home and in the World* was published recently.

Index